LCCN: 2016903047

ISBN: 978-0-692-65082-0

Printed in China

Designed by Jen Zhao

First Artvoices Art Books Publishing edition 2016

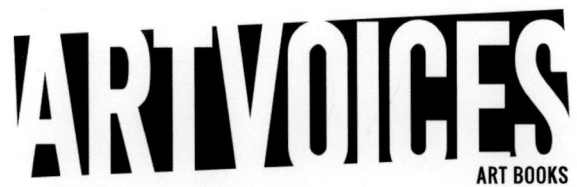

Artvoices Art Books Publishing
www.artvoicesartbooks.com

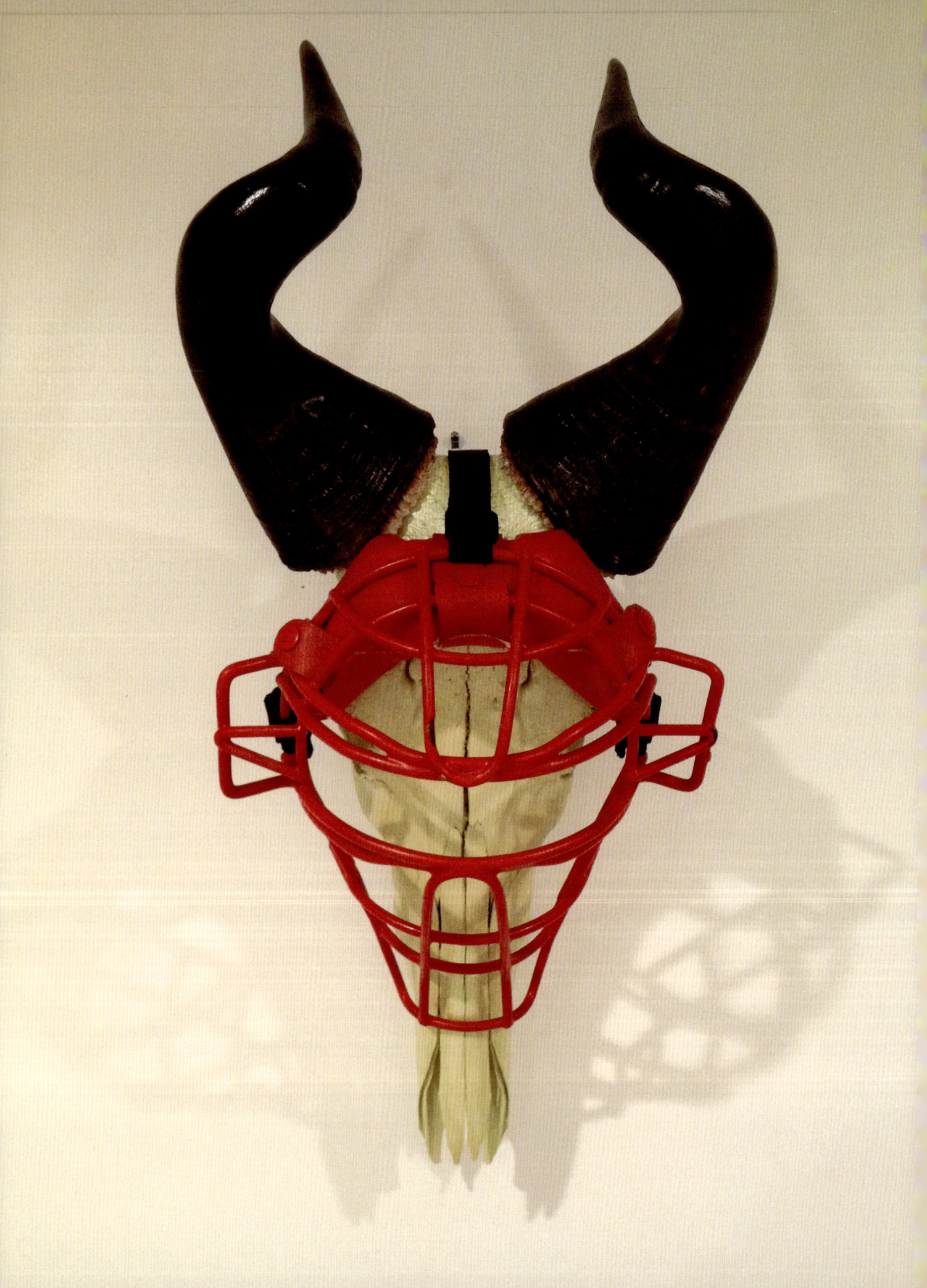

LARRY AARONS

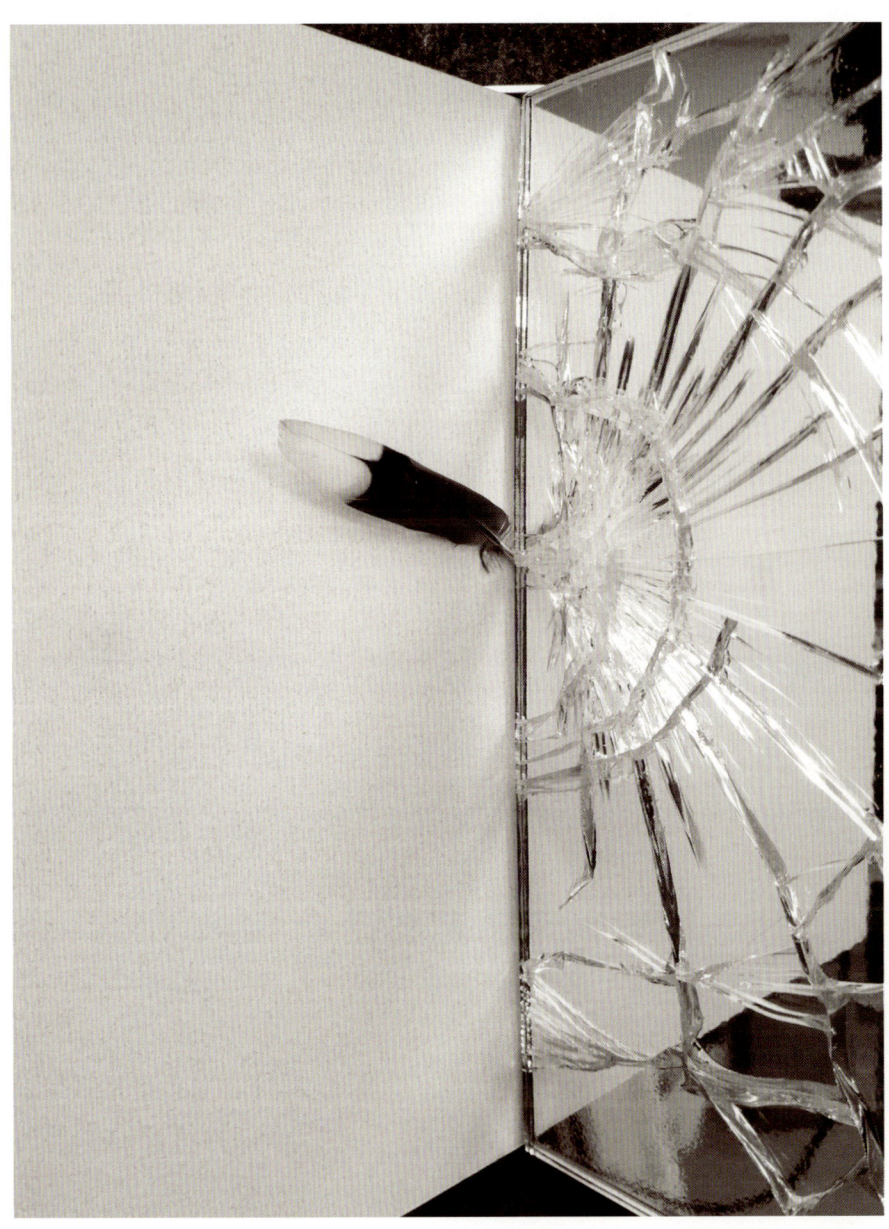

WWW.LARRYAARONSART.COM

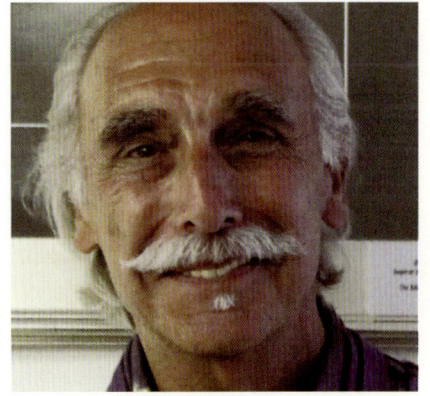

● **(facing page) Hartebeest with Mask**
Sculpture, 12 x 24 x 10 in., 2013

● **Paradise Lost**
Mixed media, 19 in. depth 9.5 in., 2015

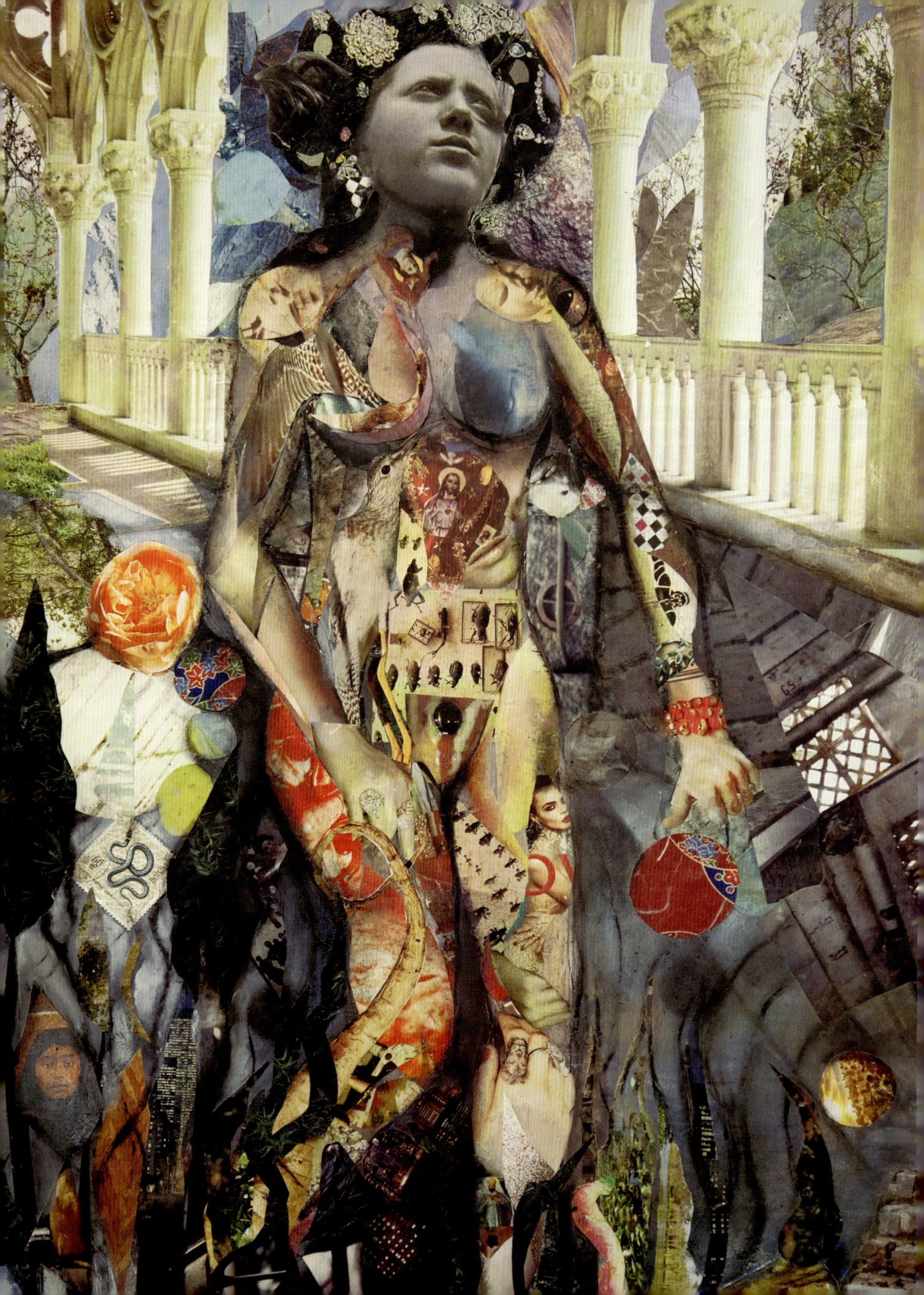

DENISE ADLER

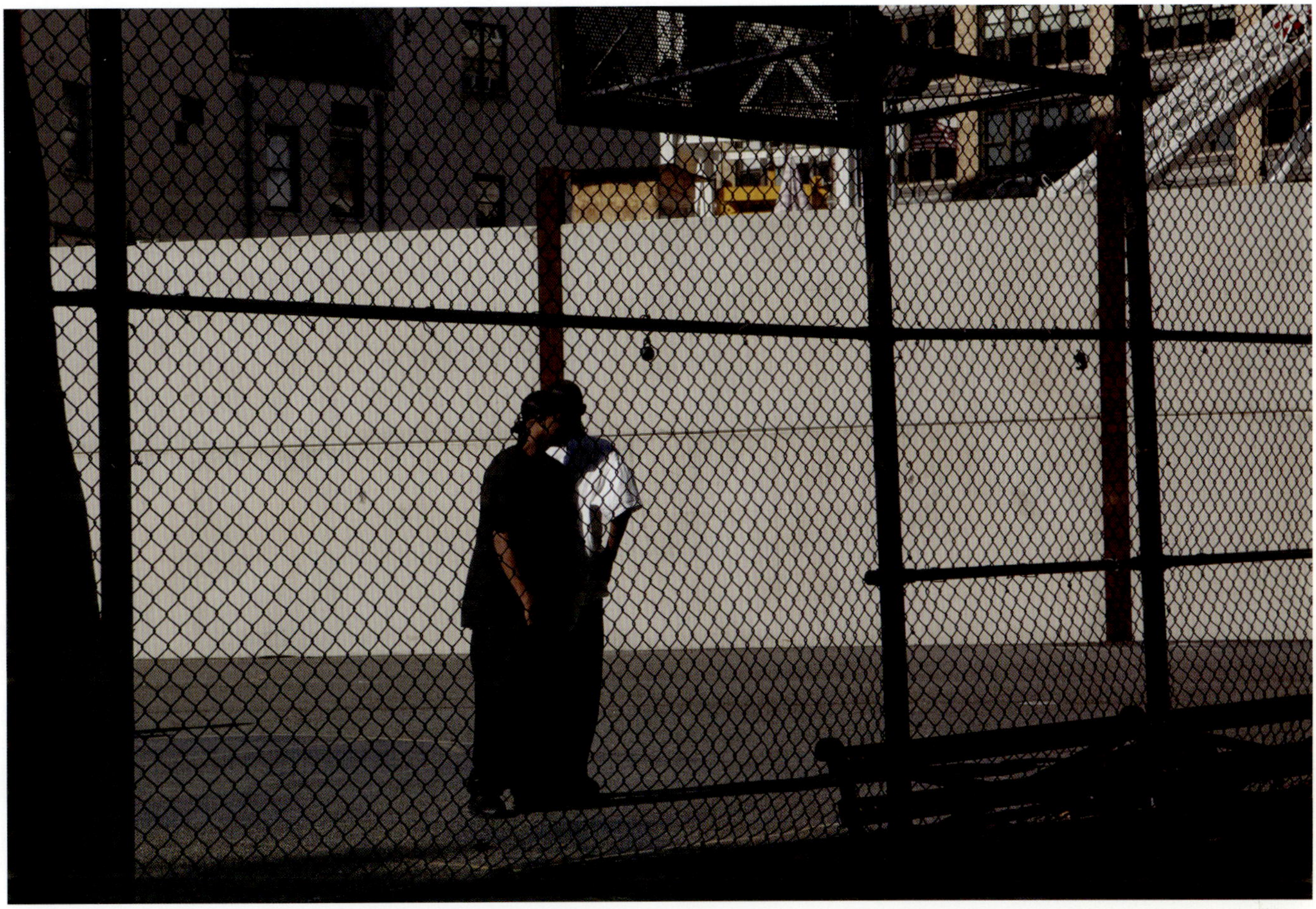

![Photograph of two figures embracing, viewed through a chain-link fence in an urban setting]

"As a child I saw faces in every fold of fabric and stories on every street corner. Today I channel this into my art, working with cut paper, paints, magazines images and photography."

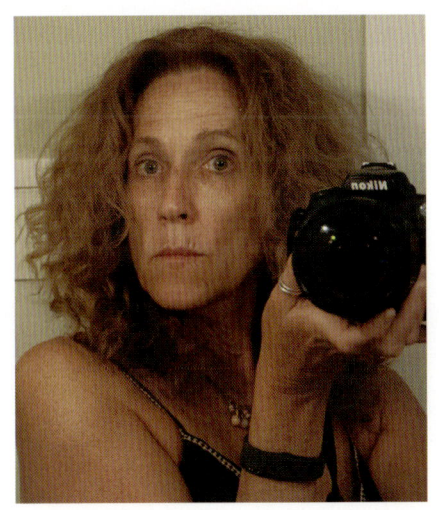

The stories develop and find their way. My collages are in homage to the religious art and icons that fascinated me as a child. My photographs are stories waiting to be told.

WWW.DENISEADLER.COM

● **(facing page) Goddess**
Mixed media collage and oil stick on wood panel, 18 x 20 in., 2014

● **Contrast**
Limited Edition Print on Archival Paper, 30 x 24 in., 2006

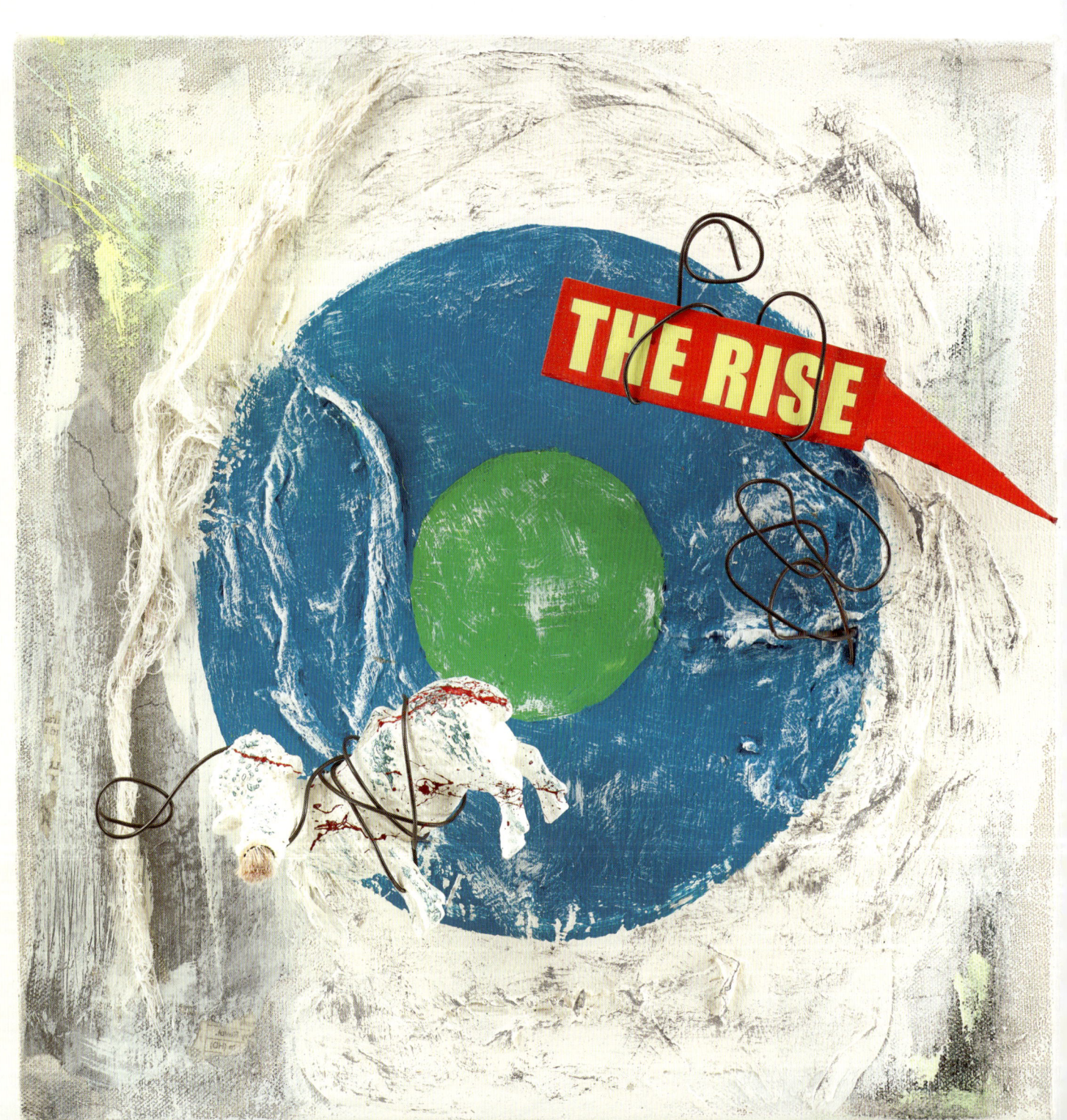

ARIANE AHLMANN

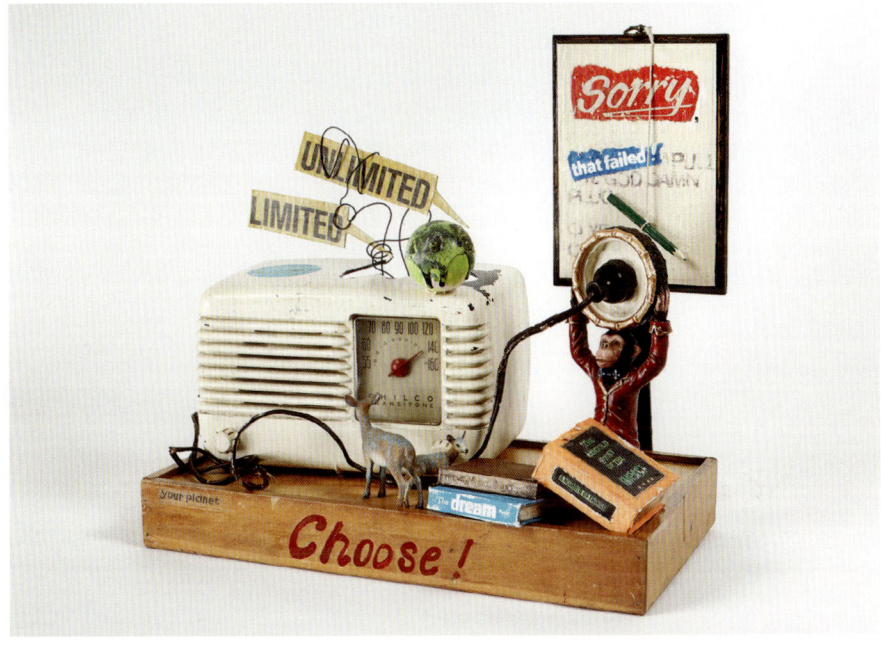

"The combination of shabby materials and unfamiliar human figures, often hybrid characters, evoke a mysterious and bizarre world in a timeless setting. The protagonists lack a clear course and their actions may seem irrational. They are lonely characters in an incomprehensible world. There is no story, just fragments of the human struggle."

Ariane Ahlmann's work is characterized by the combination of painting and sculpture. She integrates an array of different materials, such as found objects, rope and cloth. These materials are not only brought together, but processed in a unique way to achieve a look of decay and weathering. The combination of shabby materials and unfamiliar human figures, often hybrid characters, evoke a mysterious and bizarre world in a timeless setting. The protagonists lack a clear course and their actions may seem irrational. They are lonely characters in an incomprehensible world. There is no story, just fragments of the human struggle.

Ariane Ahlmann was born in 1960 in West Berlin. The city's unconventional spirit and subculture of the 1980's became her first artistic influence and inspiration. Everything seemed possible in this liberal city that was surrounded by a wall. While roaming the streets of Berlin as a photographer for the Axel Springer publishing house, the squatter movement and the art scene in the borough of Kreuzberg became Ahlmann's first artistic platform. In that hotspot of counterculture Ahlmann began to combine spray painting, textile painting and collage. There was an urge among young artists to experiment and to create something different from the minimal art and the conceptual art of that time. But most of all it was Ahlmann's need to free herself from her own conflictive upbringing. Like many of her fellow artists Ahlmann had no formal art education nor did she work as a full time artist. The teaching ground was the legendary club SO36 and the art scene around "Moritzplatz", epicenter of the German neo-expressionism.

Ariane Ahlmann lives and works in Brooklyn, New York.

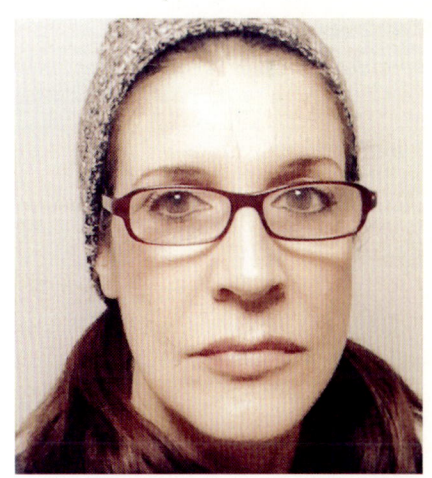

WWW.ARIANEAHLMANN.COM

SARAH AHMAD

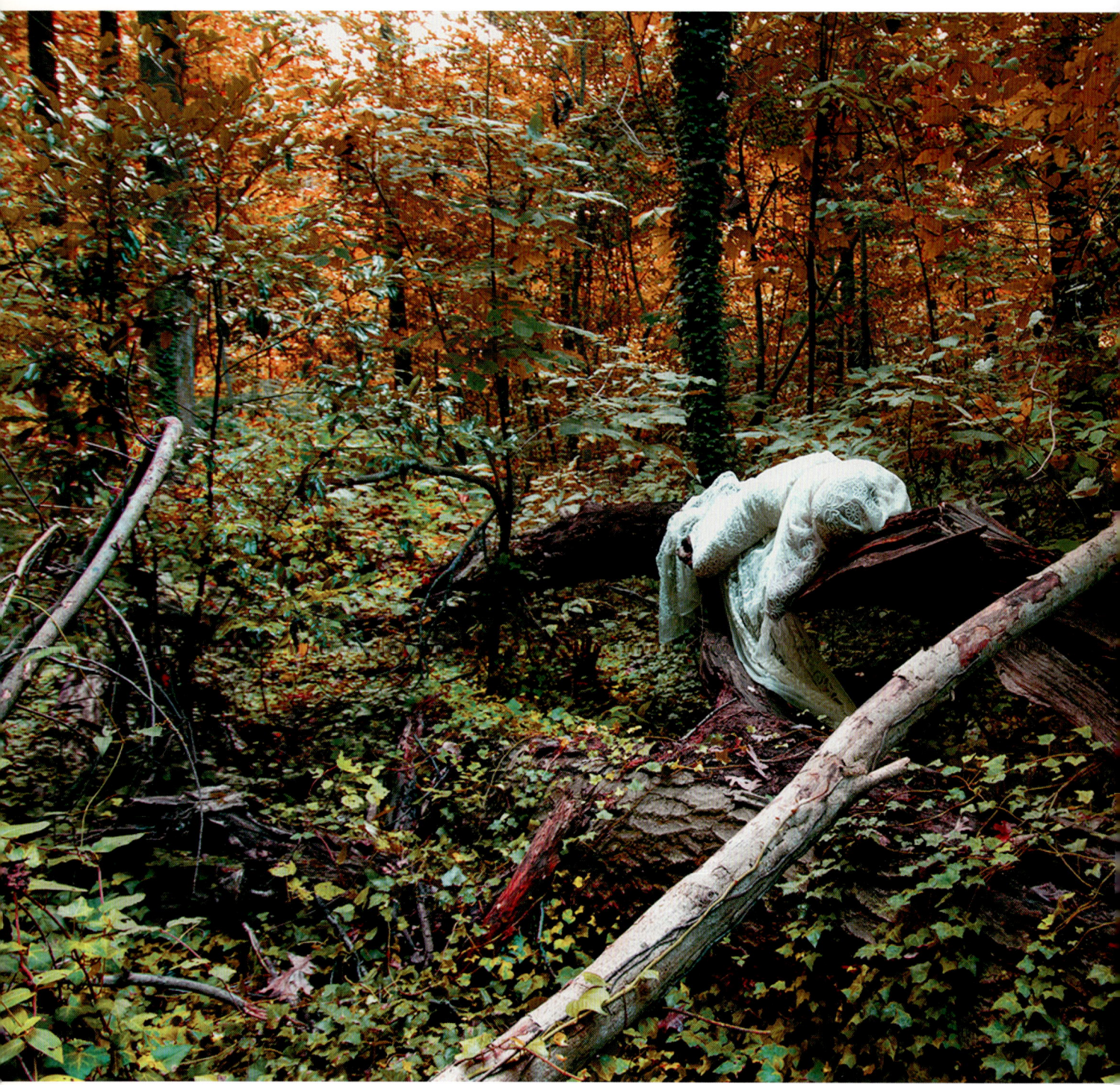

"Is she enclosed by the fabric covering her like a web or adorned by it? The web she is trapped in is beautiful, colorful, and protective. It has sheltered her through many storms evident by the fallen, ruptured trees around her. It clings to her like a lovely garment, a protective covering that refuses to shed."

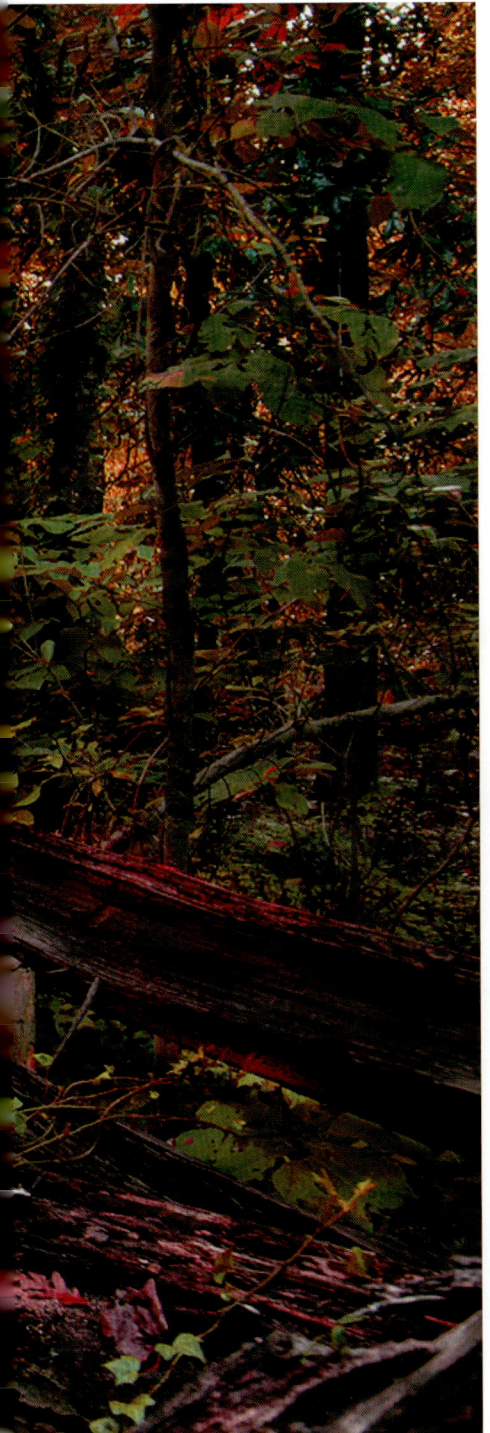

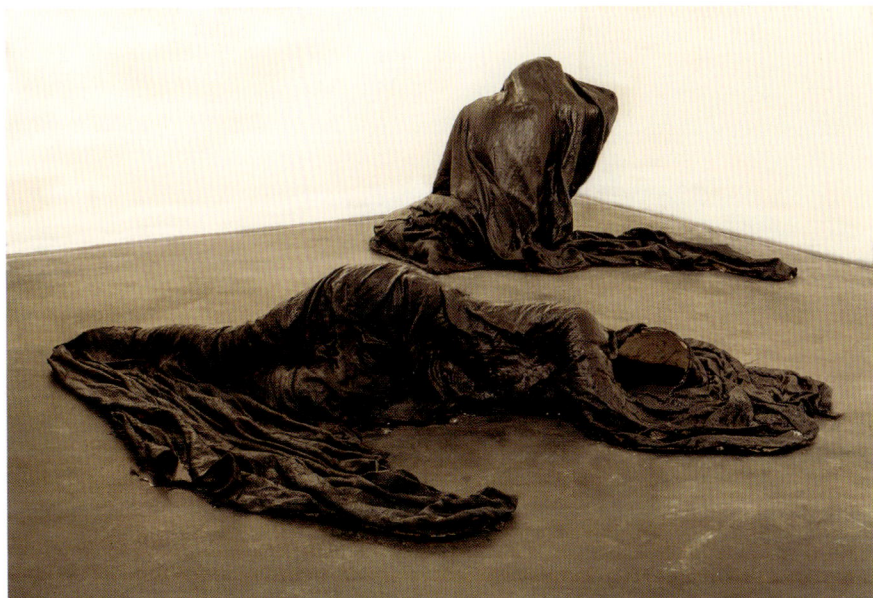

Sarah Ahmad received an MFA from the Memphis College of Art, MA Education from Union University in Jackson, Tennessee, and BA Fine Arts from the National College of Arts, Lahore, Pakistan.

"These works are part of the project "Bol" (translation in Urdu: speak. Speak for your lips are free-Faiz Ahmed Faiz) that addresses a woman's multiple, veiled, and paradoxical identities, and gaining her own voice. The woman in this series is covered in layers of chadors (fabric coverings) representing a prescribed identity. The sculptures molded in black drapery are hollow inside with no visible identity. The work raises many questions. Do the chadors bind her, hiding her true identity or are they a refuge protecting her from the outside world? Is she enclosed by the fabric covering her like a web or adorned by it? The web she is trapped in is beautiful, colorful, and protective. It has sheltered her through

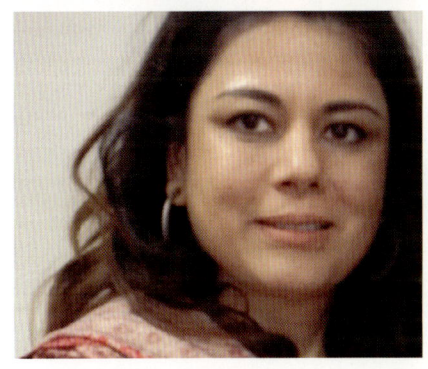

many storms evident by the fallen, ruptured trees around her. It clings to her like a lovely garment, a protective covering that refuses to shed. Is she content and accepting of her reality, or is she struggling to break free? Whether struggling to break free or surrendered to her role, she is one with the lone trees hidden in the woods… *To be one with the trees is to know Life within your own spirit* - Chief Sequoia.

WWW.SARAHAHMAD.COM

● **Bol (Speak for our lips are free - Faiz Ahmed Faiz)**
digital media photography, 17 x 24in., 2014

● **(Above Right) Bol (Sculptures)**
mixed media-resin, paint, plaster, cloth, 8 x8 x 33in., 2014

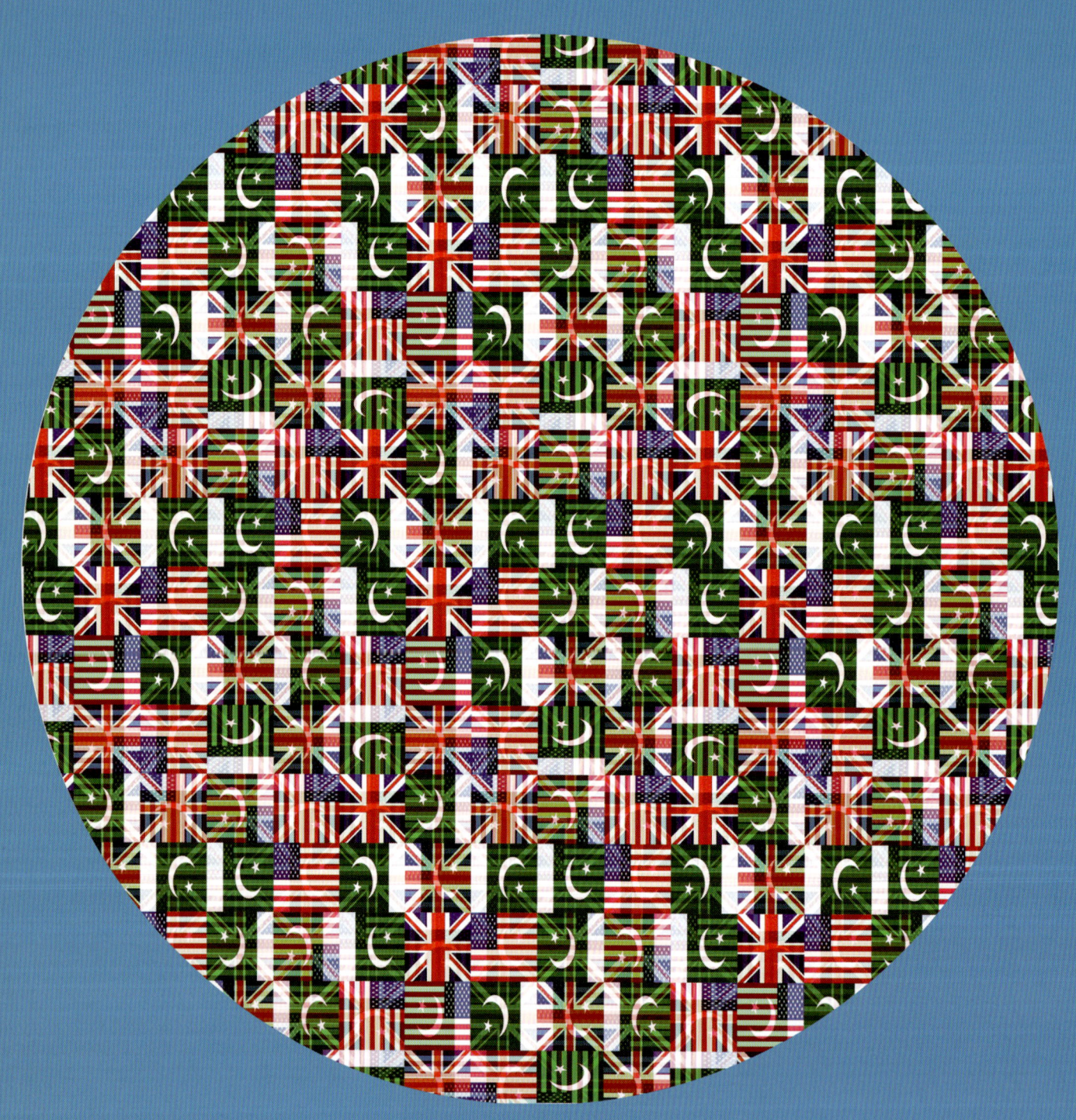

SHAFAQ AHMAD

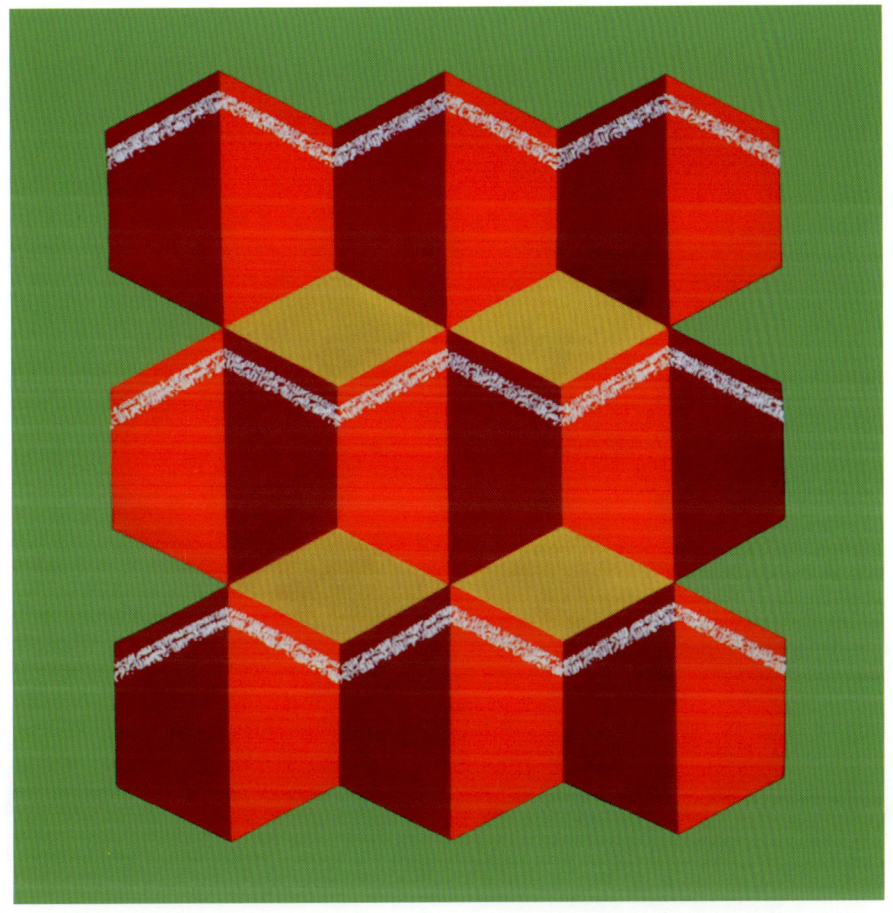

Shafaq Ahmad was born in Rawalpindi, Pakistan. After she left Pakistan she lived in the United Kingdom, Iran and Denmark before settling down in the United States. Ahmad is a multimedia artist. Her work includes painting, print making, sculpture, digital media, mixed media and art installations. Ahmad has participated in National and international group and solo exhibitions. She graduated Summa Cum Laude with a Bachelor of Fine Art degree from Virginia Commonwealth University in 1991 and a Master of Fine Art degree from Texas Christian University in Fort Worth, Texas in 2011. Her work is in the permanent collections at the Museum of Geometric and Madi Art in Dallas and Mercedes Benz Daimler Financial Corporate Headquarters in Fort Worth, Texas among other public spaces. The message of multicultural awareness is central in Ahmad's work. In her work she is intrigued and inspired by mysticism, which is to believe in the all-encompassing unity of the Creator. This belief influences both the conceptual and formal aspects of her work. Her mystical thought manifests in the physical reality of the work as it relates to our existence in the Universe. It attempts to convey the realization and acceptance of people of diverse backgrounds and cultures and bridge the disparity to convey the message of sameness and equality.

WWW.SHAFAQAHMAD.COMV

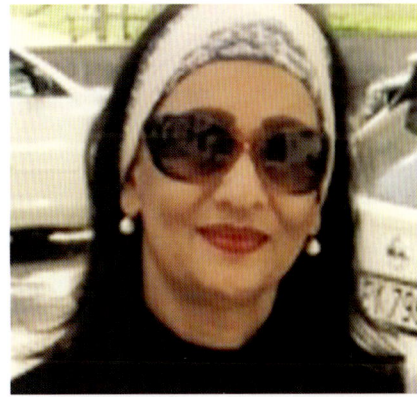

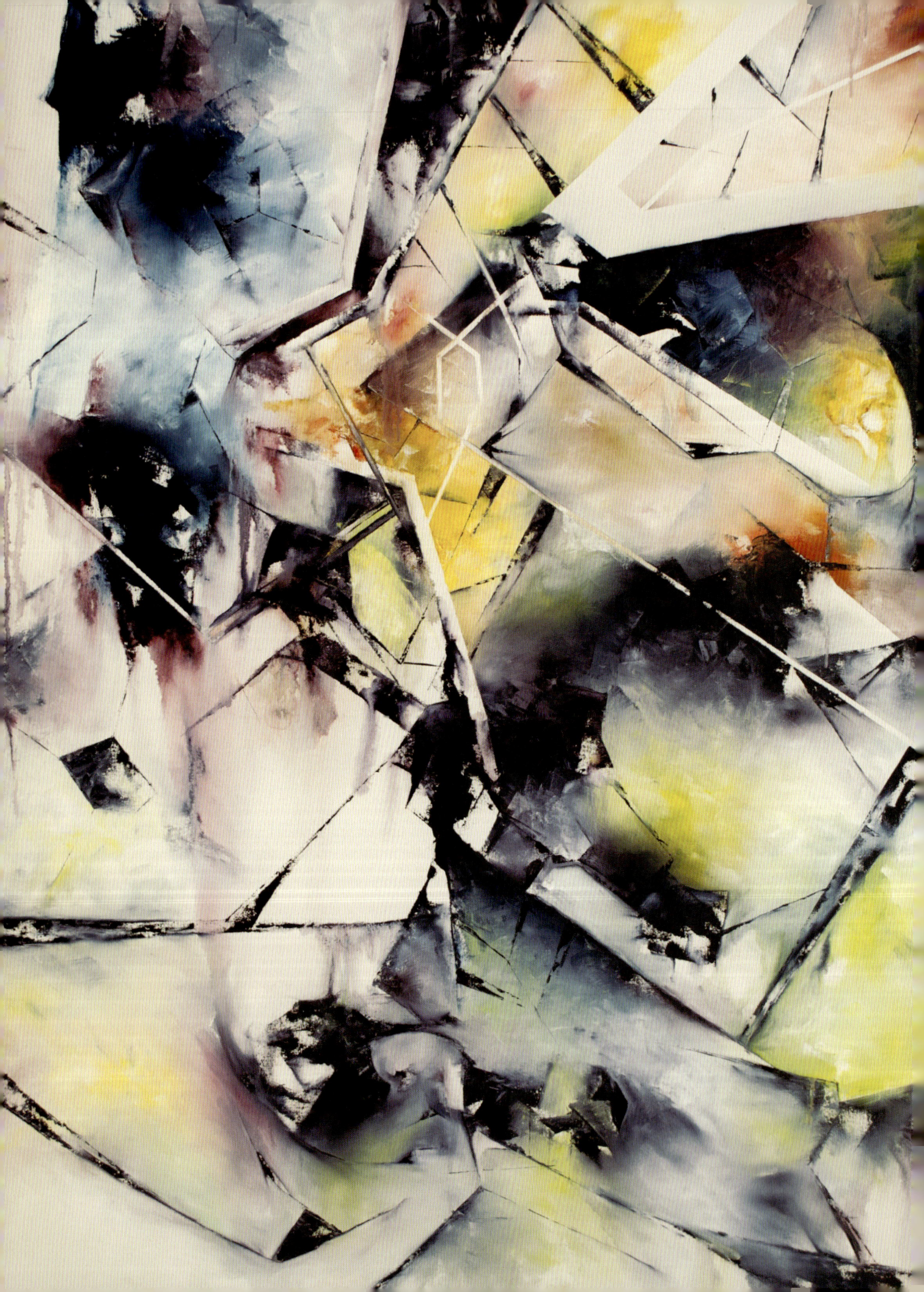

JOSÉ ALVARADO

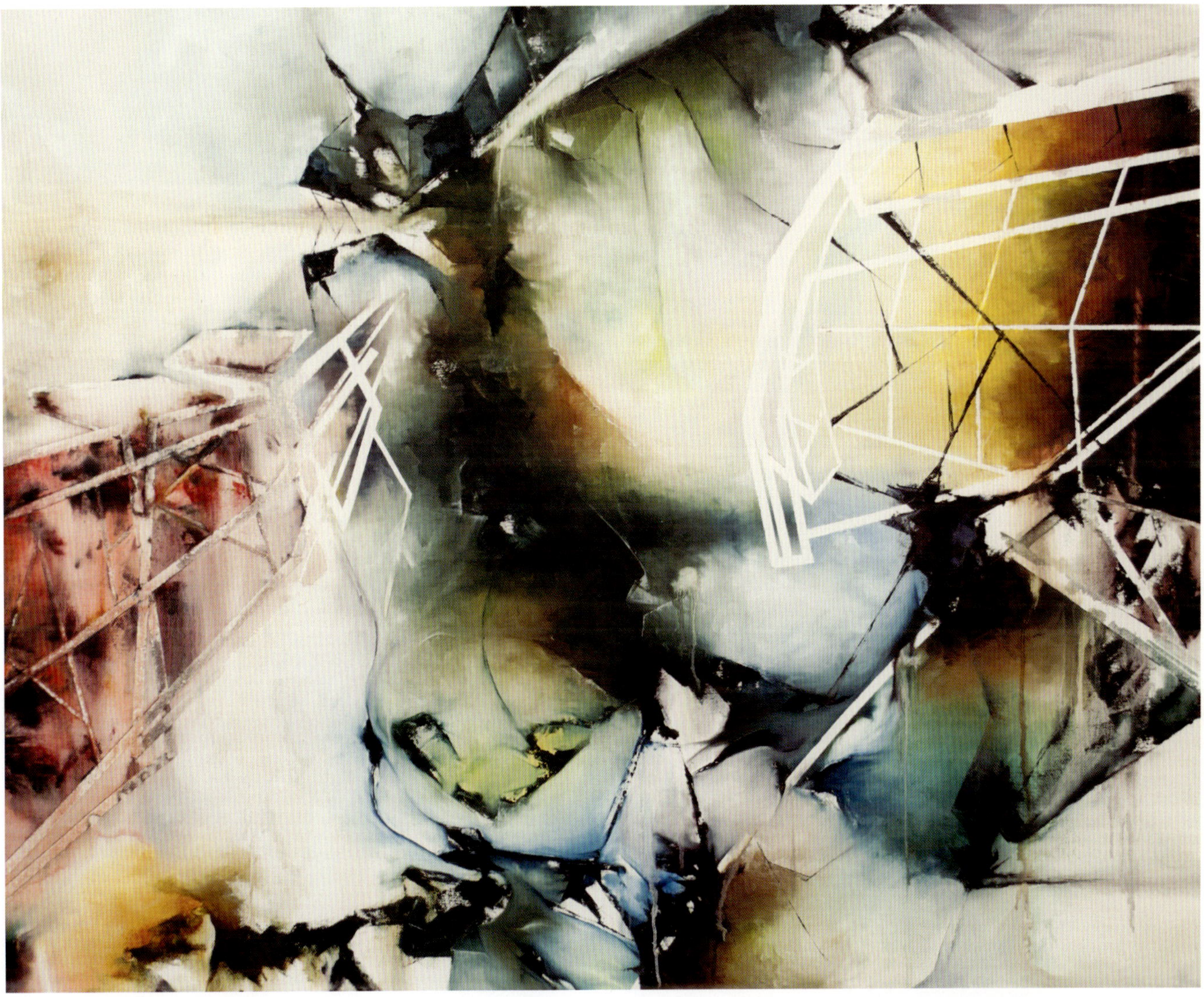

Jose Alvarado received his BA in Painting from Wichita State University and he's currently pursuing his MFA in the LeRoy E. Hoffberger School of Painting at Maryland Institute College of Art. His present work focuses on the tensions and unity between the mechanical and biological components of both the depicted entity and the physical evolution of the work itself. He tries to capture the space between these polarities and allude to processes of creation, transformation, and deconstruction. His artistic process is driven by the curiosity of science and psychology. This series of work expresses his emotional journey through the understanding and discovery of biomechanics. Alvarado is intrigued by the dichotomy developed by the fluidity of emotion in conjunction with the rigidity of the mechanical process, to seek out relational patterns composed in and around order and chaos.

JOSEEALVARADO.WORDPRESS.COM

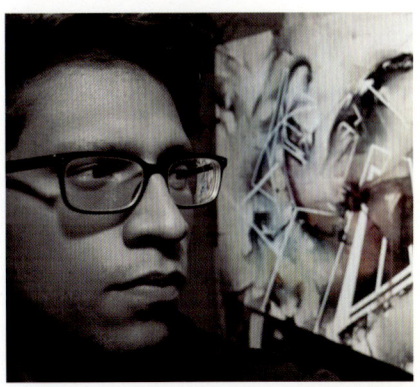

(facing page) Fractured Reality ●
Oil on canvas, 48 x 72 in., 2013

Odyssey ●
Oil on canvas, 60 x 48 in., 2013

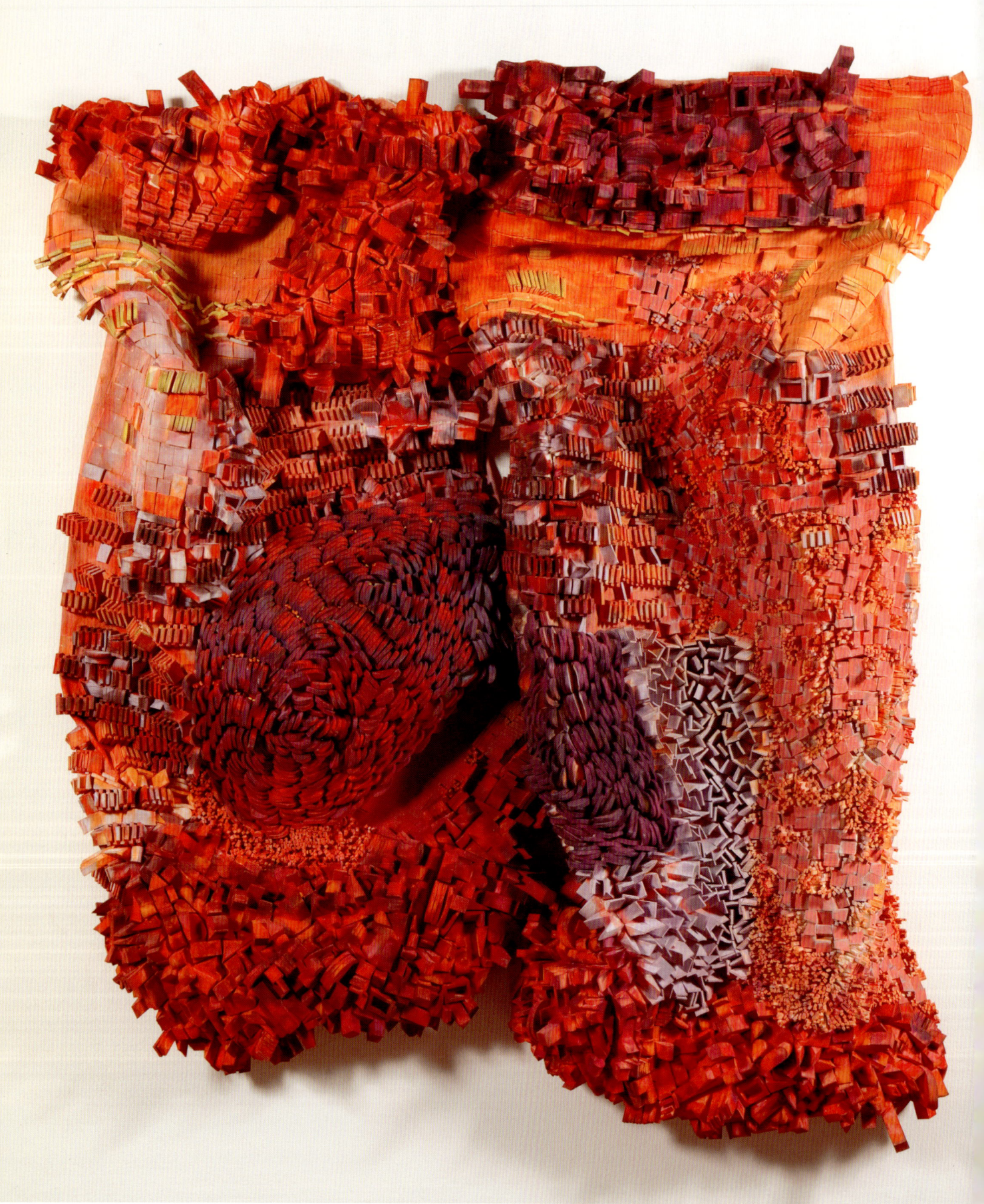

MARGERY AMDUR

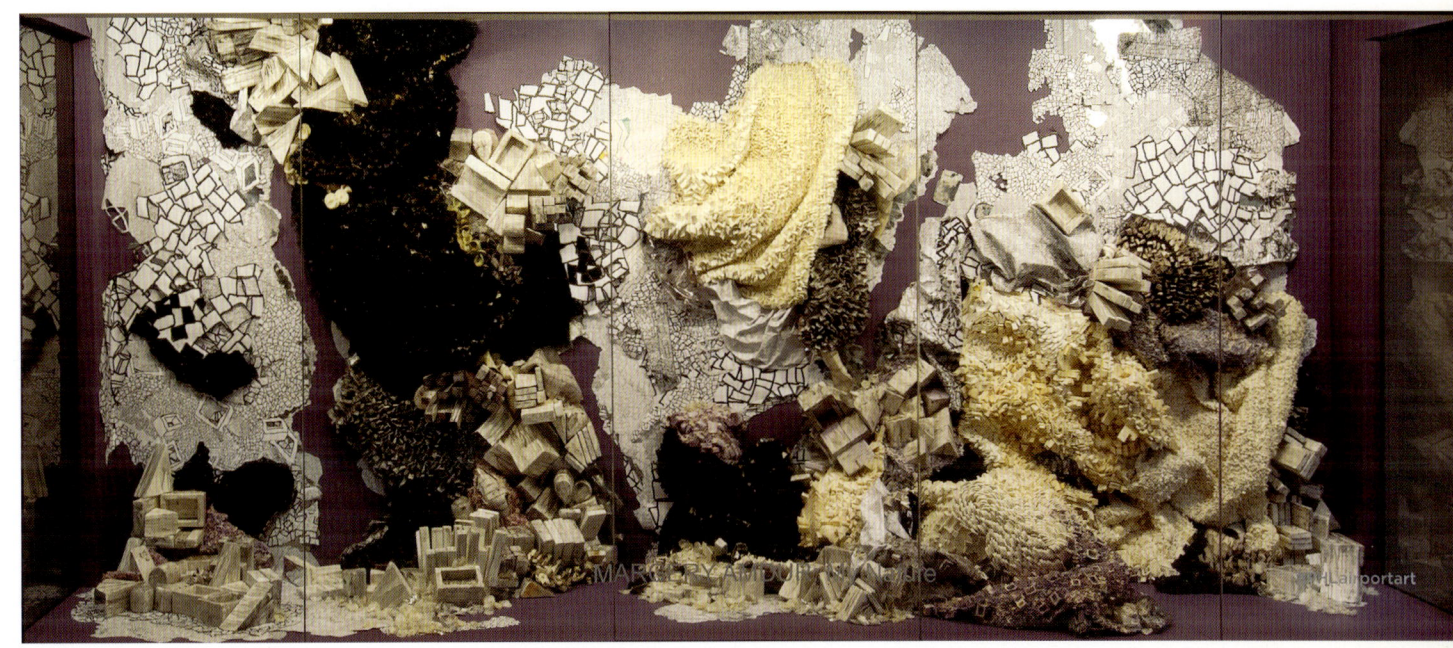

"I am a mark maker-on and off the canvas, and I don't restrict myself to any one material. I like to live in that very fluid space between painting, sculpture, and printmaking, and the idea of an obsessively ritualized process is still very prominent in the work."

Originally from Pittsburgh, Margery Amdur received her B.F.A. from Carnegie-Mellon University and her M.F.A. from the University of Wisconsin in Madison. Margery has had over 60 solo and two-person exhibitions. Her international exhibitions include Turkey, Hungary, Poland, England, and Iceland. She has been reviewed in national and international publications including Sculpture Magazine, New American Paintings, Fiber Arts, New Art Examiner, Art Papers, and in two of the Manifest International Publications. She was shortlisted in the 2015 International Aesthetica Art Prize, and an interview with the artist can be found on their site. Her next projects include an installation at the Philadelphia International Airport, and an installation at the CEU in Budapest, Hungary.

WWW.MARGERYAMDUR.NET

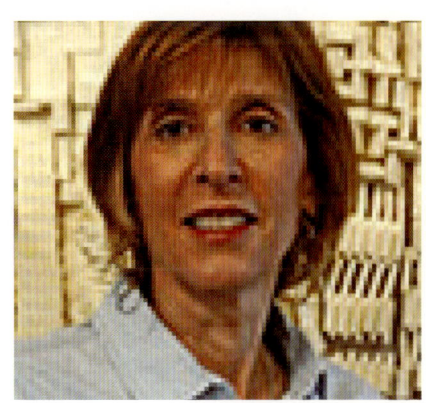

(facing page) Amass #6 ●
Cosmetic sponges coated in ink, gouache and pastel pigment , 68 x 54 in., 2014

My Nature #2 ●
Cosmetic sponges coated with pastel pigment, digital prints, styro foam, vinyl and glitter., 2015

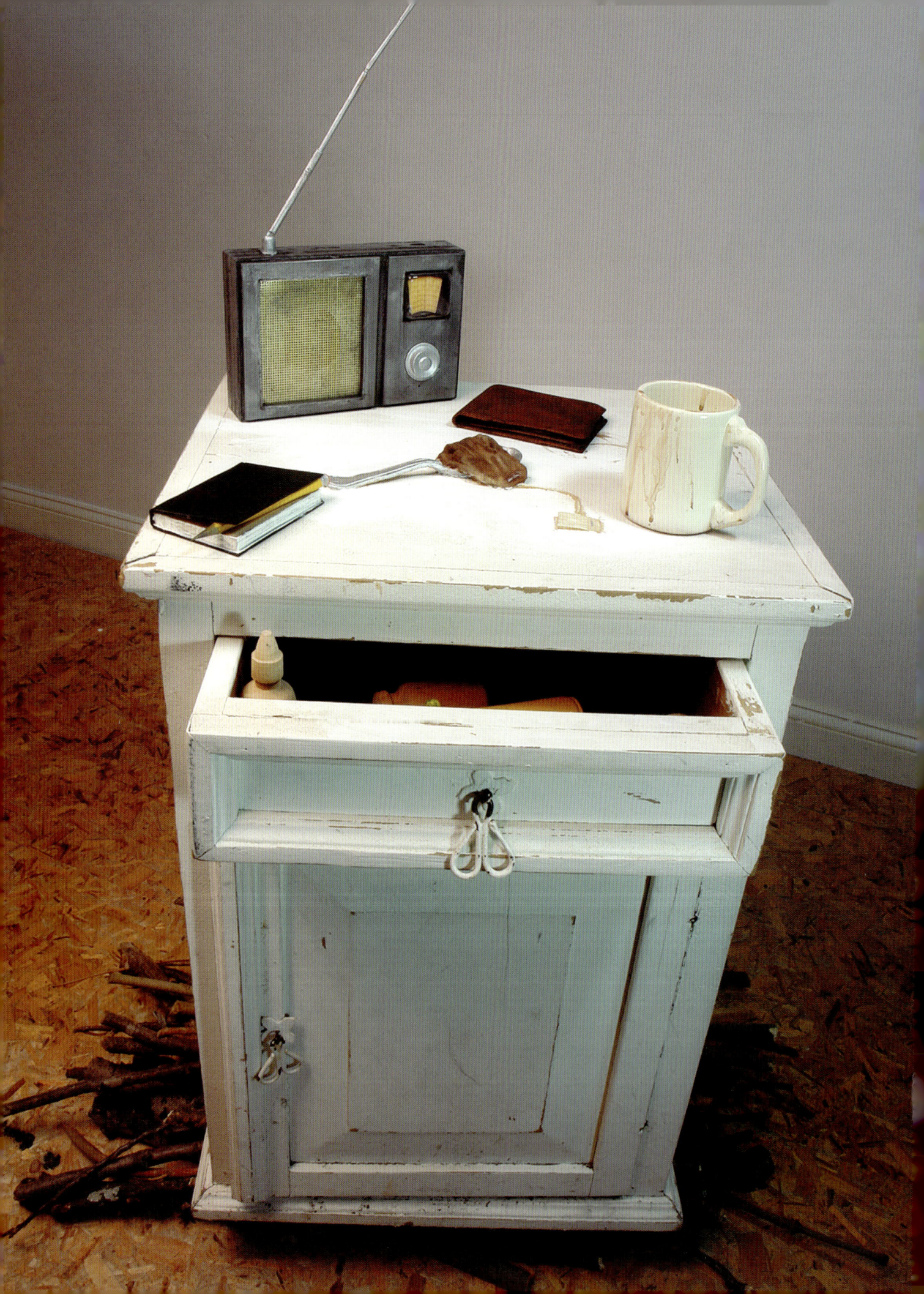

JOHN CHRISTIAN ANDERSON

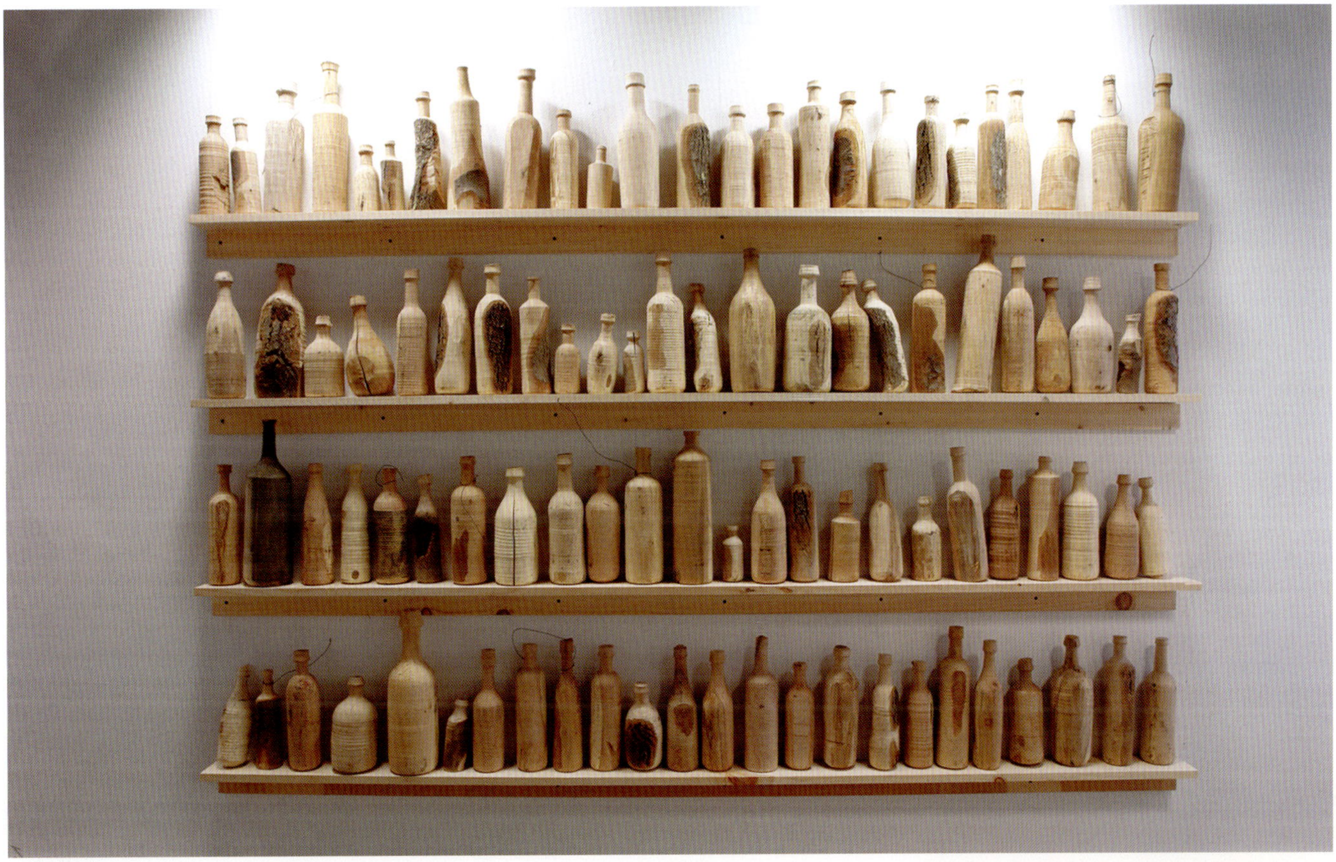

John Christian Anderson was born in Los Angeles, California. As a child his mother would take him to view Simon Rhodia's Watts Towers. These towers made a profound impact on him and, much later, became symbols of pure artistic vision, independence, and the down-to-earth attitude of using whatever materials are available. This sensibility was embraced at the San Francisco Art Institute where he received a BFA in sculpture. Subsequently, his sculpture and building expertise led to a position designing science exhibitions at the Exploratorium. Anderson eventually settled in Northern California where he secured a large barn for his sculpture and installations. He supported himself as a night custodian while during the day creating sculptures in his studio. These new art works were influenced by Indian and Buddhist sand painting, LA assemblage (e.g. Ed Keinholz), Bay Area Funk Art, Fluxus, and Minimalism.

Over time his work reflected a fusion of these aesthetic sensibilities. Anderson was especially attracted to the transient qualities rooted in sand painting. Impermanence, imperfection, and incompleteness have become fundamental to his sculpture as a way to express personal narratives while also reflecting a world that is becoming more ephemeral and out of balance.

Anderson has exhibited in numerous museums and galleries throughout the United States. This includes the Rose Art Museum, the ICA Boston, The DeCordova Museum, and the Delaware Center for Contemporary Art. His work is included in both public and private collections. He teaches at Framingham State University and lives in Boston, Massachusetts.

WWW.SCULPTUREBYJOHNANDERSON.
WORDPRESS.COM/
WWW.JOHNCHRISTIANANDERSON.COM/

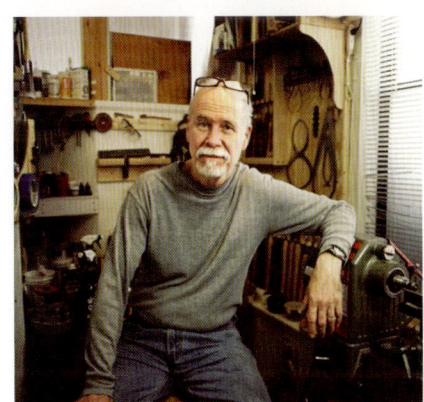

(facing page) La Noche ●
Carved, painted, and turned recycled wood and cast resin, 22 x 18 x 14 in.., 2015

My Father's Dilemma ●
Turned tree limbs & found wood, 96 x 52 x 4 in., 2012

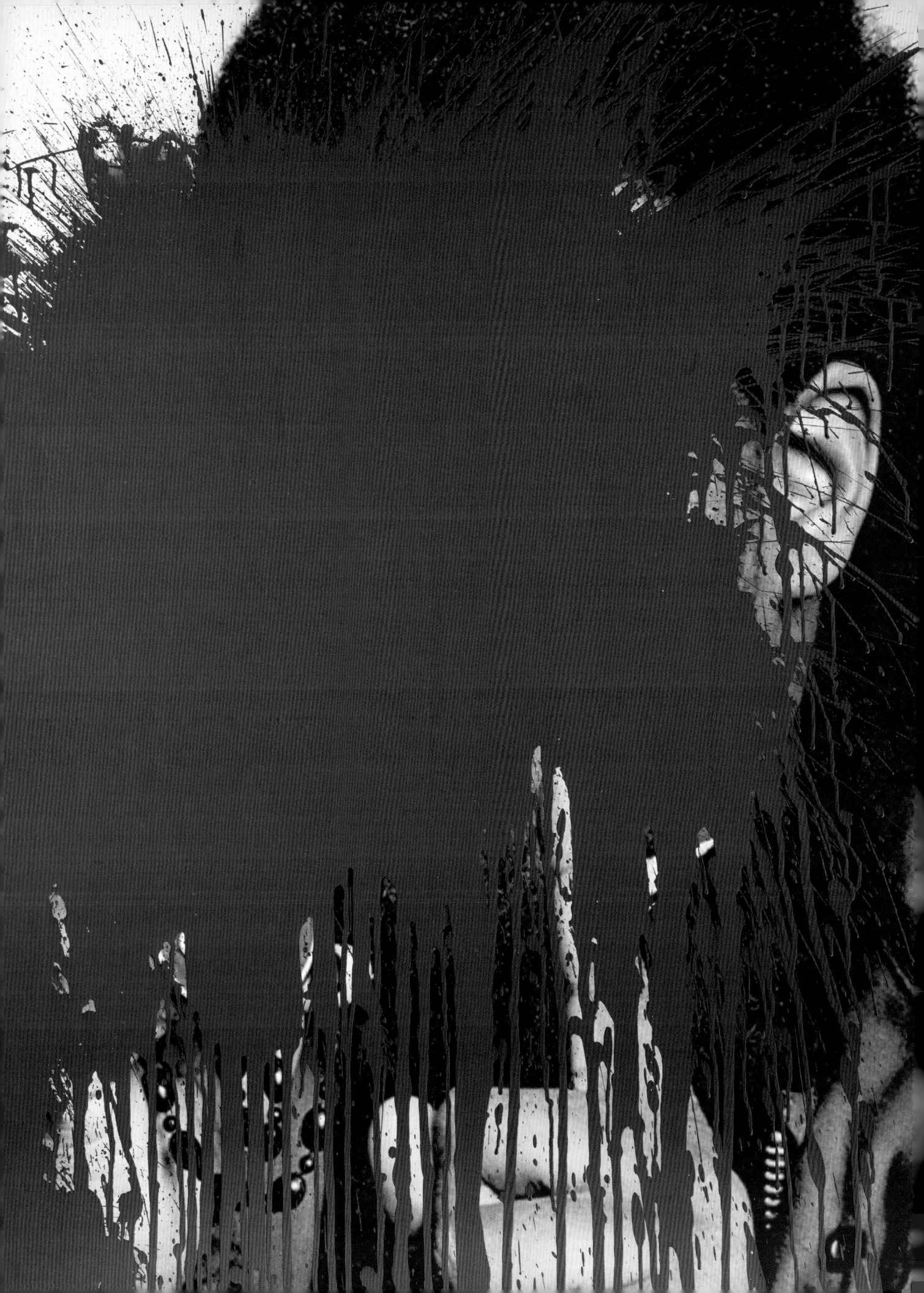

GEN ATEM

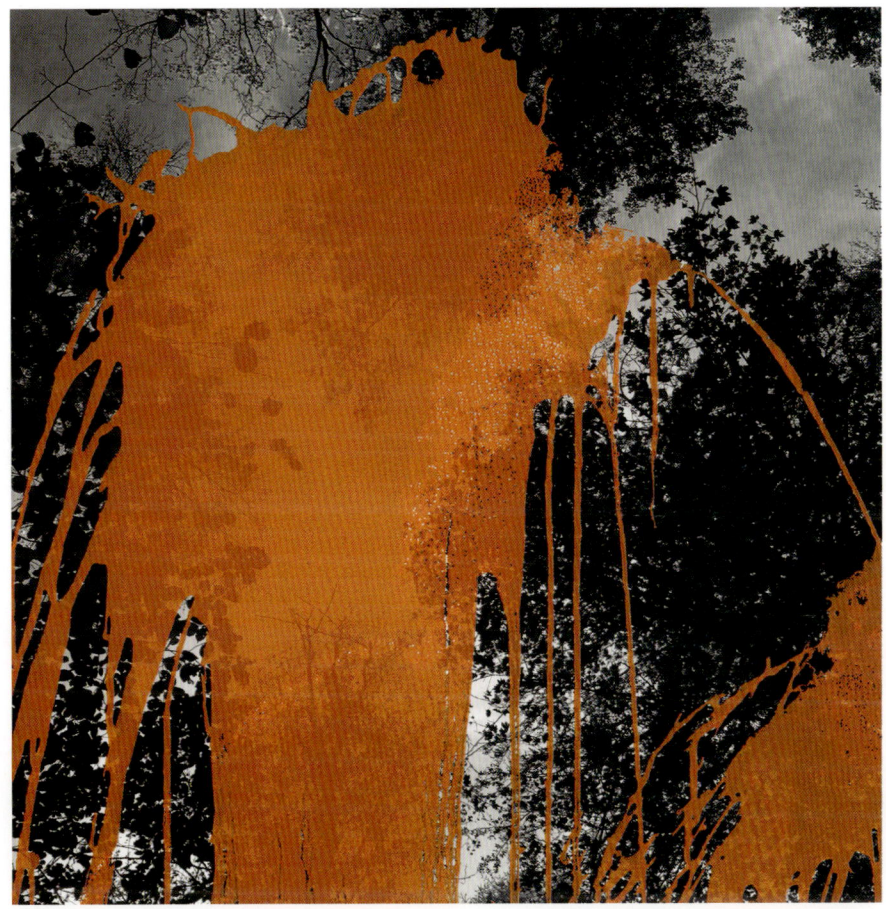

● **(facing page) Afrika Bambaataa**
Acrylic on inkjet print on canvas,
120 x 90 cm., 2013

● **Forest #3**
Fine art print on Hahnemuchle paper,
90 x 90 cm., 2015

"[Meditated Vandalism] triggers an explosive irritation, a shattering disappointment that manifests itself as iconoclastic quarrel between subject and object."

To counter the madness of identity wars, I define an asymmetric intervention strategy: Meditated Vandalism. It consists of attaining a state of tense calm emerging from the interaction between intention-free lingering on one hand and agitative intervening on the other. This state is the foundation, in which higher mental concentration is rooted. It penetrates both the subtle workings as well as the vulgar excesses of identity mania. This realization in turn triggers an explosive irritation, a shattering disappointment that manifests itself as iconoclastic quarrel between subject and object. The result is a total loss of identity. Paradoxically the concomitant fear births that force, from which my work creates and baptizes itself. Immediately afterwards, it is hung in the exhibition space and carried to its grave. Now the viewer notices, interprets and scrutinizes it - this intervention makes the viewer the vandal: not only does he disrupt the inner image of his own identity, but also the final rest of the piece and he initiates its resurrection in the realm of art. But the downfall is immediately set in motion because the personal, participative perception soon solidifies in collective delectation. Somebody come and kick it in the ass.

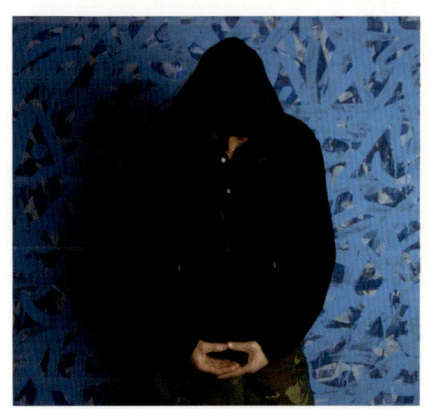

WWW.GENATEM.COM

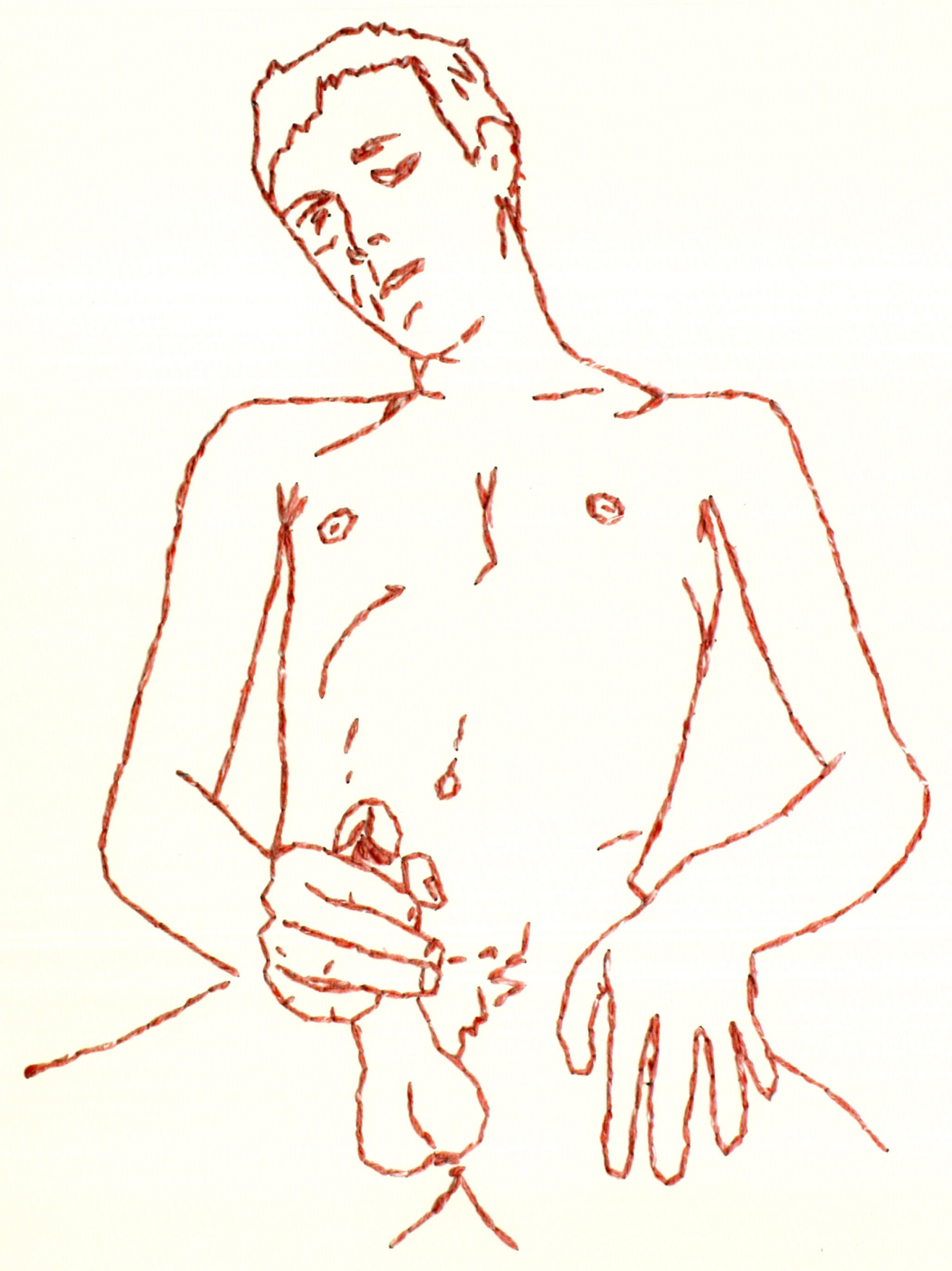

FRANKO B

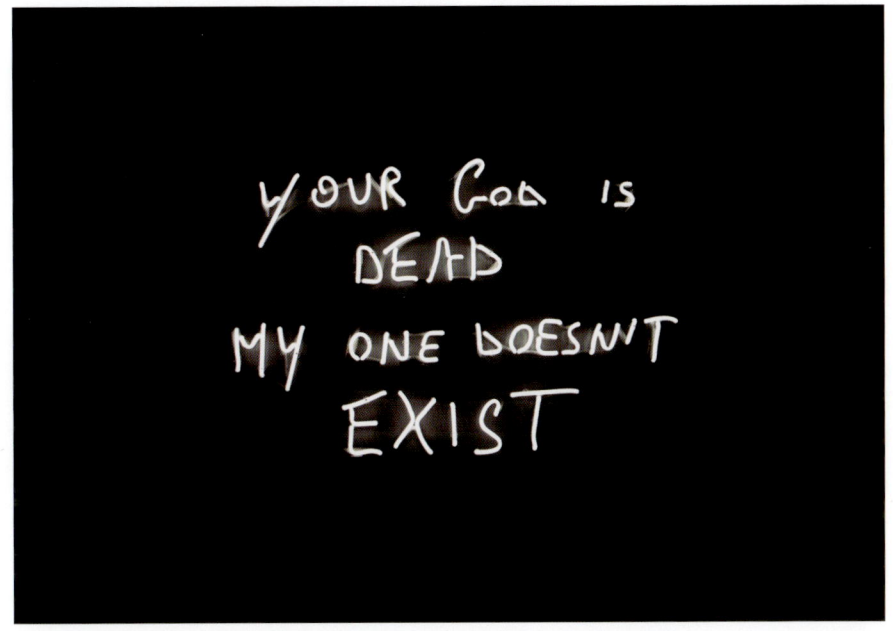

YOUR God is
DEAD
MY ONE DOESN'T
EXIST

● **(facing page) Pink Boy**
Wool stitched on paper, 2012 - 2014

● **Your God**
Neon, 2009

"The life and work of Franko B is situated somewhere between isolation and seduction, benevolence and confrontation, suffering and eroticism, punk and poetry. It is a certain type of schizophrenia that finds a balance, dramatically undermining the status quo."

Franko B was born in Milan, Italy in 1960. He moved to London in 1979, and studied Fine Art at Camberwell College of Arts from 1986-7, Chelsea College of Art between 1987-90 and the Byam Shaw School of Art from 1990-91.

Franko B has worked with many institutions across continents including at the Tate Modern, Tate Britain, Tate Liverpool, the ICA, Palais des Beaux-Arts, Belgium, Ex Teresa Mexico City, PAC Milan, RU ARTS Moscow, Russia.

His work is in respected private and public institutions, including the Tate Permanent Collection, The V&A Museum, the permanent collection of the city of Milan, Italy as examples. Franko B has lectures widely, including at St Martins School of Art, DasArt, New York University and the Courtauld Institute of Art. He has been the subject of

four monographs, most recently, I Still Love. He was appointed Professor of Sculpture at the Accademia Di Belle Arti [school of fine art], Macerata Italy in January 2009. And currently a visiting guest lecture at the royal college of arts London. Throughout his practice, he has repeatedly responded to issues of suppression, dogmatism and abuse and to the politics of performing the self.

WWW.FRANKO-B.COM

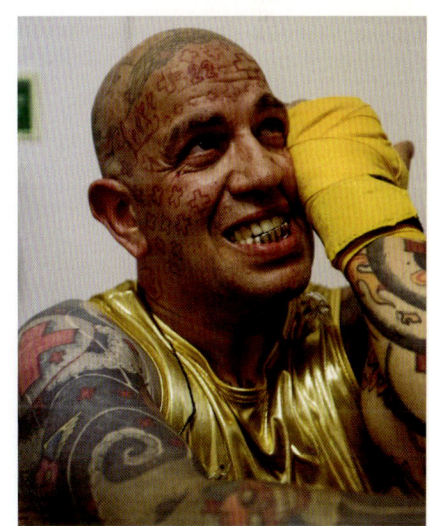

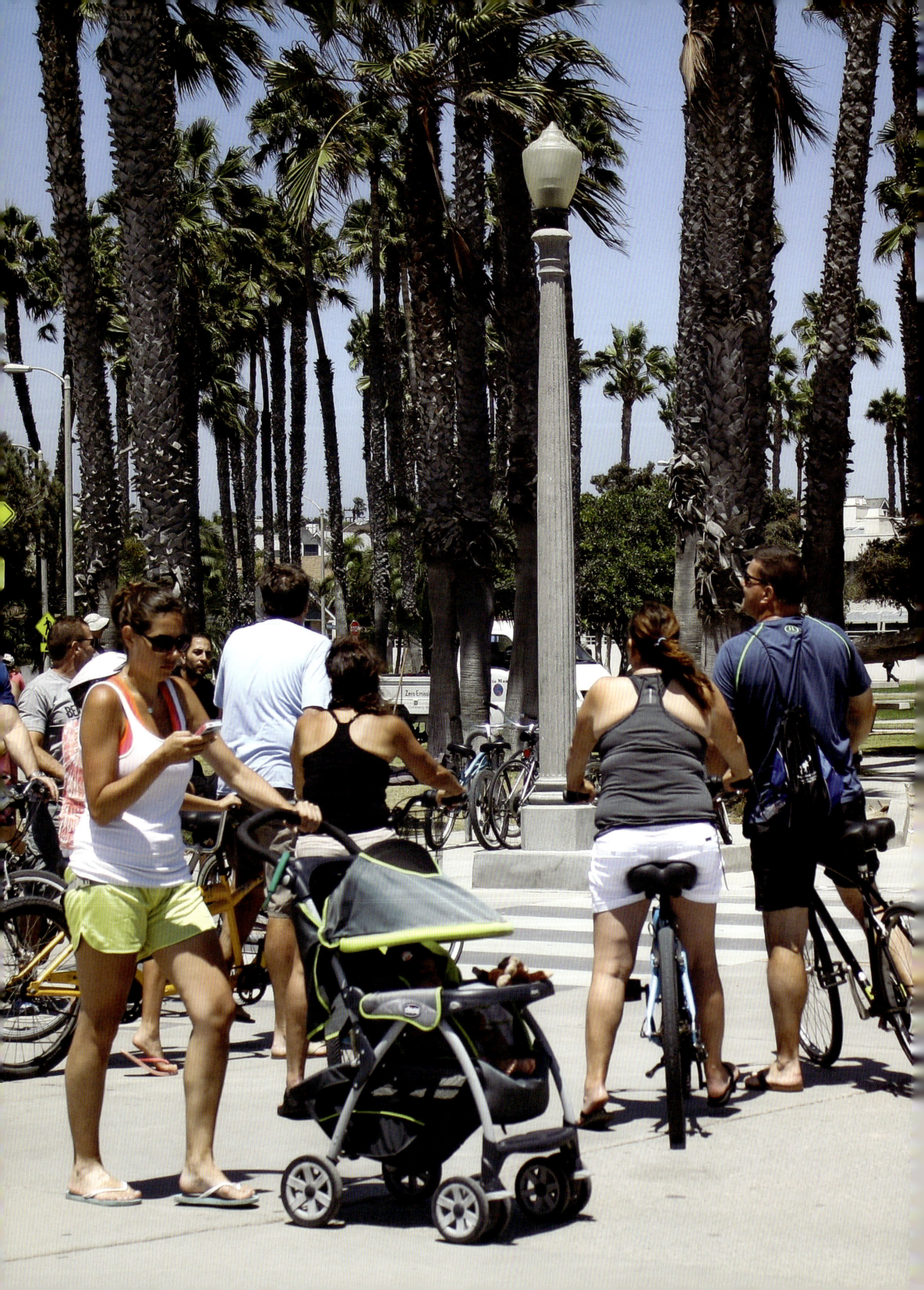

JESSICA BARROSO-GOMEZ

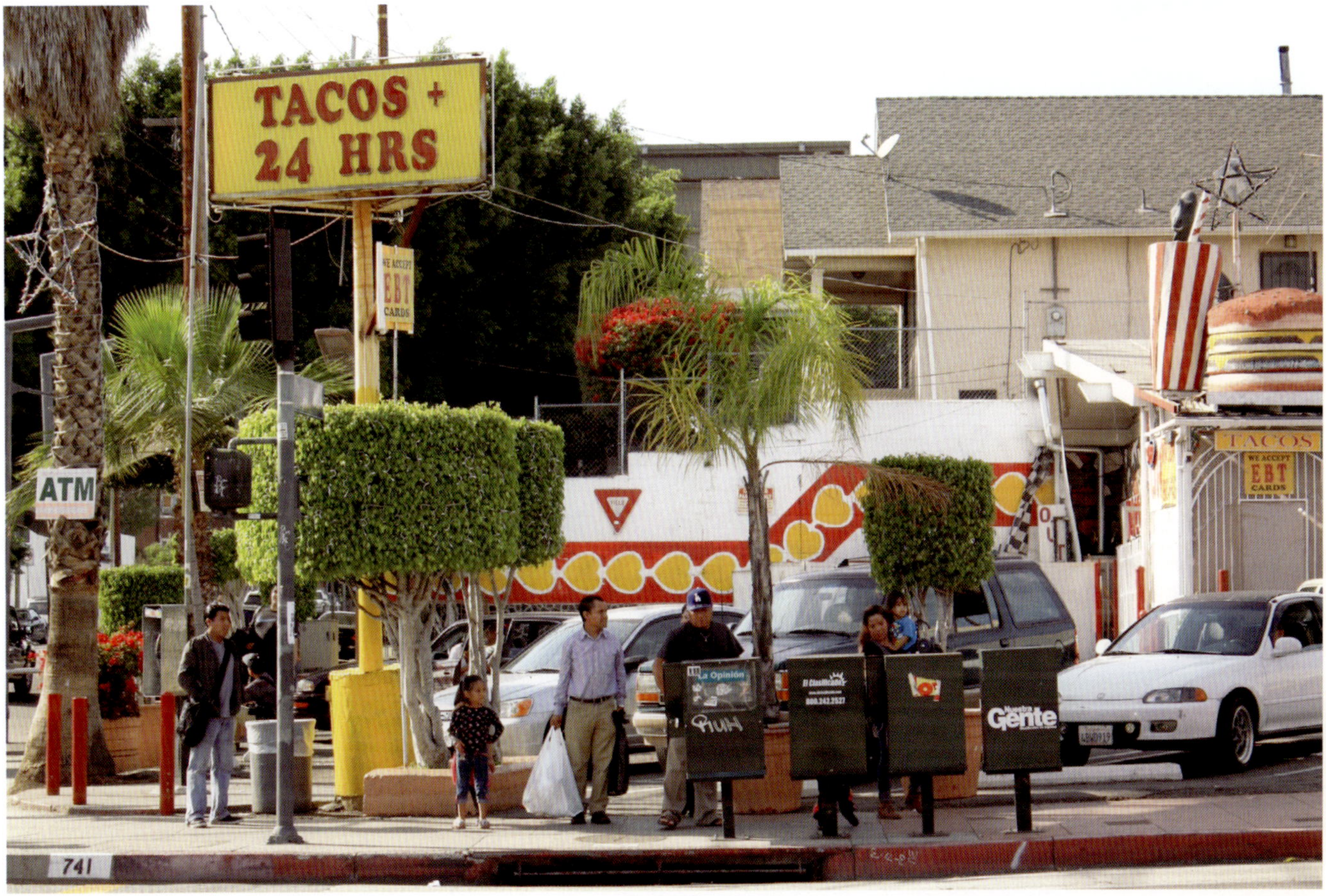

Growing up as an illegal immigrant in southern Los Angeles, I learned to live in the shadows of society. I was born into a low income family who crossed the border illegally because they bought into the American Dream. Two decades later their dream has become a nightmare. I was told that the only way out of this reality was education, so I excelled with honors only to be denied scholarships and job opportunities because of my illegal status, so I resorted to the Mexican tradition of marriage and motherhood. Two years into the marriage and one child later I became a victim of spousal abuse at the hands of an enlisted US Marine. My daughter and I escaped my ex-husband's controlling grip with literally the clothes on our back. I refused to be a victim. Somewhere in the midst of my turmoil and new beginning, I found my voice. My medium: documentary photography, my weapon of choice. My subject: family, friends my community. In documenting my life and the lives of others I found the truth that eluded me when I was lurking in the shadows. My art has literally given me a second chance. I no longer live in silence or ashamed to be Mexican. I am now an art activist, deciphering my communities' fears, self-hatred, struggles and the human condition.

WWW.JESSICABARROSOGOMEZ.COM

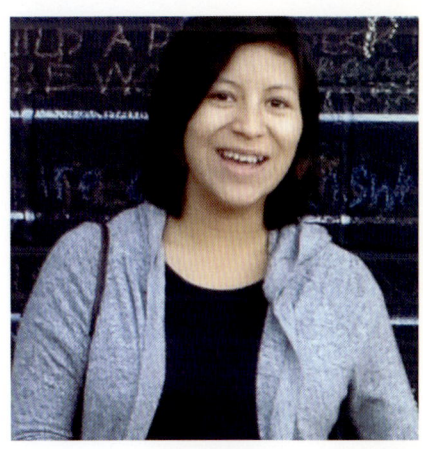

(facing page) Time Out (series) ●
Color photograph, 40 x 60 in., 2015

Waiting Room (series) ●
Color photograph, 40 x 60in., 2015

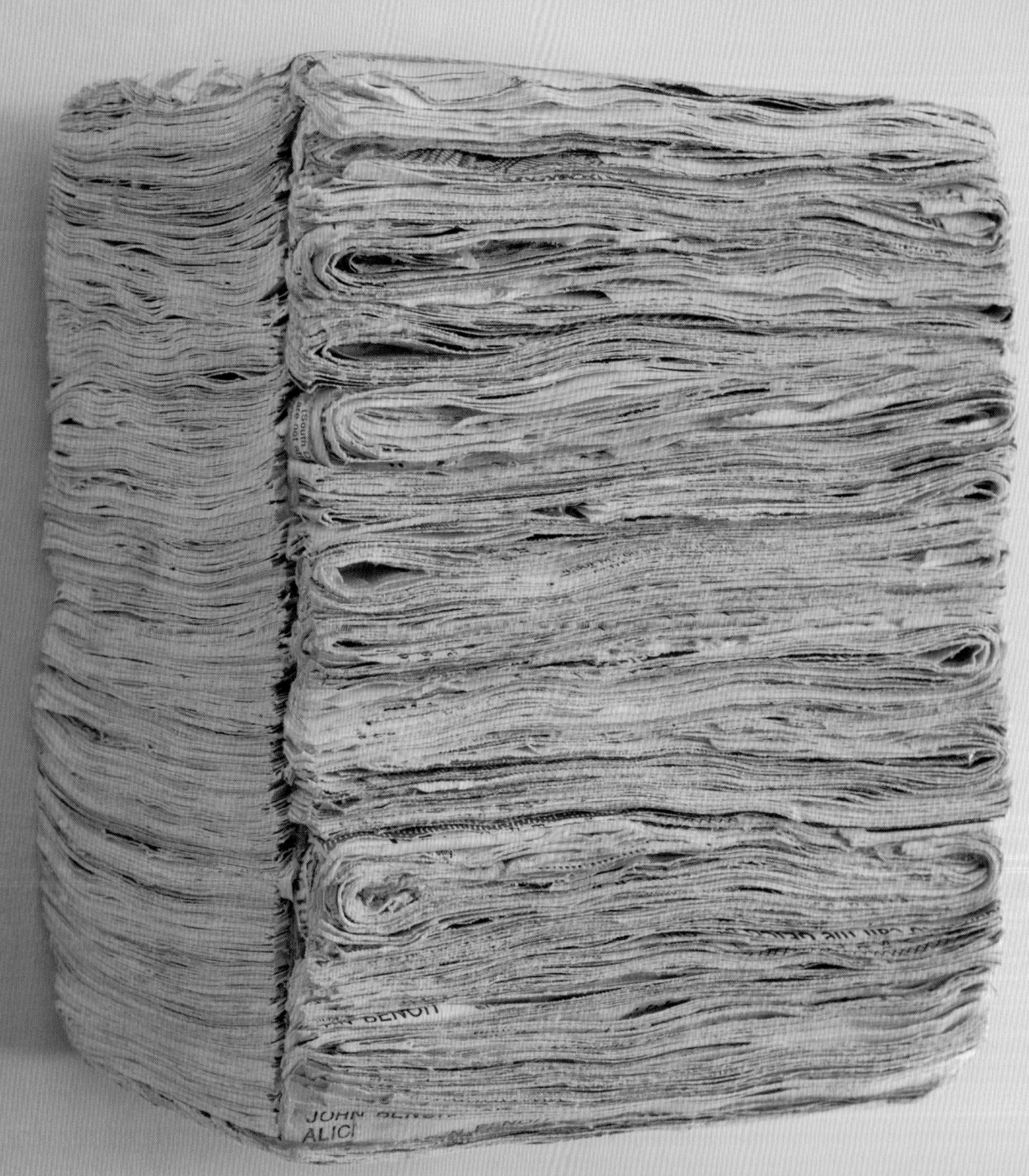

MICHELLE BENOIT

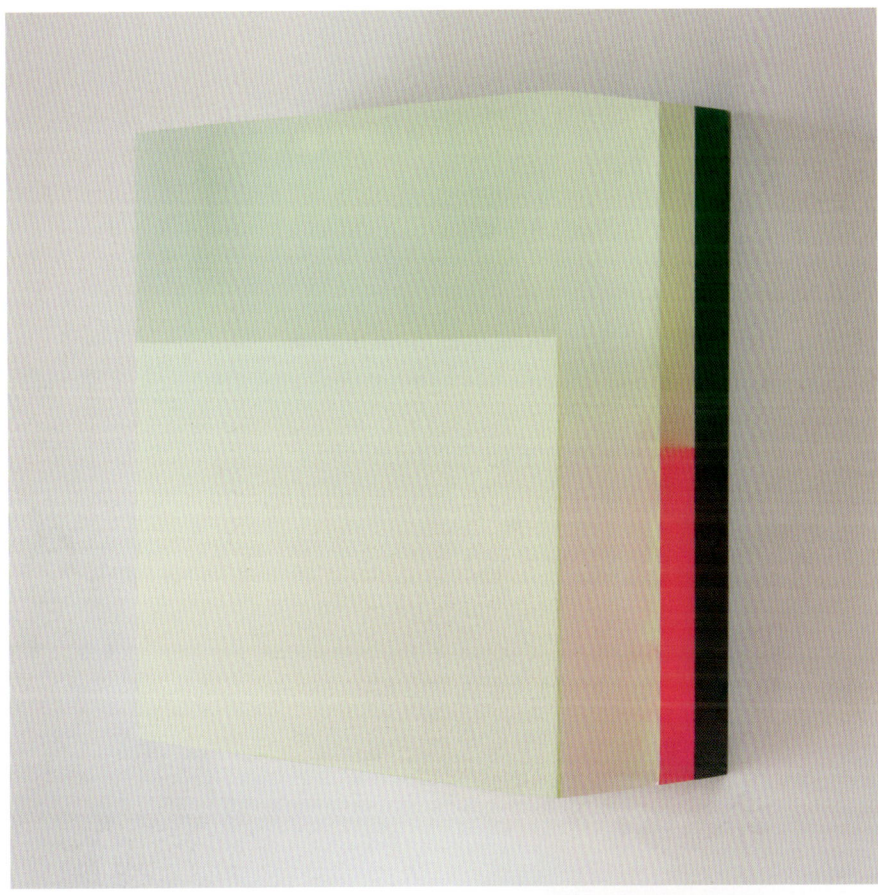

Michelle Benoit's work often utilizes recycled and reclaimed materials.

Collected, cut and painted, stacked, mortared and coalesced. Time and again appeal, experimentation and intent are embedded, revealing process and structure as image. Color combinations are coded and symbolic of and for, past events, memory and place. Frequently resulting in objects that mimic a geologic core sample. While studying in Iowa, Benoit was influenced while working under Bill Green in the archeology laboratory at the Office of The State Archeologist. Benoit currently lives and works with her husband and quite a few rescued homeless dogs and cats. They're restoring a historic 18th century farmhouse in West Warwick, Rhode Island.

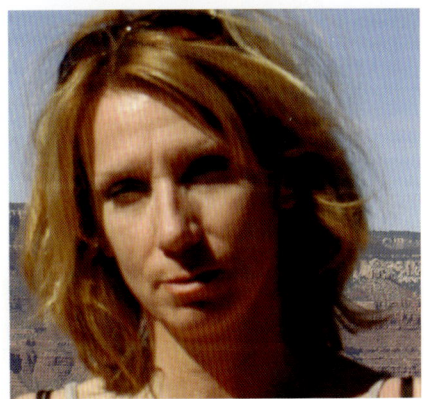

● **(facing page) Shreded Mail Series**
Written correspondence on cardboard, acrylic polymer binder, 6.75 x 5.50 x 4 in., 2014

● **The Willard Street Series; Pink Under**
Gouache and flashe paint on reclaimed bulletproof plexiglass, 6 x 6 x 2.75in., 2014

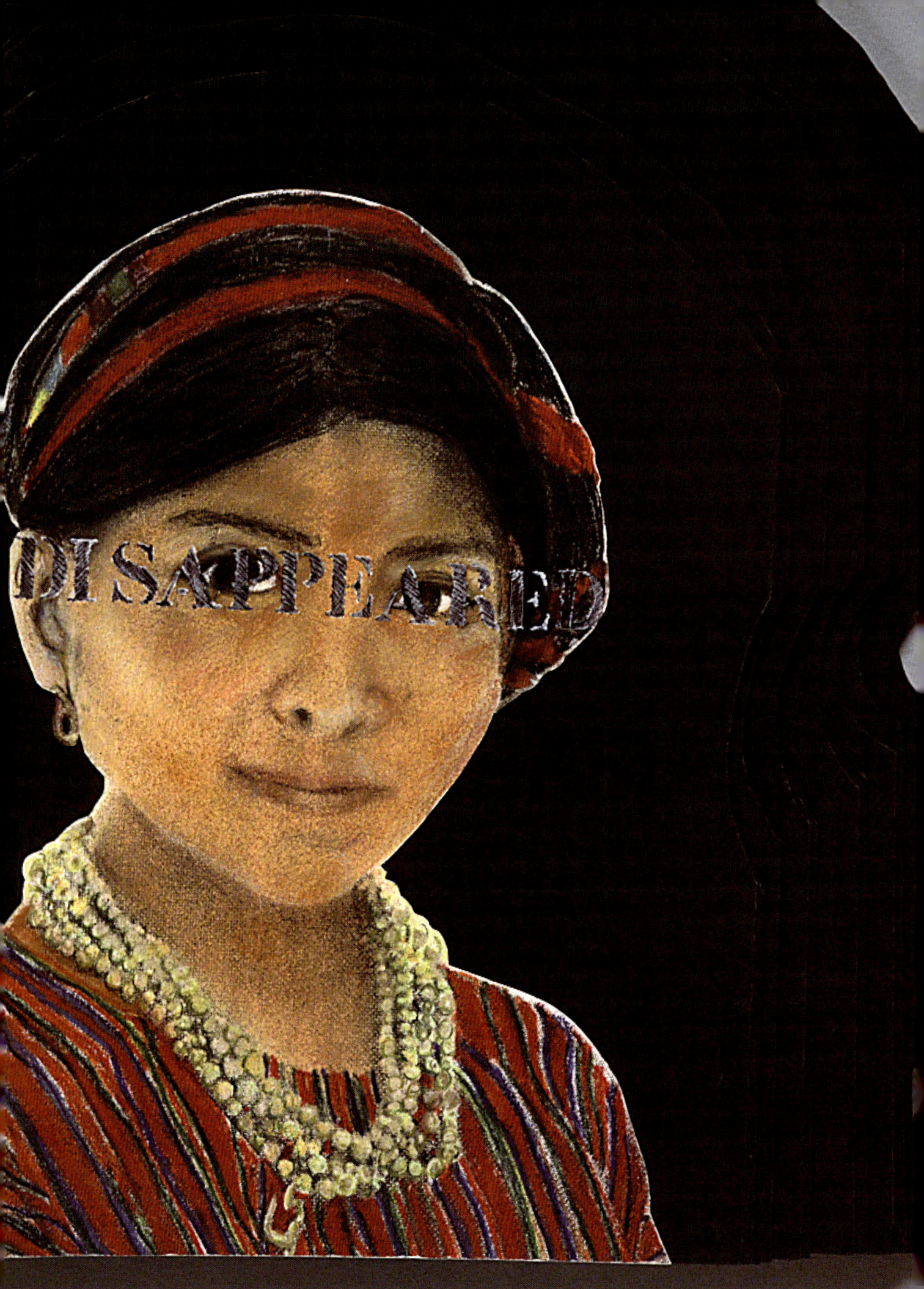

LAURA BLACKLOW

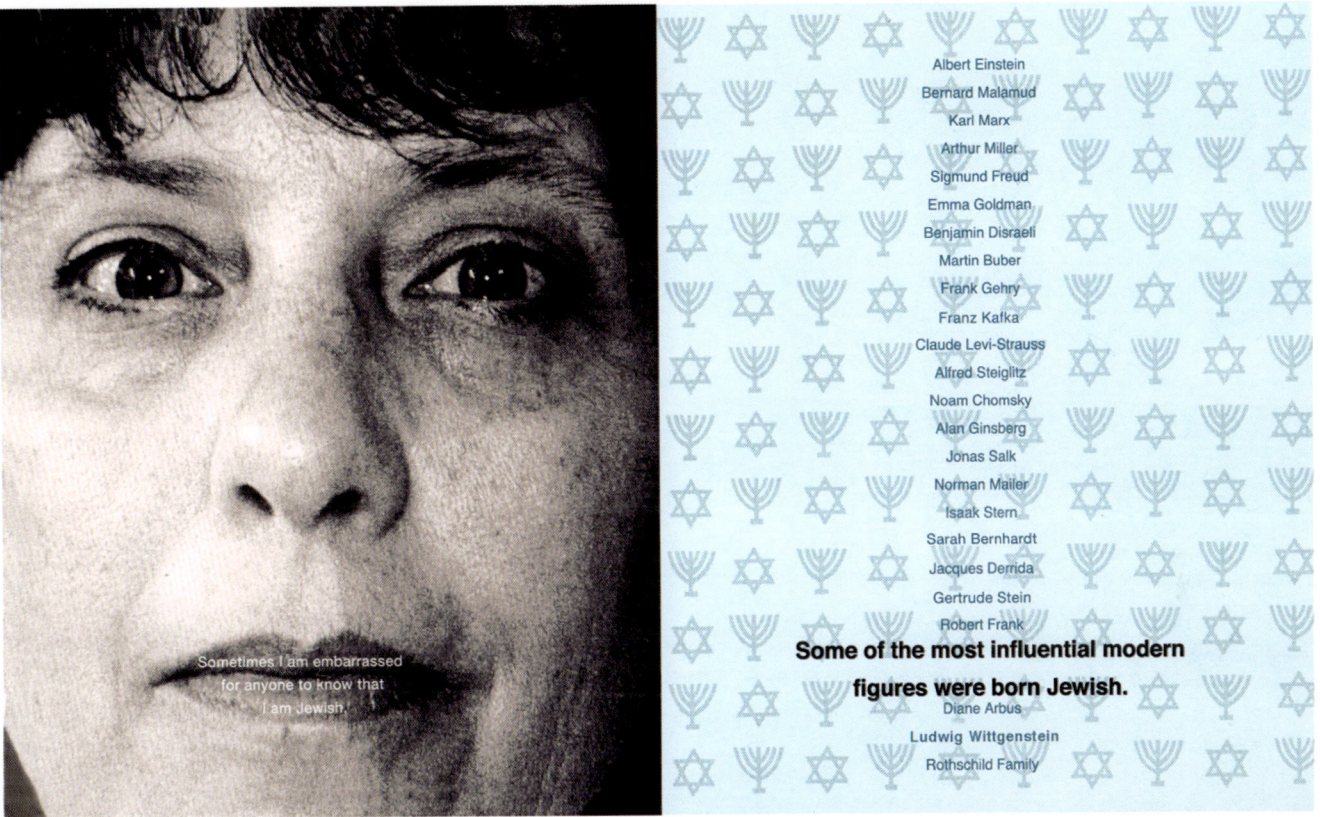

Sometimes I am embarrassed for anyone to know that I am Jewish.

Albert Einstein
Bernard Malamud
Karl Marx
Arthur Miller
Sigmund Freud
Emma Goldman
Benjamin Disraeli
Martin Buber
Frank Gehry
Franz Kafka
Claude Levi-Strauss
Alfred Steiglitz
Noam Chomsky
Alan Ginsberg
Jonas Salk
Norman Mailer
Isaak Stern
Sarah Bernhardt
Jacques Derrida
Gertrude Stein
Robert Frank

Some of the most influential modern figures were born Jewish.
Diane Arbus
Ludwig Wittgenstein
Rothschild Family

"From the moment I held a camera in my hand at an early age, I knew that somehow the medium it represented would be a big part of my world."

And so, even though I attended a conservative art school that did not recognize photography as a fine art (!), when I saw the work of Robert Rauschenberg, I was inspired to combine my training in drawing, printmaking, and painting with photography. Out of that endeavor came my interest in alternative processes and color digital photography. I am aware of the controversies surrounding the gaze. I feel the proliferation of photos in everyday life to the point that taking pictures can interfere with experiencing life. I notice the way photography is being used to exploit the viewer through advertisements and opinion media. That knowledge has led me

to use significant postmodern critiques in a new way. And so, I aim for my books and prints to be non-traditional documentary statements and often use words to provide added context.

WWW.LAURABLACKLOW.COM/

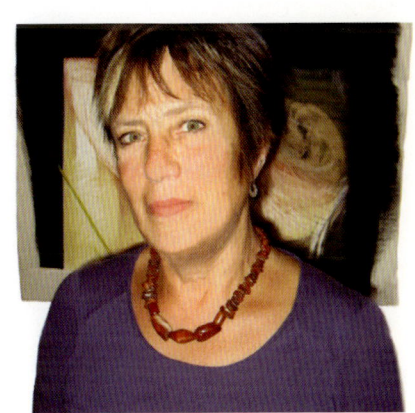

(facing page) The Disappeared ●
Black and white photocopy on rag paper with pastel, Text in Spanish, English and Braille, 12 x 18 in.

Confessions of a Jew ●
Archival inkjet print on neutral pH paper, 6.75 x 5.5 in., 2003/4

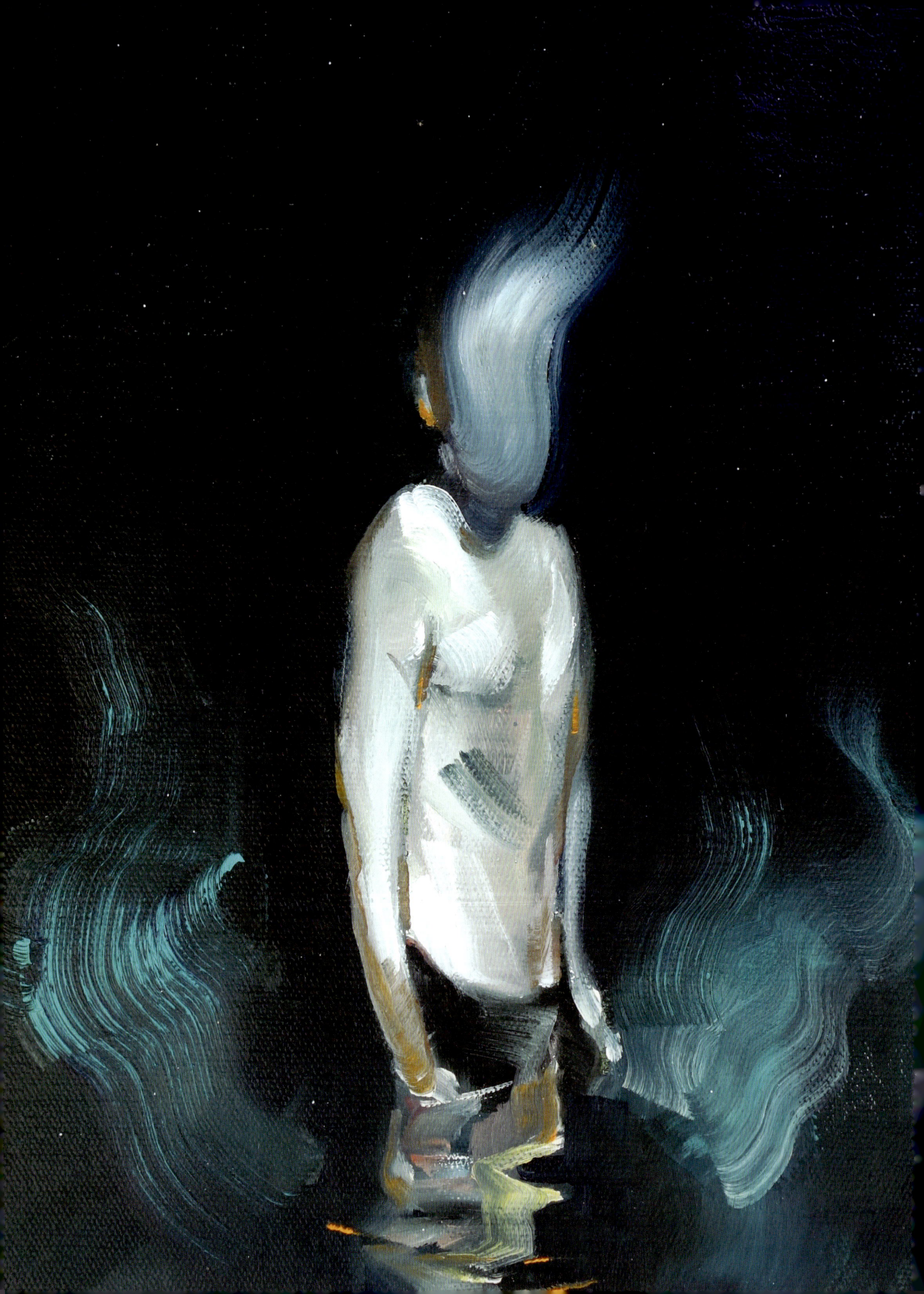

CARMELO BLANDINO

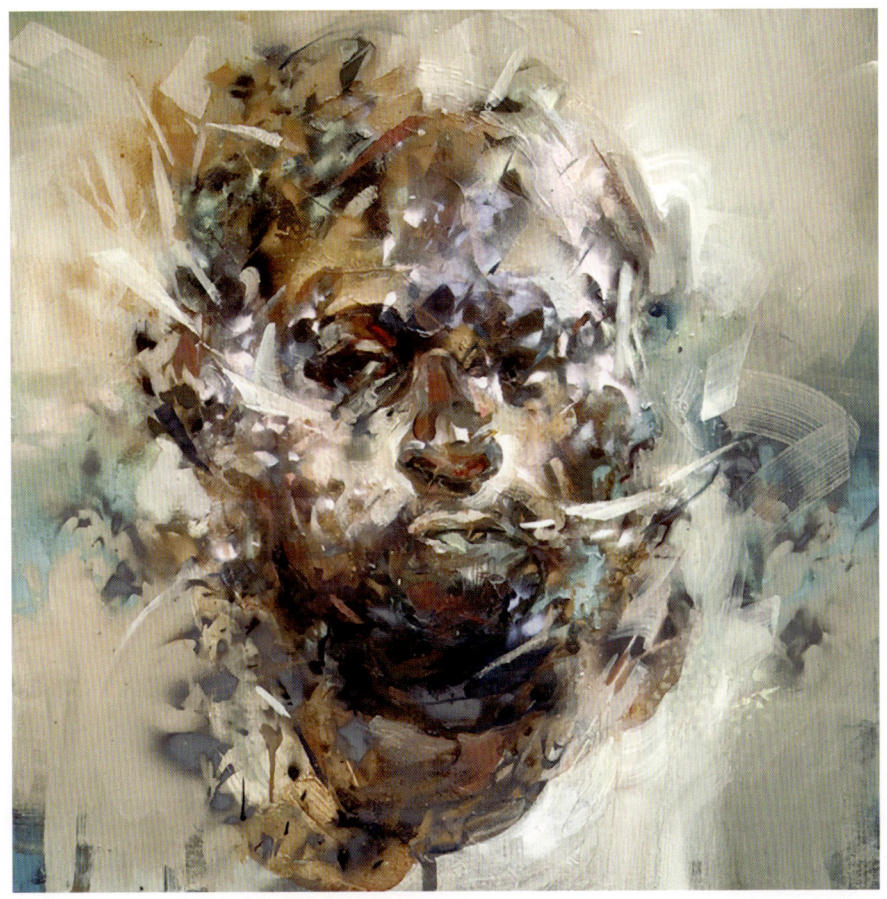

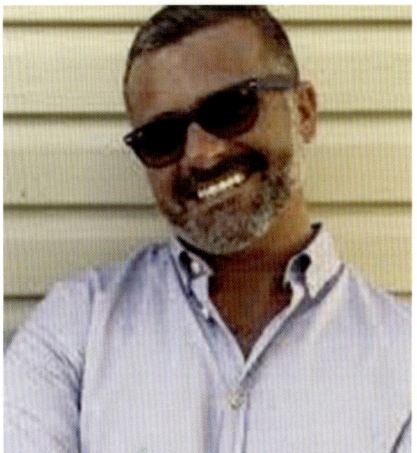

"My works are entrusted with the messages of Ages, created to impart healing and creative inspiration through beauty"

Born to Sicilian parents in Tübingen, Germany, and with a childhood spent in the cities of Montreal and Modica, Sicily, Carmelo Blandino's life journey has spanned continents and oceans. It has now brought him to the US, where he has studios and residences in both Connecticut and Wisconsin. Blandino grows his inspirational vocabulary by taking the essentialness of Home to each and every place he has made his bed, wherever he has set up easel and wielded paintbrush.

Blandino studied art and design in Montreal and enjoyed success as freelance illustrator to advertising agencies, designers and architects. A next step, borne of both

logic and calling, demanded that Blandino turn his focus on the creation of his own artistic legacy. The result is a fast growing, ever-morphing, highly personal and spiritually guided oeuvre. Informed heavily by Blandino's multicultural heritage and imbued with a sensual, expressionistic exuberance, Carmelo's paintings are renowned for their immediacy and intensity – colour, movement, and combustible forms display elemental deconstruction, rebuilt into alluring visions of harmonious appeal. The transcendental narrative, which lies at the heart of Carmelo's work, is achieved via a symbolic abstraction of the flowers, landscapes, and faces, he

renders. These images speak intimately and empathically, brilliant manifestations of what Blandino calls his "unconscious to unconscious communication." In homage to his forefathers and in service to a deeply held personal mantra, Carmelo Blandino endeavors as artist to speak through his work – heart to hand, then to the eye, then on into very the heart of the beholder.

WWW.CARMELOBLANDINO.COM

JOHN BOONE

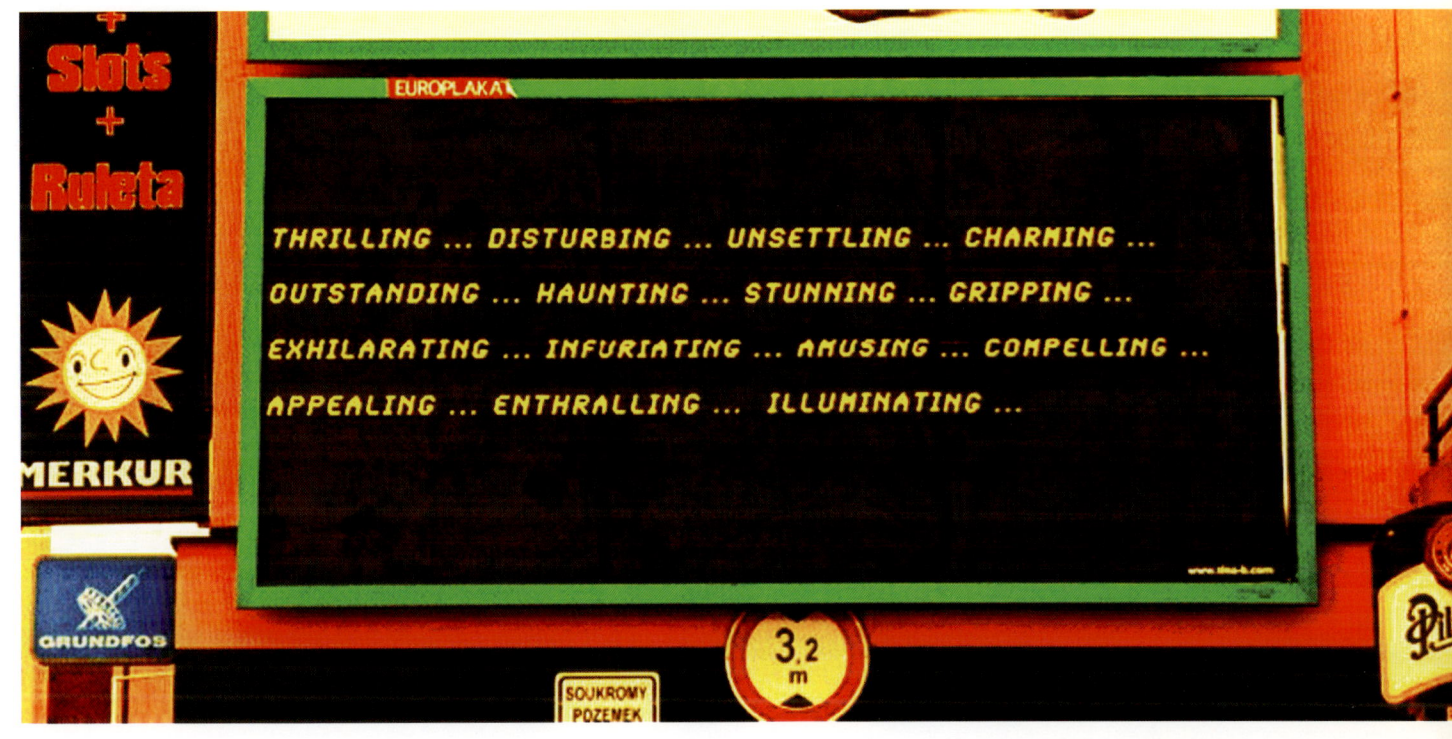

"As far as I can see, American idiomatic expressions are the perfect folk art, they belong to no one, are not authored by anyone but are used by everyone."

To make a long story short, simple words, cliches and colloquialisms in American English are the center of my art activities. Piece by piece, I take common global idioms and organize them into compositions of a single word or words or compositions of run on colloquialisms which reflect common understandings and turn them on their ear. These words are usually painted on a two dimensional surface. As far as I can see, American idiomatic expressions are the perfect folk art, they belong to no one, are not authored by anyone but are used by everyone. Often, the artwork is like the results of a Google search from a key word exposing multiple meanings. They are readymade pure media by any stretch of the imagination. They reflect common understandings back to a viewer. Throwing some light on the subject, the words are always made in a digital font which is technical, empirical and precise while the idioms are vague and have more than one meaning. My artworks include a wide variety of subject areas ranging from "speed" to "portraiture" to "time" to "taste" to "truth" to "fairness" to "freedom" to "animals" to "art" to use of the word "word." And many others. Practicing without a license, my work consists of handmade signs reflecting commonly expressed thoughts through an image of high tech. Most of these artworks are hand painted on canvas, paper or mylar. In some cases these phrases are used in message readers, live readings, etched in glass or stone or towed behind airplanes. Drawing conclusions from Dada, Pop, Conceptual, Fluxus, advertising and journalism, my artworks are signs which prompt for thinking outside the box and ahead of the curve.

WWW.JOHNBOONESTUDIO.COM/

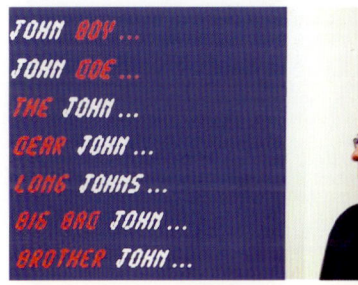

(facing page) OH 30 ●
Acrylic/canvas, 10 x 10 in., 2010

Czech Text Mural ●
Printed text for outdoor advertising, 2009

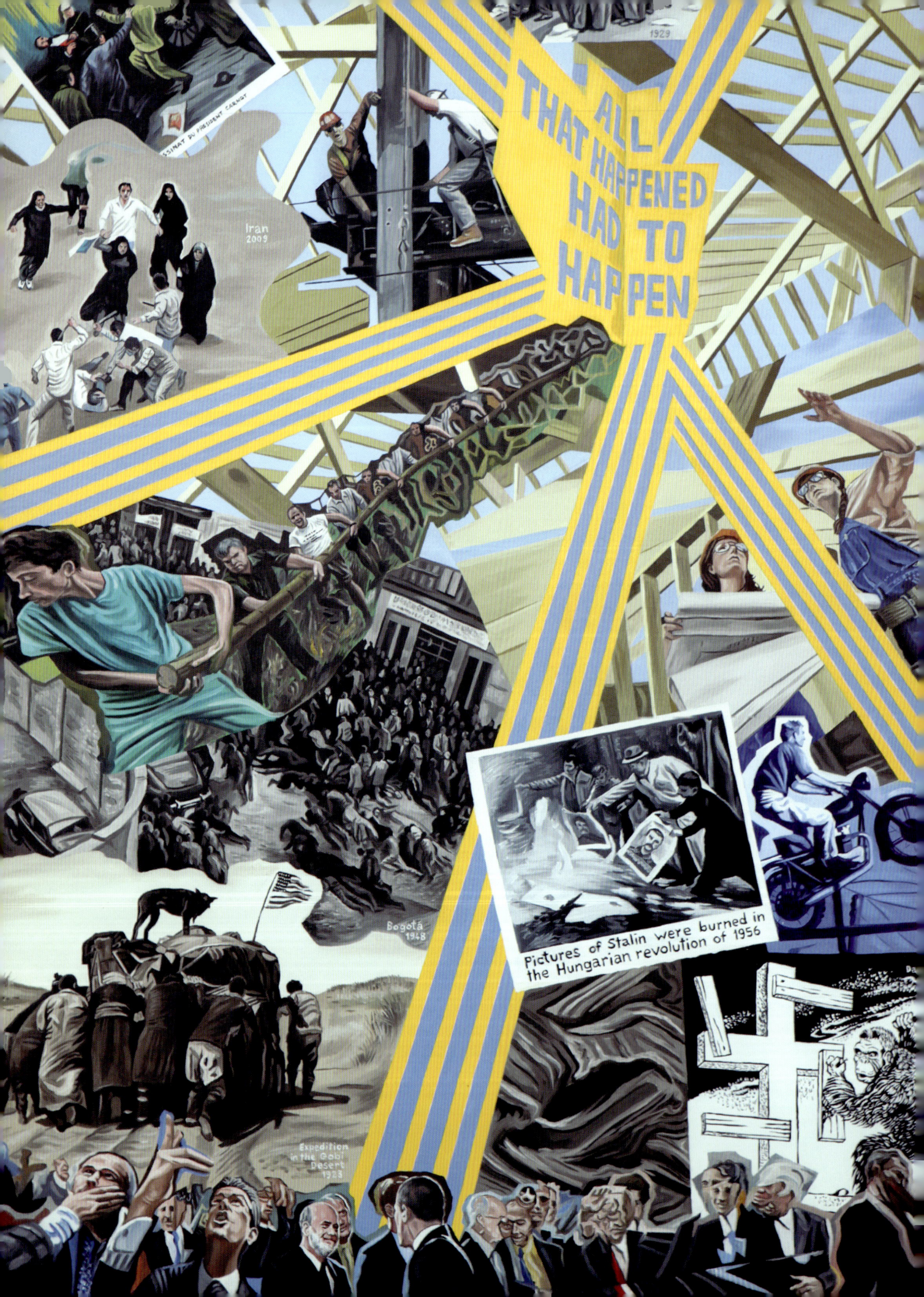

ALL THAT HAPPENED HAD TO HAPPEN

1929

Iran 2009

Bogotá 1948

Expedition in the Gobi Desert 1928

Pictures of Stalin were burned in the Hungarian revolution of 1956

WALTER BORTOLOSSI

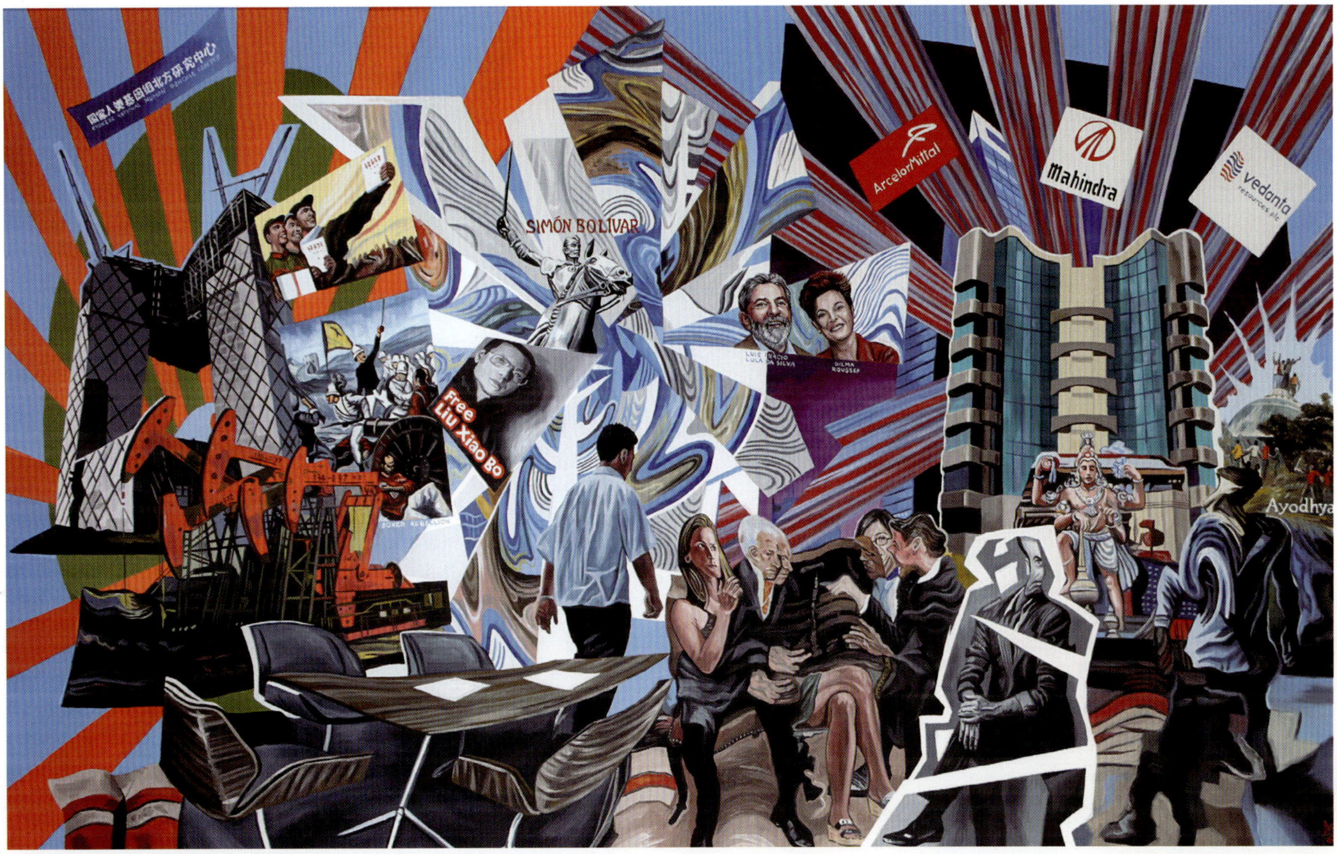

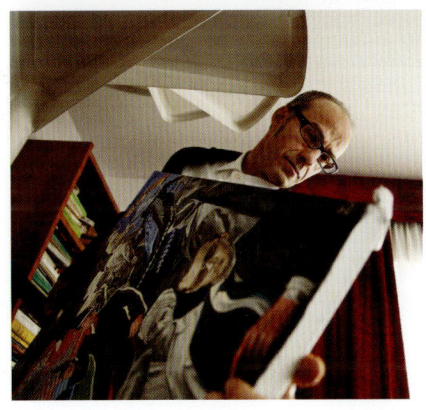

Walter Bortolossi was born in Basel in 1961. From 1975 to 1985 he lived in Venice, attending the Liceo Artistico (fine arts high school) and the Fine Art Academy, where he graduated in 1985. He presently lives in Udine (Italy) and teaches at the Liceo Artistico of Udine.

"I have often drawn on the example of the fairground mirror to describe my painting, likening the images depicted to its distorted reflections of reality. In fact I have always associated my instinctive attraction to the medium of painting with the knowledge that it enables me to choose the field of representation, and therefore a mediated rather than a direct depiction of reality.

The frame of reference provided by figurative painting offers me the possibility to present a lateral view of things, allowing me a certain degree of detachment that can, however, develop into a critical and ironic take on reality, one that goes beyond the individual facts related to general problems.

The elements and forms that appear in my paintings are not ends in themselves; they are always connected to external references from the fields of sociology, politics, economics, philosophy, etc.

The pictorial aspect of my work is nonetheless an active component and finds expression in a deformation and reconstruction of reality: the subject, while recognizable, is transformed or placed within a different context.

The main theme of my recent work has been the inexorable process of economic globalization and in my paintings I want to create images that somehow call into question the very idea of an irrevocable general trend."

HTTP://WWW.SAATCHIART.COM/
WALTERBORTOLOSSI

● (facing page) Three Focal Points
Oil on canvas, 120 x 200 cm, 2010

● All That Happened Had to Happen
Oil on canvas, 120 x 200 cm, 2010

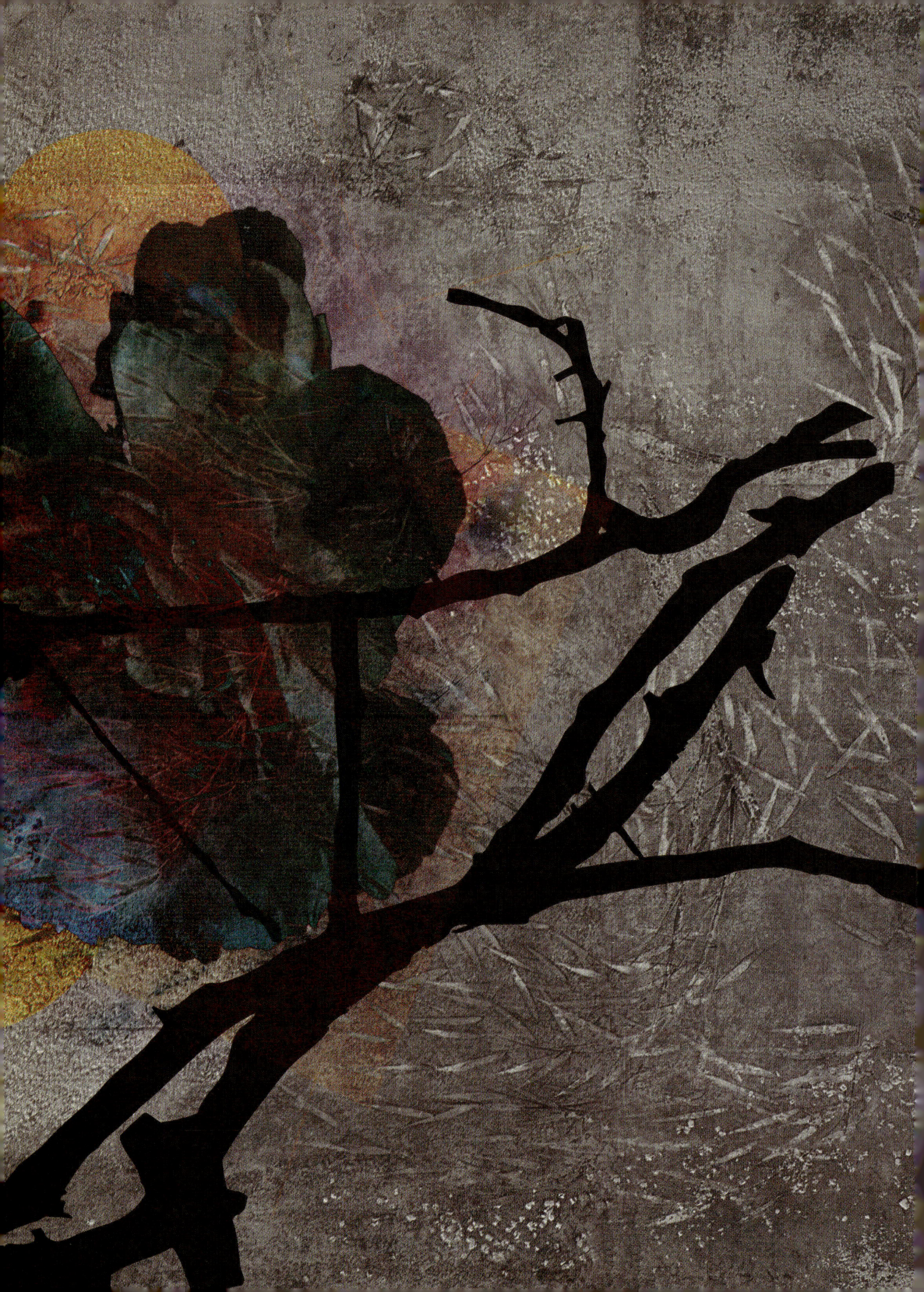

MIRIAM BOSSARD

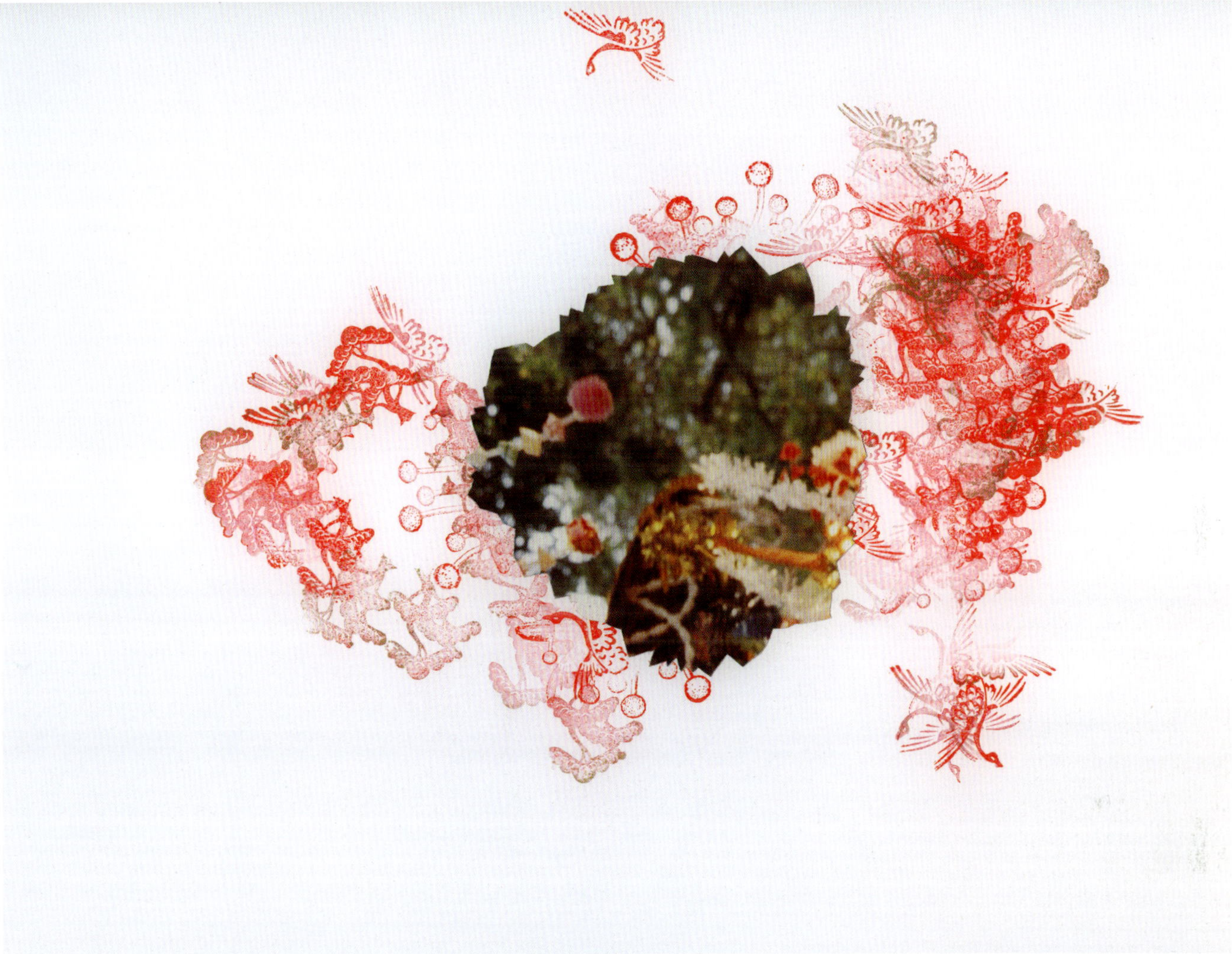

Miriam Bossard was born in Zurich, Switzerland in 1969. For several years she lived and worked in New York City, where she completed her education with a Master of Fine Arts degree. Her medium of passion is the collage. During her travels around the world Miriam Bossard collects image materials: self taken photographs or found clippings of any sort, often displaying organic objects such as tree branches, leaves, flowers, rocks and patterns. In the working process of collaging - either digitally or actual cut and paste, sometimes adding ink and paint - Miriam Bossard rearranges fragments and relationships of the parts again and again. In this procedure the coincidence is a welcome and honored inspiration. The created compositions balance carefully between abstract and precise, and manifest collages beyond memory and vision.

WWW.MIRIAMBOSSARD.COM

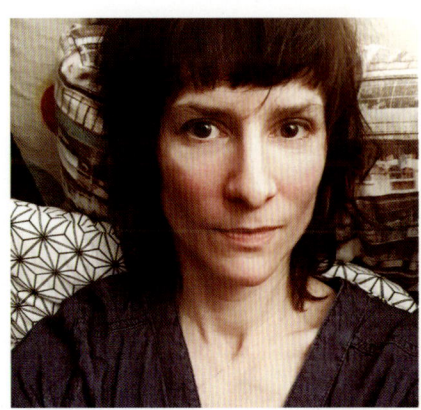

(facing page) Collage #12 ●
Fine-art-print on buetten-paper, 42 x 59 cm

Collage #9 ●
Mixed media, 40 x 50cm

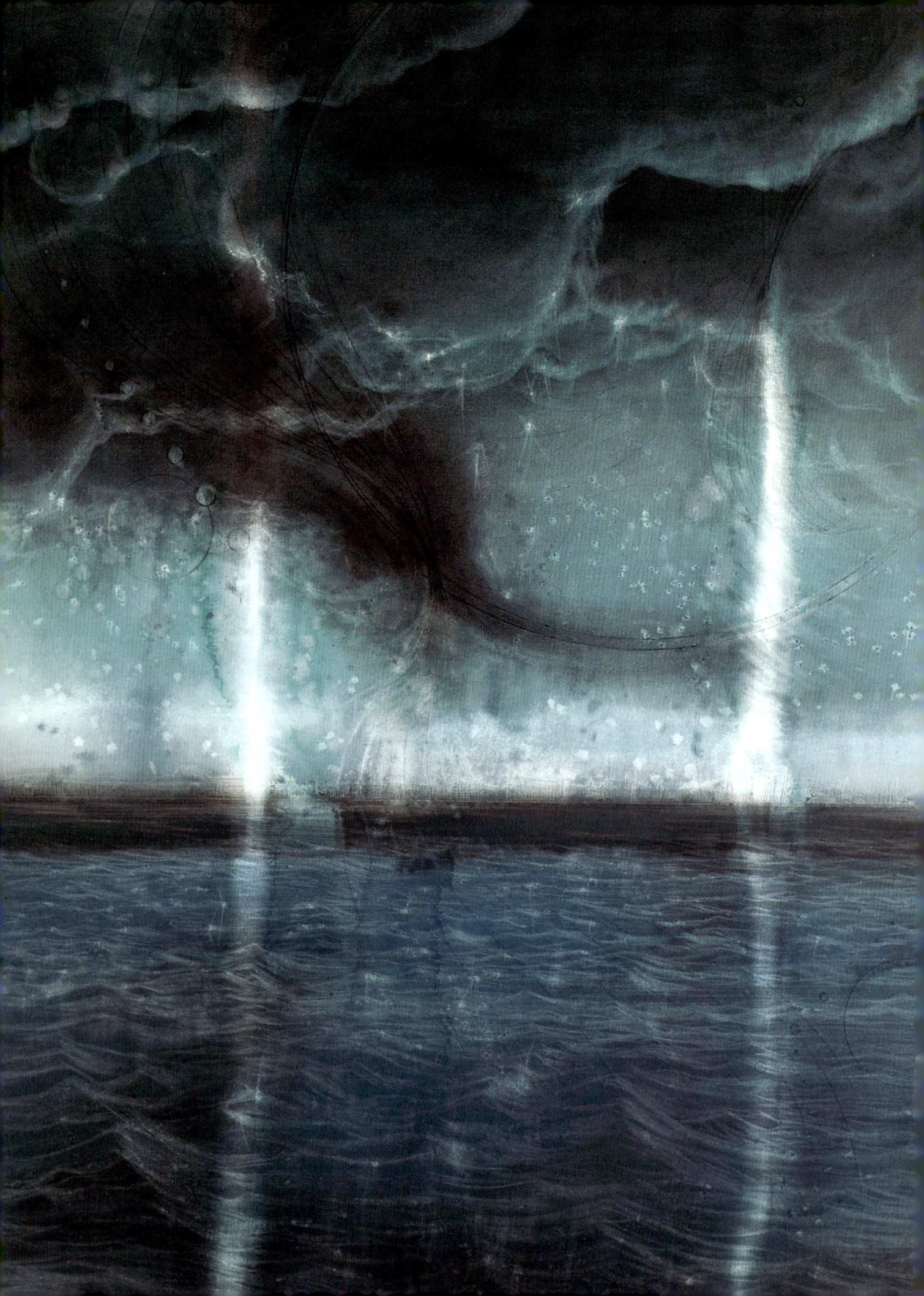

JUDITH BRANDON

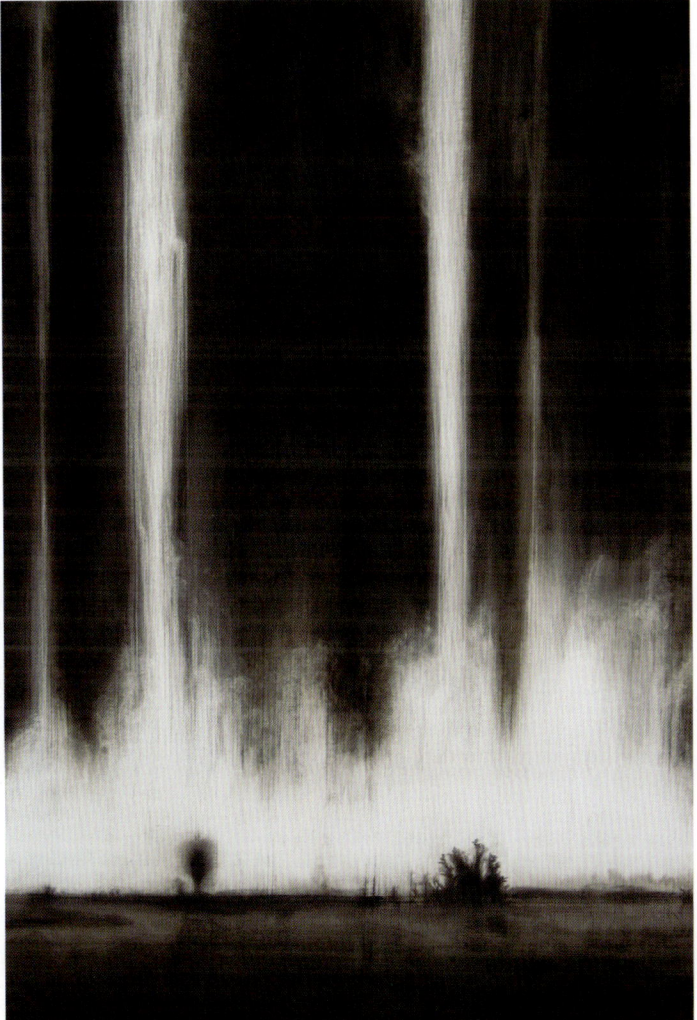

Judith Maureen Brandon was born in Indianapolis, IN 1963.

She attended the Cleveland Institute of Art where she earned a BFA in enameling and drawing. From early on she was known for her creativity and draughtsmanship. Upon meeting Judith Brandon you wouldn't imagine her to be the artist behind the large dynamic works on paper she creates. Standing at just five feet she has to be extremely inventive at how she manipulates the materials in her studio. Pieces are often worked on upside down because it is one way to reach the upper edges of her paper.

She is currently having her third solo exhibition, Super Natural, at the Kenneth Paul Lesko Gallery. In September of 2016 her work will be included in a four person exhibition at the Canton Museum of Art in Canton, OH.

WWW.JMBRANDON.COM/

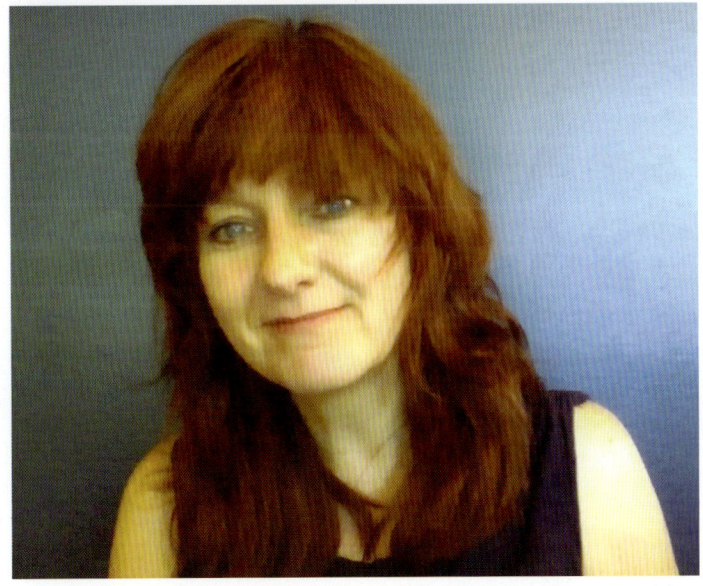

● **(facing page) Light Pillars in Cyan**
Mixed media on paper, 54 x 40 in., 2009

● **Ascension**
Mixed media on paper, 51 x 42 in., 2011

SHANNONDOAH BUCKLEY

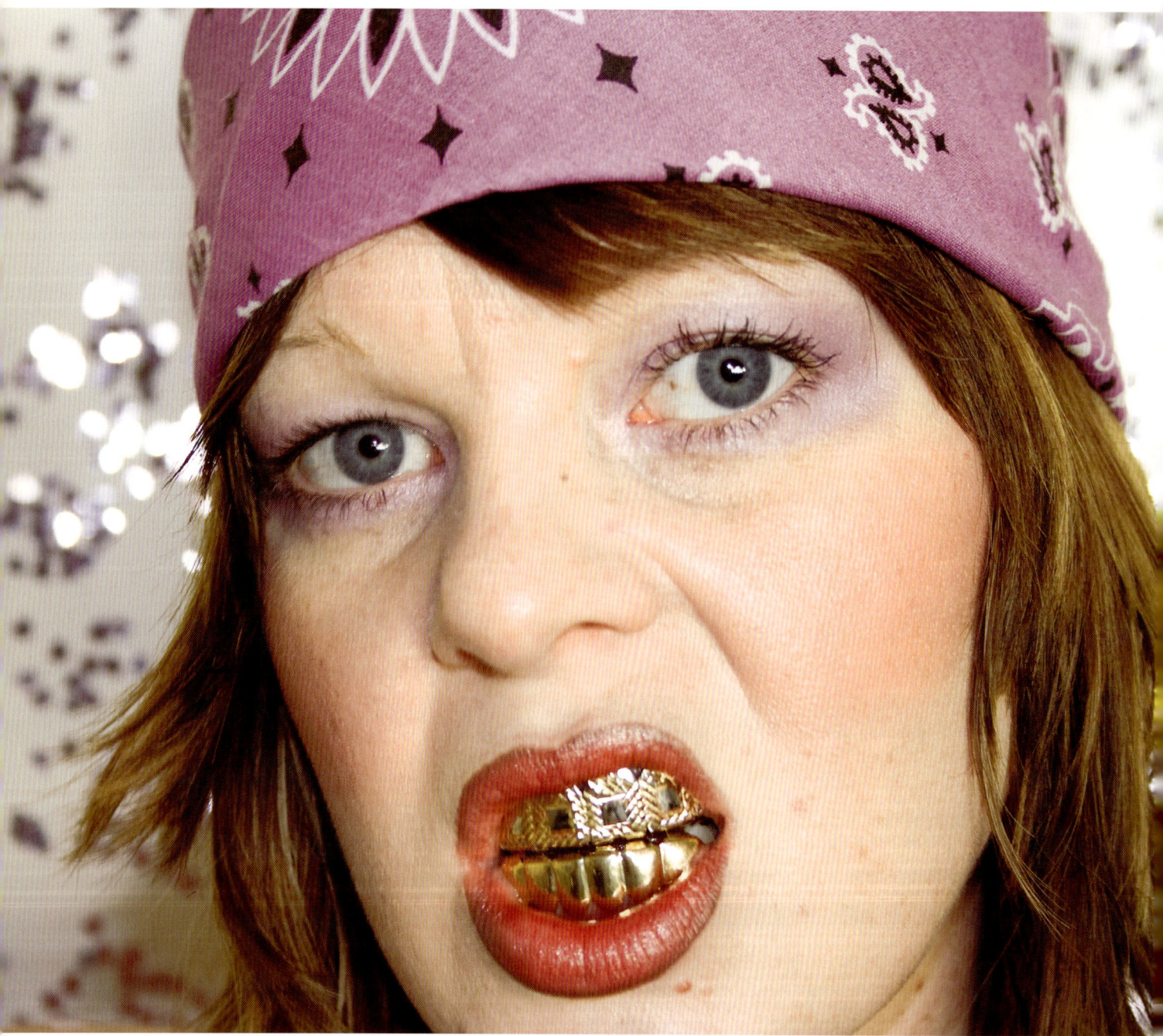

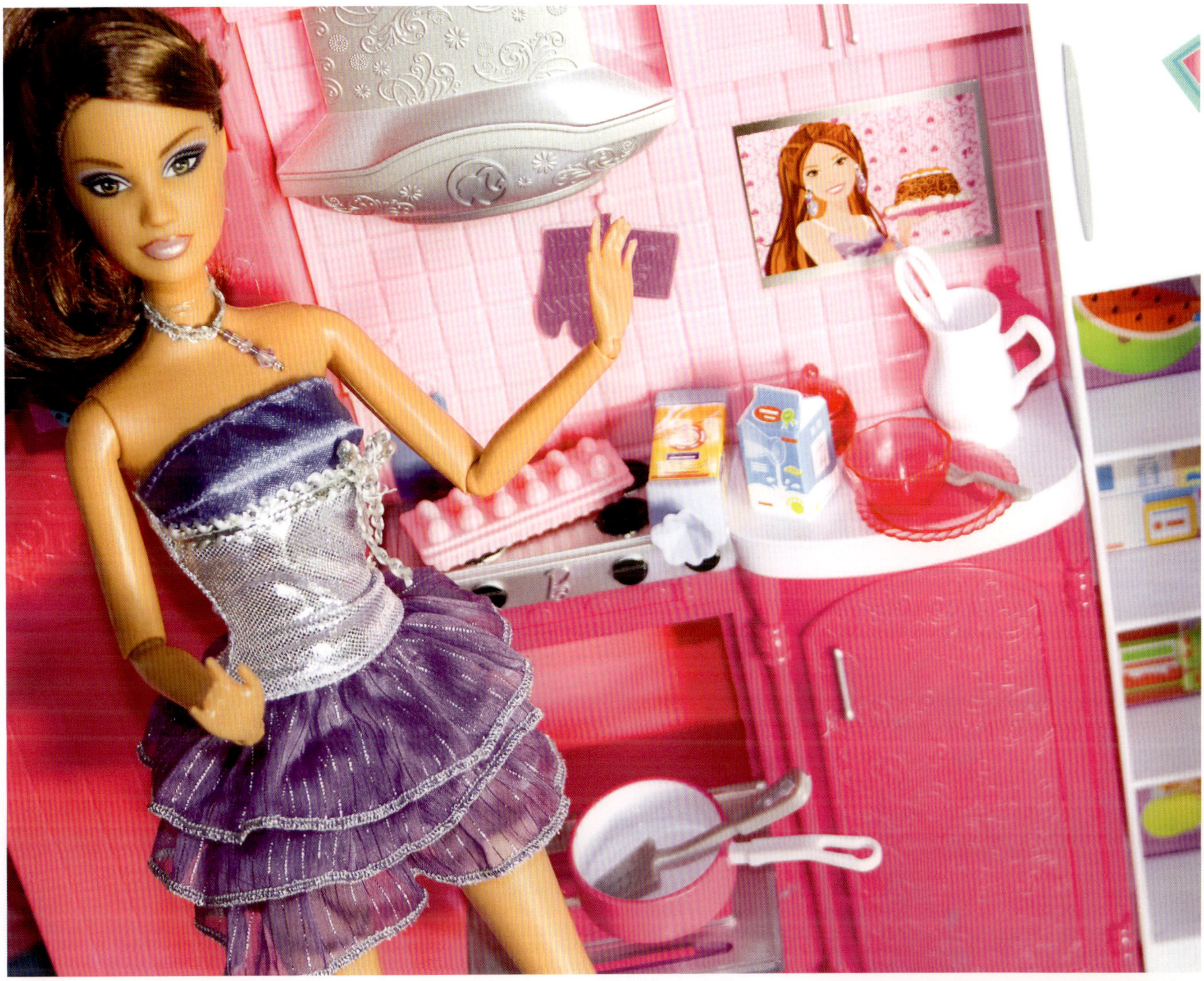

I am a multi media artist who makes photographs, paintings, drawings and sculptures. I am a Native New Yorker who has been living and working in California for the past 10 years. The photographs I currently create are mostly Digital, although I do enjoy shooting with 120mm film using the Holga and Diana cameras. Currently all of my photographs are digitally printed. I prefer making straight photographs, getting what I want in camera, therefore utilizing photoshop as little as possible. I typically focus on making color photographs but do like working with black and white photography at times. Self Portraiture and Still Life photography are where I communicate my socio-political ideas about Identity, Beauty, Race, and Gender. My Street and Nature photographs are more intuitive as opposed to the extremely composed Self Portrait and Still Life images I make. All my photographs are either printed very small like miniatures or like more traditional sized photographs. My oil paintings and multi medium drawings feature composited images of plants, animals and text which are definitely influenced and inspired by gardening, wildlife and poetry. The sculptures I make are conceptual and typically made from found objects which consist of every day things like commercial vegetable crates, cardboard boxes, and glass jars. My sculptures often reference farming and the commercial production of food as well as the education of children using children's learning objects and toys. All of my work explores Identity and Materialism.

SHANNONDOAHBUCKLEY.BLOGSPOT.COM

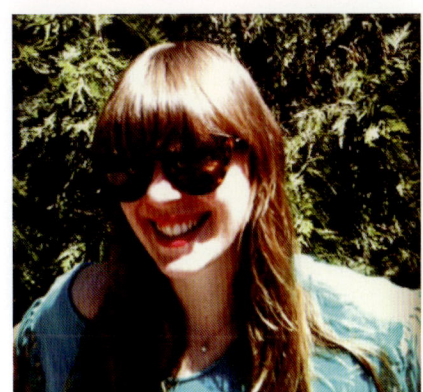

(facing page) Over It ●
Digital photograph and print, 8 x 10 in., 2013

Kitchen ●
Digital photograph and print, 8 x 10 in., 2013

CLAYTON CAMPBELL

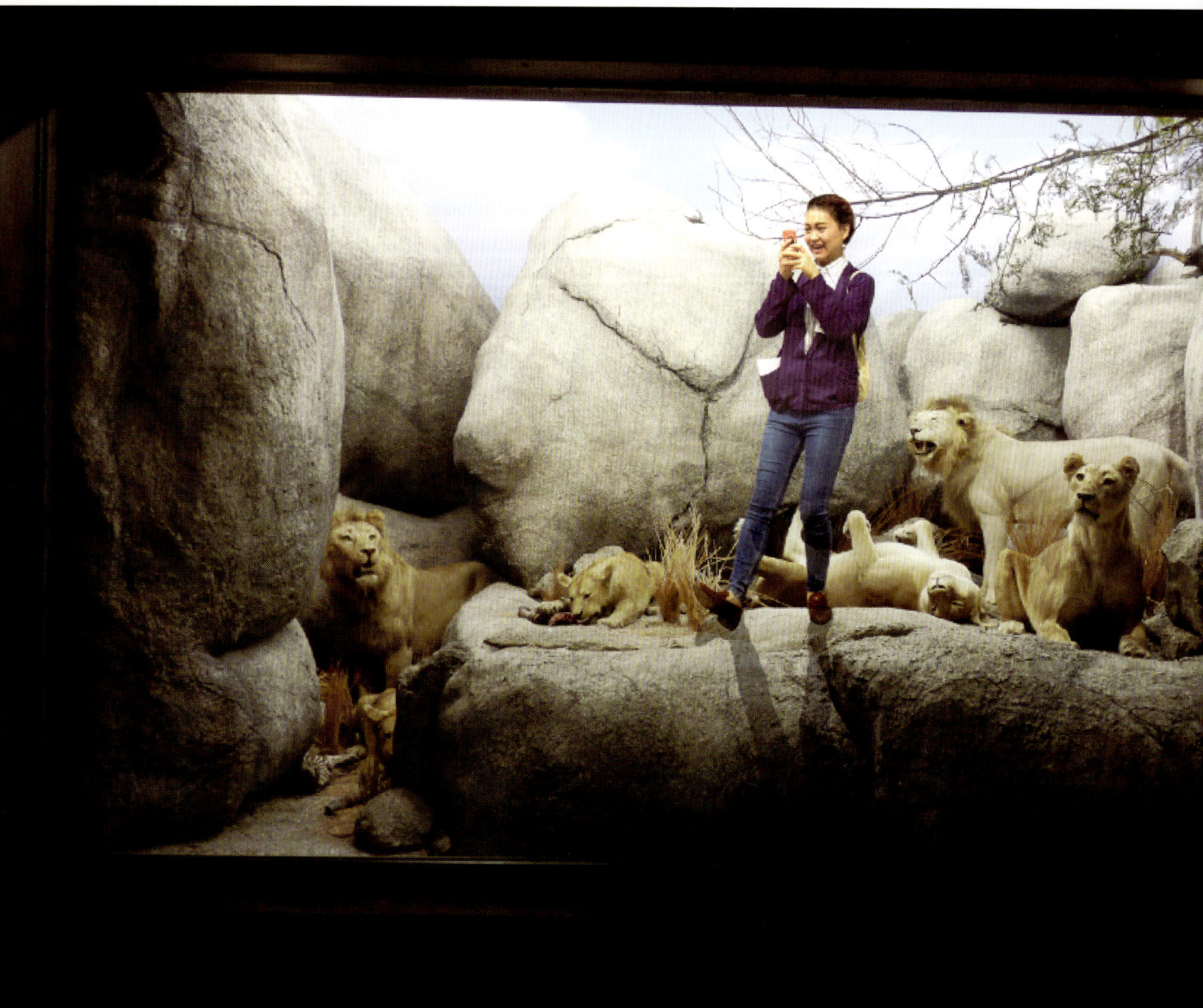

● **Selfie Self Satisfaction Dance Before Dinner**
Digital print, 2015

● **(facing page) Words We've Learned Since 9/11 #2: Religion is Fear, Hate, Sandnigger**
Color photograph, 17 x 22 in. (triptych), 2005 - 2013

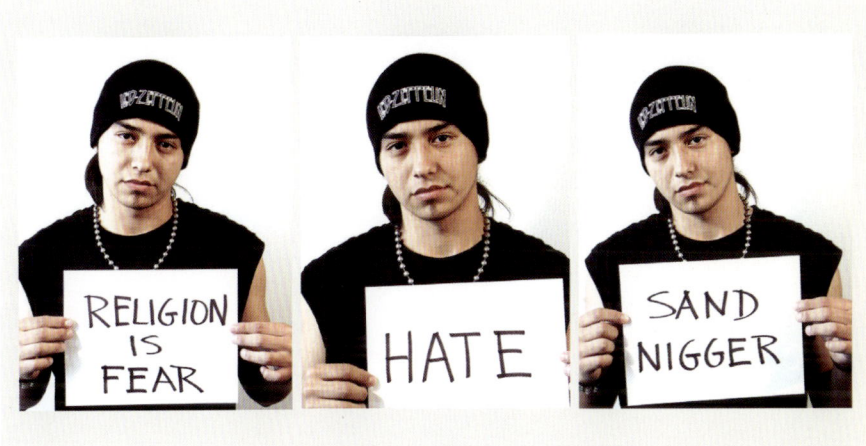

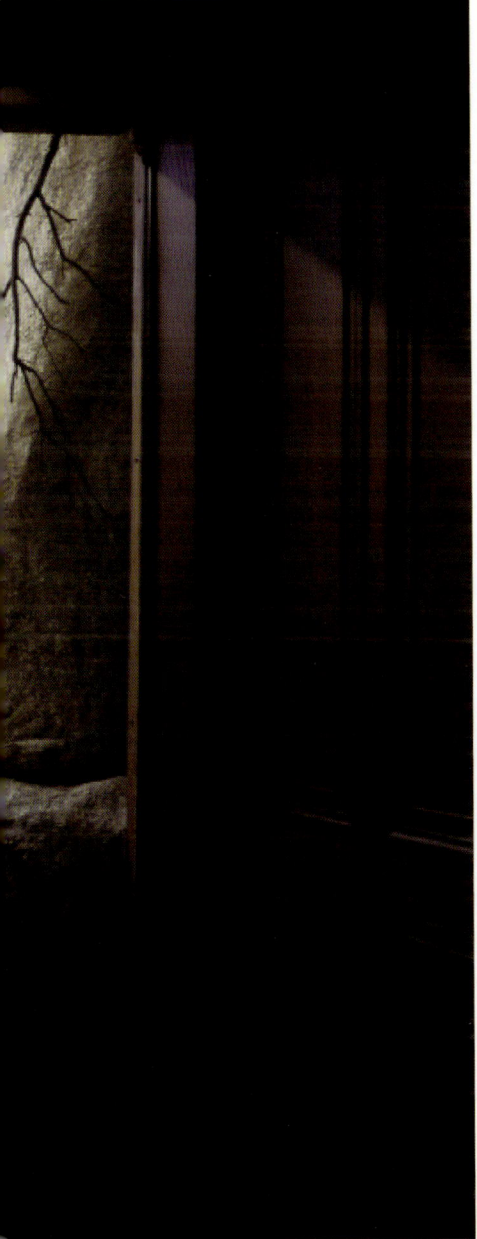

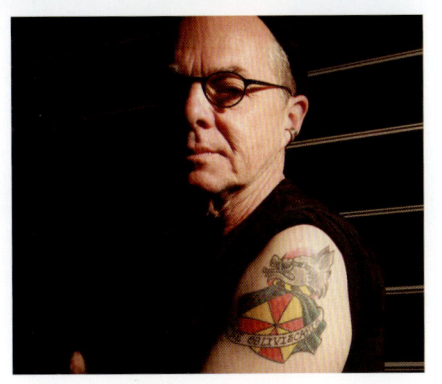

Words We Have Learned Since 9-11 is a unique participatory photographic project by Los Angeles artist Clayton Campbell. His non-partisan project establishes intercultural dialogue between diverse populations about cultural difference and how persons view their future.

In 2013, a decade after September 11, 2001, the artist says that the most important word in the title of the project is "since". "Words We have Learned Since 9/11 is not directly about 9/11, but about everything that has happened to people since then. What is happening now, where are we going, how do we feel? What new words are we learning, what words have changed for you? It becomes a legacy of this decade since the first major event of the 21st century that everyone anywhere remembers."

I was sitting in a Paris cafe last summer, the kind of convivial place where people get together to solve and identify the worlds problems over glasses of wine sopped up with bits of bread. But things seemed to have changed. Not that many people were talking, they instead were on their cell phones. Every other person walking by were on their phones too, navigating the street and metro stairs with uncanny sense of direction even while being totally disconnected from their environment, and the people around them. Wild Kingdom consists of diorama's where the human species is placed, self absorbed and woefully unawares of what is happening around them.

Clayton Campbell is a visual in Los Angeles, California. He studied painting and printmaking with artist Ernst Fuchs in Vienna, Austria and at the Art Students League of New York. He is recognized for his art works and project s involving social commentary, and has been director of several important arts organizations including long time Artistic Director of the 18th Street Arts Center, Los Angeles. He is the former President of Res Artis, the international association of residential arts centers and consults with many artist residency programs worldwide. A widely published arts writer, he contributes to Contemporary Magazine and Flash Art International. In 2002 Clayton Campbell was awarded the distinction of Chevalier in the Order of Arts and Letters by the French Government for his work as an artist and arts organizer.

WWW.CLAYTONCAMPBELL.COM/

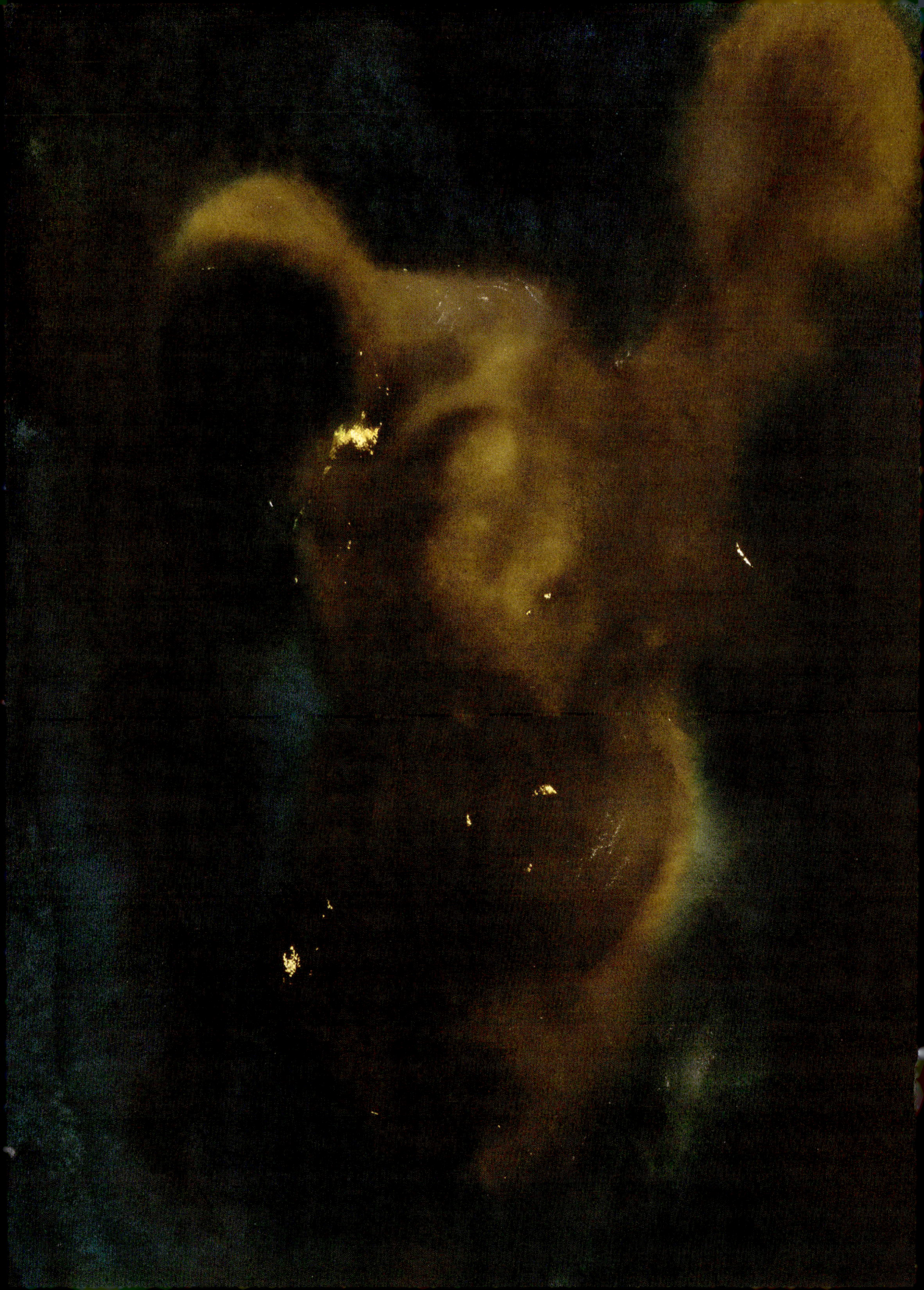

KATHLEEN CAPRARIO

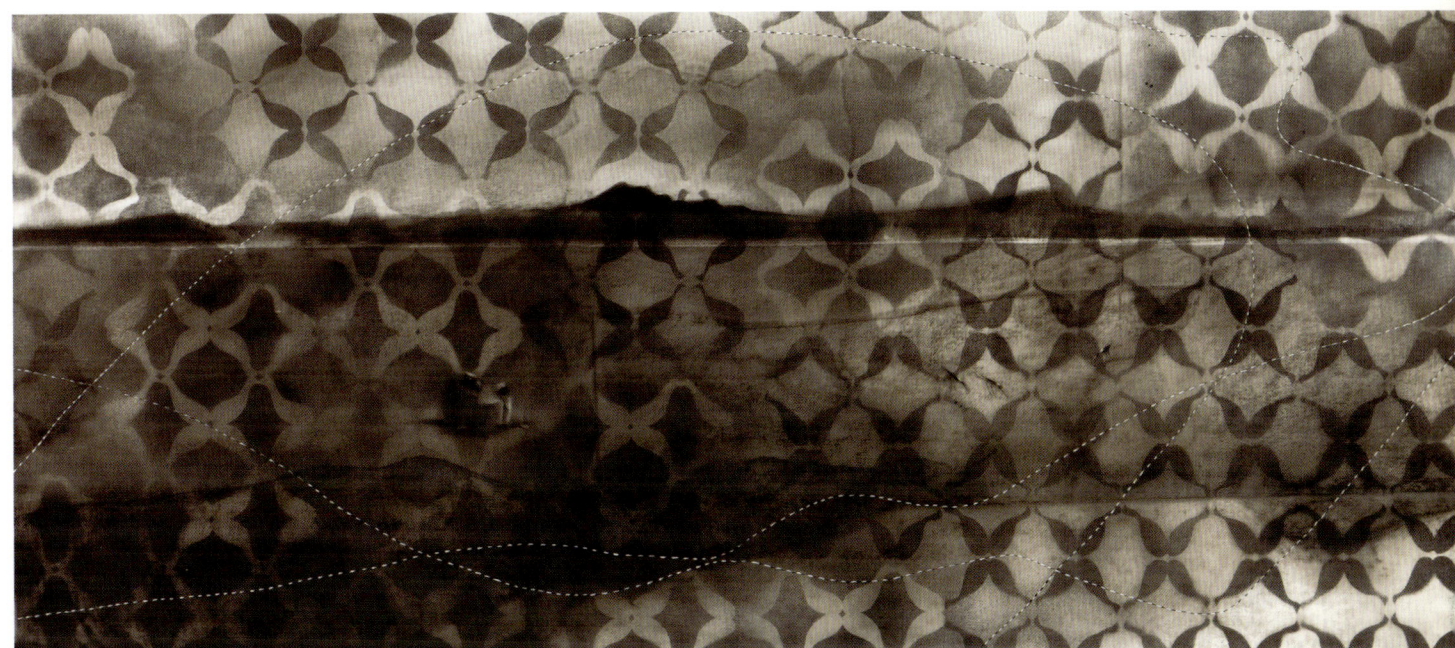

Kathleen Caprario traded the concrete canyons of New York City for the real canyons and broad skies of the Pacific Northwest where she found her life-long subject—the land. Her process is similar to the spontaneous and organic growth of a forest with underlying layers of organizing pattern that metaphorically ground and visually describe the interconnected relationship of self to nature. Caprario's early career in textile design focused her attention on repeated motifs and she developed an interest in pattern and its cultural associations to feminine identity and landscape. Her work continues to evolve from the question, "How am I shaped by my environment?" Caprario's work is exhibited nationally and has received awards including an Oregon Arts Commission Individual Artist Fellowship and the Modesto Lanzone Award. Artist residencies at the Ucross Foundation, Jentel Foundation, Morris Graves' Foundation and Playa Foundation as well as living and working with Aboriginal children in Central Australia (2010), have informed her work.

WWW.CAPRARIOART.COM

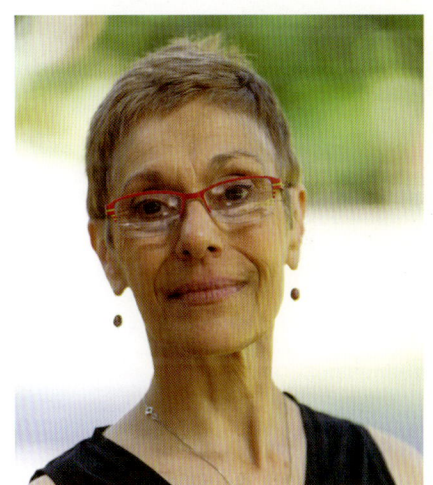

● **(facing page) Waterbodies I**
Watercolor on paper, 30 x 22 in., 2009

● **Avocet Dreaming**
Graphite, spray paint, chalk on vellum,
42 x 83 in., 2011

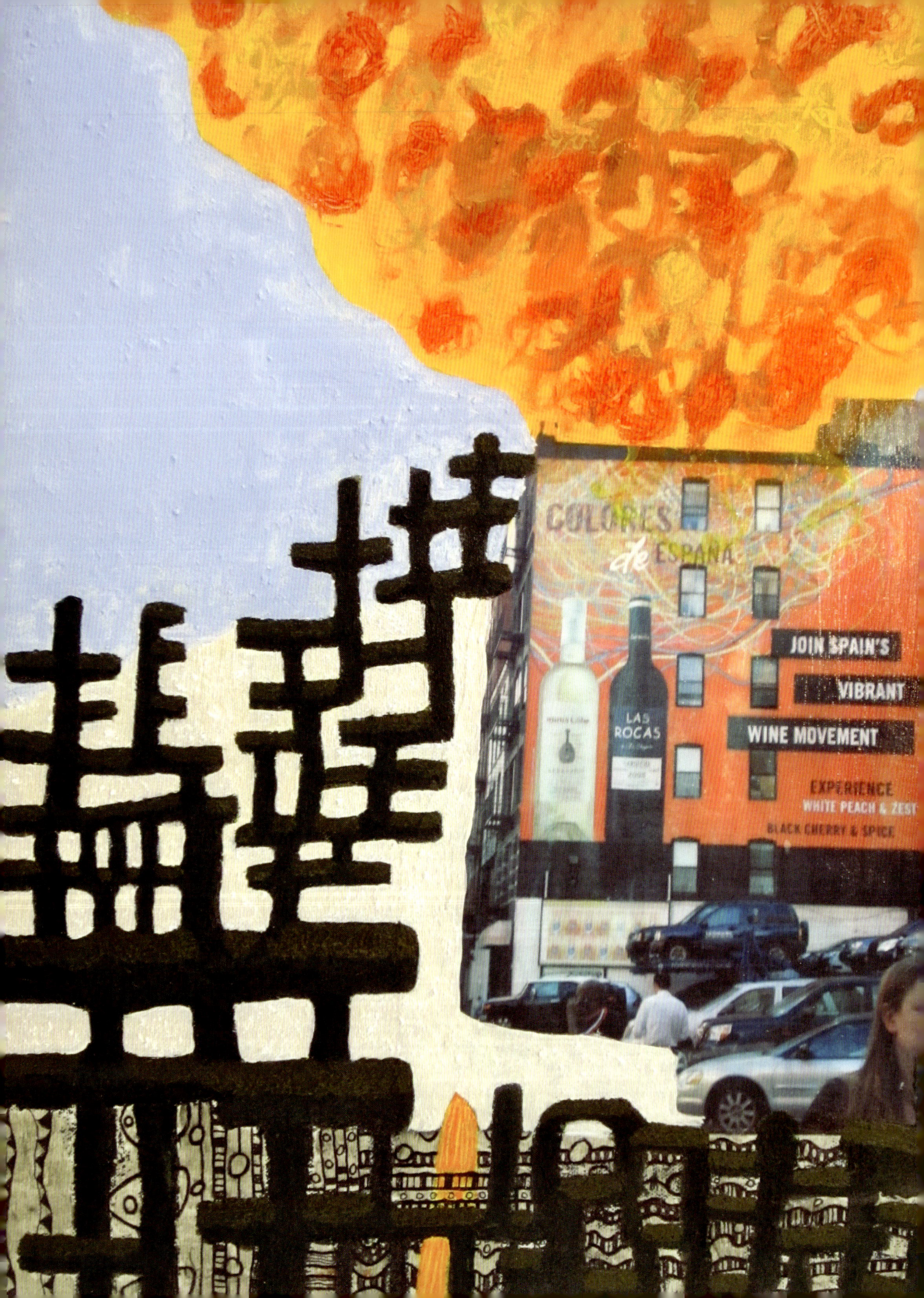

IRENE CHRISTENSEN

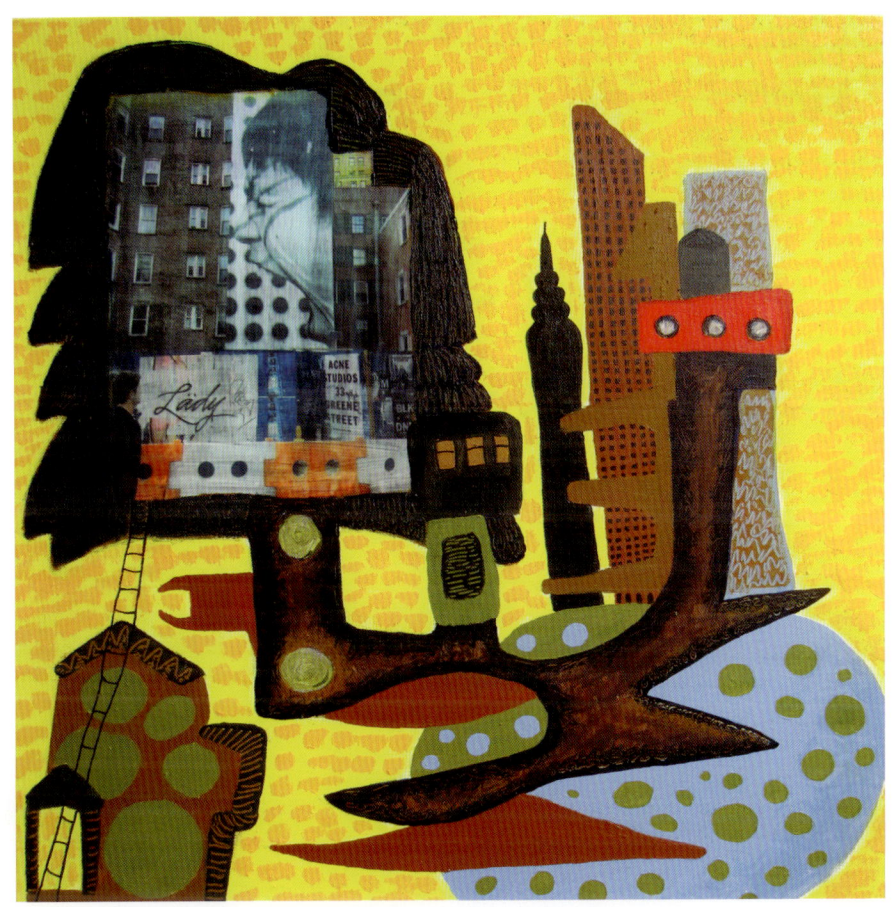

"Having experienced life as a New Yorker both before and after 9/11, the time came for me to reflect upon the city as I saw it then and as I see it now. For years, my daily walks downtown took me beneath some of the outdoor public art of Manhattan - those enormous not-to-be ignored billboards above Lafayette Street. These mixed media paintings express my interpretations of New York City."

Irene Christensen manages to divide her time producing her work not only in her studios in New York City as well as in Oslo, Norway, but also for one month each year in Costa Rica. She is an artist who has for years developed both organic and constructive imagery. She is involved in creating a personal iconography. These symbols are rooted in the figurative and landscape images with colours setting moods rather than copying nature.

In her recent series called "From SOHO to NOHO" inserts of city life, photos of trash cans and urban dwellings are collaged onto the canvas.

Irene Christensen has exhibited in Europe, the United States, Costa Rica, Brazil, Israel and Argentina since 1983. Her work is represented in museums and personal collections. She is a member of Norwegian Association of Professional Visual Artists (NBK), Newark Art Council, National Arts Club in NYC and Adviser to Everglades Artists in Residence (AIRIE), Florida and Board Member to Artists Talk on Art (ATOA), New York City.

WWW.MARLOW.NEOIMAGES.NET

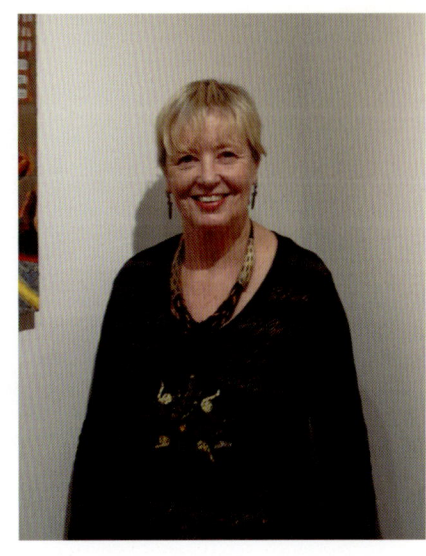

CECILIA CHARLTON

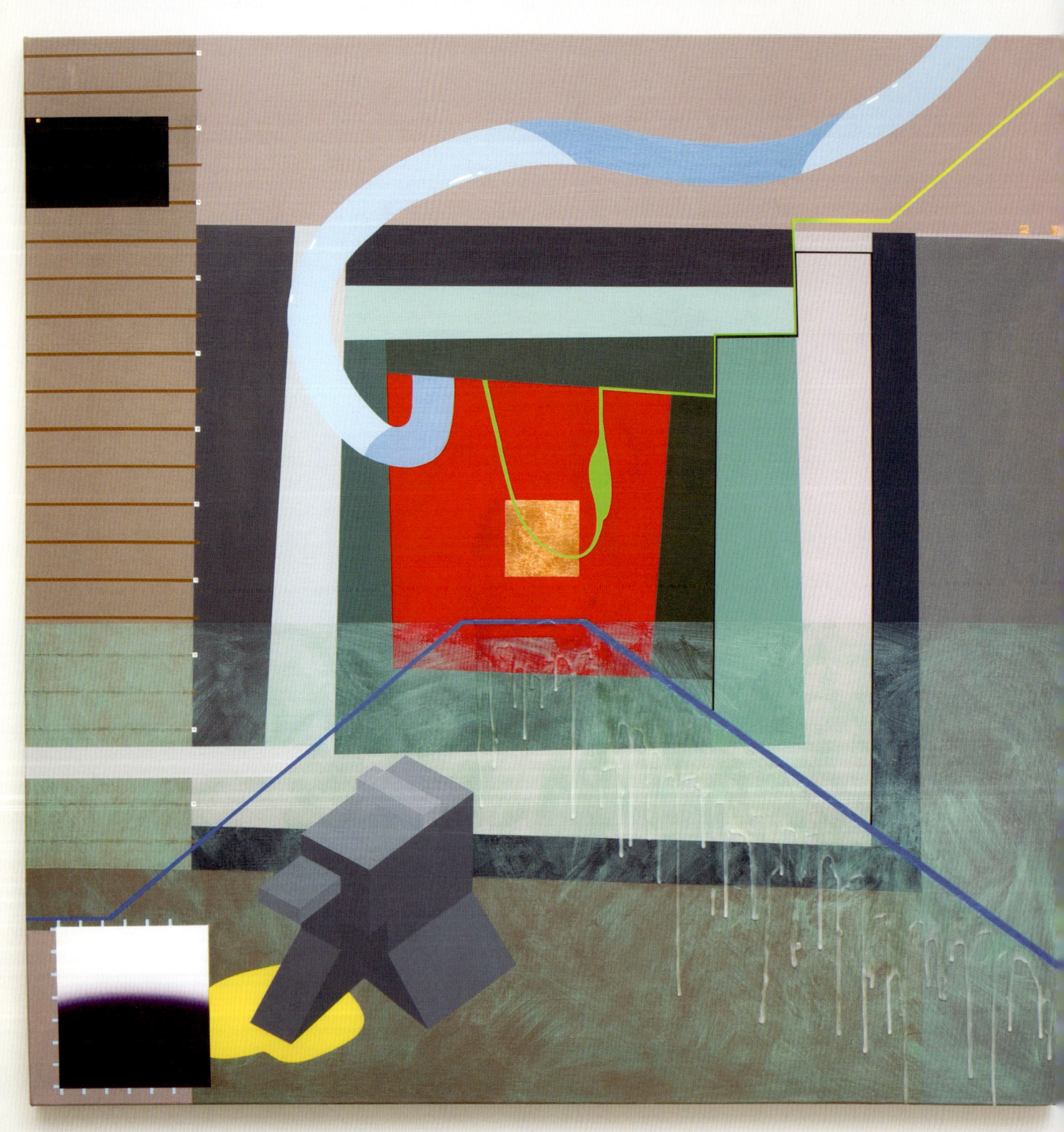

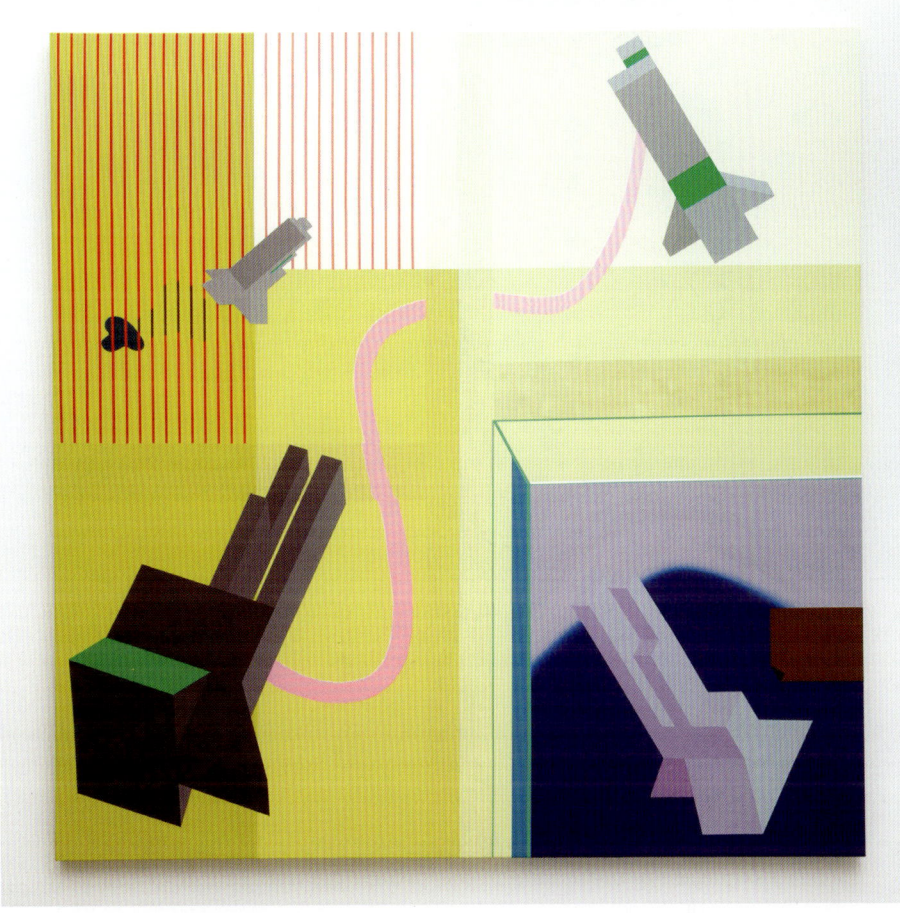

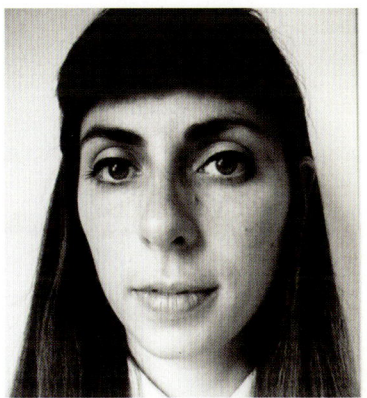

● **(facing page) The Anvil**
Acrylic paint and metal foil on canvas, 60 x 60 in., 2015

● **Hemispheres (Inversion I)**
Acrylic on canvas with metal foil, 72 x 72 in., 2015

"Working in a new genre which I am terming reductive scientific surrealism, I create forms that are potentially anthropomorphic yet unrecognizable, well-ordered yet extemporaneous. Contradictions enable subjectivity and personal inquest, while encouraging dialogue about the languages and symbols that I am initiating."

From a childhood heavily steeped in needlework and infused with scientific and technological research, I create paintings that evoke patchwork, phenomenology and poetry. I was born in Corning, NY and I lived in a dozen places before settling in New York City to study fine art at Hunter College.

Through a neat application of acrylic paint and the implementation of deceptive abstraction, I create a platform from which we can experience and discuss issues of human perception, history, and social convention. Working in a new genre which I am terming reductive scientific surrealism, I create forms that are potentially anthropomorphic yet unrecognizable, well-ordered yet extemporaneous. Contradictions enable subjectivity and personal inquest, while encouraging dialogue about the languages and symbols that I am initiating. Susan Sontag asks in her 1965 journal, "What are the sensory mixes of the future?" Present in my artworks is the space where science and humanity overlap and eerily begin to speak the same language, in an attempt to answer this question.

Within the digitized appearance of the paintings there is a sense of spontaneity – suggesting the presence of a person.

Paramount is the implication of disarray, buoyed by the neurotic meticulousness with which the elements are constructed. I am interested in innovating and crafting new visual languages to discuss issues pertinent to today. Through my paintings, I transform the real world, suspending time and sound, and offer a meditation on dualities: individuality/ homogeneity of the person, contemporary/ archaic thought processes, and real/ digital space.

WWW.CECILIACHARLTON.COM

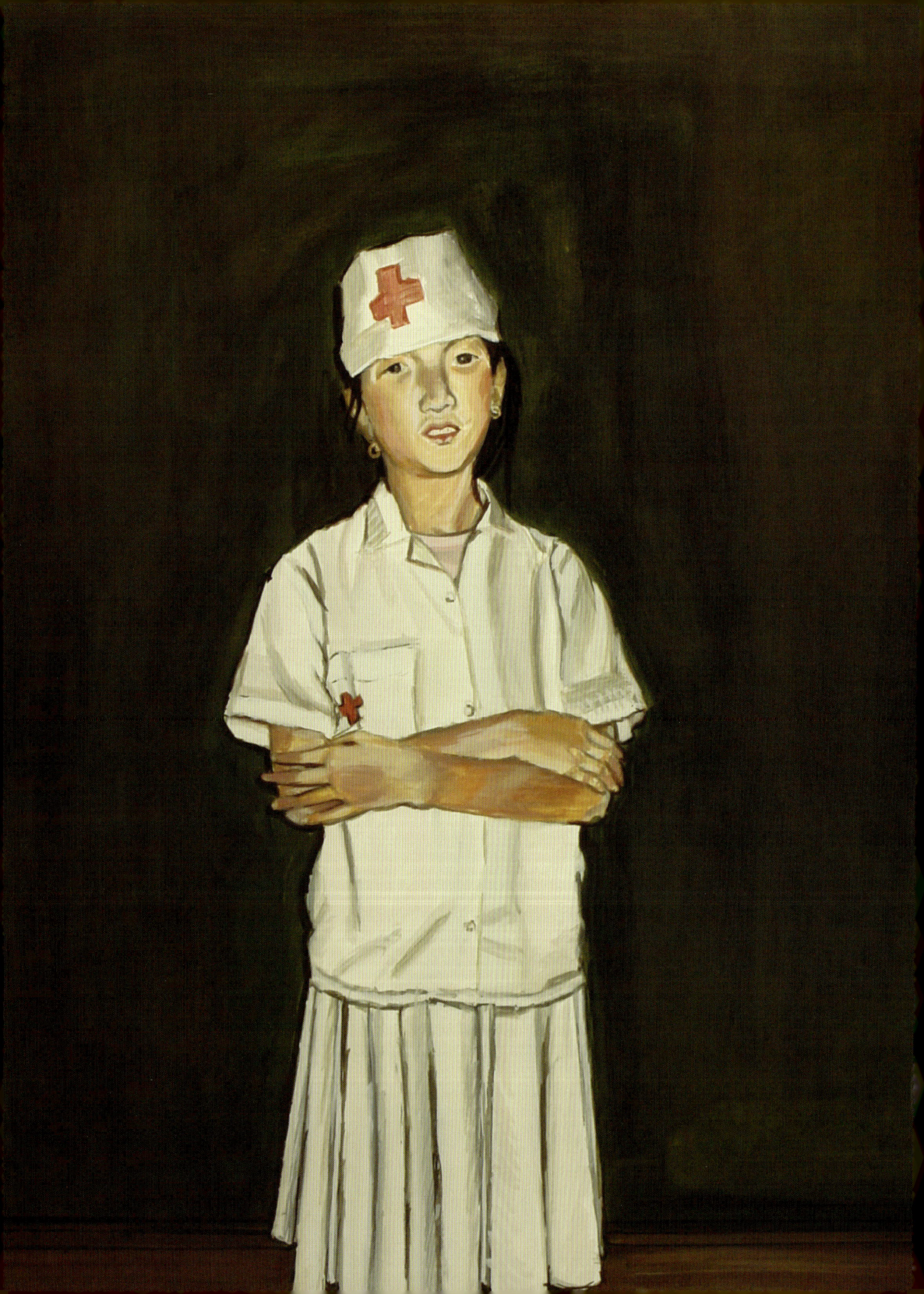

LAURA CHASMAN

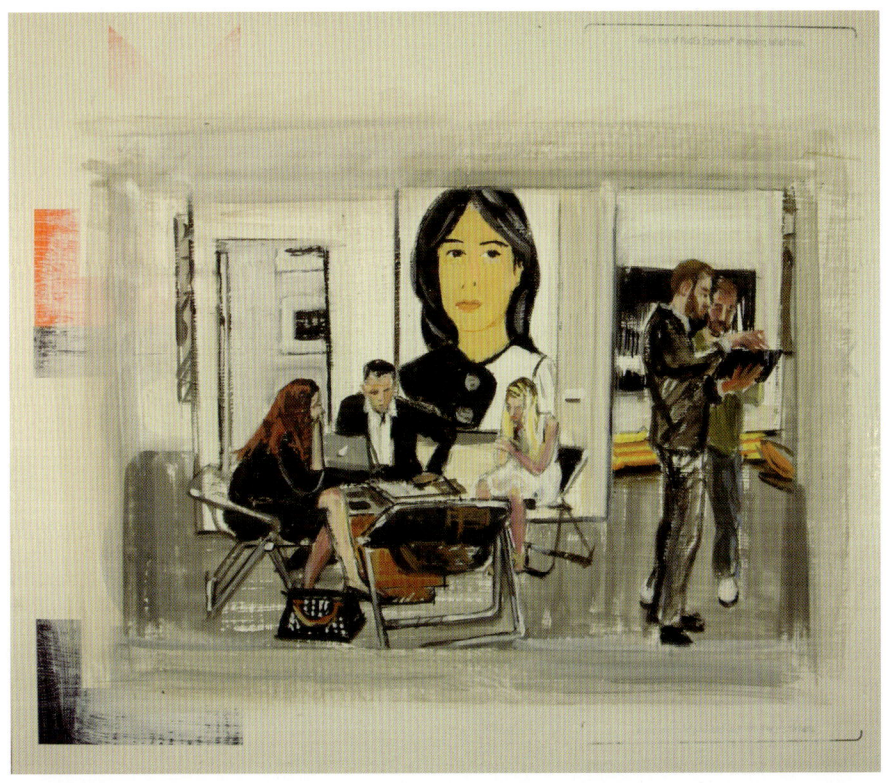

Laura Chasman grew up in Brooklyn, N.Y. From an early age she was captivated by color and imagery. Manhattan was just a train ride away and Chasman went often. She visited museums and attended classes at art schools, as well as studying at the Art Students League- a liberating experience for an aspiring young artist from Brooklyn. She is a graduate of the Boston Museum School, as well as Smith College School of Social Work. Chasman was a practicing psychotherapist, as well as a geriatric social worker. Her interest in people has always gone beyond an outward manifestation of the self. Her figurative paintings are narratives that express how her subjects look, as well as how Chasman experienced them. Both individuals and groups of people fascinate her. Her gouache portraits are based on inspiring situations combined with odd or eccentric, humoristic elements.

She has exhibited in Boston area galleries and institutions for over 30 years. In 2000,

The Addison Gallery of American art invited the artist to participate in a panel discussion on the contemporary portrait in conjunction with the exhibition Alice Neel. Neel has always held a formidable place on her roster of influential artists. Chasman has received numerous awards including the Eighth Maud Morgan Prize and exhibition awarded by the Museum of Fine Arts, Boston. She was an Artadia finalist in 2009, and her portraits were included in the National Portrait Gallery's Boochever Competition in 2009 and 2013. Chasman's work is in both public and private collections.

WWW.LAURACHASMAN.COM

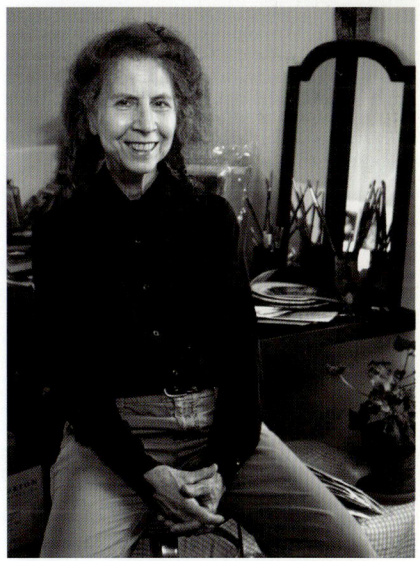

ETERI CHKADUA

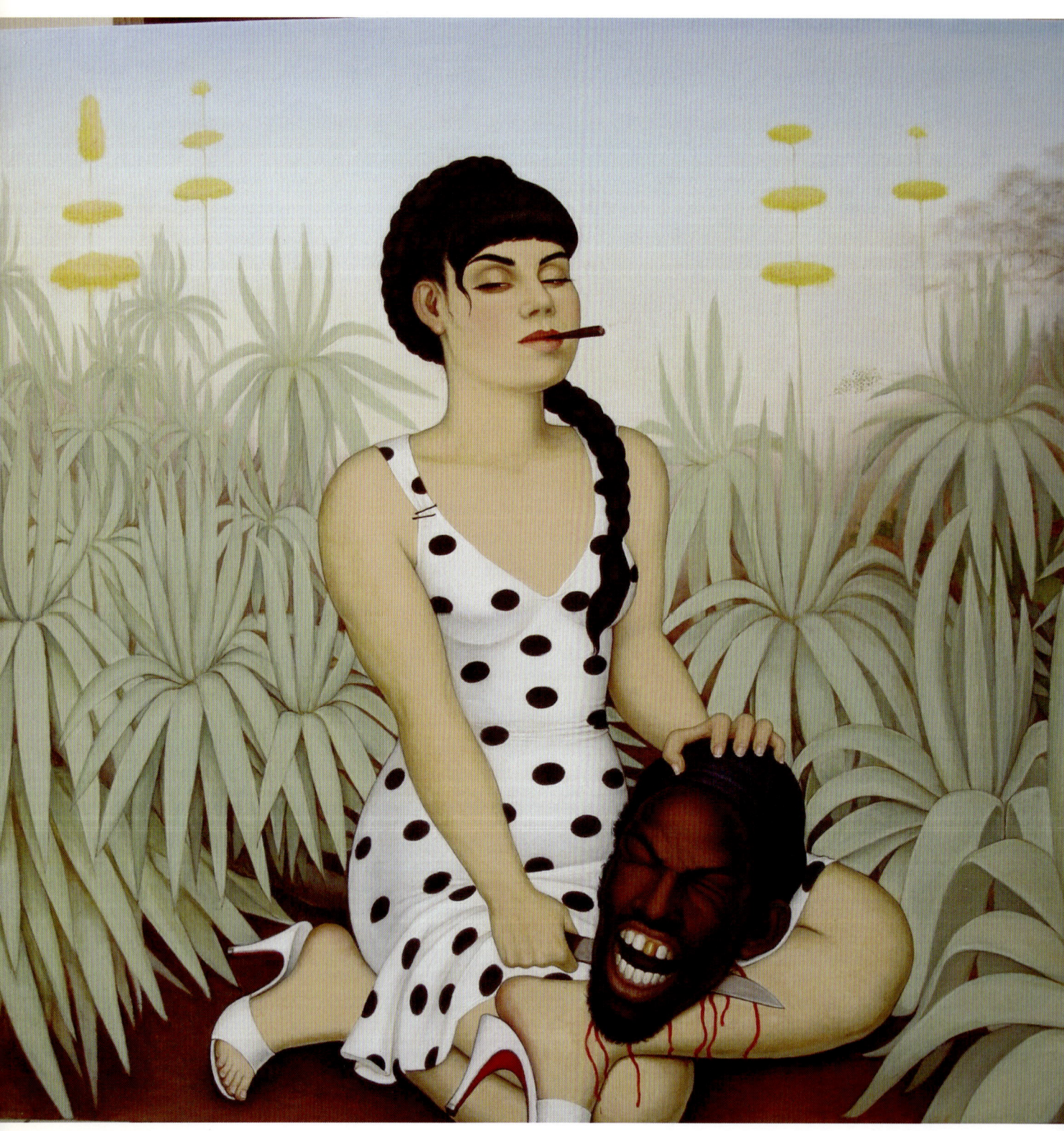

● **Salome**
Oil on linen, 48 x 52 in., 2005

● **(facing page) Ice Cream**
Oil on linen, 52 x 76 in.

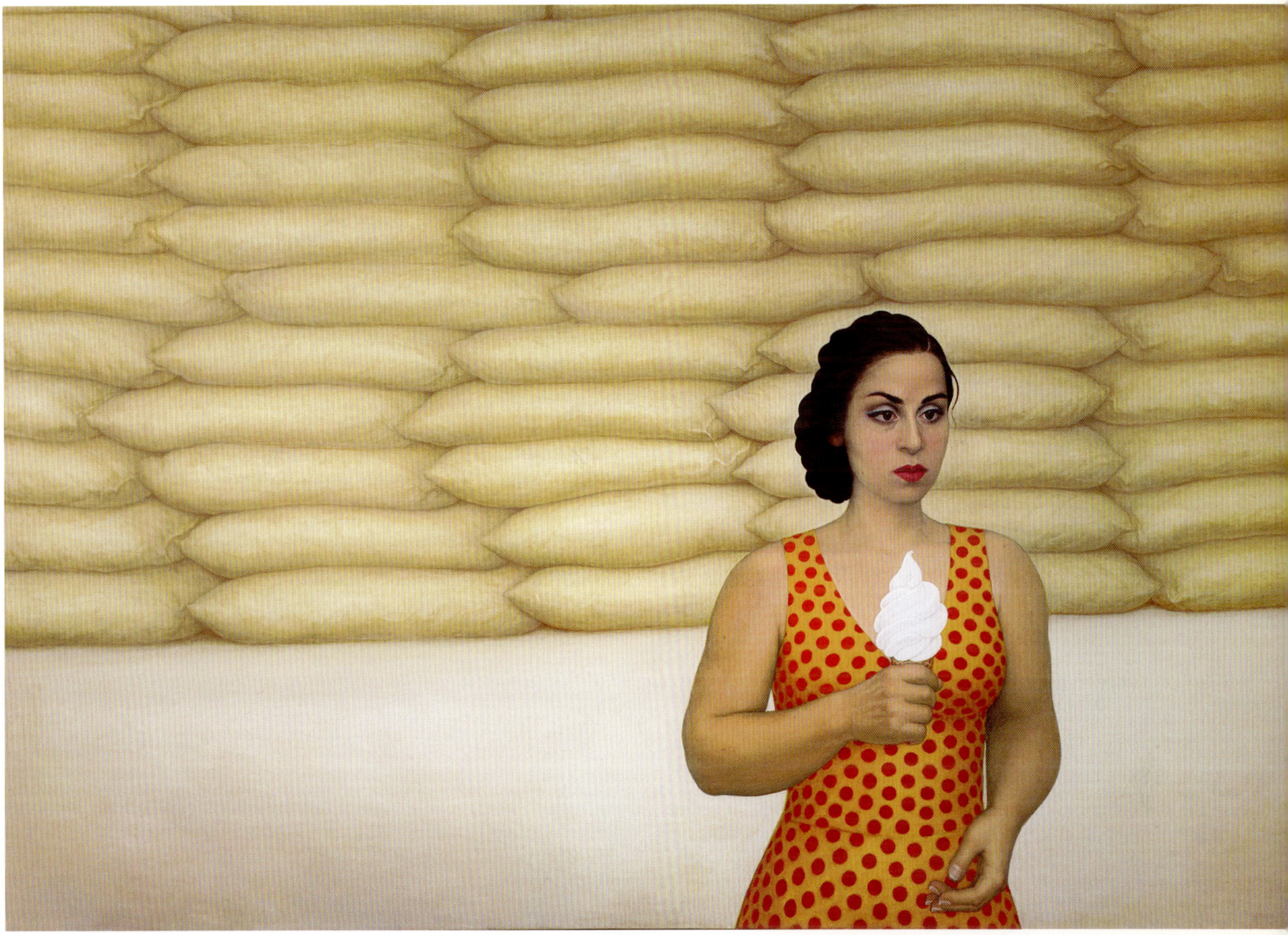

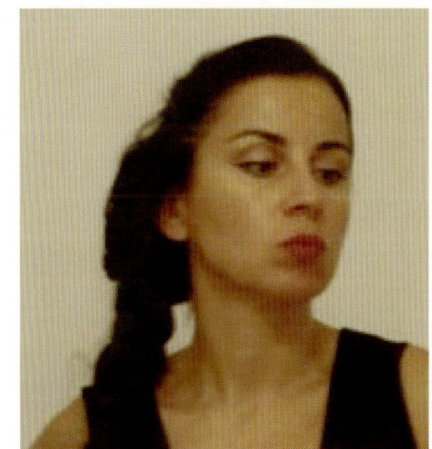

Eteri Chkadua was born in 1965 in Tbilisi, in the capital of the Republic of Georgia, (former Soviet Union). Eteri studied Fashion Design and Monumental Painting at the Tbilisi Academy of Arts. In 1990 Maya Polsky gallery in Chicago hosted her first exhibition. The same year, Eteri was invited as an Artist in Residence and Visiting Professor at USCB, (University of California, Santa Barbara, CA.) In 1996 Eteri was invited to Instruct Painting and Composition, at the Academy of Arts, in NYC. Eteri is the recipient of the Pollock-Krasner grant. Her paintings have been displayed at Indiana University (Northwest) Museum, Buffalo State college Museum of Art and Archeology in Missouri, Aldredge Museum in Connecticut, Museum of Modern Art in Vienna and LUNA Kulturhus Konsthallen, Sweden. Eteri Chkadua represented her native country Georgia at the Venice Biennale in 2007.

WWW.ETERICHKADUA.COM

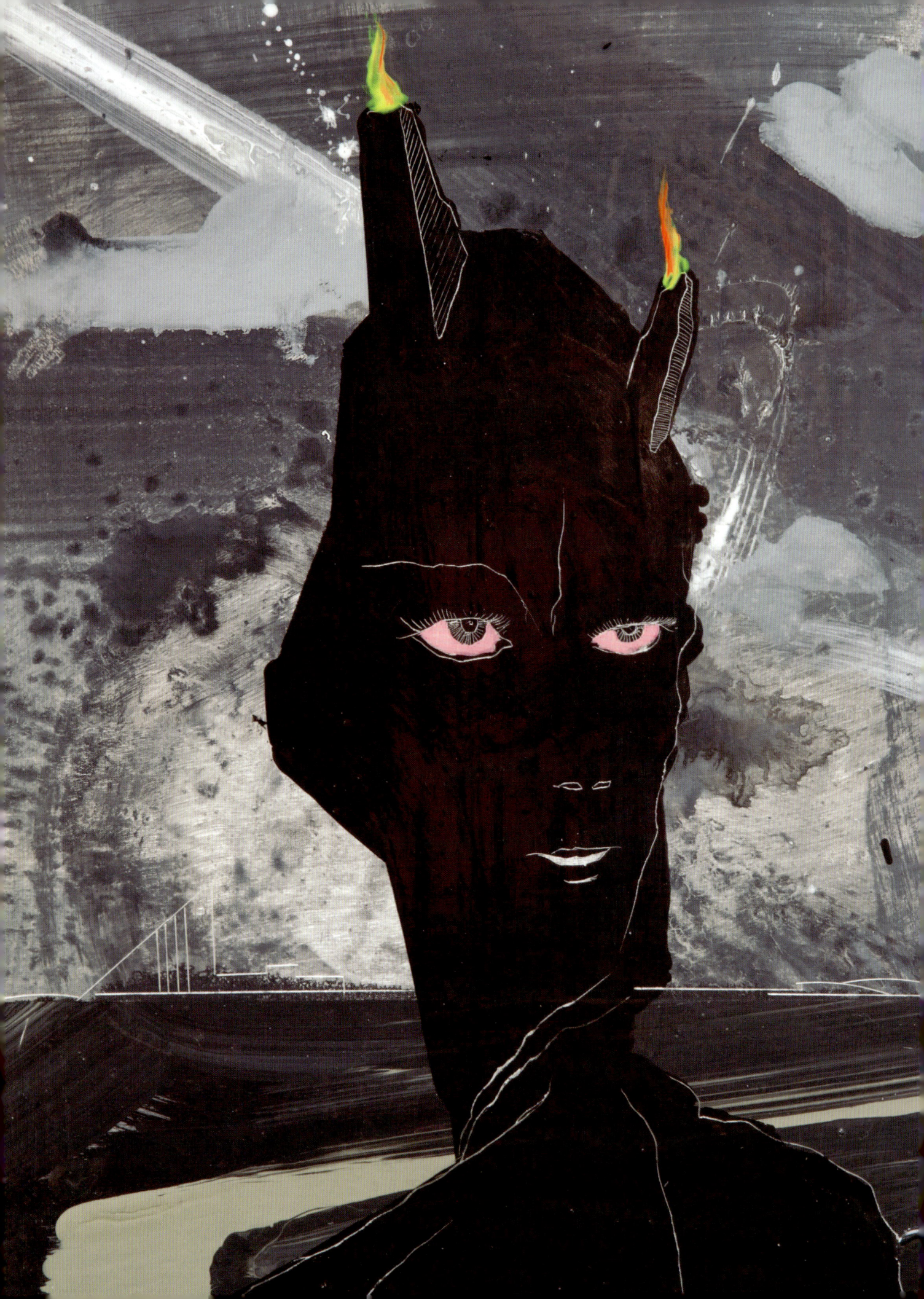

MICHAL CIMALA

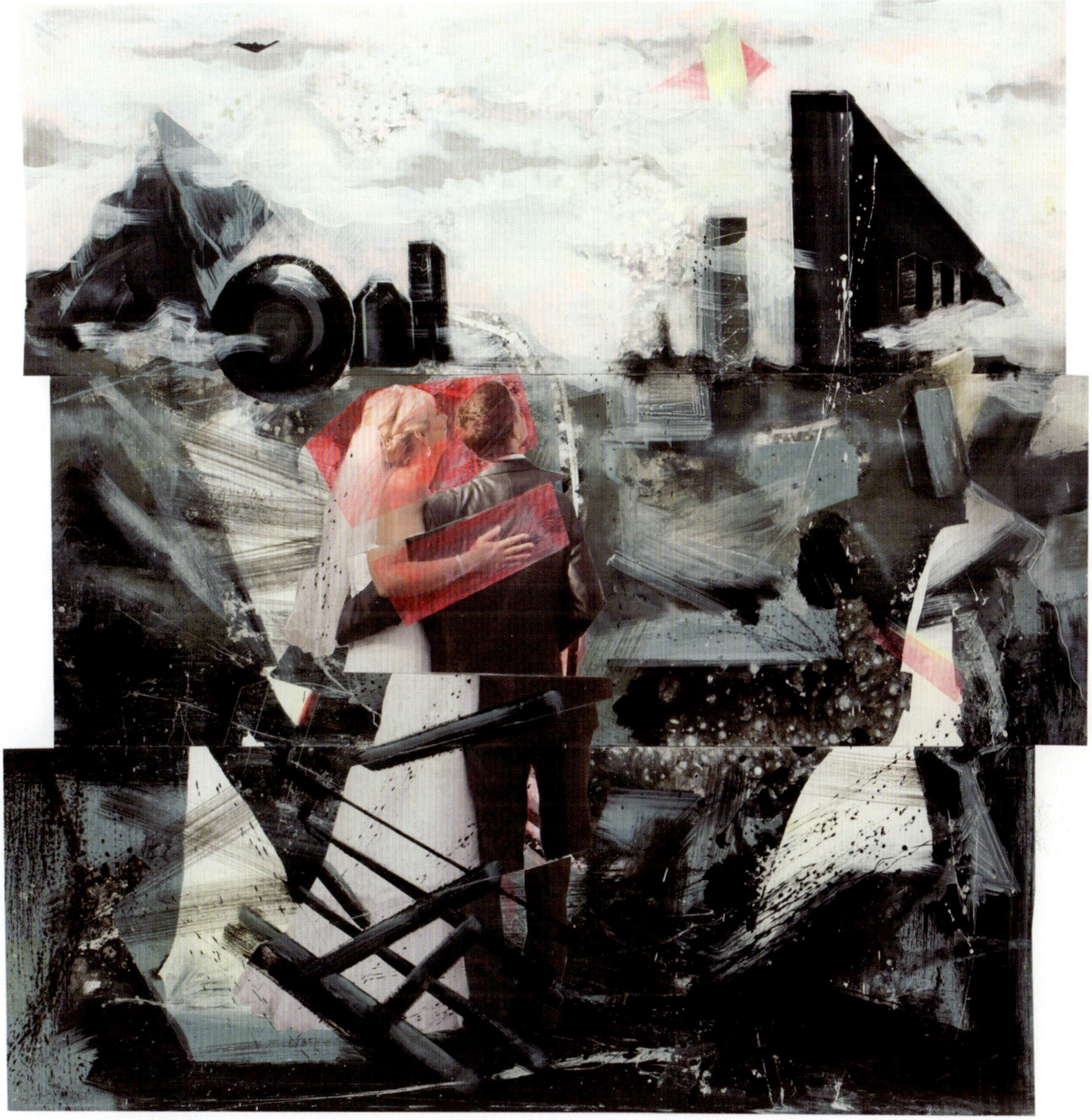

Lives and works in Prague. Since 2006 he works as an assistant at the Academy of Fine Arts at the Atelier Sculpture 1 led by Jaroslav Róna. Co-founder of Trafačka ateliers and Trafo Gallery.

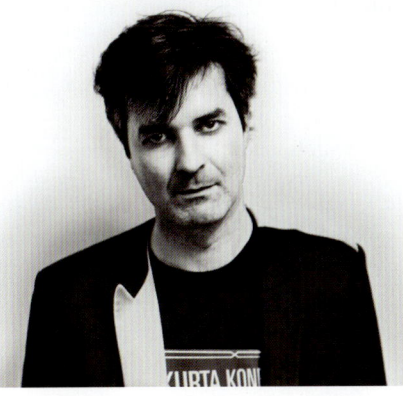

● **(facing page) Satan with burning chimneys of eternity**
Acrylic on skybond, 10.5 x 14.5 in., 2013

● **Great expectations in front of a factory – a wedding night**
Acrylic on skybond and digital print, 54 x 57 in., 2013

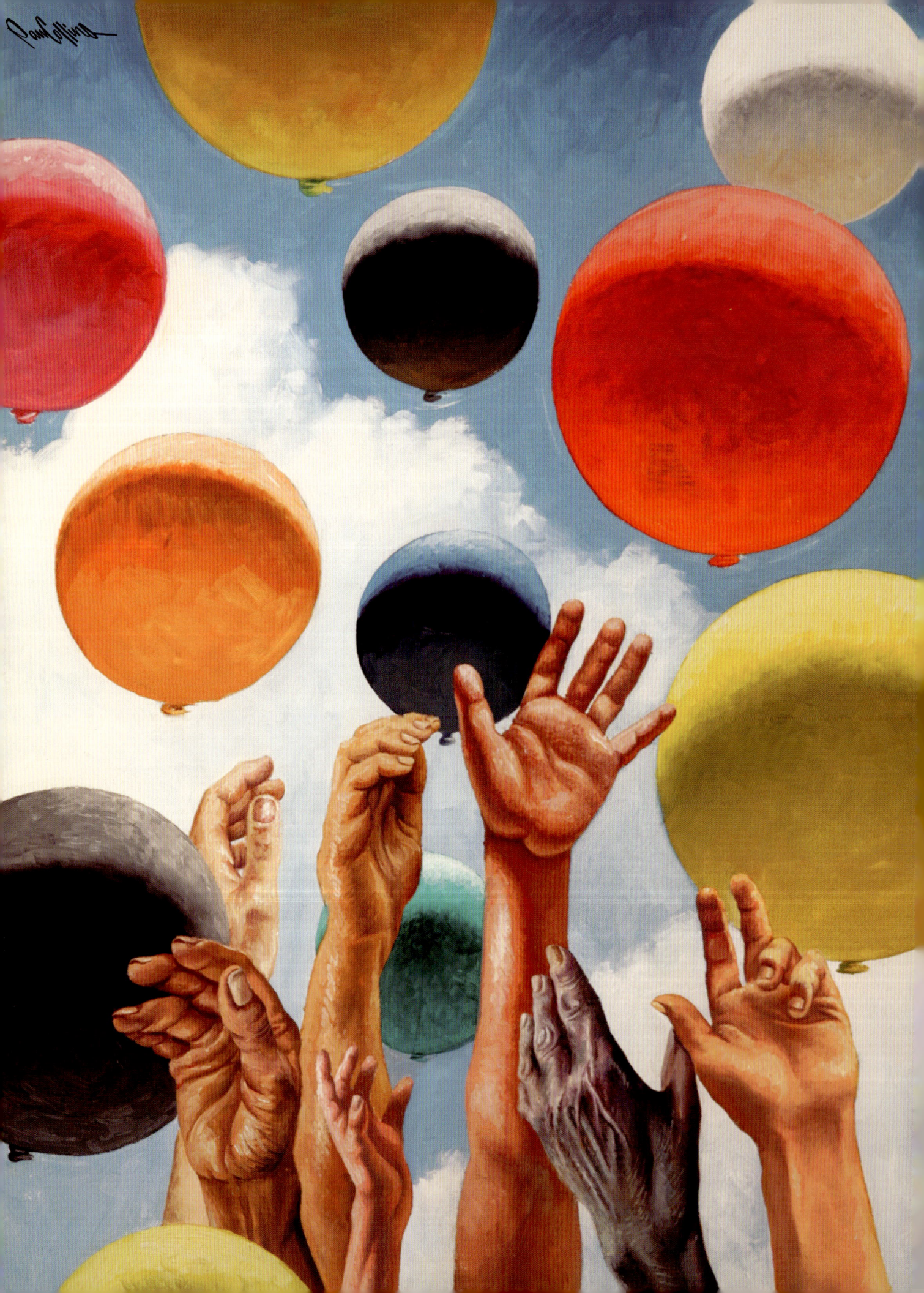

PAUL COLLINS

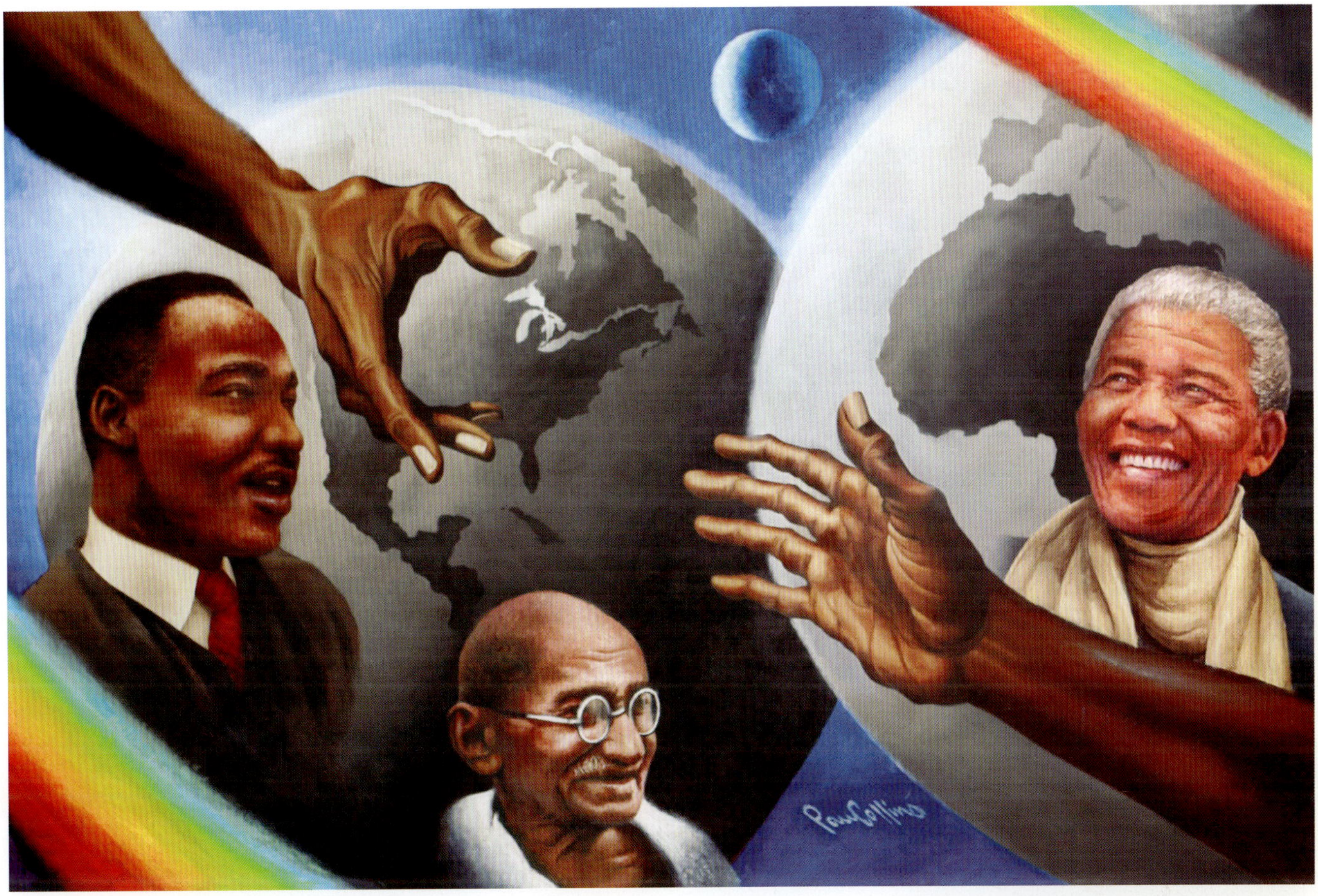

Paul Collins was selected as one of the top twenty most eminent figure painters in America by Watson-Guptil Publications. His works portray strong people and places that push us emotionally. With over 100 solo exhibitions he continues his quest to unite us. Collin's first collection of paintings from his sojourn to Senegal propelled him to international notoriety. He was the first artist of color to paint a sitting president, creating "The President Ford Mural". Eunice Shriver viewed him as the official artist of the Special Olympics. He was commissioned by Coretta King to create the Martin Luther King Peace Prize Medal, by President Carter to create the Presidential Fitness Poster and by NASA to design the space patch commemorating the first American women in space. The Association for Tourism in Israel commissioned him to create their 40th Anniversary Mural. A steady climb to international recognition has been punctuated by exhibits and hangings in several prestigious museums, galleries and cultural centers. Several commissioned works for Amway, Anheuser Bush, Bartech, Blue Cross and Meijer can be viewed around the world and in a wide variety of media. Collin's achievements have won him many national and international honors. He served on the board of the John F. Kennedy Center for the Performing Arts, the Martin Luther King Jr. Center and Kendall College of Art and Design. Throughout his career he has painted in Cuba, France, Gambia, Israel, Japan, Kenya, Key West, Mexico, Senegal, and the Pine Ridge Reservation while keeping roots in Michigan.

WWW.COLLINSART.ORG

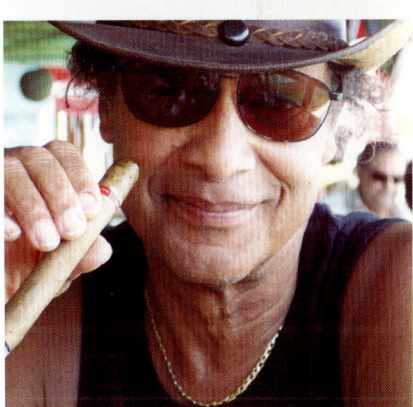

(facing page) No Strings ●
Oil on hardboard, 42 x 54 in., 2000

Blessed are the Peacemakers ●
Oil on hardboard, 70 x 106 in., 2015

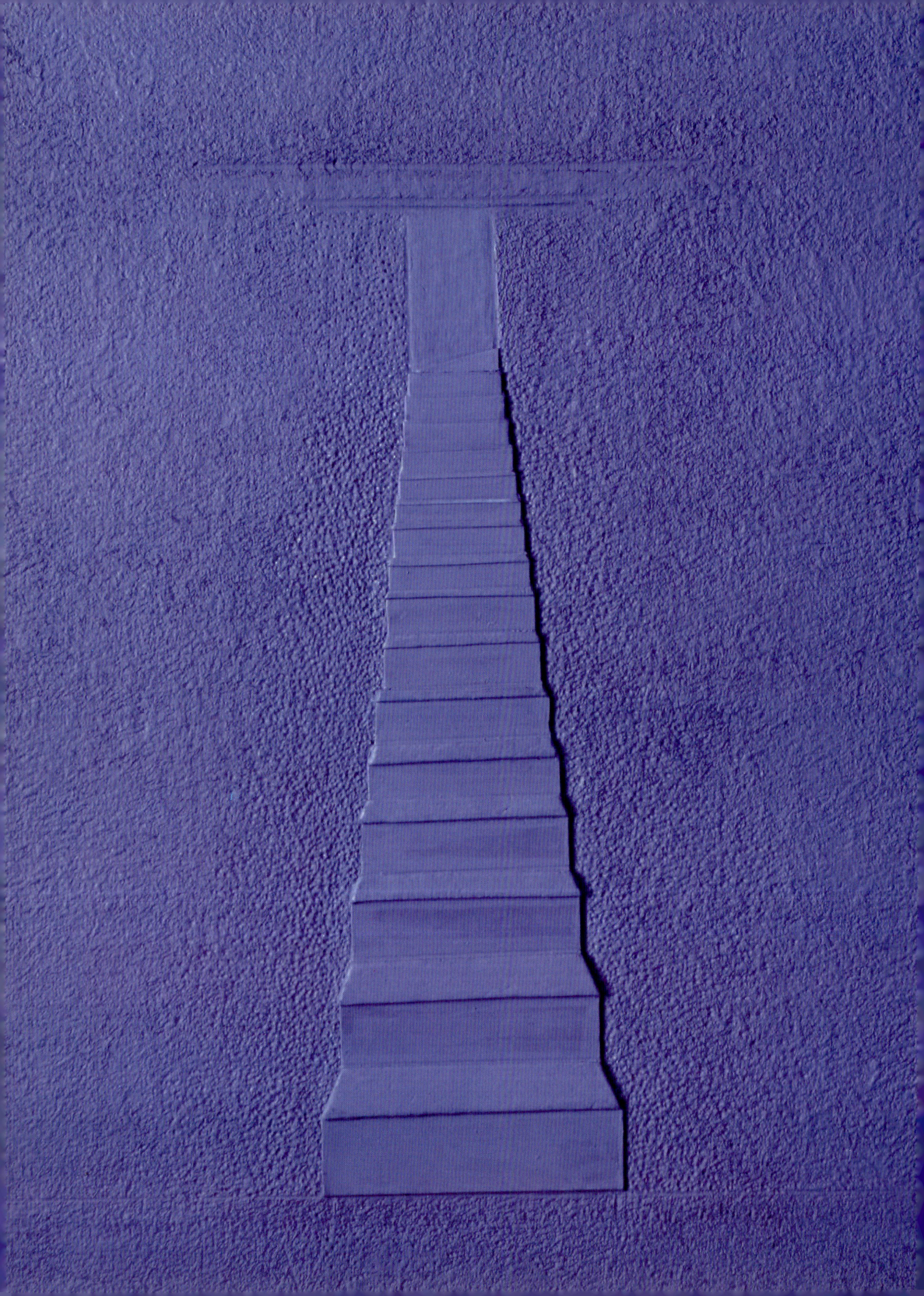

GLENN CONNELLY

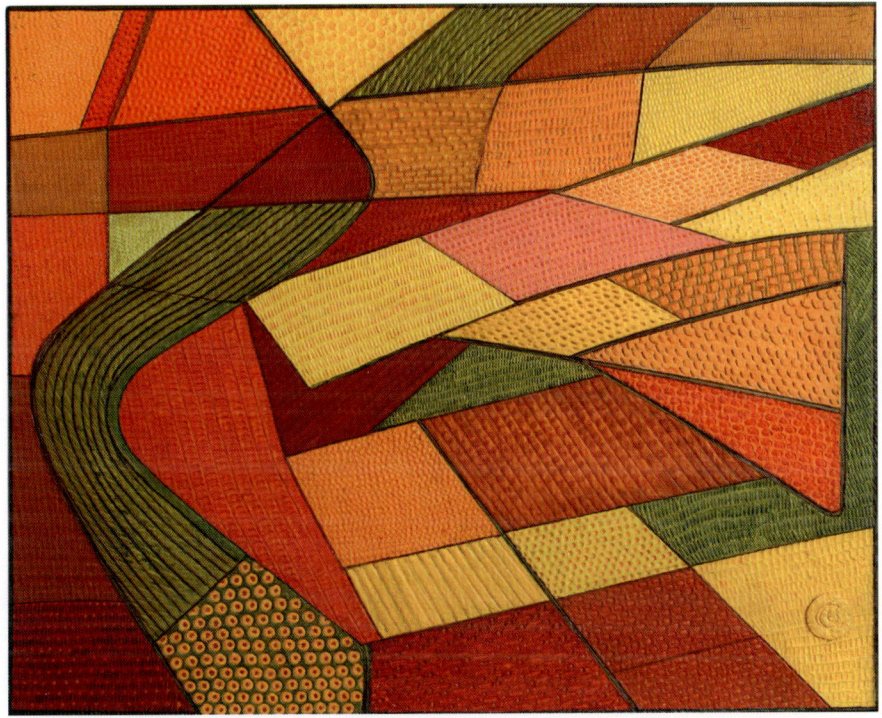

● **(facing page) Purple Blue Staircase**
Acrylic on incised handmade paper. One image from teh color series of 29 Paintings each with a different sculptured design and color. 2010

● **Provence Patchwork**
Abstracted patchwork styled view of Provence, France flower fields. Acrylic on incised handmade paper, 22 x 28 in., 2007

Glenn Connelly is a New York based artist specializing in paper based art. This specialization has resulted in a collection of over 100 paintings over the past 15 years. The works are diverse in subject matter, style and technique. The paintings revolve around a stylized representation, not realism. They include abstracts, allegorical, animals, flowers, landscape, figurative, aerial views of the Earth, and other subjects. The works have evolved from flat paintings on commercial paper to paintings on hand-made paper with incredible detail combined with texture and sculptural qualities. These sculptural paintings are literally sculptural pieces with texture, depth, height, and color as key characteristics. The technique used to create these paintings is analogous to sculpting combined with painting.

The techniques used to produce the sculptural textures are many. One technique involves incising multiple tiny patterns by hand into paper plates producing a result similar to chasing and repousse. The incised patterns vary in shape, design, size and even texture. In some paintings the incised patterns add depth to an otherwise flat painting, whereas in many other paintings, small incised patterns create multiple patterns inside larger patterns inside the overall image. The unique result of the incising technique is that the effect of light and shadow on the paint produces two tones for each color. Only hand tools are used. Molds are not used.

WWW.ARTONPAPER.BIZ

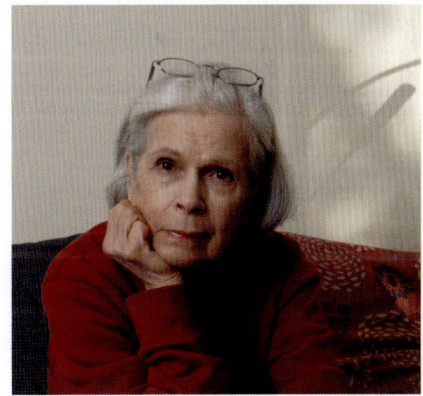

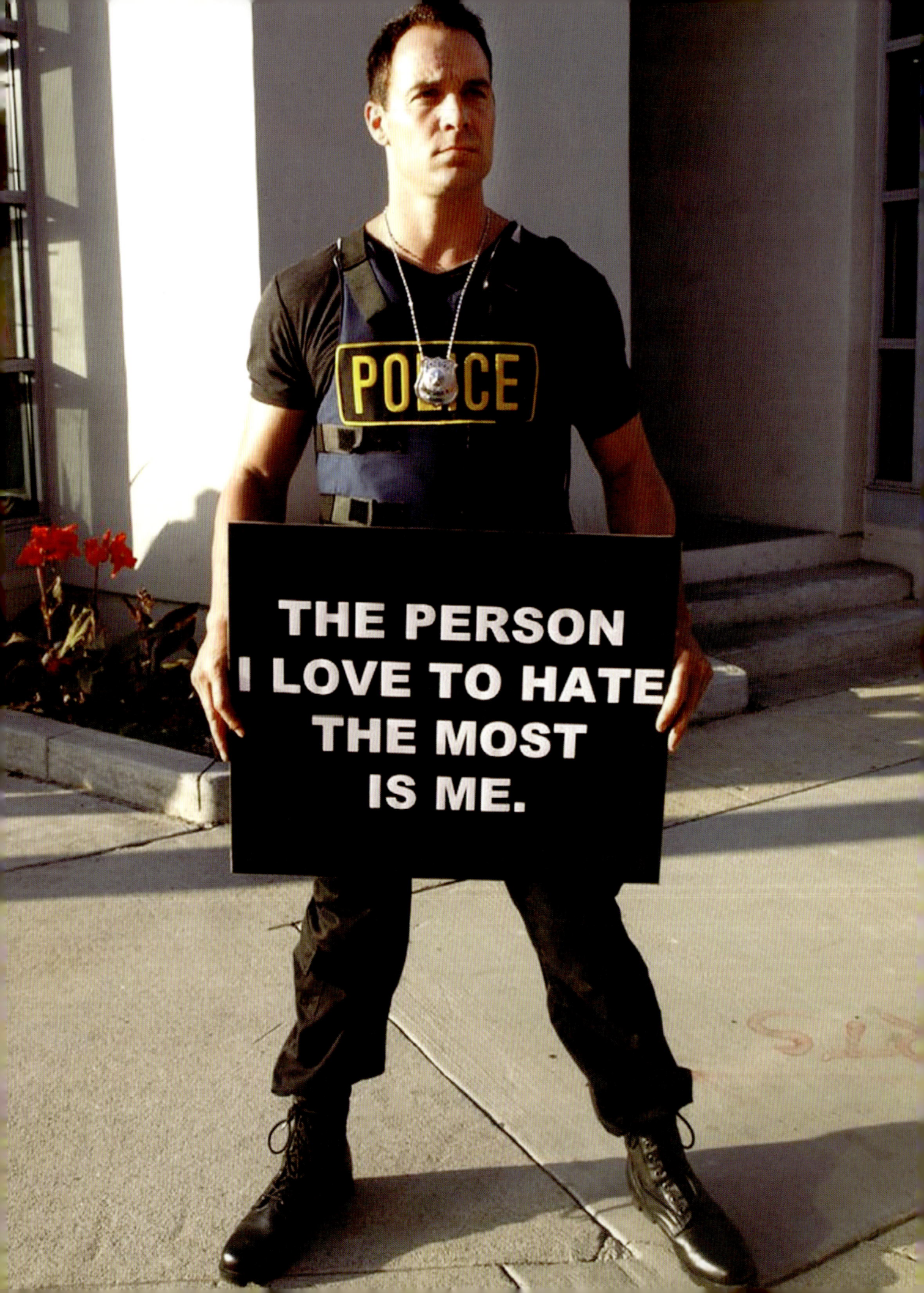

CITIZEN X

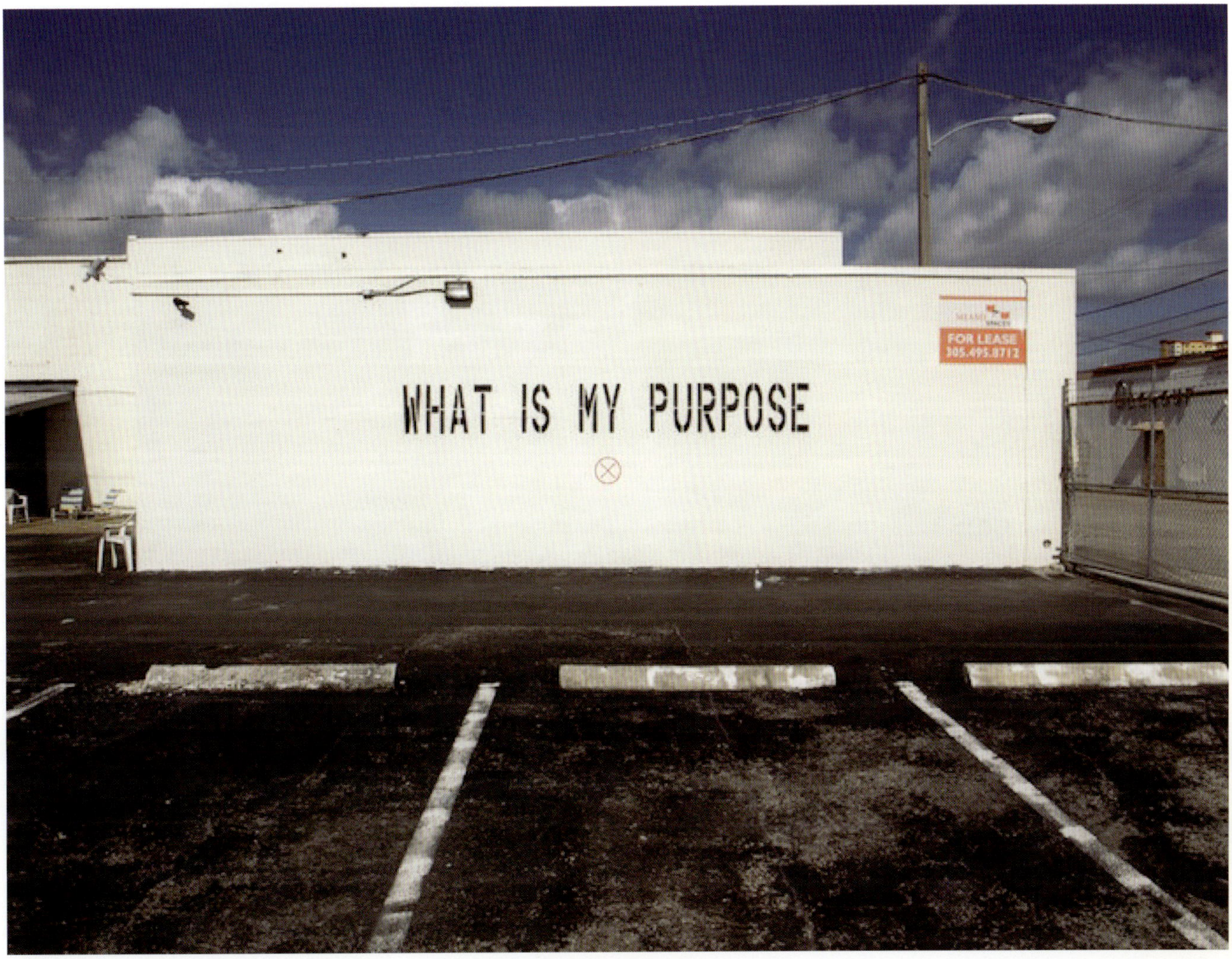

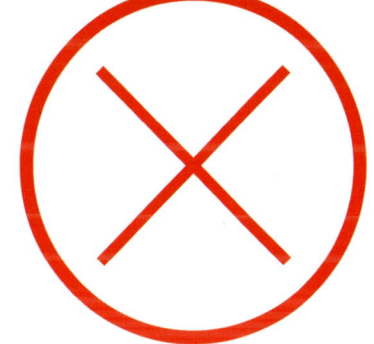

WHAT IS MY PURPOSE

Citizen X was conceptualized to expose what has been suppressed in the darkest corridors of our psyche. Confessions for the World to examine of what defines us as human and our humanity and lack thereof. Citizen X is a collaboration between four contemporary Los Angeles artists, each using a unique voice to initiate a text-based public dialog.

WWW.THE-CITIZEN-X.COM

● **(facing page) The Person I Love to Hate**
C-Print on archival paper, 20 x 24 in., 2013

● **What is My Puprpose (mural)**
Spray paint on cement, 2013
Fountainhead Residency Studios (Miami Florida)

BIBI DAVIDSON

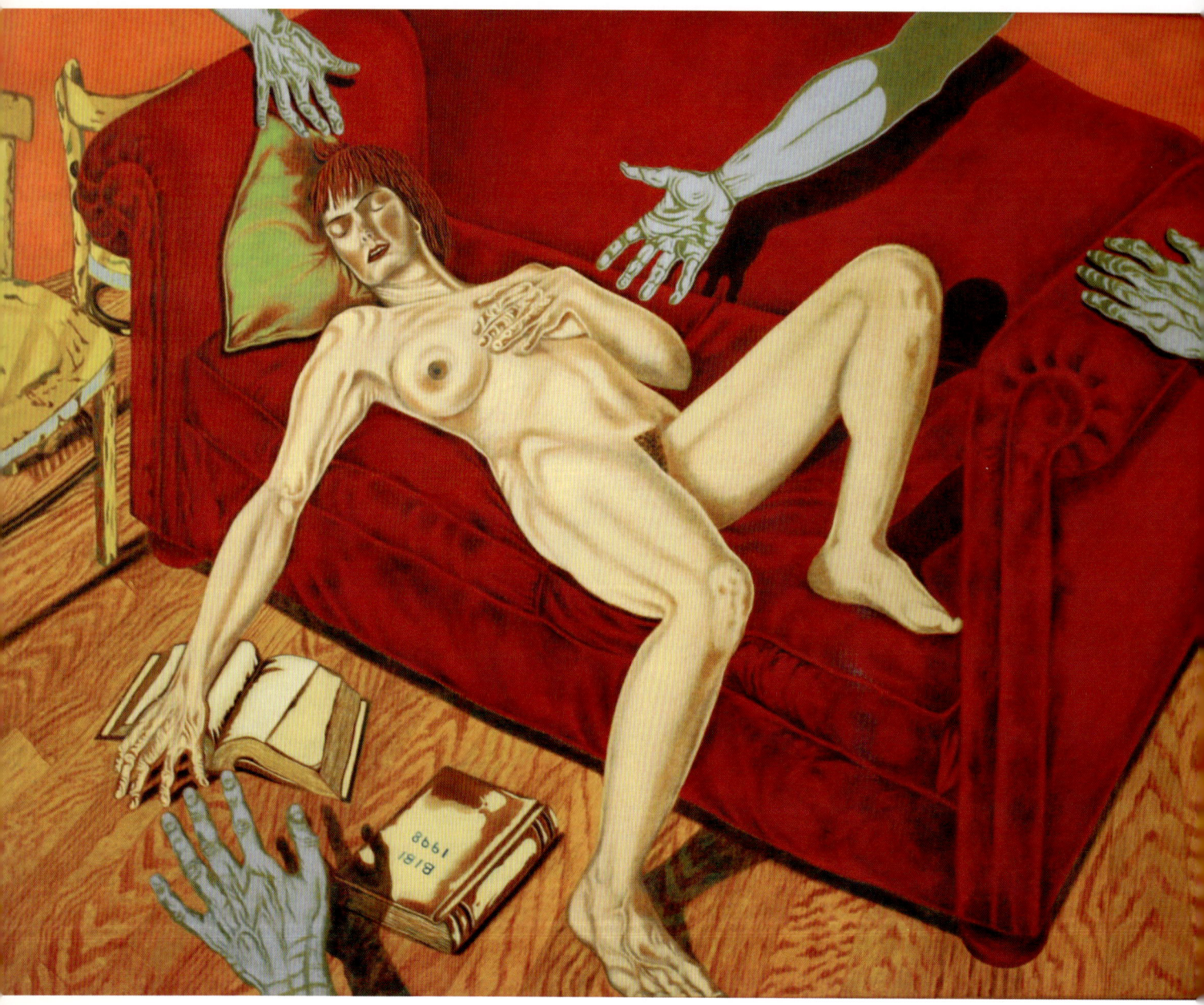

● **In the Spotlight**
Oil on wood, 31 x 22 in., 1998

● **Adolescence I, II, III**
Oil on wood, 20 x 20 in., 2005

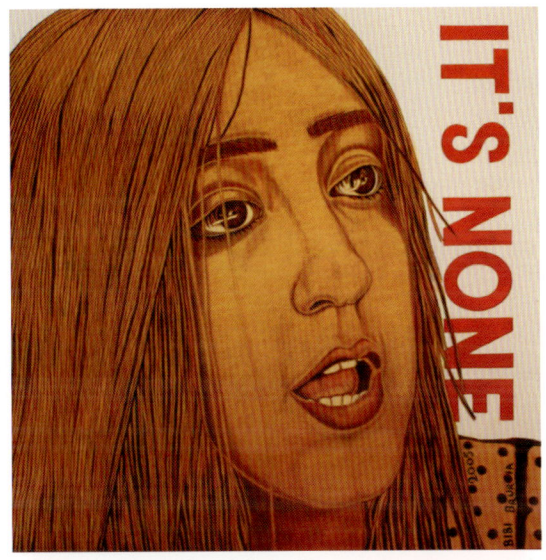

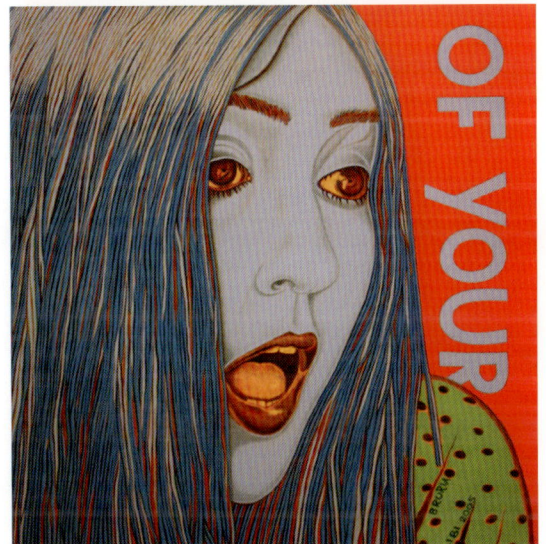

One is born to a certain talent and passion, which either is in his/her genes, past life or the influence of their environment. At a very early age I observed the surroundings around me and put them on paper, I love hair. I always paint it as if a magnified glass magnifies it. A certain color can make me breath better. I love the color red. For years I'd been doodling a character on every piece of paper I had. All of a sudden I realized that it was the subject of my art. It became the "stories of my life" series; it's all the silly thoughts and dreams of my being, from the past, from the present and from the future. It's My Girl..........
it's me.

WWW.BIBIDAVIDSON.COM

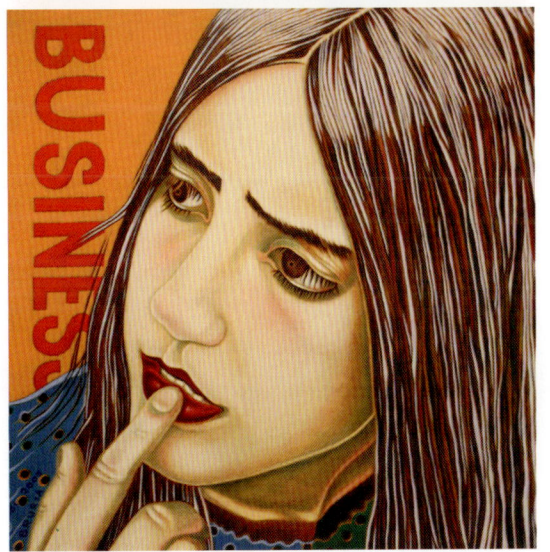

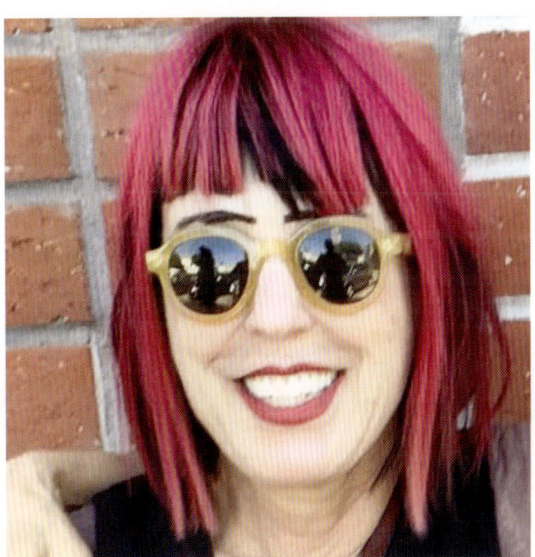

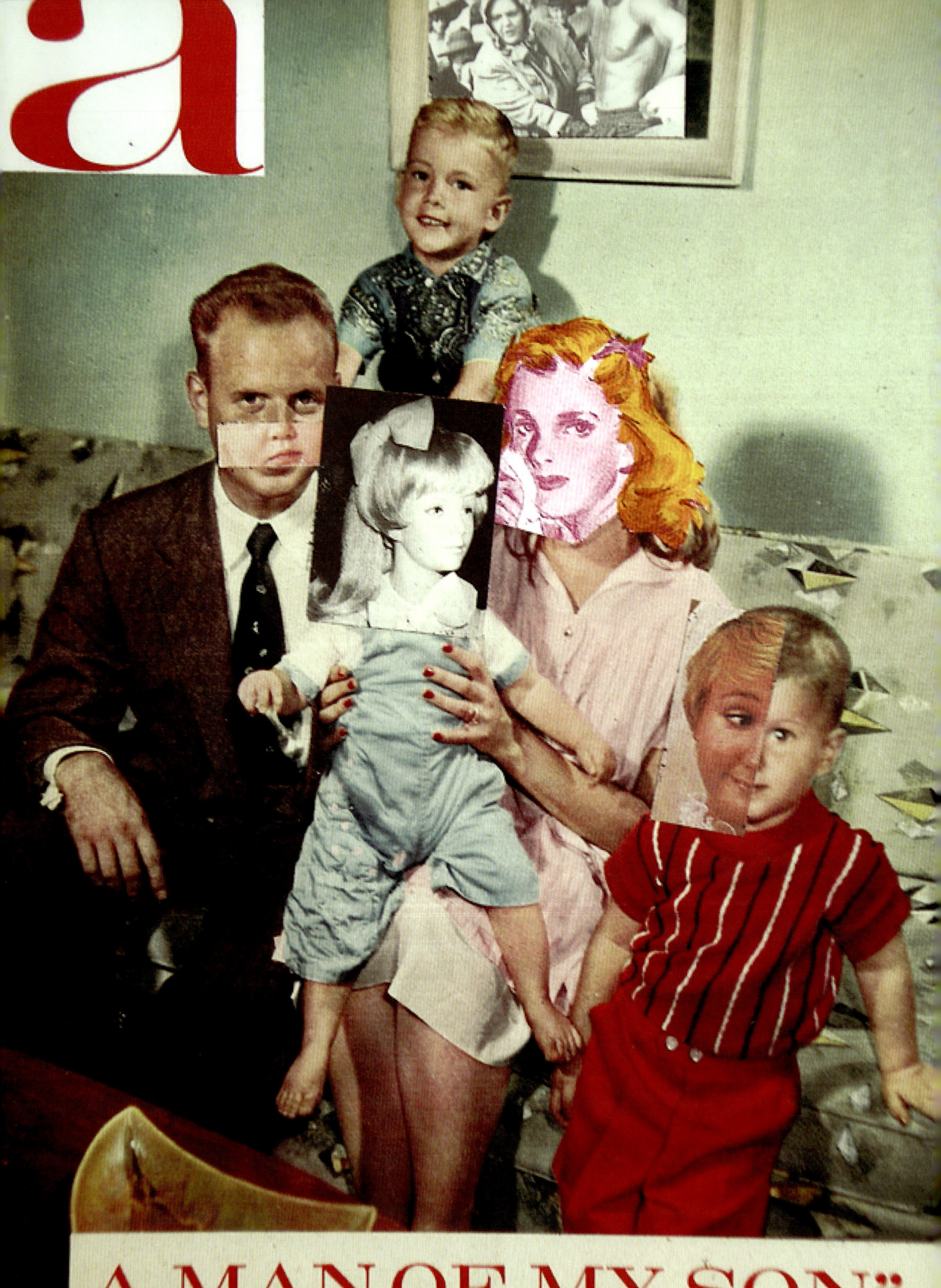

SID DANIELS

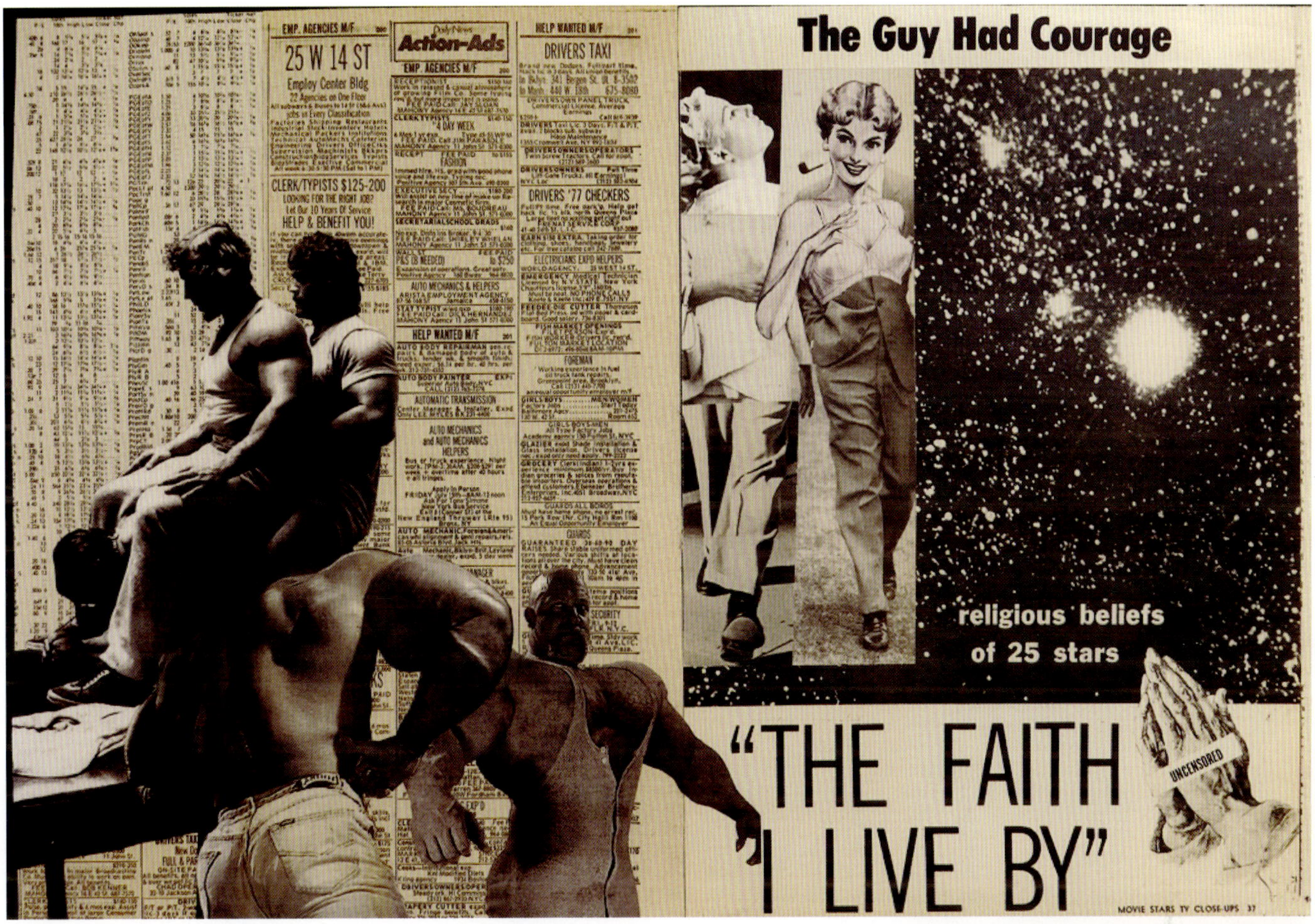

Sid Daniels was born in Toronto, Canada, and as a boy he worked in his uncle's shoe store. This is where his fascination for shoes began, which led to his passion for fashion, Brazilian music and 1930s and '40s Hollywood movie musicals. These were important catalysts that resulted in his hallmark 'showgirl' theme paintings, a signature to his style which he coined 'Latin Deco'. Sid relocated to new York City in 1979, and throughout the 1980s, his large scale canvases were staged vignettes of stylized sexy women in platform shoes, symbolically representing an architectural form. And throughout the 1990s, his women in heels were integrated into his restaurant and nightclub murals in New York City, Philadelphia and Japan.

In 1997, Sid relocated to Miami Beach, the Art Deco capital of the world, creating posters for the US Ballroom Championships, 'Flamingos on the Beach' (Art in Public Places) and First Night Miami Beach. In 2010, Sid introduced the square format, with an Art Deco contemporary twist, paying homage to 1930s choreographer Busby Berekely. That same year, his series of contemporary collages, explored the human condition and our dysfunctional society at the Sol Gallery, Miami Beach. In 2013, Sid's Parasol Series juxtaposes inventive surface textures and pop geometry with an image he repeats over fourteen canvases. An experiment in camouflage and repetition.

A new paradigm shift emerges in 2015. The figure is eliminated and his focus is all about architectural and geometric imagery The palette is now deeper, darker and monochromatic.

WWW.SIDDANIELS.COM

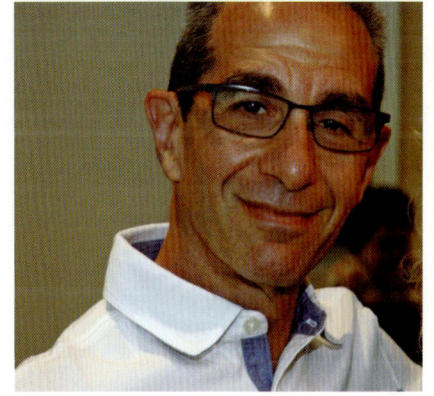

(facing page) Gonna Make a Man Out of You ●
Collage on board, 14 x 16 in., 2010

Secret Society ●
Collage on board, 14 x 20 in., 2010

CHRISTOPHER PAUL DEAN

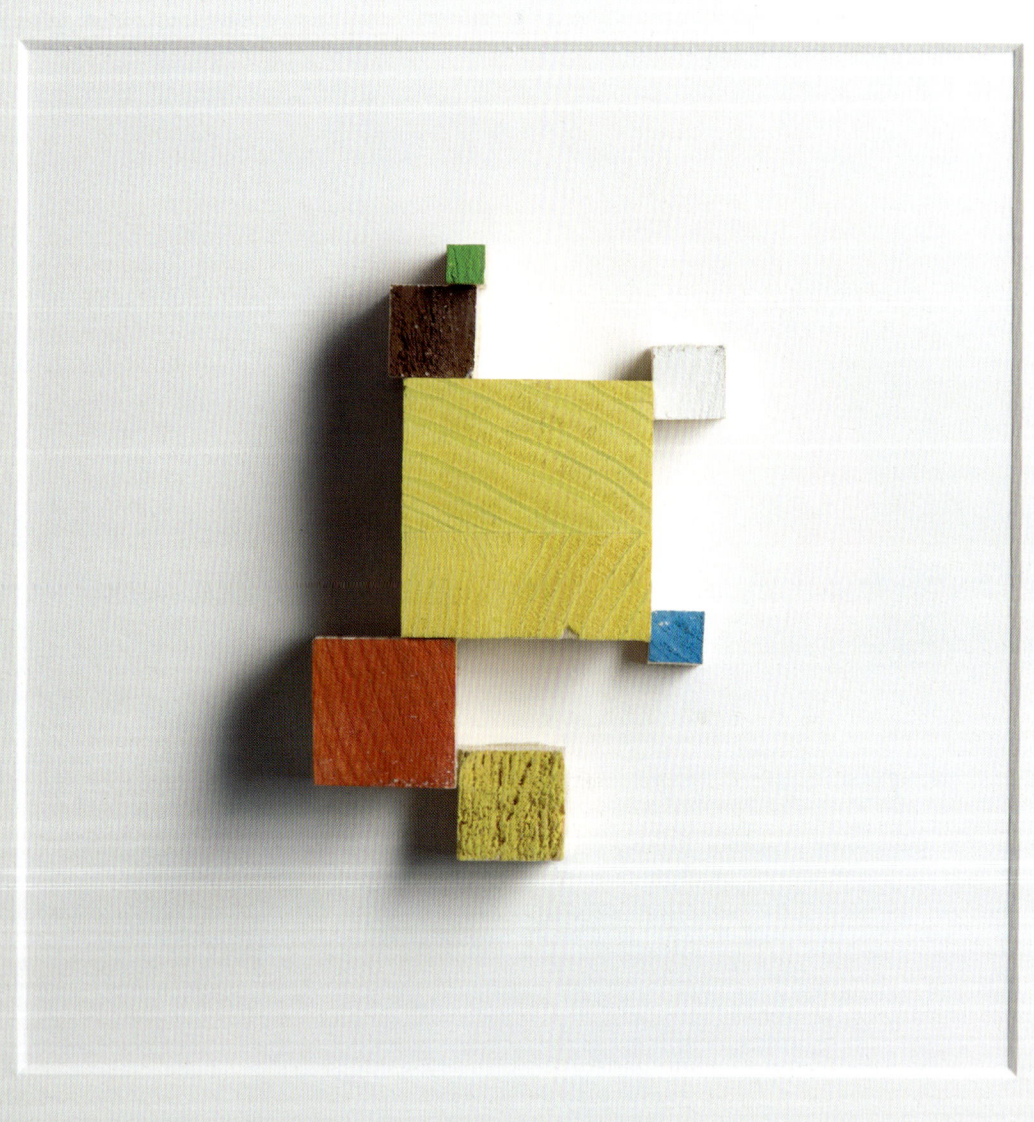

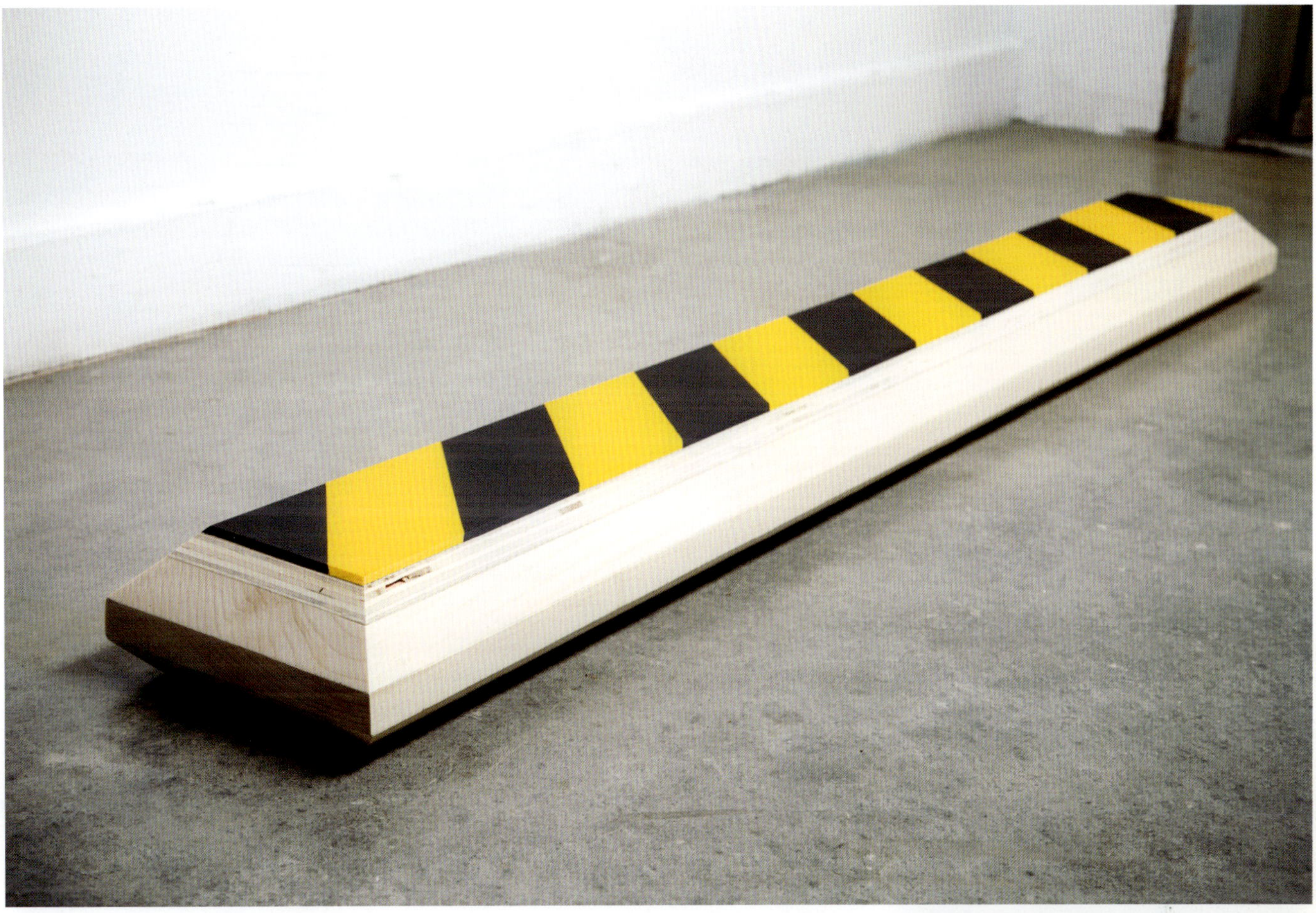

Christopher Paul Dean (December, 1983) was born in Milton Keynes, England. At the age of 21, with no academic qualifications and leaving a full-time job, Dean pursued and completed a National Diploma in Art & Design with Triple Distinction. Following this, he earned a B.A. in Contemporary Applied Arts from the University of Hertfordshire, receiving a First Class Honors. Dean is currently pursuing his M.F.A in Sculpture at the Savannah College of Art and Design.

Since 2010 Dean has worked alongside a number of artists in both Scandinavia, and America. The first of which was Christin Johansson, where he spent 3 months at, 'The Folk Art School' in Holbæk, Denmark. Following this, in 2011, he travelled to 'Cranbrook Academy of Art', where he assisted Danish artist Anders Ruhwald.

In 2012, Dean began working as an Art Handler for SCAD Museum of Art, Savannah, Ga. It was during this time he met Dallas-based artist, Gabriel Dawe. Dean was Head Assistant for Dawe's installation, 'Plexus 21', at Gutstein Gallery, Savannah. In 2014 Dawe invited Dean to Mexico to assist with an installation at the U.S Consulate in Monterrey.

Throughout his years of study Dean has been awarded a number of merit-based scholarships, bursaries, and grants. Most recently, for the second year in a row, Dean was selected from a number of candidates as the most worthy of receiving a, 'Sculpture Endowment Scholarship'.

WWW.CPDEANART.COM

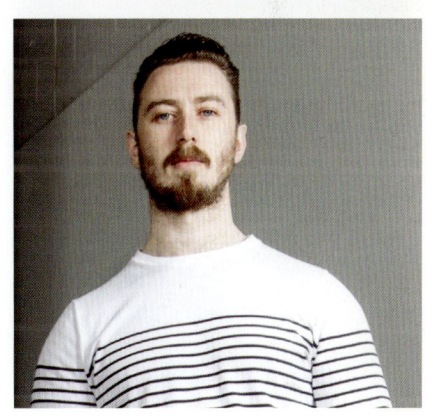

(facing page) Square Dowel Composition ●
No. 1" dowels, 21 x 21 x 2 in. (framed), 2015

Caution ●
Wood, masonite, paint, 6 x 46 x 3.5 in., 2014

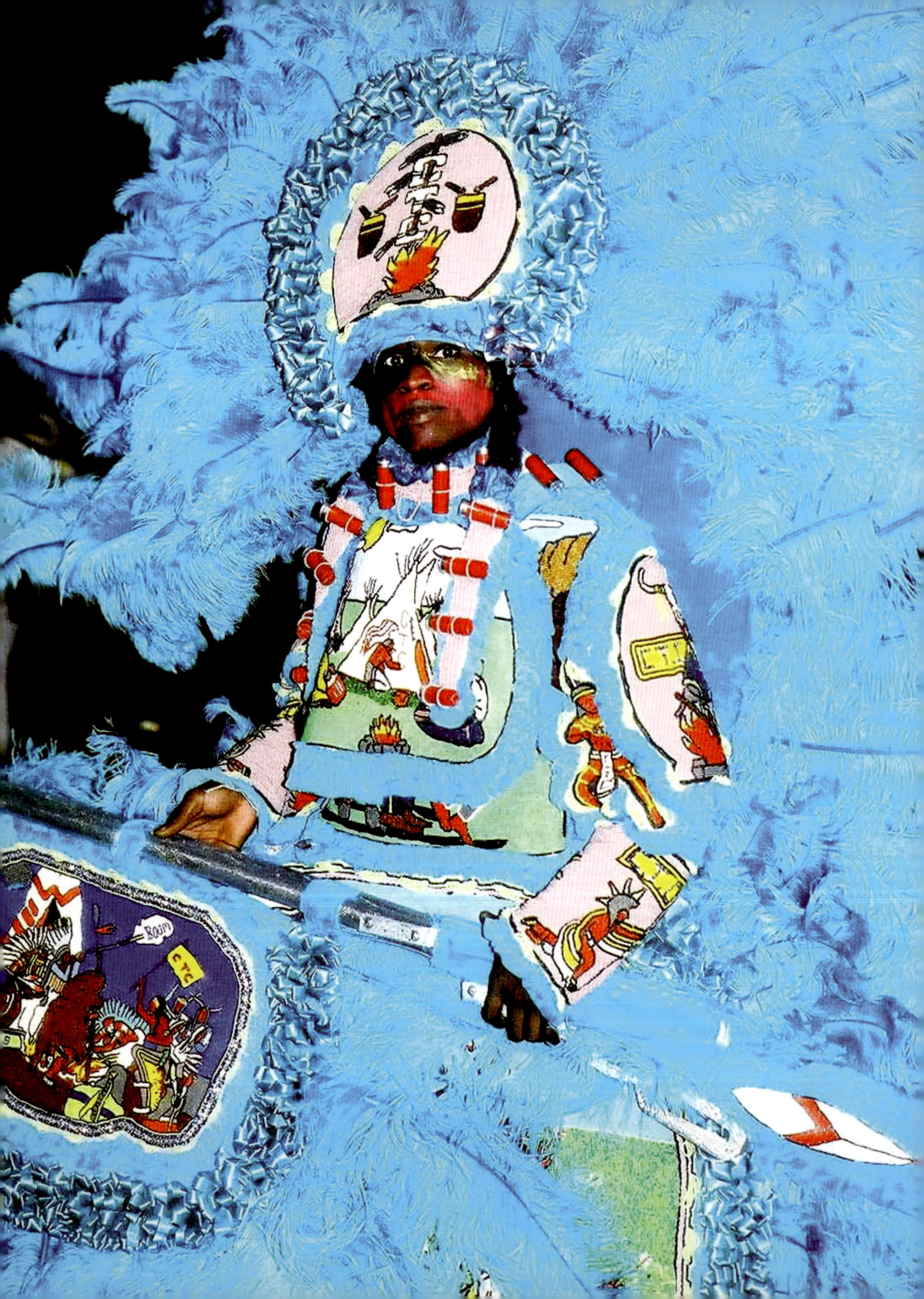

MICHELLE ELMORE

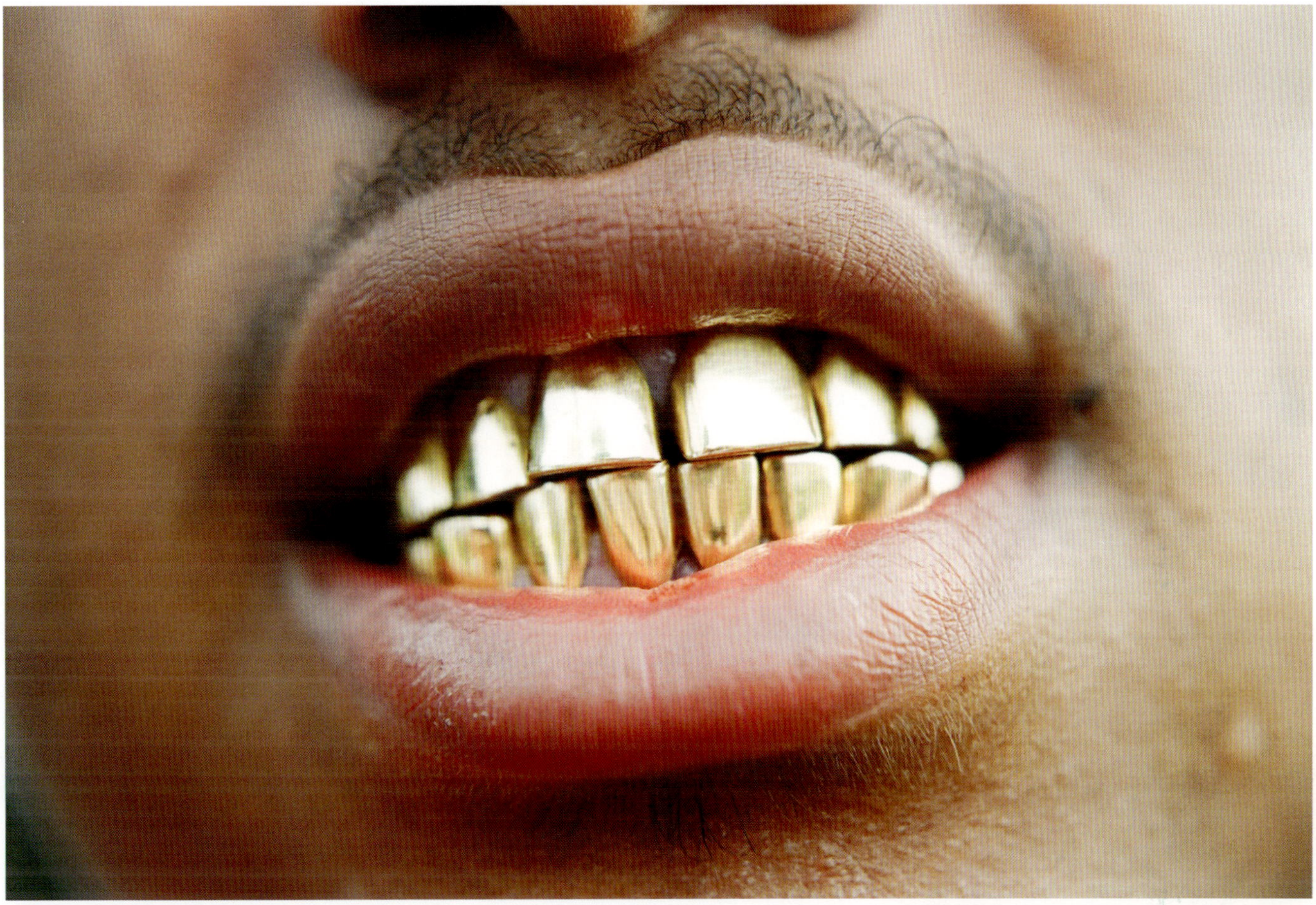

Armed with three magnifying filters on my 50mm lens and no tripod, I started out visiting barbershops in New Orleans on Friday afternoons. Many of my subjects were Gangsta Rap artists, and this led to many commissions documenting their day-to-day lifestyles in the neighborhoods they were from.

In the two years leading up to Katrina, I did over 200 "Southern Pop" photographs, Spending some much with these young people, I quickly realized that the moniker "soldiers" by which they refer to themselves and each other is not an affectation. The average live expectancy in this demographic is 25 years. They speak, live and interact with an urgency that I would imagine exists on battlefields.

I have personally witnessed over 50 shootings. One day, one of my "Southern Pop" subjects was shot through the chest. The bullet passed through his body, missing both his heart and spine by fractions of an inch. Apparently, the slug was so hot that it cauterized the wound on the way through and it didn't even bleed. He went home and lay down for a few hours and was back on the street the next day.

WWW.MICHELLEELMORE.COM

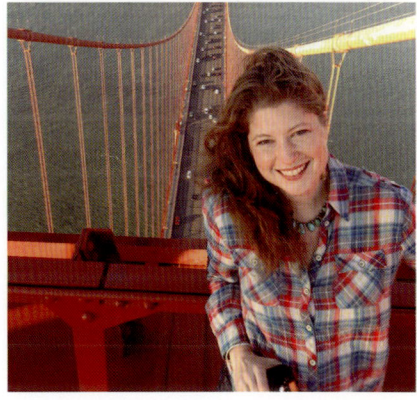

(facing page) Black Mardi Gras Indians of New Orleans (series) ●
Color photograph, various dimensions, 2008

Bling Bling a/k/a Southern Pop (series) ●
Color photograph, various dimensions, 2008

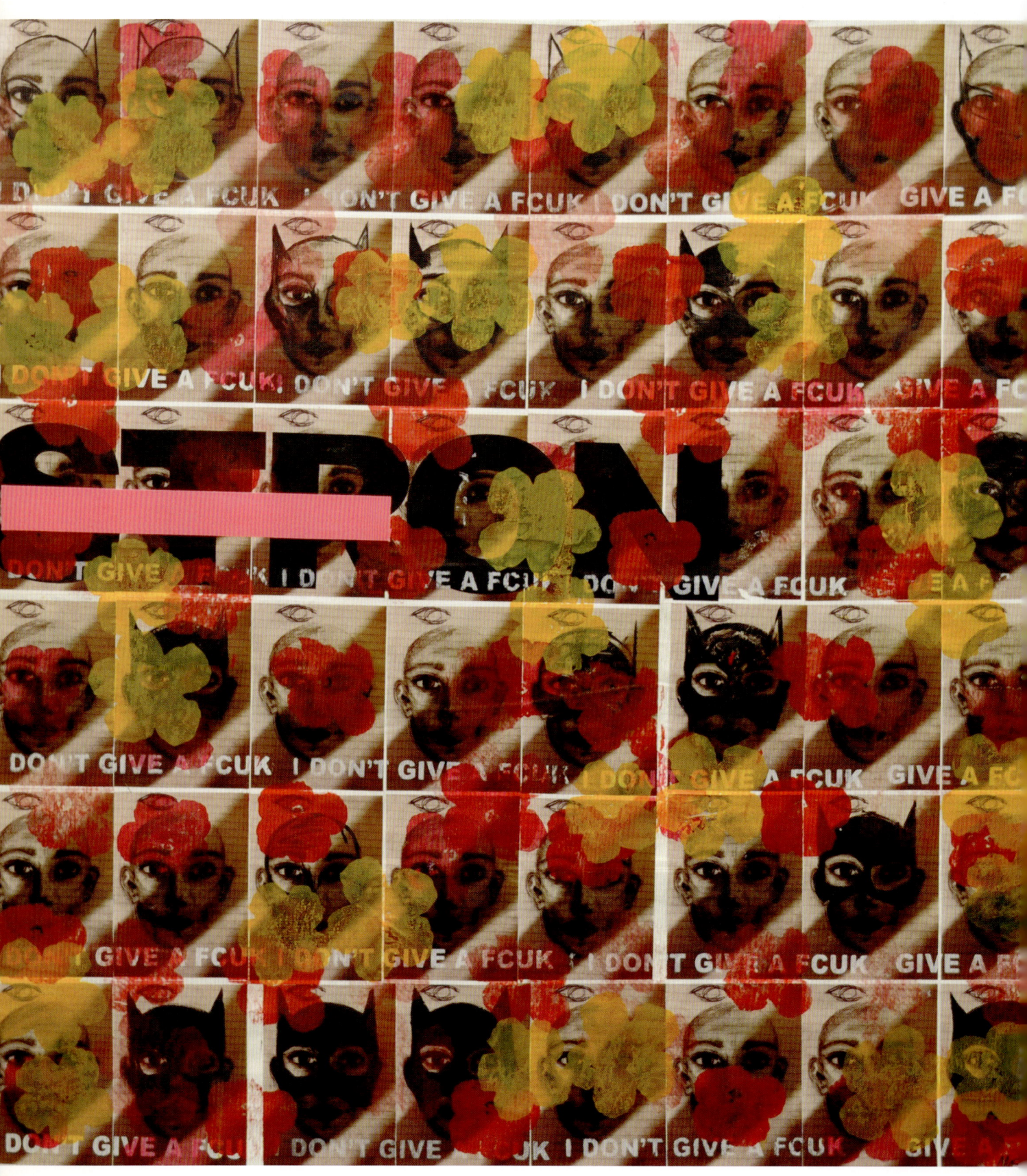

MARIA FRAGOUDAKI

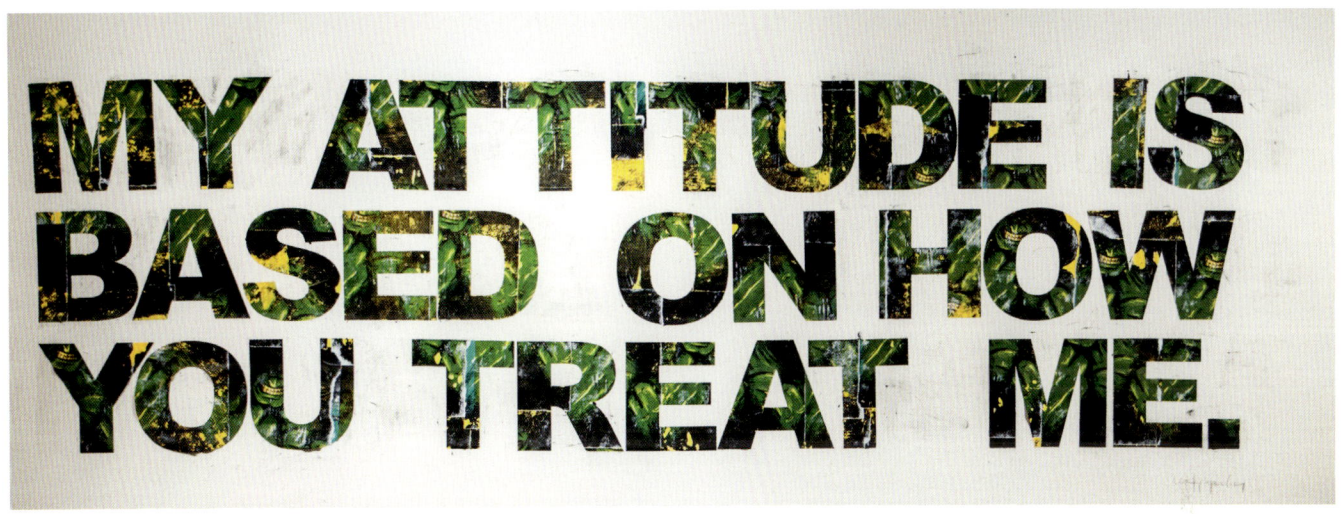

"All her paintings are composed through multiple dense, textured layers of color which is characteristic of her expression mode, creating a personal style that is both fresh and highly promising" said Olinka Miliaresi-Varvitsioti, an art historian."

Maria Fragoudaki was born in Athens, Greece in 1983. She studied Chemistry, Pharmacology and Business management in London, UK where she subsequently worked for a few years. Over the last 7 years she attended various art residences, courses and seminars in painting & fine art in London and New York.

Maria Fragoudaki has presented her work in numerous group and solo shows throughout museums, art fairs and galleries in New York, Switzerland, Belgium and Greece, including the Goulandris Natural History Museum in Athens, the Historical and Folklore Museum of Aegina in Greece, and Scope Basel in Switzerland. Since moving to New York in 2012, she has attended three art residencies at the School of Visual Arts,

and has exhibited at WOP gallery (2015), Ca D'Oro gallery (2015), 103 Allen St. (2015), Luhring Augustine gallery in partnership with Visual Aids (2015), New Century Artists (2014), One Art Space gallery (2012), 4 N. Main Gallery (2012) in Southampton NY, and Kouros Gallery (2011) in New York. Her work has been acquired by private and corporate collections around the world.

WWW.MARIAFRAGOUDAKI.COM

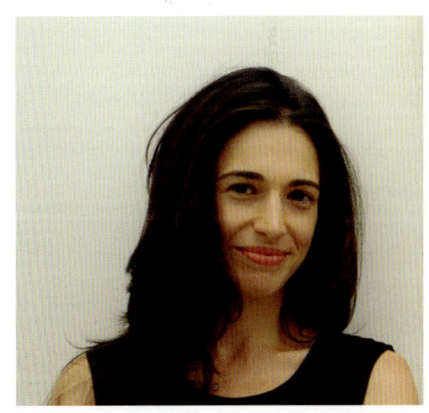

(facing page) WISE to Be ●
Mixed media on canvas, 51 x 50 in., 2014

Attitude II ●
Collage on canvas, 90 x 40 in., 2013

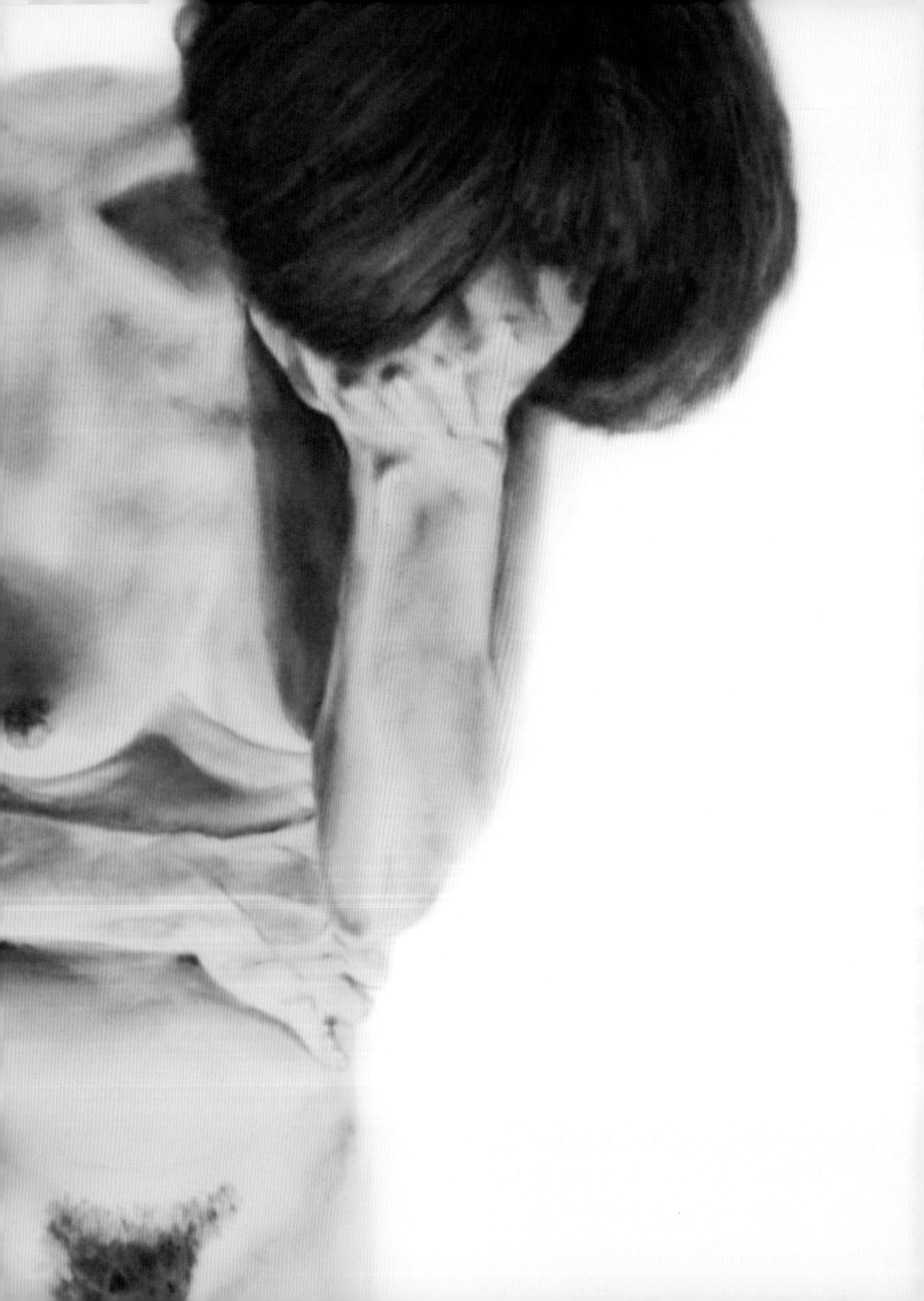

COLLEEN GARIBALDI

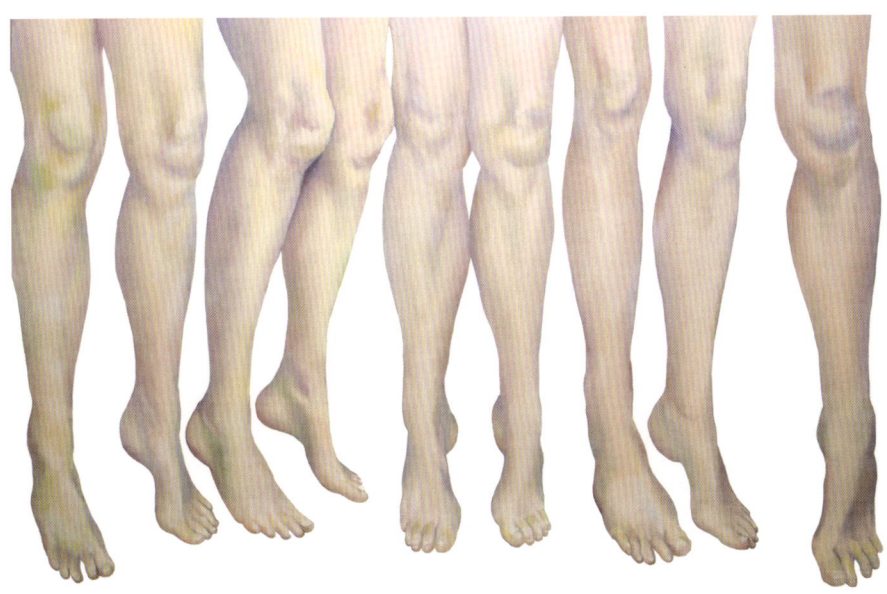

"For me making art leads to awareness, bringing to the surface that which is going on inside. Oftentimes it is a literal journey; for example, an examination of influential patterns in life got transformed into works exploring patternmaking using limbs, pictures of nonsensical and purely graphic configurations devoid of connotation. "

Influenced by the lessons learned as a child traipsing about with my military family of balancing a solid foundation with the enrichment of new challenges and experiences, I've been working in a variety of media, focusing mainly on the figure. Primarily a painter, I've also been exploring 3D, video and stills while maintaining a drawing and photography practice, always pushing my familiarity with materials and methods, trying old and new alike.

Recently I've been looking at the body as object and using it as my tool, exploring my world while questioning cultural norms of viewing the body as mere carnal commodity. For me making art leads to awareness, bringing to the surface that which is going on inside. Oftentimes it is a literal journey; for example, an examination of influential patterns in life got transformed into works

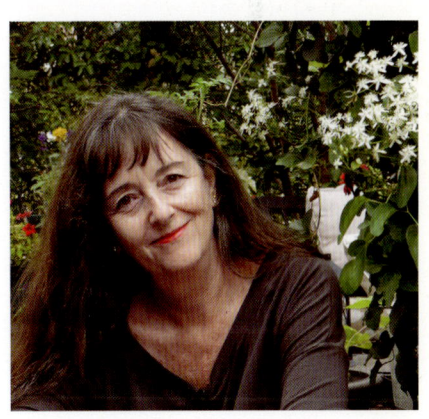

exploring patternmaking using limbs, pictures of nonsensical and purely graphic configurations devoid of connotation. Concurrently, through making work with limbs or the figure in a more narrative manner, such as illustrating feeling like slabs of meat being inspected, I'm ruminating on the omnipresent nature of story, endeavoring to find a way to stay true to my desire to work with abstracted representations of the figure.

My work has been exhibited regionally and nationally and is in multiple private collections. I have been awarded grants and scholarships from the Pennsylvania Academy of the Fine Arts, the Vermont Studio Center and Cloud Farm and was recently in a residency at the Vermont Studio Center.

WWW.COLLEENGARIBALDI.COM

(facing page) Series 1, 4 ●
Graphite on paper, 22 x 30 in., 2015

Being Reviewed ●
Oil on canvas, 30 x 40 in., 2015

SCOTT GENGELBACH

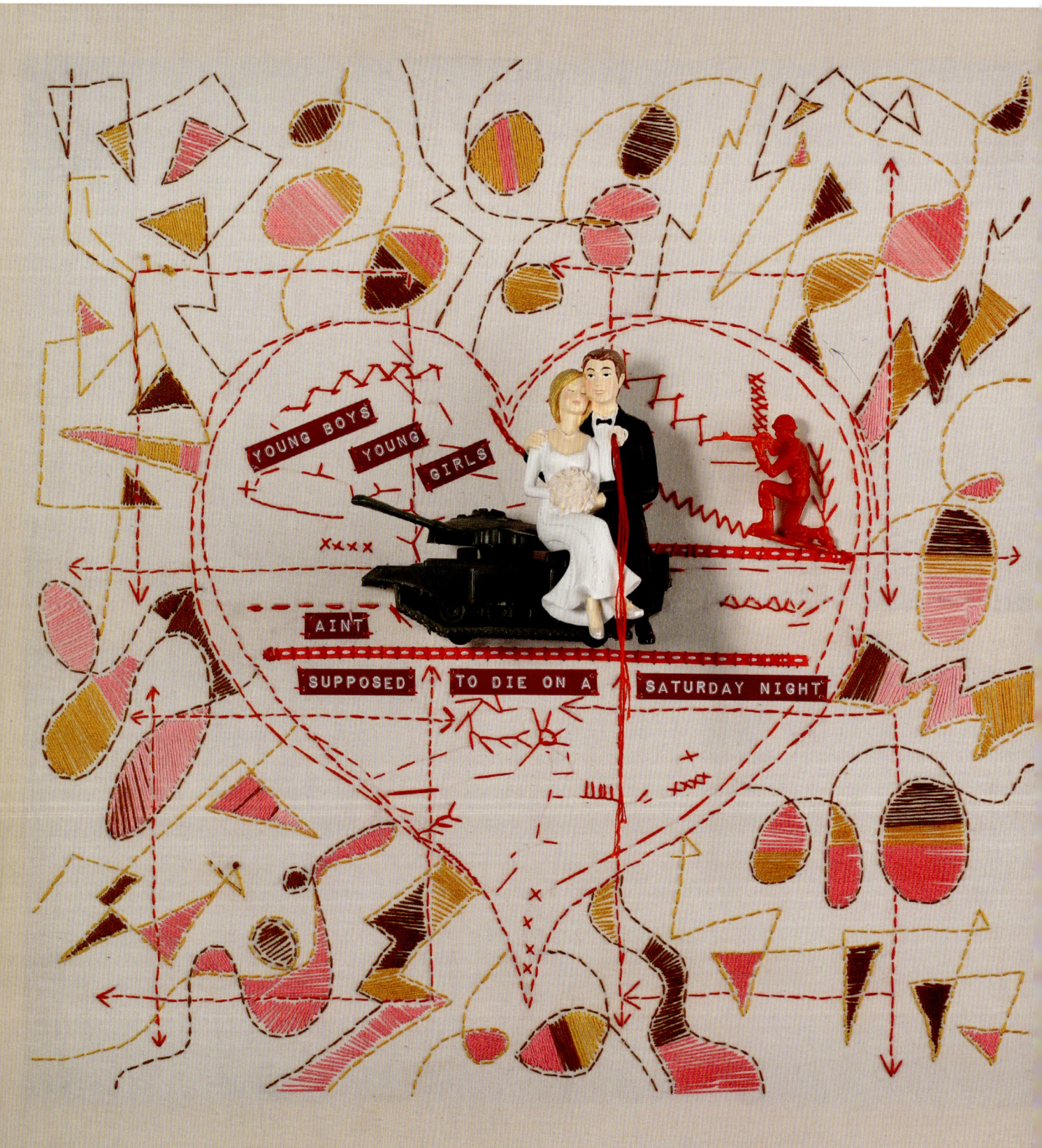

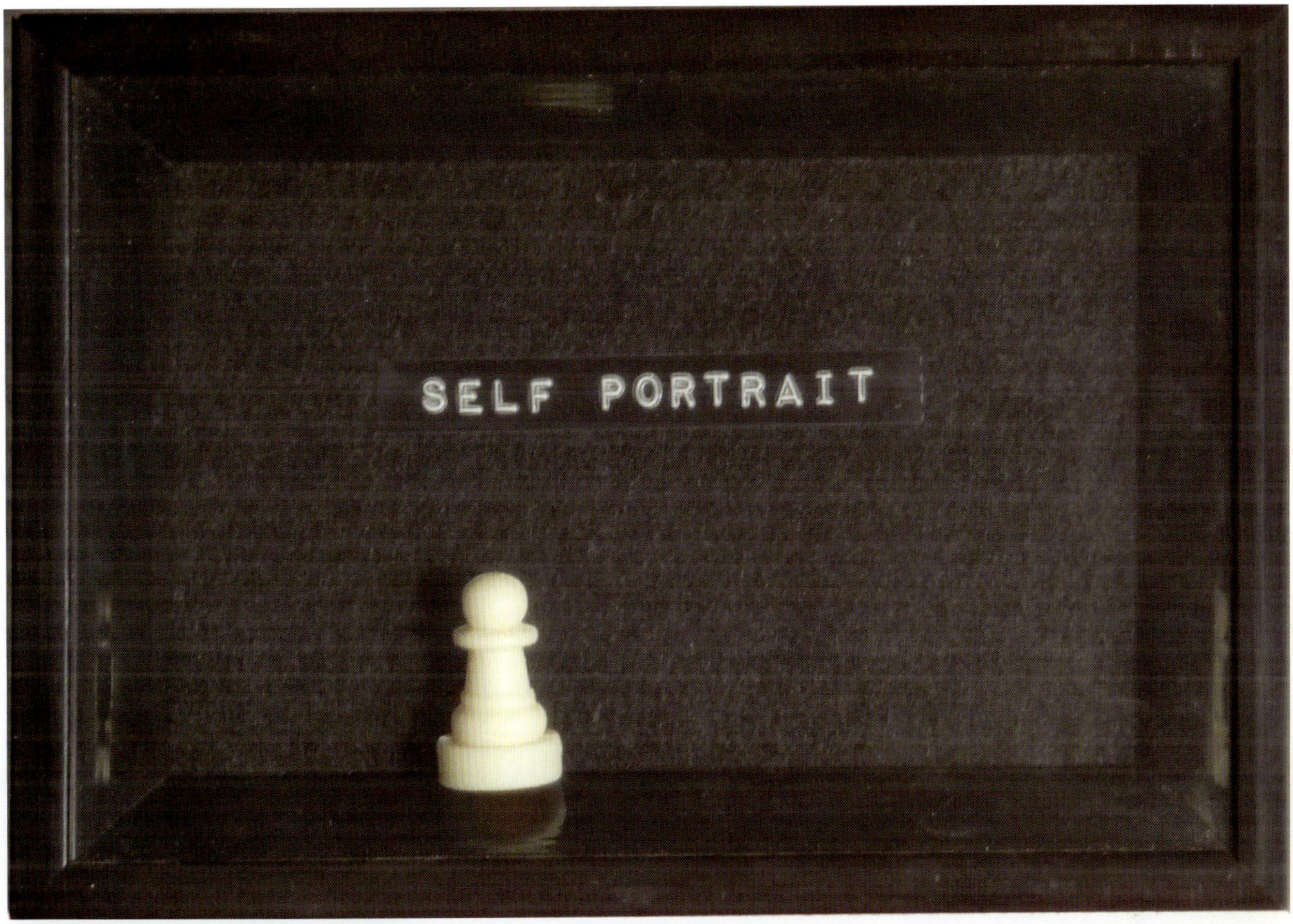

SELF PORTRAIT

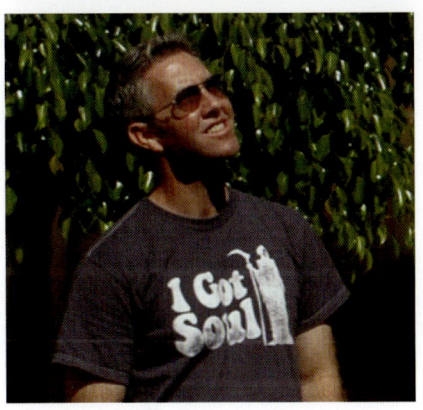

Scott Gengelbach is a mixed media artist currently working and residing in San Diego, California. He has a BA in Applied Design from San Diego State University where his focus was fiber arts.

WWW.SCOTTGENGELBACH.COM

● **War Is Love (#21)**
*Hand embroidery and mixed mediums on muslin,
16 x 16 x 4 in., 2009*

● **Untitled**
*Chess piece and punch label in shadow box,
5 x 7.25 x 1 in., 2011*

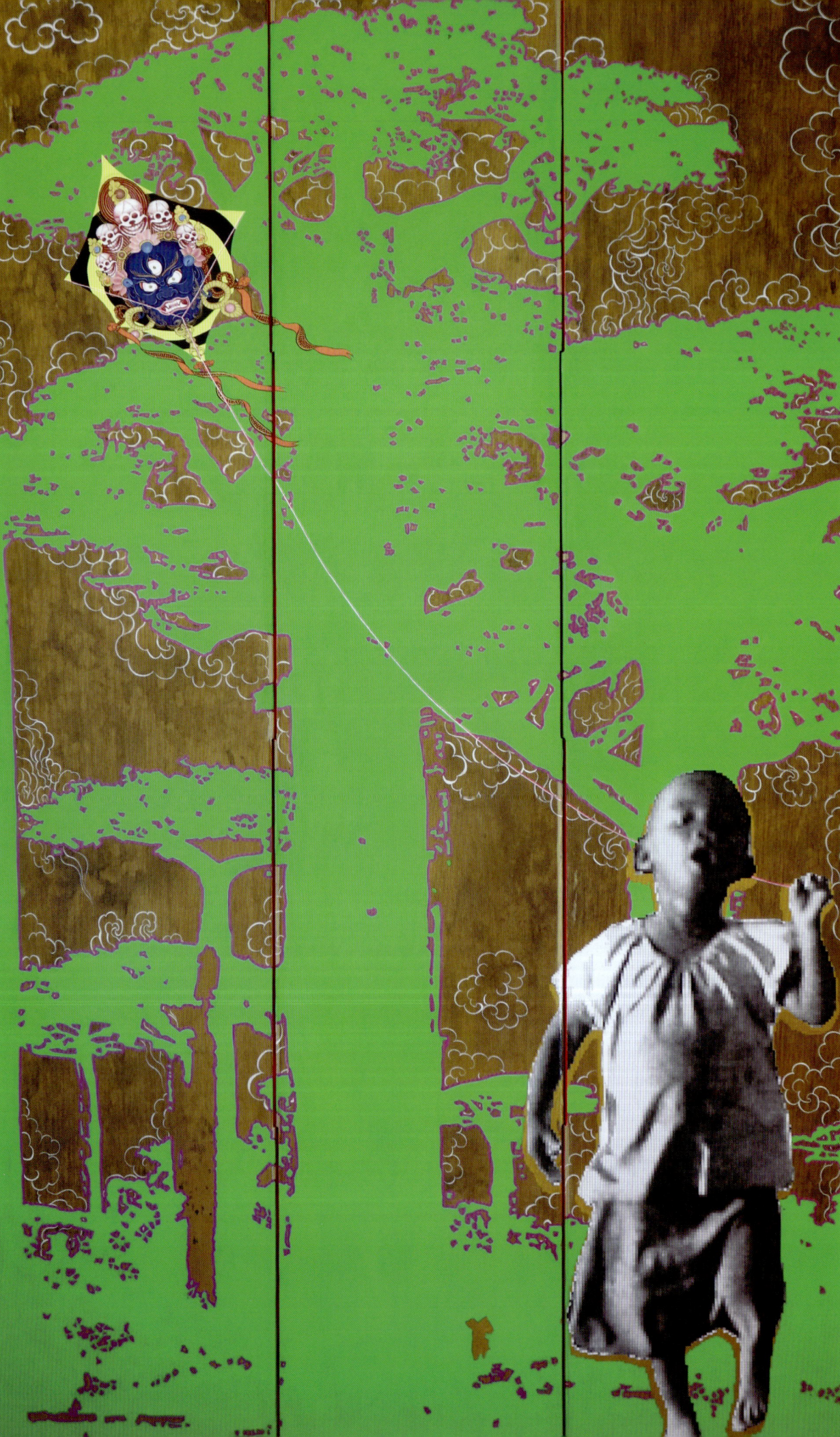

KEVIN CONNOLLY GILLESPIE

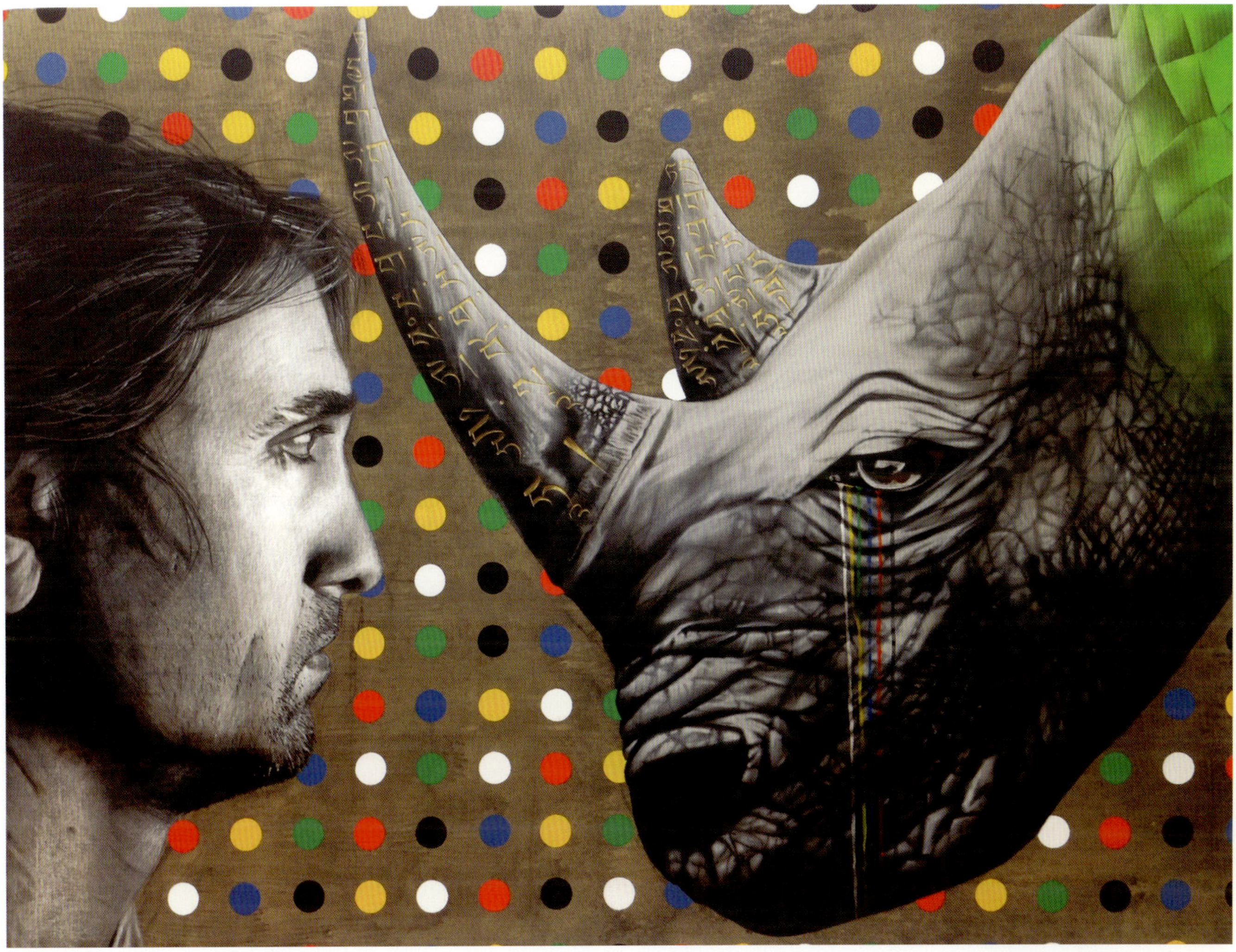

Kevin Connolly Gillespie was born in Johannesburg, South Africa, on February 13th, 1975. After completing his academic studies at King Edward the Seventh School, Kevin decided to refine his studies at Parktown Collage, focusing on fine arts. Having learned the traditions of figure painting, Kevin was eager to move to Cape Town to establish is career in fine arts. He worked as a fine artist, receiving commissions, murals, and his first solo show. In an effort to grow as an artist, Kevin moved to New York City in 2000, where he currently lives and works. Kevin continues to grow as an artist by honing on his skills. He has been influenced by asian art traditions of old including Thai, Japanese and Tibetan; as well as the new, street art traditions. Kevin's art is collected internationally with collectors based in the United States, United Kingdom and in South Africa.

WWW.SIGNEDCONNOLLY.COM

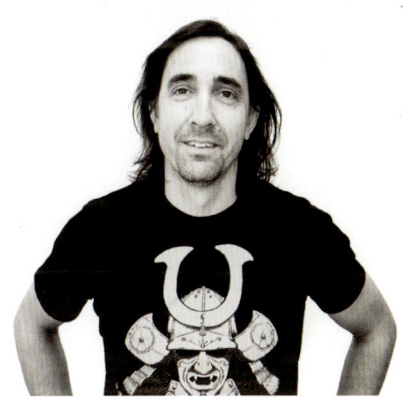

(facing page) Mahakala Kite ●
Vinyl, acrylic on wood panel, 84 x 60 in., 2014

Self Portrait with Rhino ●
Acrylic, charoal on canvas, 58 x 50 in., 2014

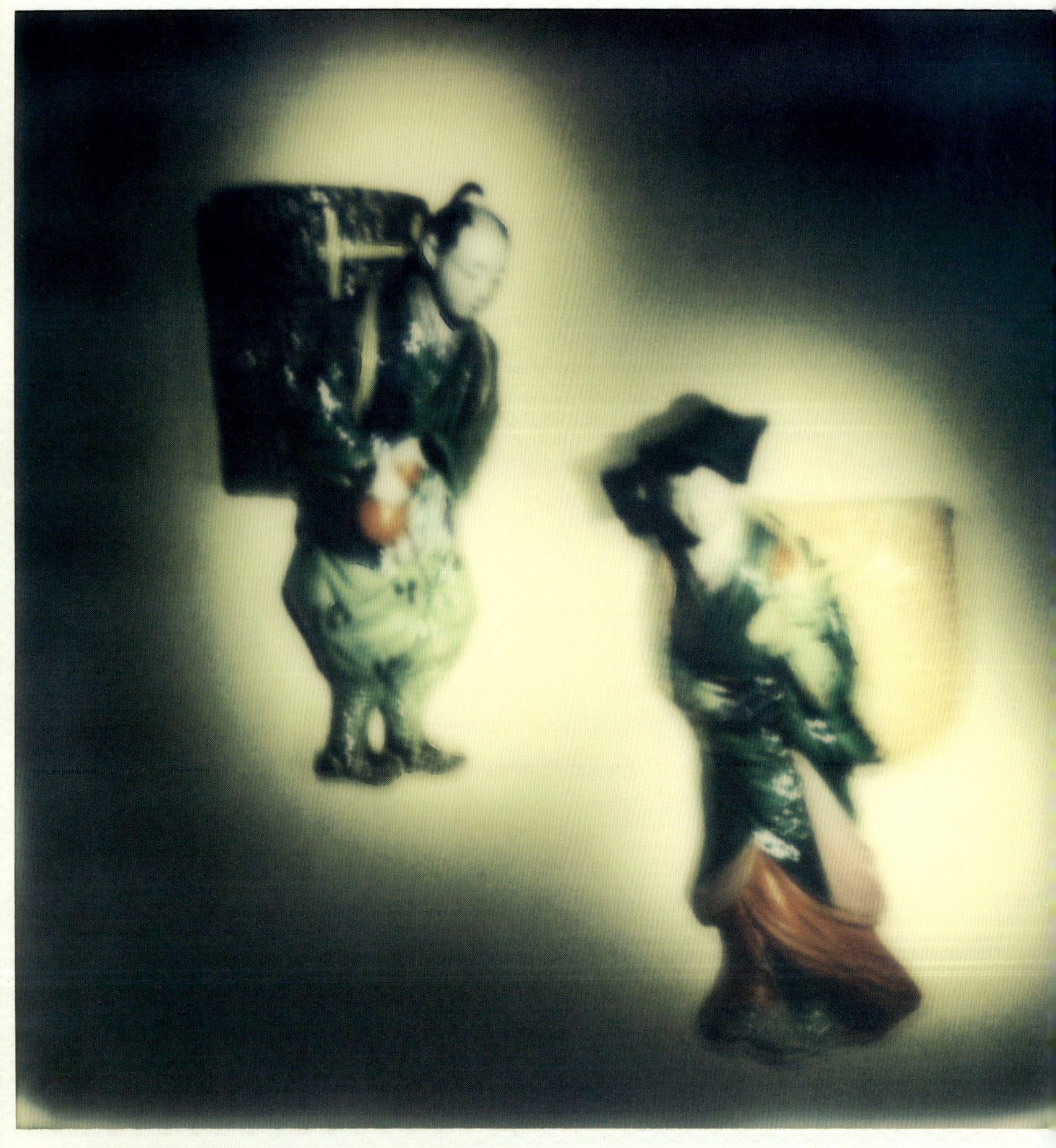

My Paris Japanese Wall Vases

Bill Cadwuning ©2014

PETER GLENDINNING

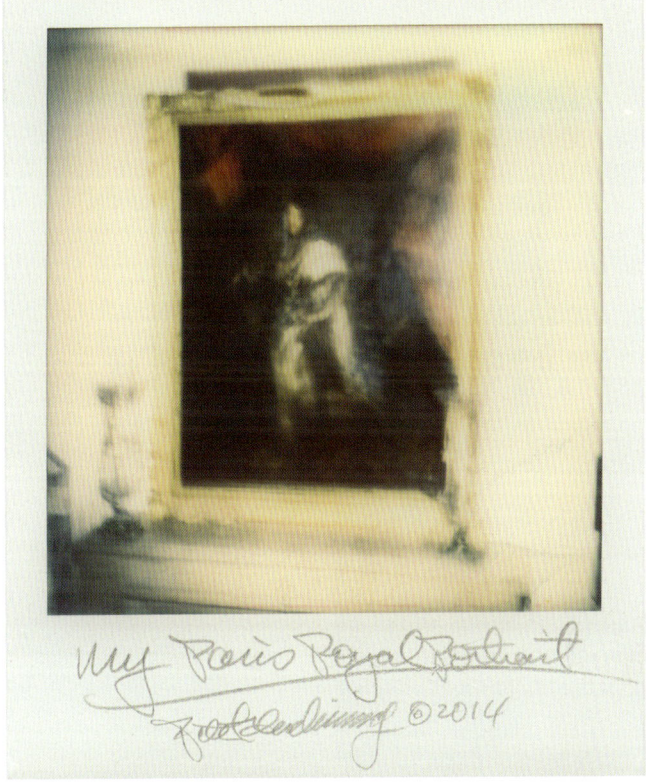

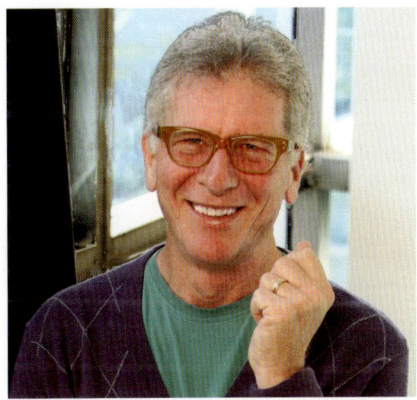

🔴 **(facing page) My Paris Japanese Wall Vases**
SX-70 print, matted and framed in black wood to archival standards, 2014

🔴 **My Royal Paris Portrait**
SX-70 print, matted and framed in black wood to archival standards, 2014

"Connecting in a tangible manner with another man through the experience of adopting his domicile as my own, becomes an opportunity to recognize a resonance that is both sympathetic and real. In every sense, they reflect on and reveal essential natures in another, in me, and in that place of imagination that may well be shared by many others, *My Paris*."

""I have rented an apartment in the Marais district of Paris for 2 weeks each summer for several years. The environment is eclectic, romantic, nostalgic, of another era but of today as well.

The patina of the life of the owner that becomes part of my being during this time, is the subject of these "portraits en creux," a typically evocative French term that means "hollow portraits," meaning a portrayal through symbol, without the appearance of the subject. That is particularly important in this series, as the works are portrayals of myself, of another man, and in a way of others who share the same sensibilities."

Peter Glendinning's works in photography and video had their first gallery exhibit at Alex Coleman's FOTO Gallery on Broome Street in NYC, in 1978. His most recent exhibit was held in 2015 at LOFT Gallery in Brussels, Belgium. In between those events his artwork has been exhibited in over 100 group, 2-person, and individual exhibits, and earned recognition through awards such as Individual Artist Grants from the Michigan Council for the Arts and Unicolor. The series "My Paris" (represented by the two images reproduced here) was selected for the prestigious "Best of the American Society of Media Photographers 2015 Award." His work is represented in numerous public and private collections, including The George Eastman House, University of Arizona,

Tweed Museum of Art among others. His commissioned work in creative photography has been accomplished for clients as diverse as Fuji Photo USA, General Motors, United Auto Workers International, Calumet Photographic, and Genovese Drugs, to name but a few. He is regularly called upon for service as a juror of exhibits and reviewer for photographers' portfolios in national and international venues. A published author (Color Photography from Prentice Hall), and former President of the Photo Imaging Education Association and Midwest Region Society for Photographic Education, he also serves as Professor of Art, Art History, & Design at Michigan State University.

WWW.PETERGLENDINNING.COM

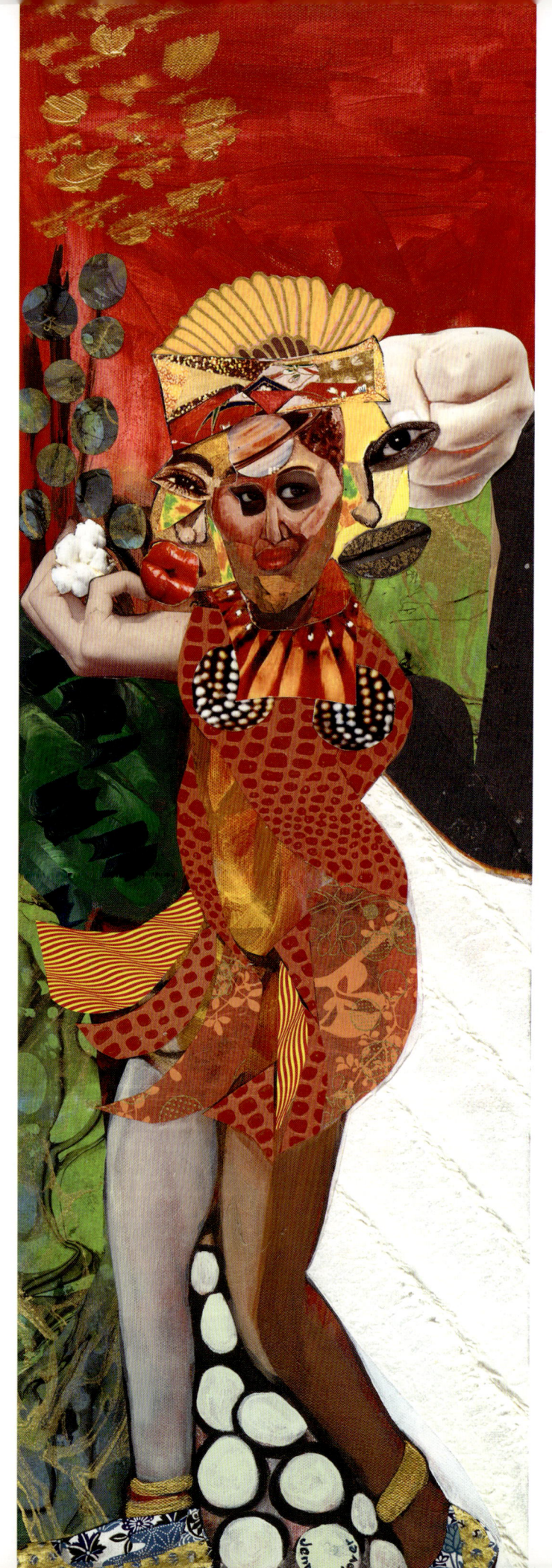

JENNE GLOVER

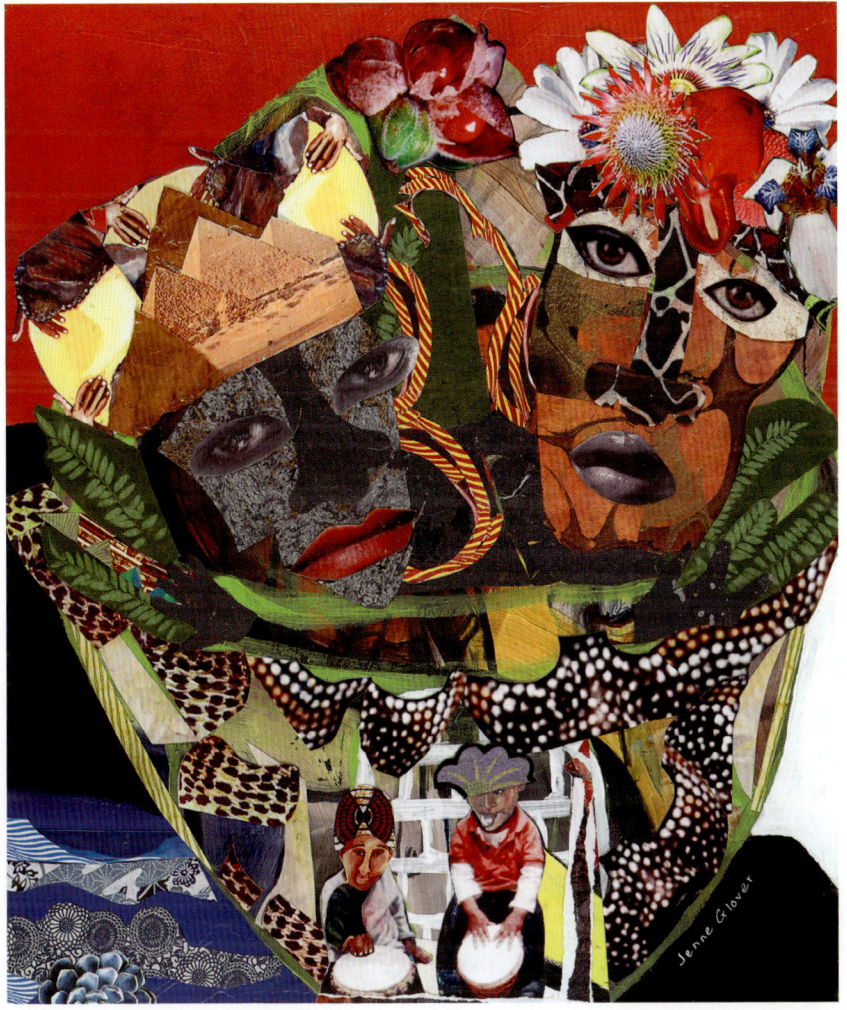

● **(facing page) Omo B. Me**
Mixed media collage, 30 x 10 in., 2014

● **Out of Africa (Eden's Ritual Bow)**
Mixed media collage, 24 x 18 in., 2013

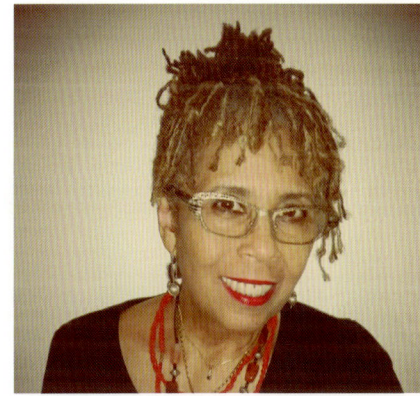

"Art has transformed my life and keeps me in touch with the kid inside of me."

My evolution as a figurative, expressionist painter to a mixed-media collagist has occurred over 30+ years. Born and raised in Washington, DC, my appreciation for the fine arts began as a child thanks to my dad who made gallery and museum visits a regular part of our Sunday activities. I create art to pay homage to humanity, family, memory, history, and spirit. I am fascinated with the free-flowing, abstractness of collaging; and seek to find the pulse of the concept, and go with the flow. Working from an Afrocentric framework, I am releasing my emotional connection to the African American journey by creating commentary on life from bondage to freedom. I am designing ritual bowls to celebrate and honor life, the ancestors, and the environment. I am exploring humanities relationship with music, by creating visual rhythms.

My art is colorful, infused with textures, patterns, rhythm, and repetition. Compositions are constructed of magazine cutouts, ready-made materials, paint, fabric, oil pastels, and altered pictures from earlier works that are repurposed. It is difficult for an artist to break new ground, but I hope to achieve this by producing work that is unique and has both femininity and subtle power. I want my attention to detail and flair for storytelling to bring fluidity, movement and a cinematic characteristic to my collages with each piece reading like the part of a greater whole.

WWW.JENNEGLOVER.COM

GRAHAM GODDARD

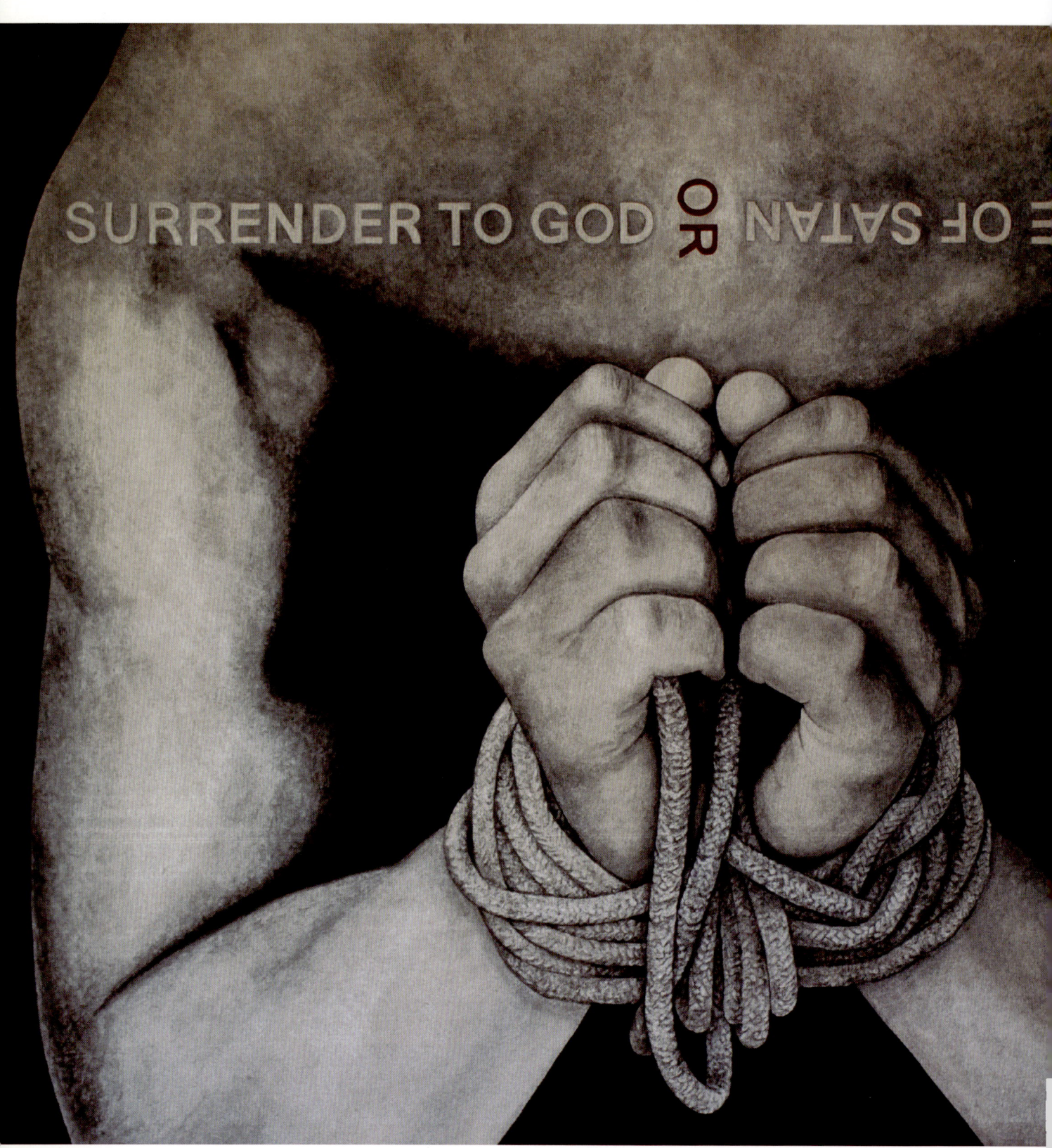

SURRENDER TO GOD OR ƎƆ OF SATAN

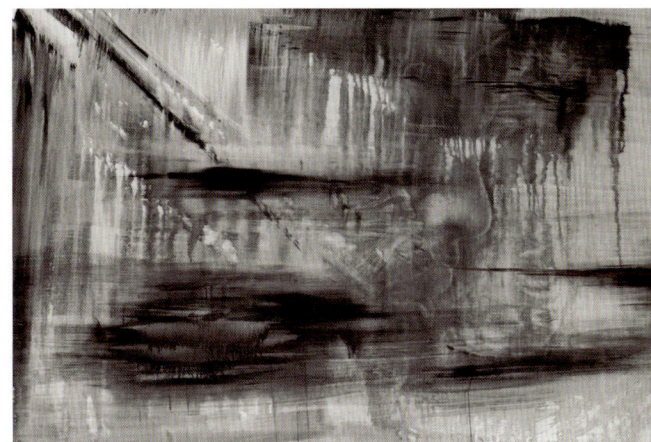

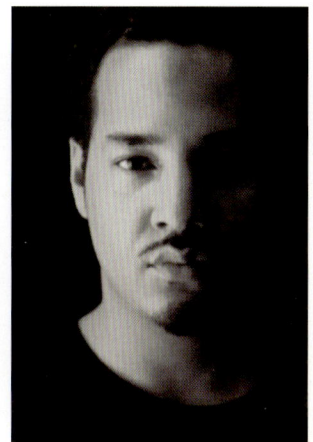

"The notion of dualities within the spectrum of dynamic relationships that emerge when the image is turned and disrupted is particularly interesting to me. I believe that the viewer participates in a pure and direct manipulation of the image, consequently unveiling a variety of aesthetic perspectives that inhabit the multidimensional landscape of the canvas."

Graham Goddard (born April 12, 1982) is a Trinidadian-American conceptual artist making visual statements about self-discovery, the environment, spirituality and commodification through painting, sculpture and site-specific land art installations. Goddard's work has been exhibited at the Skirball Museum, the California African American Museum and numerous art galleries in the United States and abroad.

In 2003, Graham Goddard developed the Rotating Canvas, which allows the viewer to turn the painting 360 degrees, exposing the power of imagery while exploring the nature of viewer interaction. Goddard's work focuses on the canvas as the object while using inverted images to activate it's functionality. As viewers insert themselves into the evolution of the imagery featured in the Rotating Canvas, the process of viewing and interacting with the work can be seen as demonstrative of the continually transforming relationships between content and context.

WWW.GRAHAMGODDARD.COM

● **(facing page) The Great Emancipation**
Acrylic on canvas, 48 x 60 in., 2010

● **Run to the Light**
Acrylic on canvas, 60 x 72 in., 2015

MICHAEL GRIESGRABER

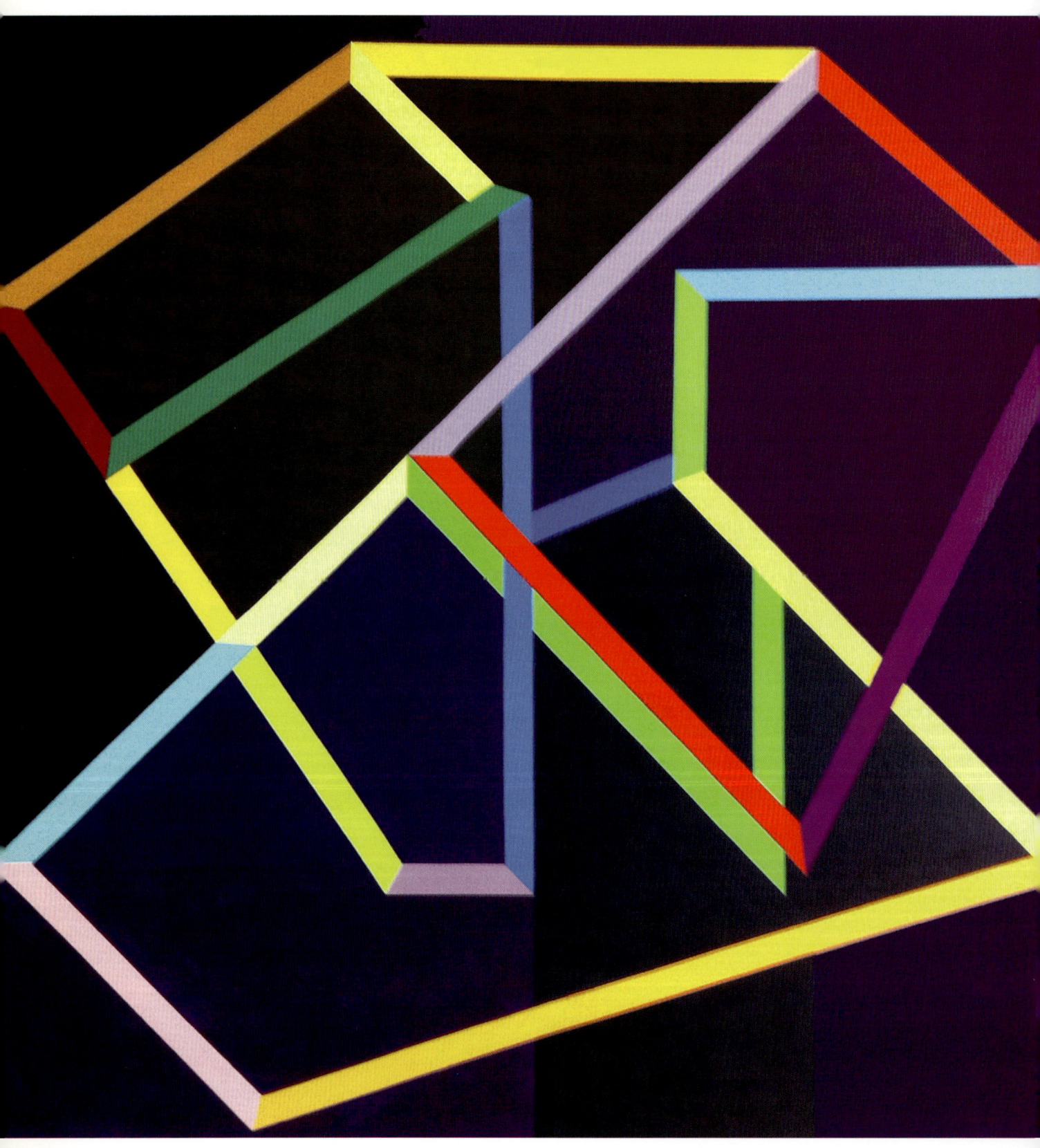

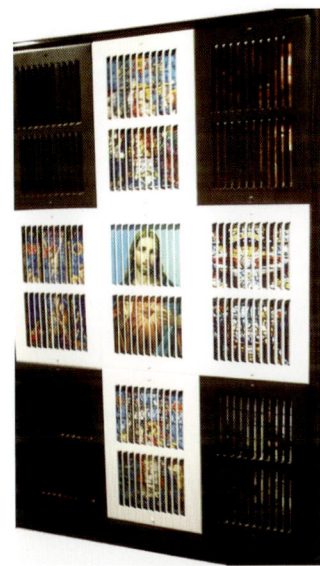 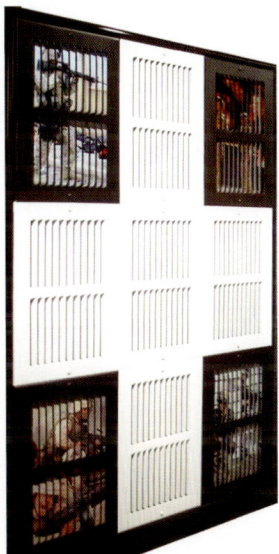

War and Peace
24" x 36"
Stained Glass photos
Metal vents
right view

War and Peace
24" x 36"
Iraq War photos
Metal vents
left view

Born in St Paul, Minnesota, Michael Griesgraber attended the University of Minnesota, earning a BFA in studio arts, studying with Professor Peter Busa. New York School painter Busa mentored Griesgraber and put him in touch with the contemporary art world, including introducing him to Willem de Kooning and visiting his studio in the Hamptons.

While in college, Griesgraber was the assistant designer for Peter Seitz, the Walker Art Center's estimable first design director. In the early 1970's Griesgraber was elected president of the Minnesota chapter of Artist's Equity, a nonprofit with the mission of improving conditions for fine artists.

He earned his Master of Fine Arts Degree from Syracuse University in New York in 1977, and subsequently spent several years in the advertising field, first with the BBDO agency, then with several technology companies. After various high-level positions in Minneapolis, Singapore, Boston, and Los Angeles, he finally left marketing to pursue painting full-time. He paints seven days a week in his downtown Las Vegas studio, located within the Southern Nevada Museum of Fine Art annex.

In 2014 Griesgraber was honored when 20 of his paintings went on display for a two-year stint at Las Vegas City Hall. That same year his painting "No Direction Home" was selected by Lauren Hinkson, curator of the Solomon Guggenheim Museum, for the 2014 national show "COLOR" at the BWAC Gallery in New York.

WWW.MGRIESGRABER.COM

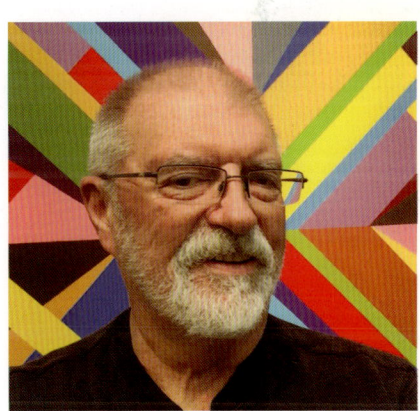

(facing page) Zig Zag ●
Acrylic on canvas, 48 x 48 in.

War & Peace ●
Stained glass and photos (l), Iraq photos (r) and metal vents, 24 x 36 in.

HOLLIS HAMMONDS

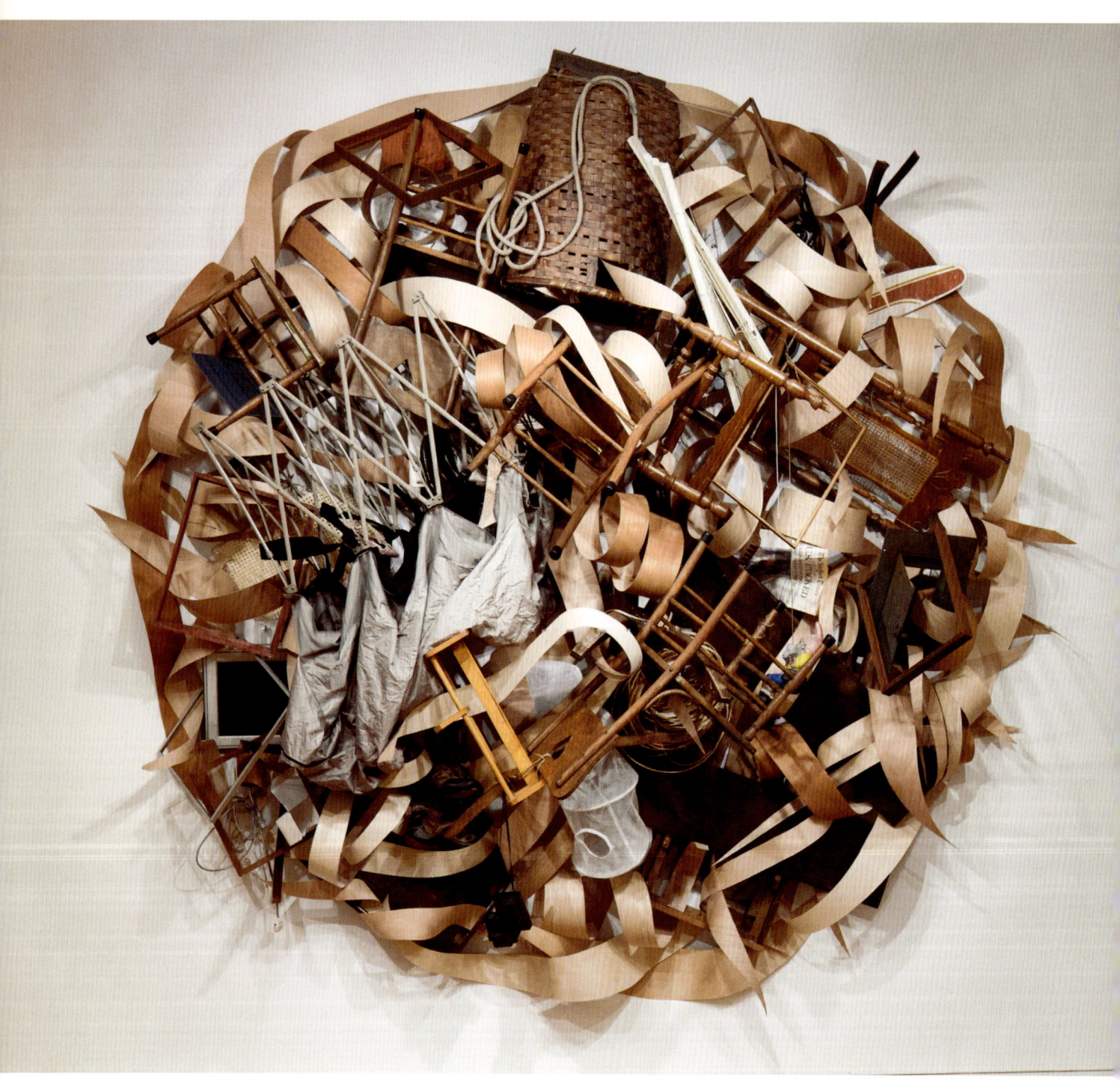

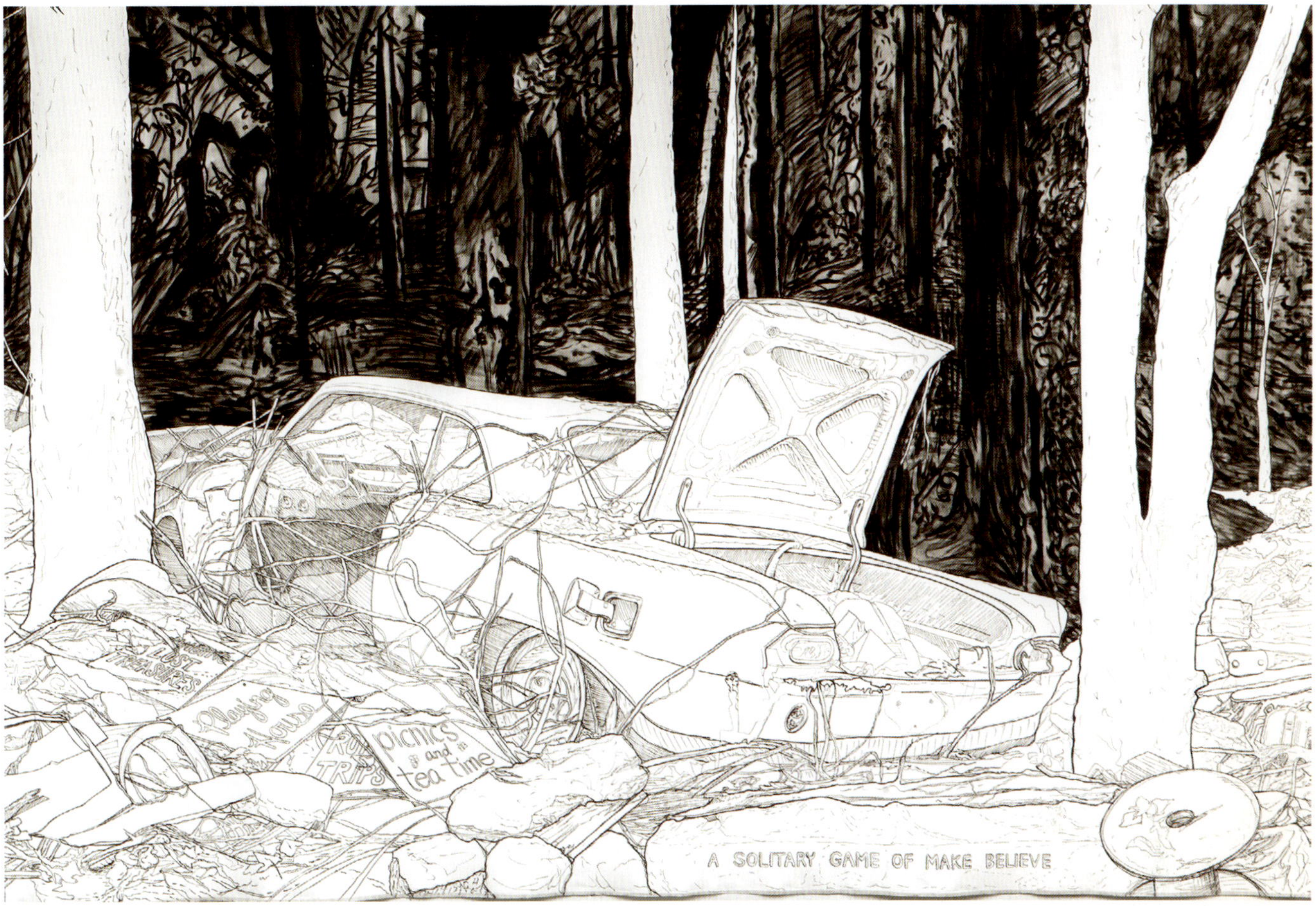

A SOLITARY GAME OF MAKE BELIEVE

Hollis Hammonds is a Kentucky born artist who has been living and working in Austin, Texas since 2007. Hammonds received her MFA from the University of Cincinnati. In 2001, and her BFA in drawing from Northern Kentucky University in 1998. Her work crosses media from drawing to sculptural installation, and has been exhibited throughout the U.S. including recent solo exhibitions at Redux Contemporary Art Center in Charleston, SC; the Reed Gallery at the University of Cincinnati in OH; the Museum of Art at Southern Mississippi University in Hattiesburg, MS; the Hiestand Galleries at Miami University in Oxford, Ohio; Texas Tech University in Lubbock, TX; Indie Grits Film Festival in Columbia SC; and at Women and their Work gallery in Austin,

TX. She is the author of Drawing Structure: Conceptual and Observational Techniques, and has had her creative work published in New American Paintings #114, INDA 4, INDA 7, INDA 8, Studio Visit Magazine, and Uppercase Magazine. Currently she is the Chair of the Department of Visual Studies at St. Edward's University in Austin, TX.

WWW.HOLLISHAMMONDS.COM

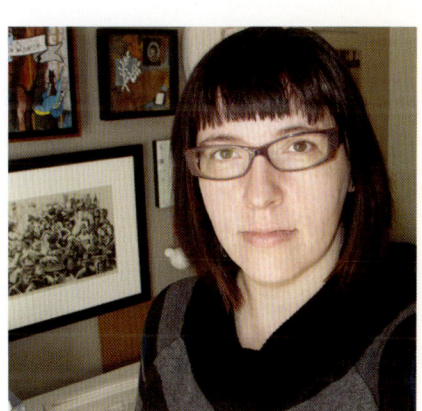

(facing page) Worthless Matter: ●
Forgotten Home
Found and donated objects, wood veneer, 12 x 12 in., 2014

The Dark Forest (detail) ●
Charcoal, acrylic medium and ink on canvas, 8 x 36 in., 2015

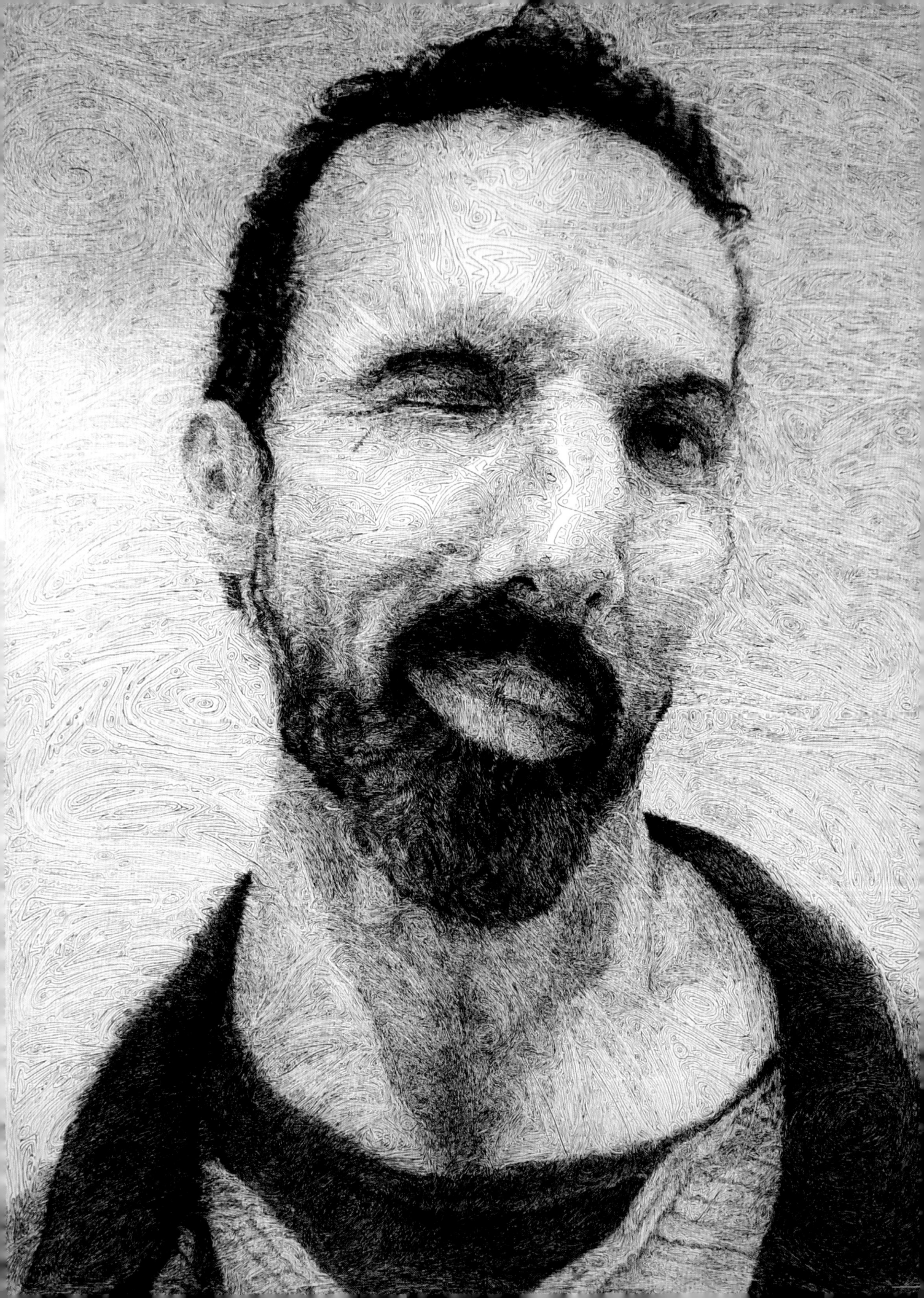

JOHN HAMPSHIRE

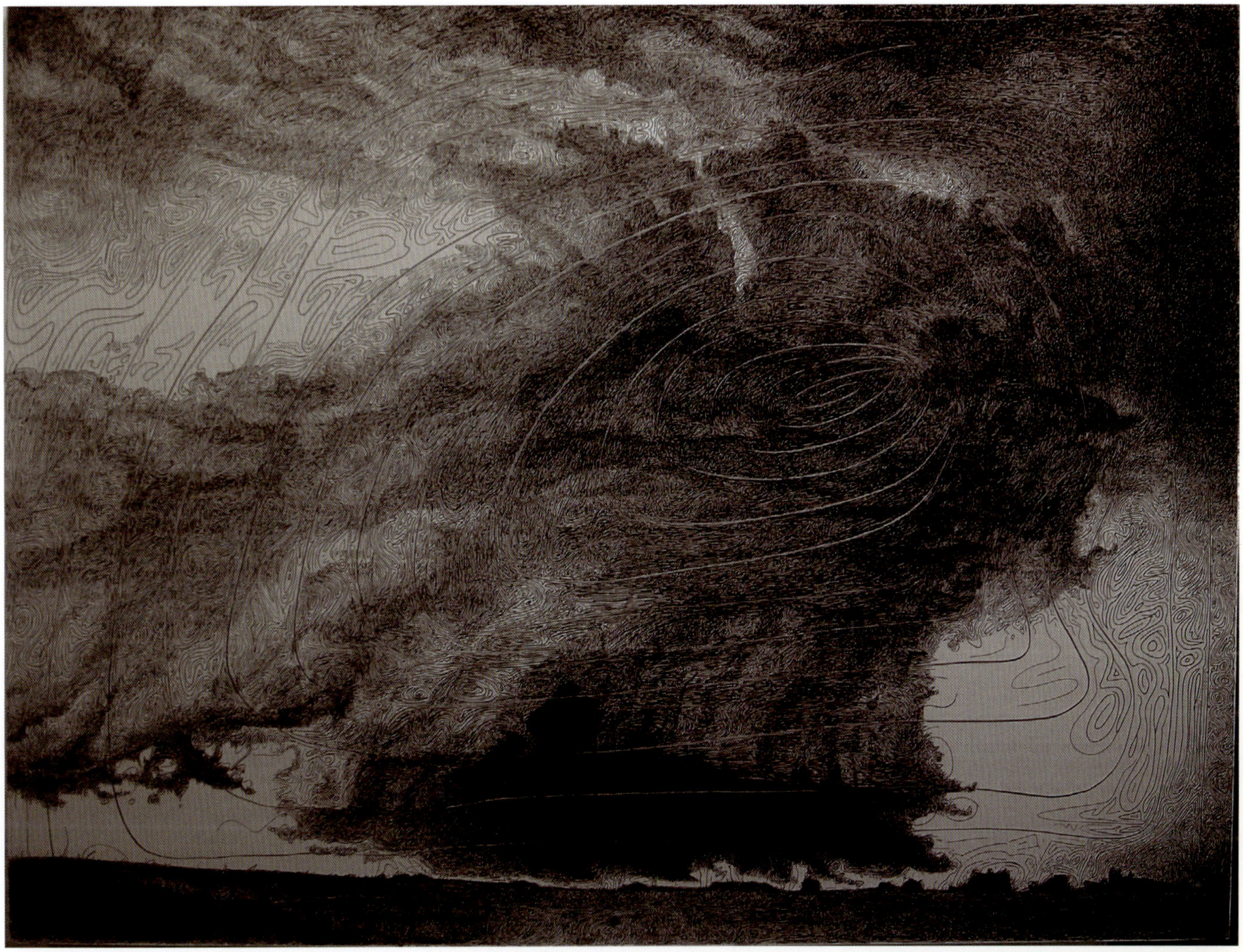

John Hampshire was born 1971 in Chicago, IL. He received a BS from Skidmore college 1994 and a MFA SUNY Albany 1997. John is currently Associate Professor of Art at SUNY Adirondack and he lives and works in a former church in Troy NY. Recent awards include 2011 NYFA Fellowship in Printmaking/Drawing/Book Arts, the SUNY Chancellor's Award for Excellence in Scholarship and Creativity, and the Dr. Arthus C. Collins '48 Purchase Award, University at Albany Alumni Association. Selected solo exhibitions of his work include "Layers and Labyrinths" at The Show Walls, 1133 Avenue of the Americas, NYC (2008), "Expressive Eccentricities", State College of Florida (2009), and "Labyrinthine" in

The Project Room at the Phoenix Gallery, NYC (2005). Selected group exhibitions include "Black and White". Lana Santorelli Gallery. NYC (2010), International Small Works Exhibition. 80 Washington Square East Galleries. New York University. NYC. (2001-2009), and "International Works on Paper". Soho20 Gallery, NYC (2001). John's work is in permanent collections: The Hyde Collection, the State University of NY at Albany Museum Collection, and the SUNY Adirondack Art Collection.

WWW.JOHNHAMPSHIRE.WEEBLY.COM

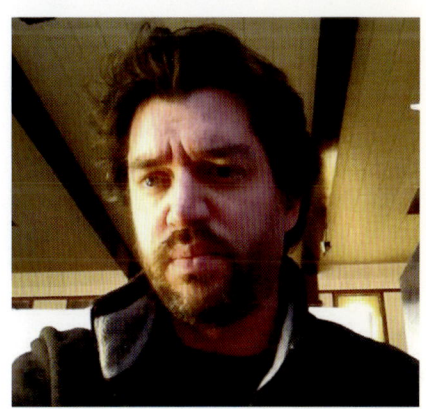

(facing page) Labyrinth 113 (Brian) ●
Ink on canvas, 48 x 36 in., 2005

Labyrinth 220 ●
Ink on canvas, 36 x 48 in., 2009

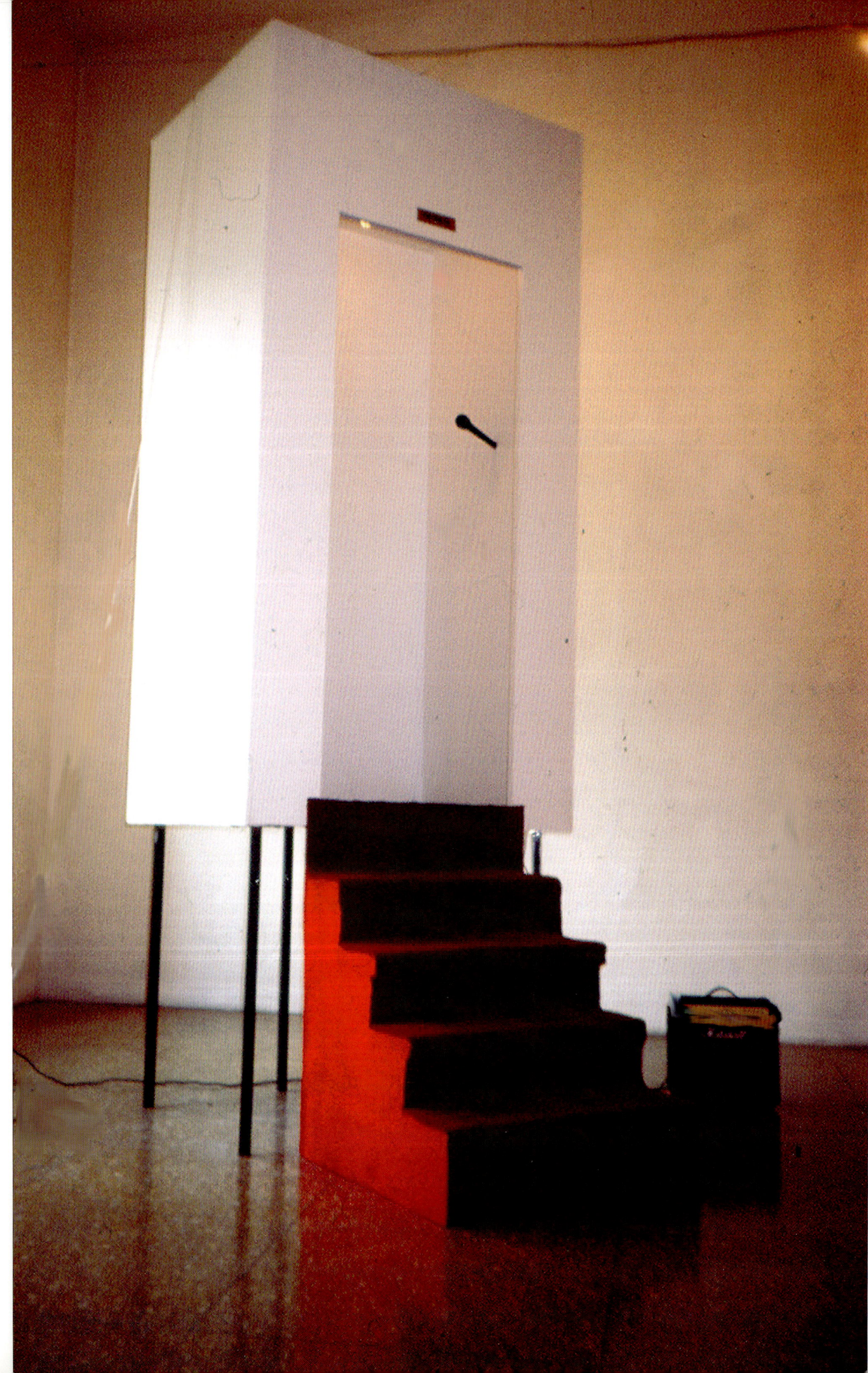

JERELYN HANRAHAN

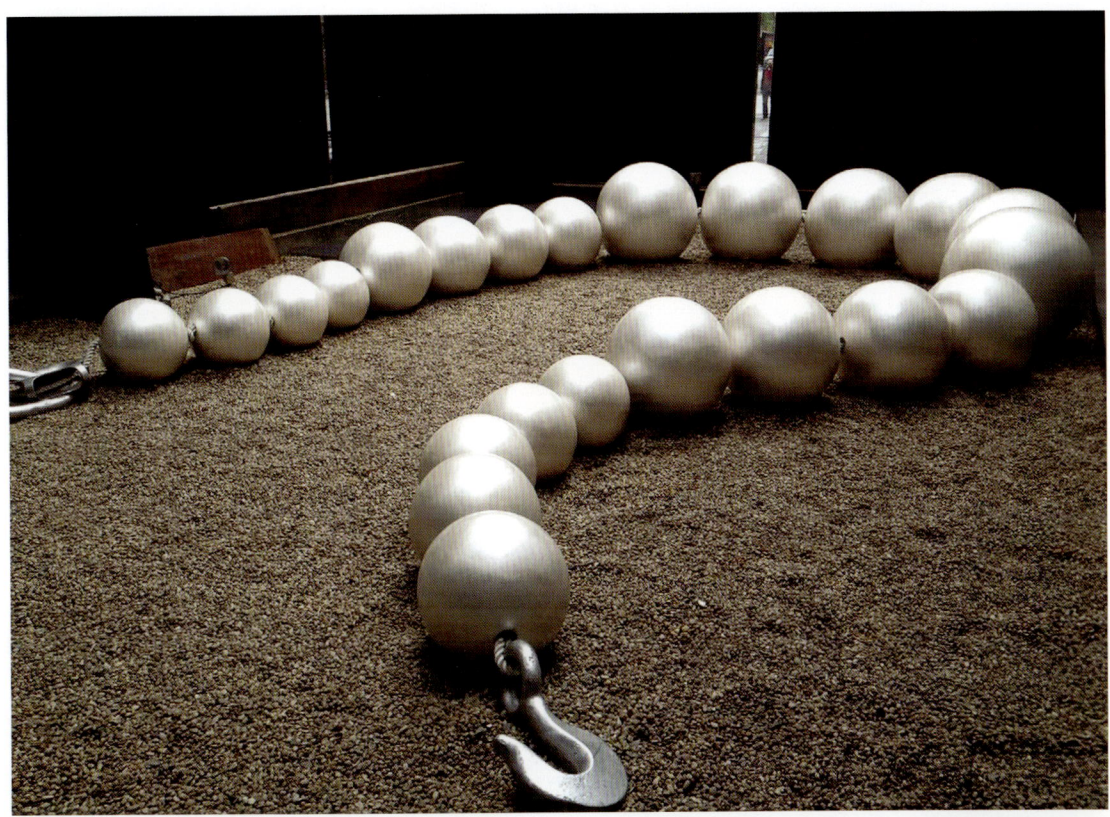

Jerelyn Hanrahan work is a conceptual dialogue developed through 2 dimensional works and public art projects. Interviewed on three occasions for the PS1 / Museum of Modern Art radio station, National Public Radio with Margo Adler, BBC in New York and London, Telli –Bern in Switzerland, Air Canada in Toronto and on Havana T.V. in Cuba, Art Dirt, web based radio. Her work has been reviewed by Sculpture Magazine, New York Times, Newsday, neue bildende kunst, Time Out Magazine, Village Voice, NY Arts, Brooklyn Rail, Tages Anzeiger, Kunst Bulletin, Art Observer, Adbusters and The Resident, as well as numerous international publications. Graduated Pearls, a fifty-foot public sculpture exhibited at Jim Kempner Fine Arts, Chelsea, New York, initially was sited in Theodore Roosevelt Memorial Park, Oyster Bay, New York. The project was part of the New York Foundation for the Arts, Fiscal Sponsorship Program. Her works on paper have been exhibited in the Aargau

Kunsthaus, Switzerland, Venice Pavilion, Venice, Italy, and Beijing, China, Galerie Rohmer Apotheke, Zurich, Switzerland ,The Andy Warhol Museum, Pittsburg, the National Arts Club, New York, solo exhibition at the Van Der Plas Gallery, New York. Hanrahan's drawings (97 works) were published by Andrea Zust in Notations In a Trek, The book was accompanied by a solo exhibition of drawings at Art Magazin, Rolf Muller Galerie , Zurich, Switzerland, and a reading of the text by Max Blagg at the Drawing Center in New York. Hanrahan's history of grants include Special Opportunity Stipends and Sponsorship from the New York Foundation for the Arts, Lower Manhattan Cultural Council, NCR Media Systems, Creative Time Inc., LMCC, Thundergulch, Pro-Helvetia Arts Council of Switzerland, Puffin Foundation, Switzerland's Fondation Nestle, and Stadt Bern.

WWW.JERELYNHANRAHAN.COM

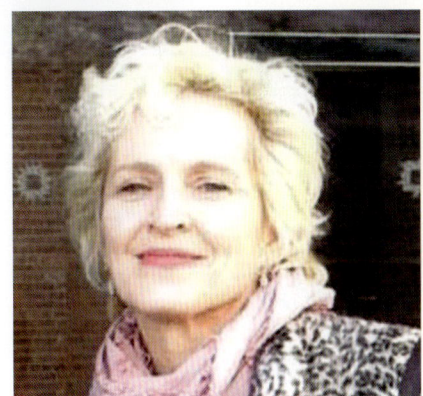

(facing page) A.W.O.L. ●
(Assente Sensa Permesso)
Wood, parkett floor, track lightening and audio,
18 x 6 x 6 in.

Graduated Pearls ●
East portland cement, cast steel, mariners rope,
50 x 40 x 30 in., 2012

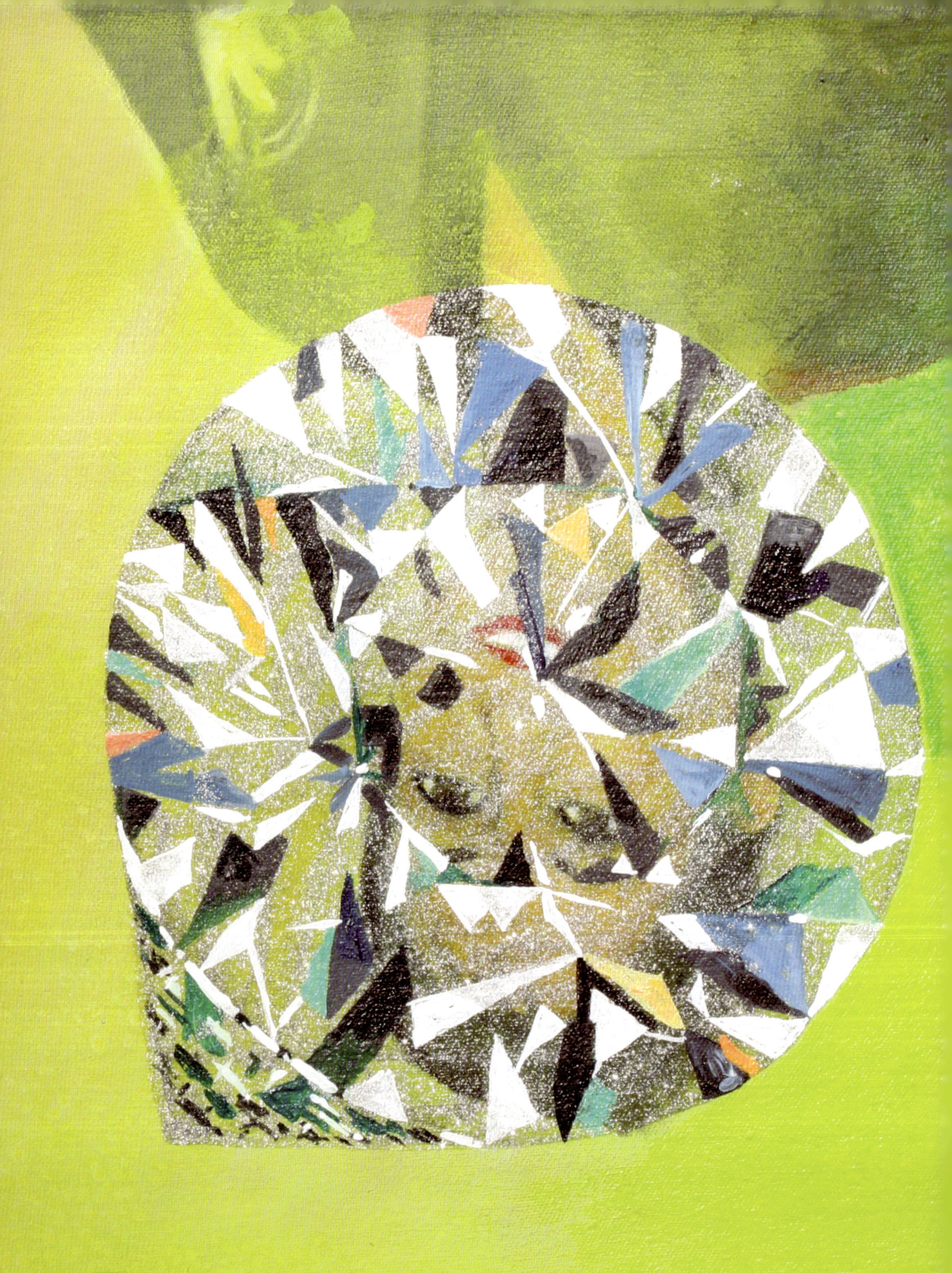

S. P. HARPER

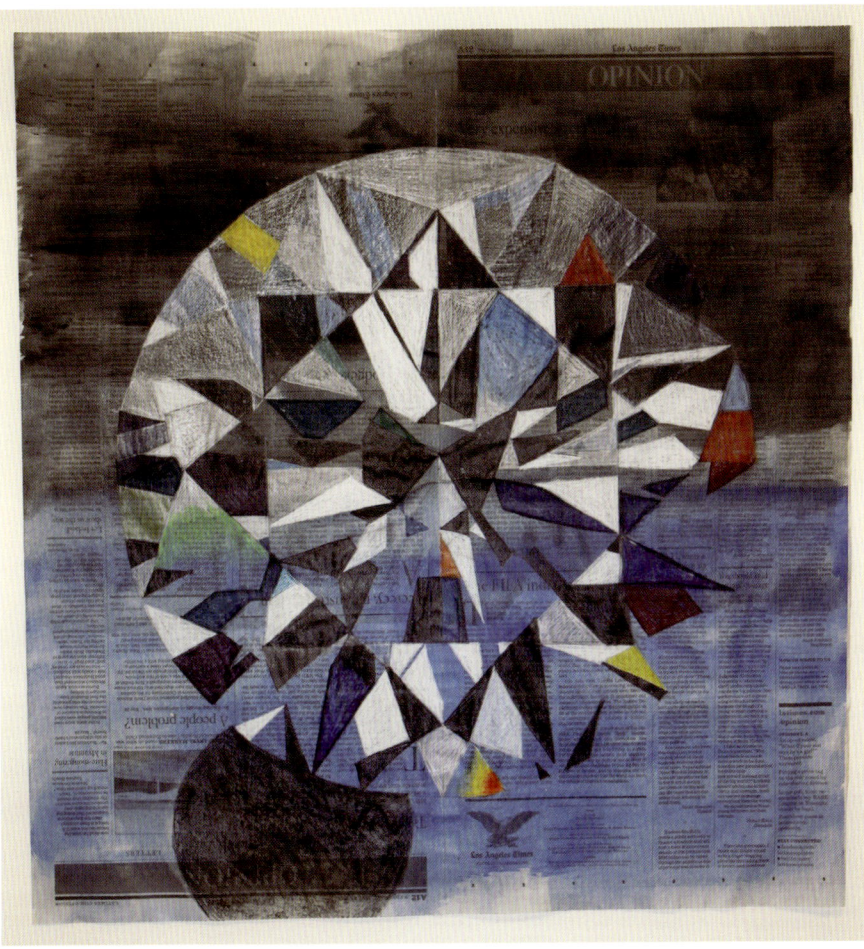

S. P. Harper paints images of cut gemstones on recycled materials. What begins as a bit of refuse is repurposed, transforming base materials into noble objects. Focusing on the intersection of rummage rubbish and object d'art, showing how materials change from valuable to worthless and back to valuable again, the work explores layers and levels of reality. The surface first layer is a discarded scrap, formerly a door, made from wood, which originates from a tree. A photograph from a jewelry catalogue taken of a precious stone instigates the gem painting.

An existing printed background partially disappears behind an acrylic wash as well as disappearing all together behind opaque oil paint rendering. Background recycled patterns appear and disappear through the transparent and reflective facets in the jewels. Diverse mediums such as wall lath and plaster rubble, tablecloths, discarded canvases and metal scraps are surface materials. By reforming and re-employing, the work fits into the green movement to reduce, reuse and recycle. Harper studied art at the American University in Paris, France, the University of Southern California (Bachelor of Fine Art, summa cum laude) and advanced studies at Art Center College in Pasadena, California. After spending 12 years in New York, Harper returned to Los Angeles. Since returning, Harper spent time teaching art before concentrating on eco-art.

WWW.SPHARPER.COM

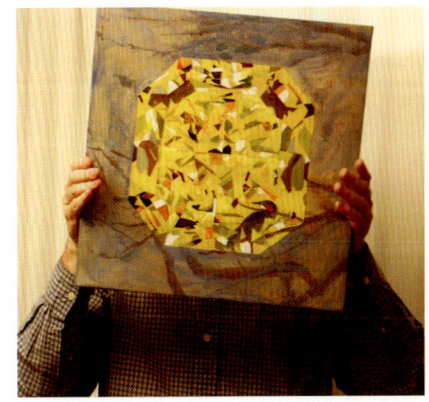

(facing page) Diamond on Persian Portrait ●
*Oil and acrylic on portrait painted canvas,
12 x 12 in., 2014*

Brilliant-cut Diamond on Newspaper ●
*Acrylic, oil pastel, ink & pencil on paper,
27 x 25 in., 2015*

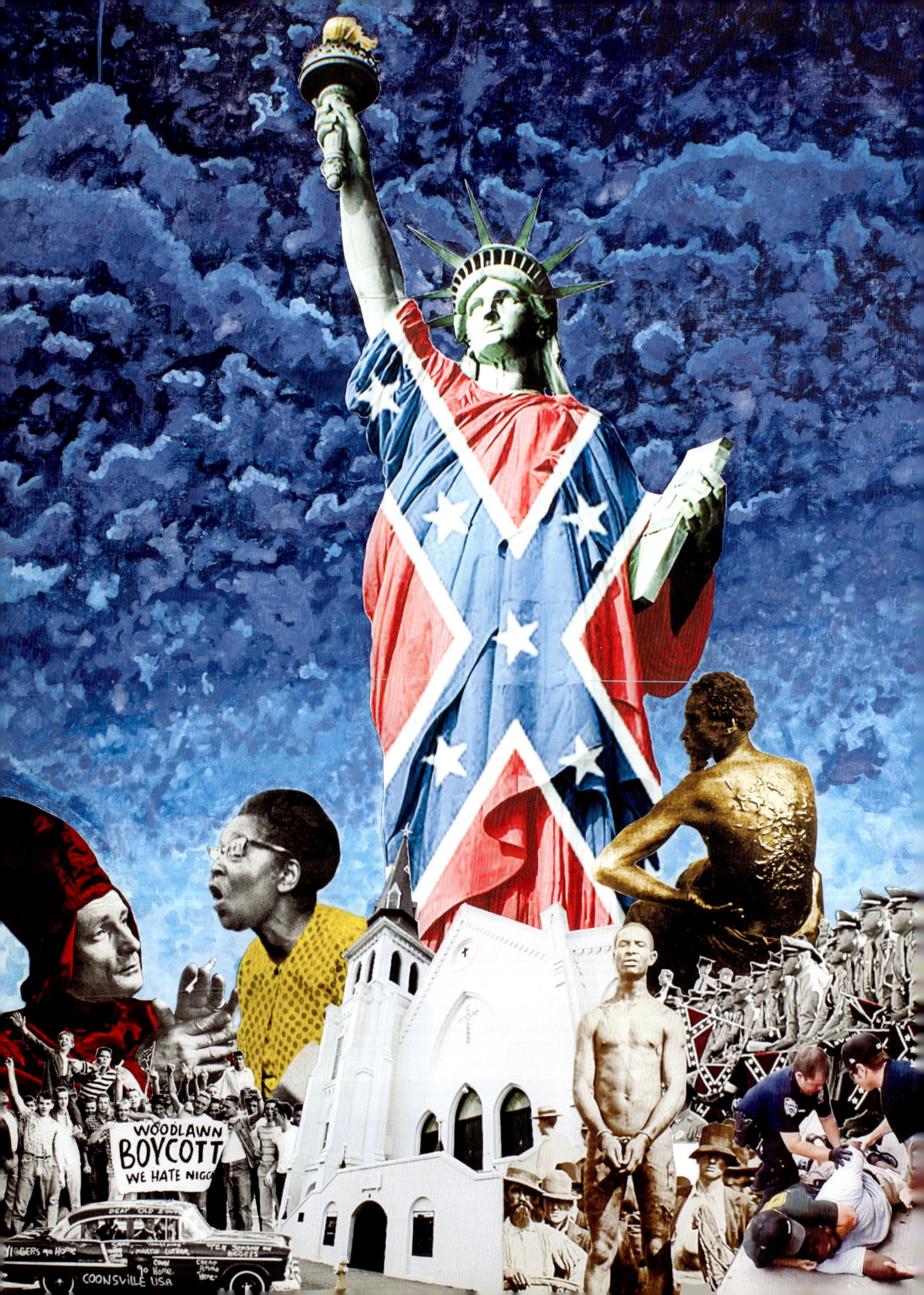

MARK HARRIS

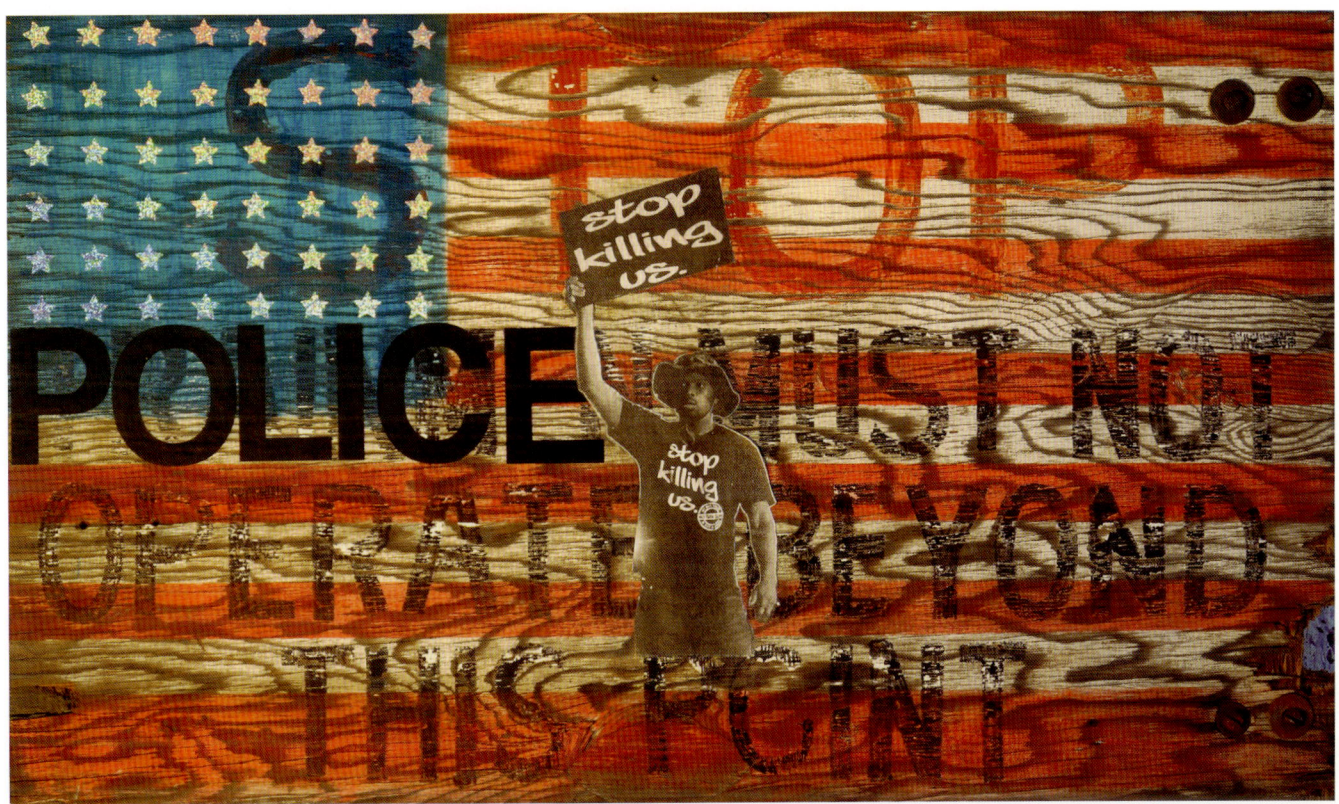

San Francisco, California-based artist Mark Harris has been actively exhibiting his work for over fifteen years. A native of Durham, NC, he grew up in Atlanta, GA and has lived in Tampa, FL, and Santiago, Chile. Harris has combined his passions for social justice, activism and art making to create a unique visual vocabulary that he uses to engage his audience on some of the most critical issues facing society today. Harris is equally passionate about working with youth, and has taught in both public and private schools in San Francisco and the surrounding Bay Area. He has expanded this practice to include mentoring at-risk youth through art education programs. Harris has recently taught youth at the Beacon Center, the African American Art & Culture Complex and has also worked with the ArtSpan Youth Open Studios program as an Artist Mentor for youth artists all in San Francisco.

Harris has exhibited at the USF Thacher Gallery in San Francisco; Rock, Paper, Scissors Collective, Oakland; 111 Minna Gallery, San Francisco; Linn Benton College, Albany, OR; Marin Museum of Contemporary Art, Novato; Triton Museum of Art, Santa Clara; and The Whitney Young Cultural Center, San Francisco; among others.

His work is included in numerous collections both domestically and internationally from Chicago to London to South America.

WWW.ARTOFMARKHARRIS.COM

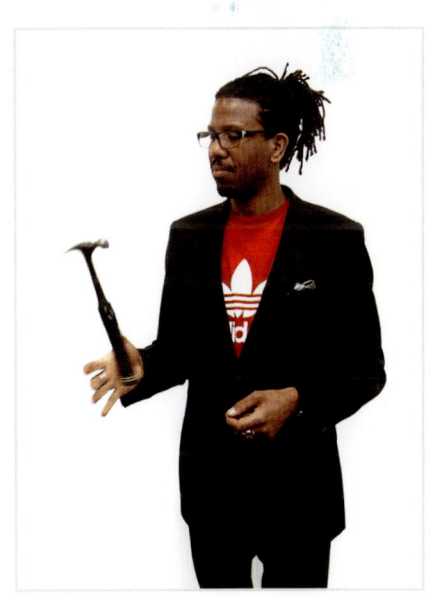

(facing page) Pride and Prejudice ●
Mixed media on panel, 30 x 40 in., 2015

Untitled – American Flag ●
Mixed media on found wood, 17 x 29 in., 2014

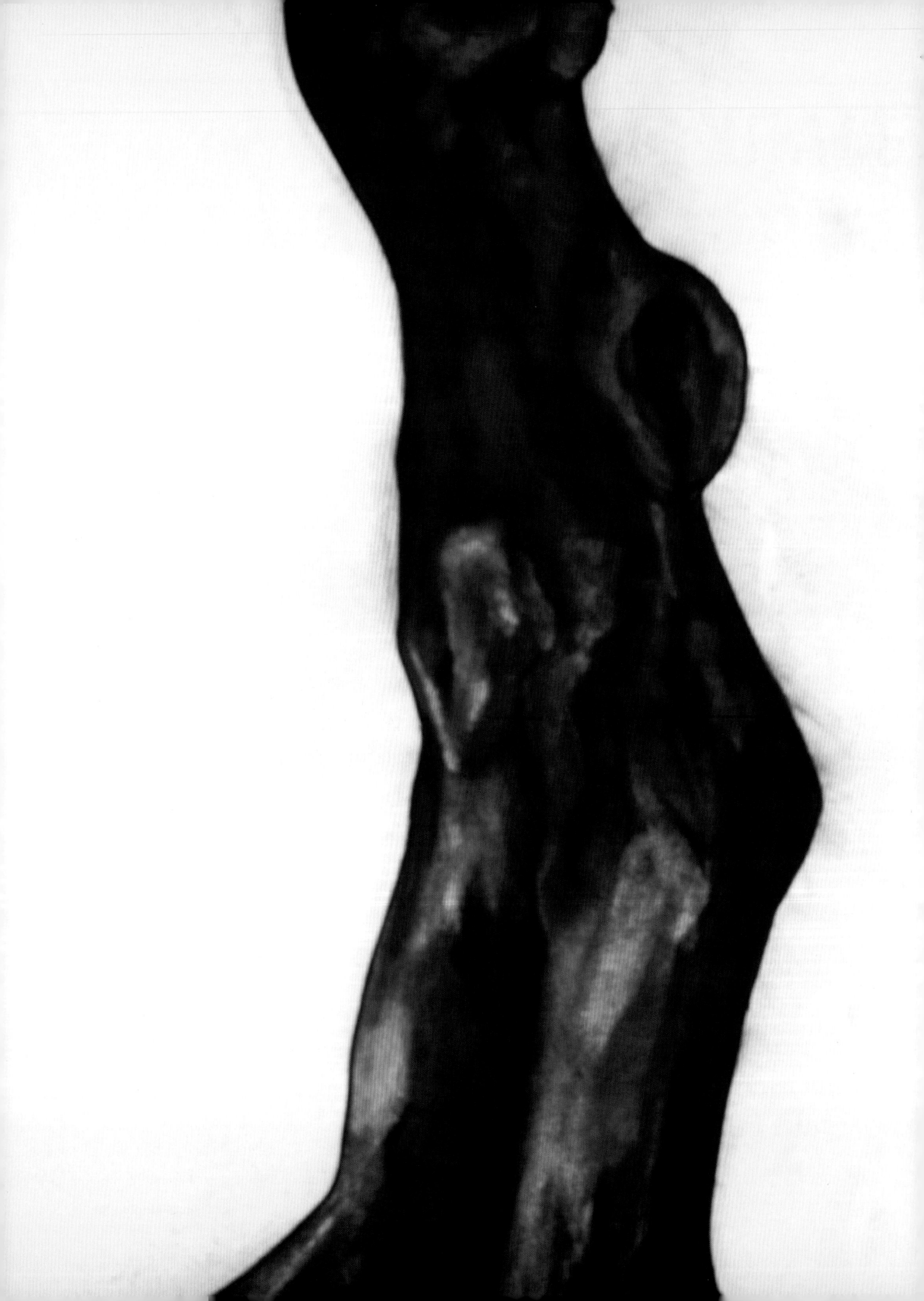

MARY HRBACEK

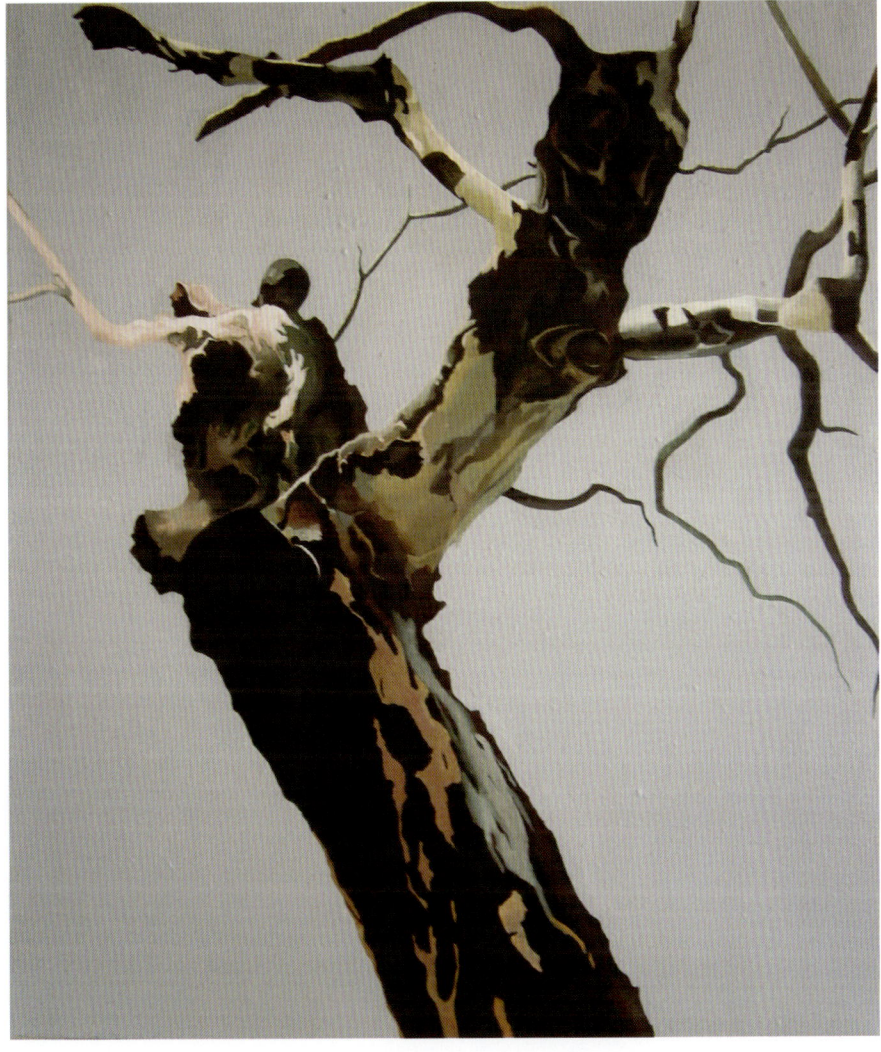

● **(facing page) Monumental**
Charcoal on paper, 22 x 30 in., 2006

● **On My Back**
Acrylic on linen, 42 x 46 in., 2007

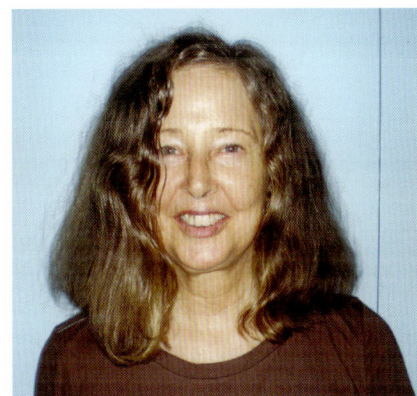

MARY HRBACEK, an artist and critic based in NYC has exhibited at The Parrish Art Museum, the National Academy Museum, and internationally in China, Korea, Kyrgyzstan, Greece and Canada, where Lynn Ruscheinsky, the "Drawn Festival," selected her for a two-person show at Elliott Lewis Gallery, Vancouver. She is a member of AICA (International Association of Art Critics). At Roger Smith, Dominick Lombardi curated a solo installation of her "Black on Black" human-tree charcoal drawings, engendered by her drawing at "The American Drawing Biennial VI," Muscarelle Museum (College of William and Mary), VA, awarded the Juror's Prize from Ann Philbin of the Drawing Center. Edward Rubin chose her work for his exhibit "At the End All That Remains Is A Good Story: Eight New York Artists Figuratively Speaking," at the Fran Hill Gallery in Toronto. She exhibited in "Covert Narratives," curated by Thalia Vrachropoulos at the Tenri Cultural Institute, NYC. Of her various university exhibitions, the most recent is "Baruch Small Works" curated by Richard Timperio at Mishkin Gallery, Baruch College, 2015. Elga Wimmer curated her 2013 solo show entitled "Peopled Forest of My Mind;" her April exhibition, "Life Before Life" marks her fourth solo exhibition at CREON. She is participating in the Mykonos Biennale, Greece 2015; her drawings are included in "Whispers," at the Museum of Contemporary Art of Crete. Hrbacek's hybrid paintings take transformation to the borders between imagination and belief, testing the similarities between human anatomy and tree forms, to symbolize the ultimate interconnectedness between mankind and nature.

WWW.MARYHRBACEK.COM

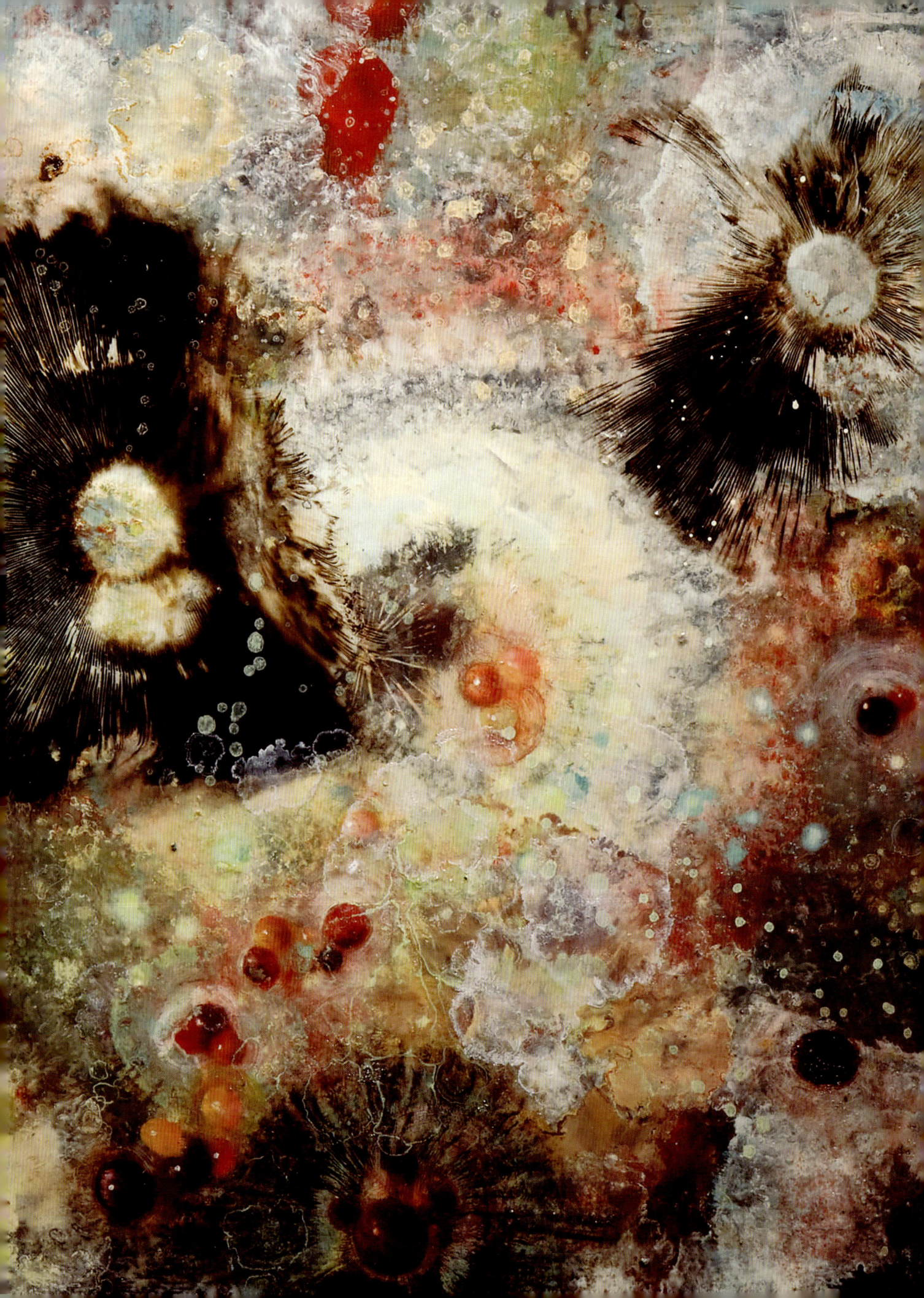

MARLANA STODDARD HAYES

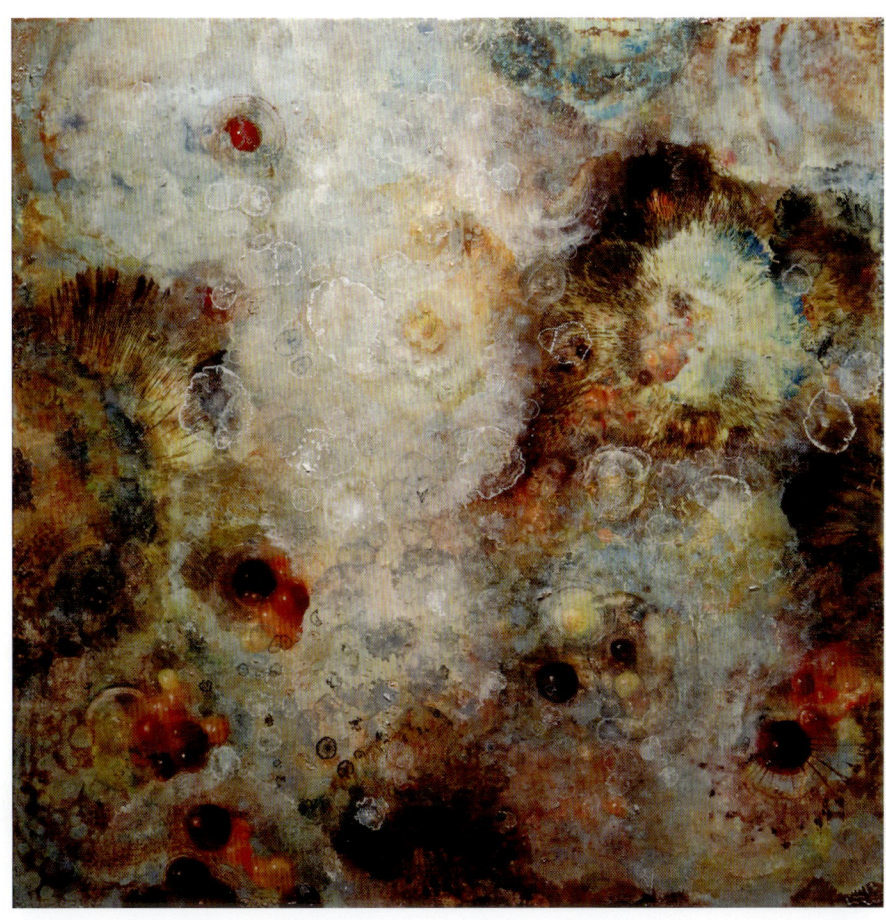

Marlana Stoddard Hayes is an artist based in Portland, Oregon. She has taken the advice of Wes Jackson and "dug in, making oneself a native through exploration of the land." The relationship she has developed with an acre tract near the Willamette River has come to inform the work she currently makes, which explores the intersections between soil communities and the various fungi that inhabit this area, especially flush with the fall rain cycle. The careful tending of organic life and its reflective capacity on shaping human life are values she has strived to incorporate into this visual work. There are reverberations in the visual field that have been inspired from the soil beneath and our connection to it.

Painting's depth of field has been another interest for over 35 years.

Gradual discovery of this atmosphere allows access to the inner reaches of the mind to find transformation, illumination, and equilibrium. Trained as a printmaker, she has adapted methods of transferred touch to apply pigment to surface using acrylic mediums that hover between opacity and transparency.

Marlana teaches in the School of Graduate Studies at Marylhurst University, which explores aspects of the spirit in creative work, as well as gives intensives in painting at the Sitka Center for Art and Ecology. Work in collections includes: Scripps College, Spencer Museum of Art at University of Kansas, University of Iowa Hospitals and Clinics, The Kansas Health Foundation and The Dept. of Education in Washington, D.C.

WWW.MARLANASTODDARDHAYES.COM

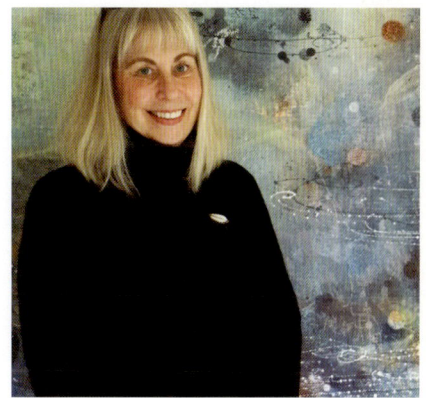

(facing page) (43) Koan ●
Oil on panel with spores (Agaricus Agustus),
14 x 14 in., 2010

(45) Koan ●
Oil on panel with spores (Agaricus Campestris),
14 x 14 in., 2010

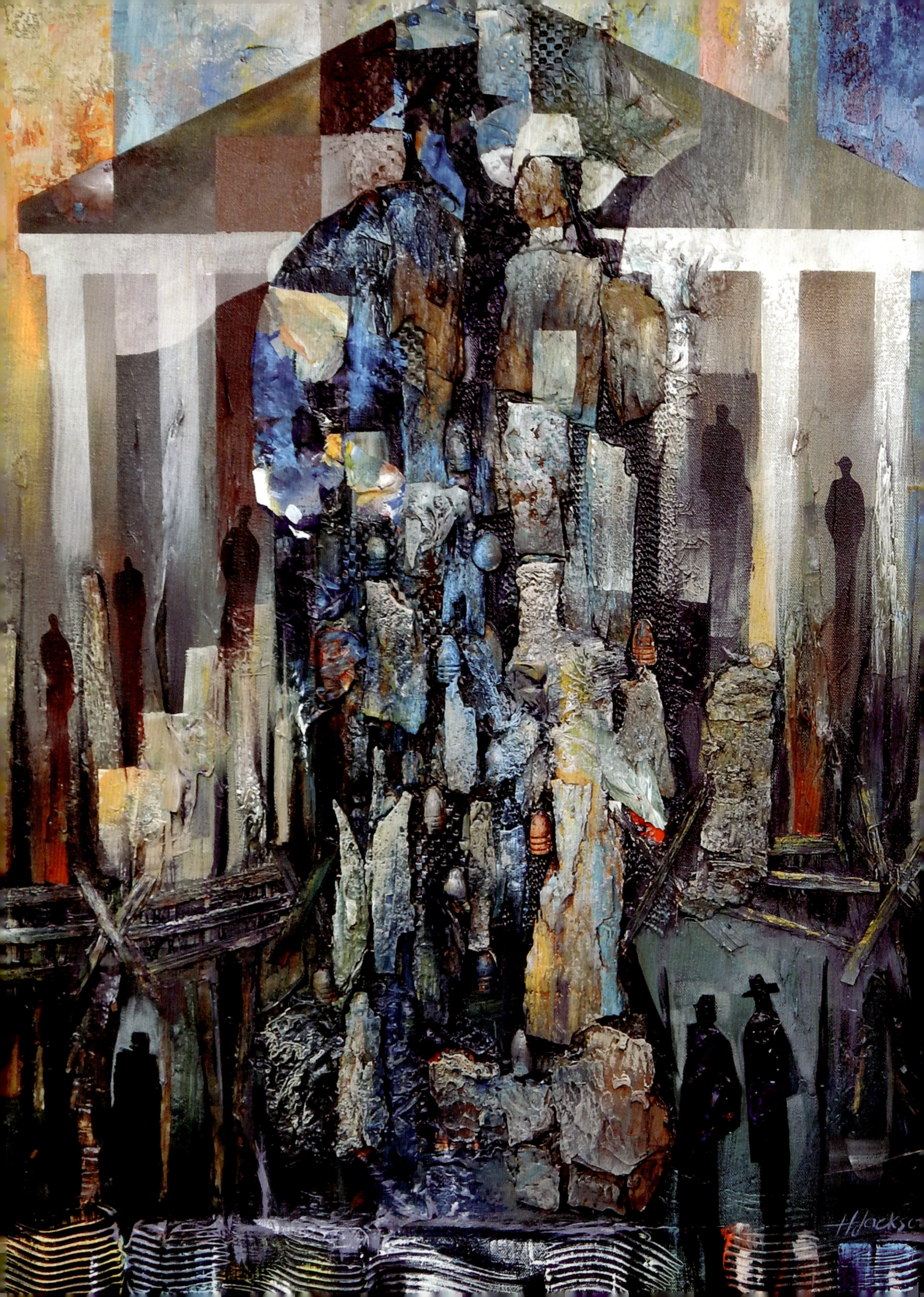

HUBERT JACKSON

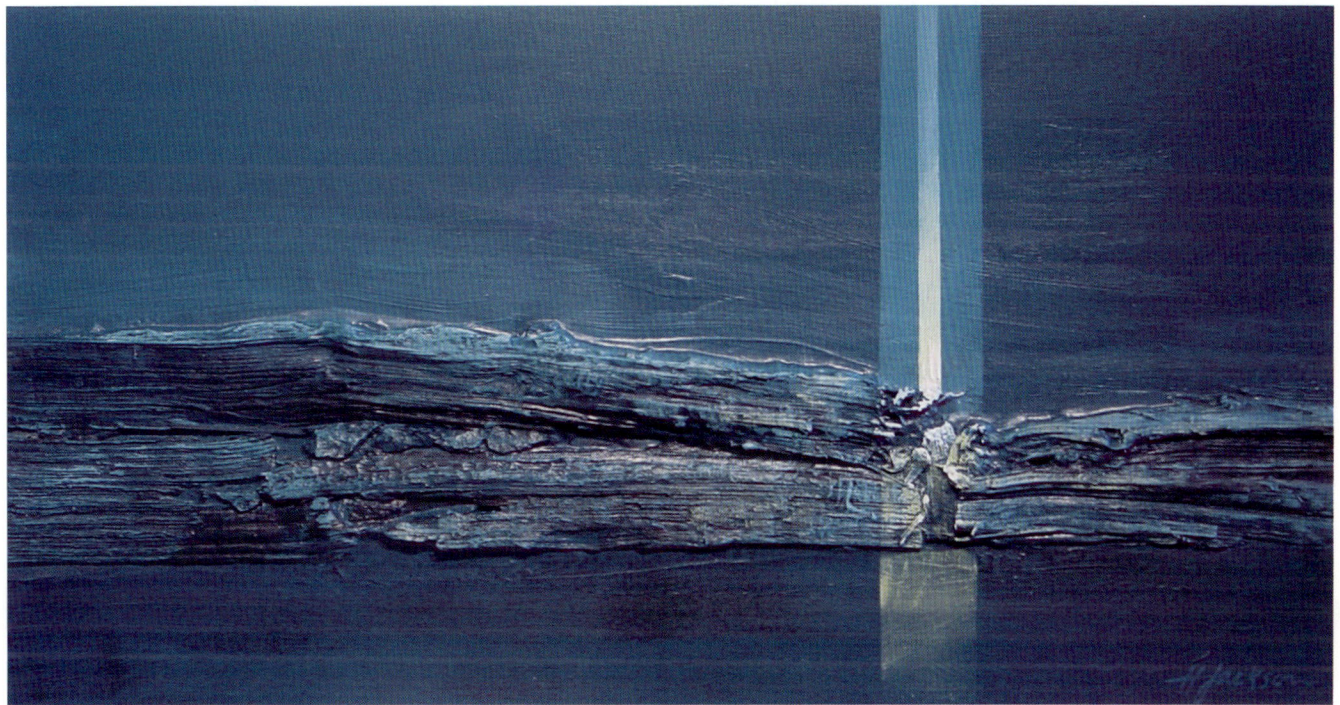

Hubert Jackson was born in 1943 in Culpeper, Virginia. He earned his Bachelors in Fine Arts Education at Virginia State University in 1965. After graduation, he moved to Washington D.C. It was during these postgraduate years that he really intensified his painting education. By 1971 he earned his Master's degree in painting from Howard University. At Howard, he enjoyed studying with James Porter, Lois Jones, Ed Love, Jeff Donaldson, and Starmanda Bullock. Other prominent DC artists contributed to his aesthetic growth, including Gene Davis, Morris Louis, Alma Thomas, Lucille Malkia Roberts and Sam Gilliam. In the early '70s he participated in the historical national movement of community based mural projects under the advisement of Hughie Lee-Smith.

Jackson has exhibited extensively. His work is in a number of private collections, not only in the U.S., but also outside the U.S. These include ambassadors of foreign countries such as Lesotho, Ghana, Guinea and New Guinea, through the Artist in Embassies program. In July 2015 Jackson exhibited at the U.S. Embassy in Rome, Italy. His exhibition, Spirits of the Journey, commemorated the 150th anniversary of the end of the American Civil War.

WWW.HUBERTJACKSON.COM

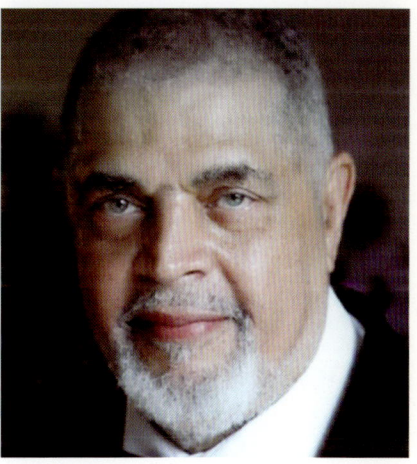

(facing page) Spirits of Appomattox ●
Acrylic/mixed media, 36 x 24 in., 2015

Still Morning ●
Acrylic/mixed media on panel, 12 x 24 in., 2012

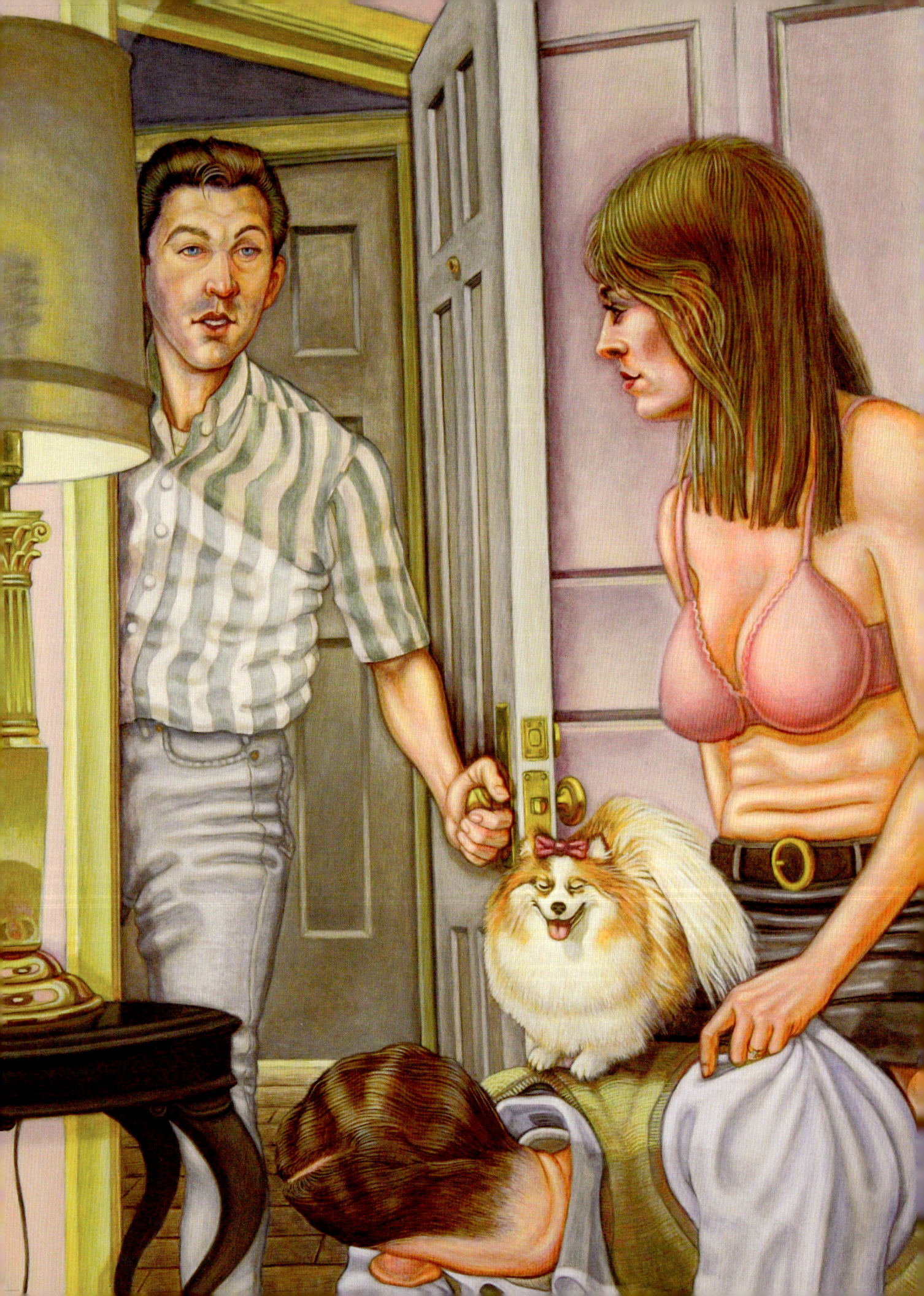

JED JACKSON

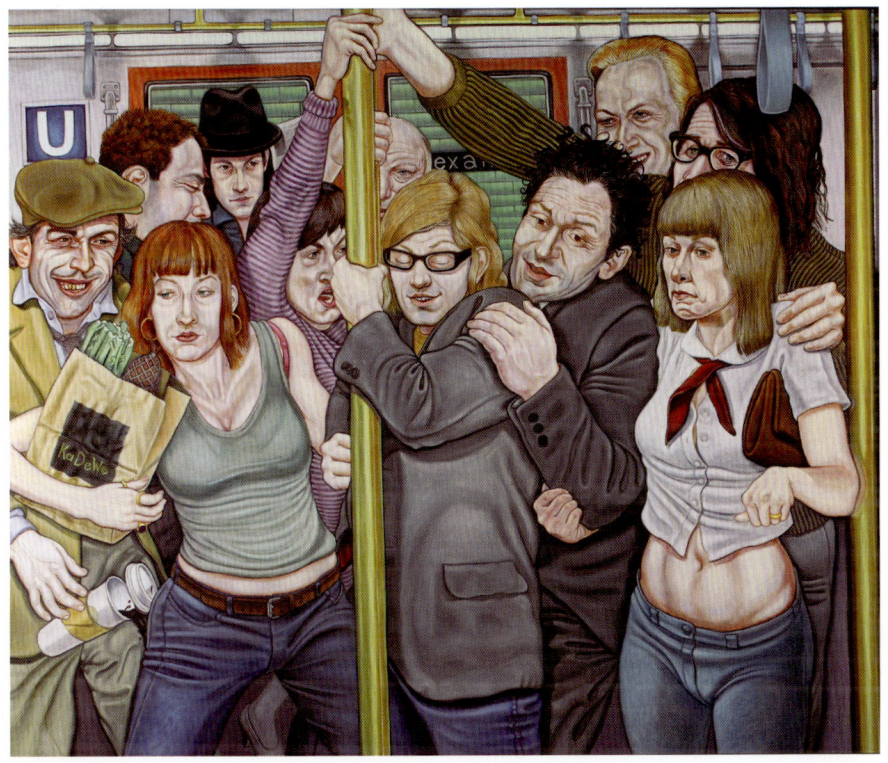

Jed Jackson studied art at the Memphis College of Art (BFA 1977), the Skowhegan School of Painting and Sculpture and received an MFA from Cornell University in 1980. He has exhibited his work in France, Holland, Switzerland, England, New York, Chicago, St. Louis and many other centers. His work has been recognized with 12 fellowships from Arts Midwest/NEA, Tennessee Arts Commission, Arkansas Arts Council, MidAmerica Arts Alliance, Cornell University and recently the Rocheforte-en-Terre residency sponsored by the Maryland College of Art and the Department of Morbihan, France. In 2006 he exhibited his work in a solo exhibit at the Institut Franco-Americain in Rennes, France. He has taught at the college and university level for 28 years and is current Professor of Painting at the University of Memphis.

Jed Jackson makes paintings that traffic in ideas from politics to social culture—from serious to not so serious(funny).

He counts amongst his muses the spirits of Mark Twain, Stanley Kubrick, Jack Kerouac, Erich von Stroheim, Christian Schad, Otto Dix, Ernest Hemingway, Gloria Swanson, Maynard G. Krebs, W.C. Fields, Billy Wilder, John Huston, Winston Churchill, Buster Keaton, Leni Riefenstahl, Nick Cave, Tom Waits, Arthur Conan Doyle, Arnold Schoenberg, Gustav Mahler, Ulf Timmermann, Rainer Maria Rilke, Ezra Pound and most of the painters in the history of western civilization and some who hail from other locales. He considers the work he does as a kind of image sorting—a kind of improvisation. Convincingly painted images are necessary to bring the whole collage of ideas and references off. He thinks paintings are still more important than movies.

WWW.JEDJACKSON.COM

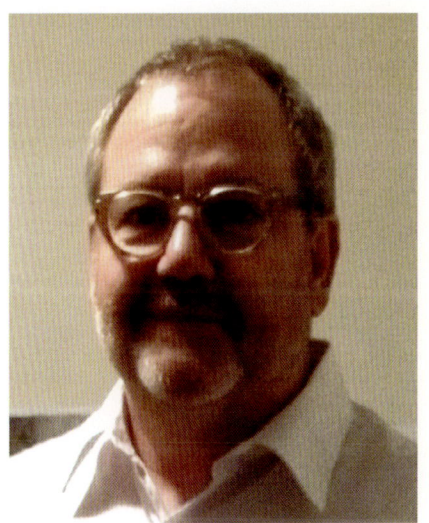

(facing page) Horsey ●
Oil on wood, 18 x 18 in., 2014

UBAHN/Young Pioneers ●
Oil on wood, 35 x 40 in., 2008

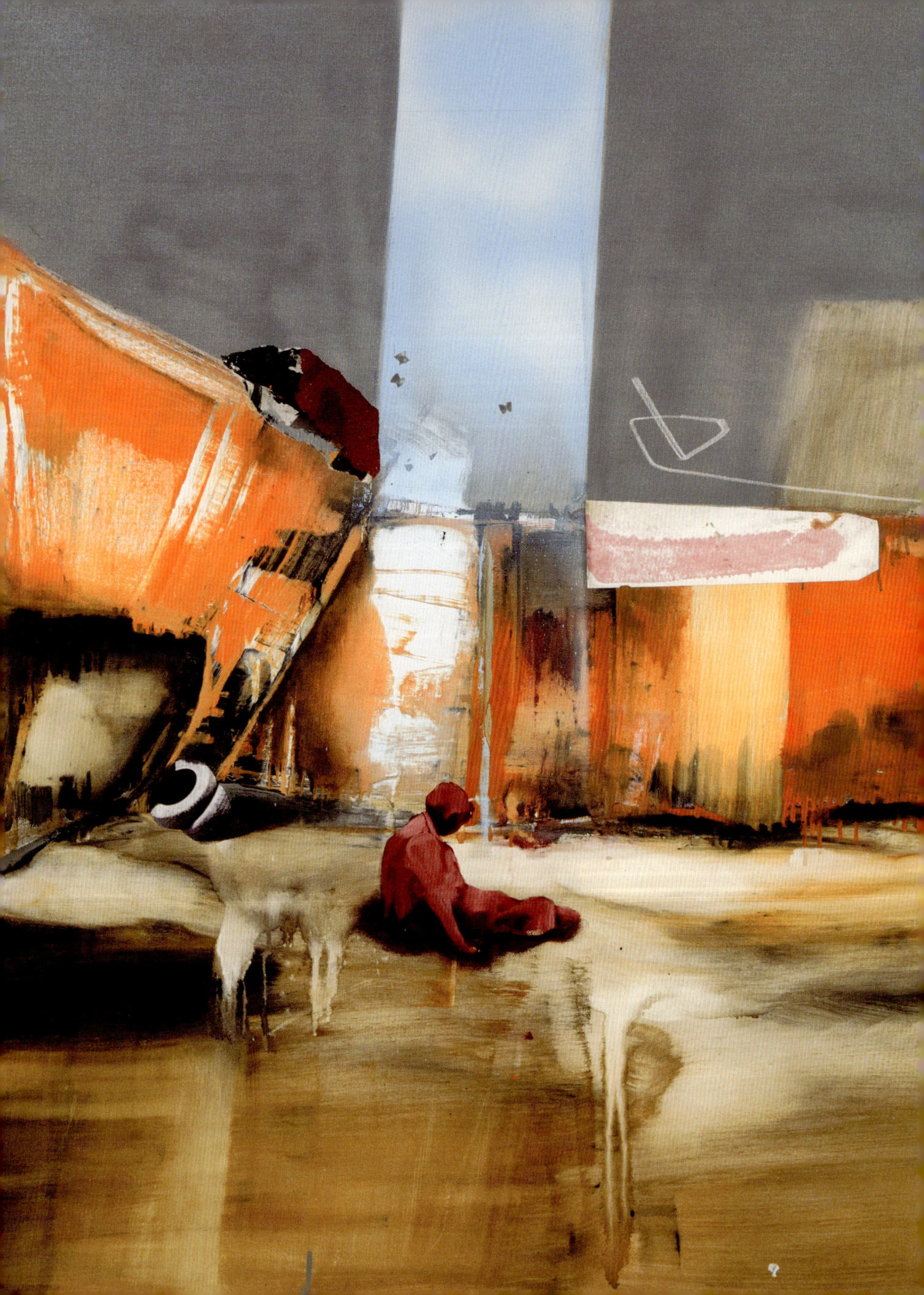

MARCUS JANSEN

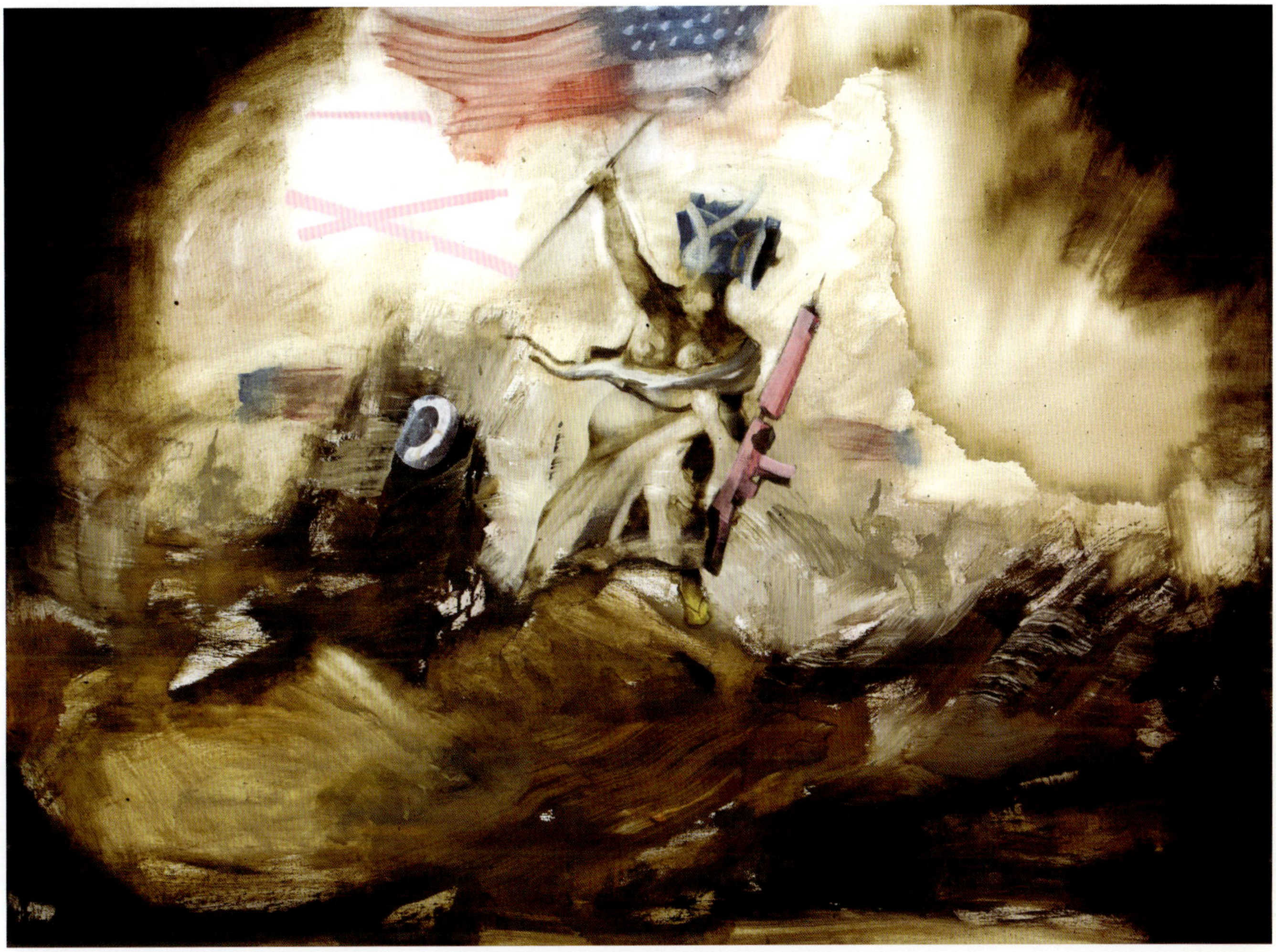

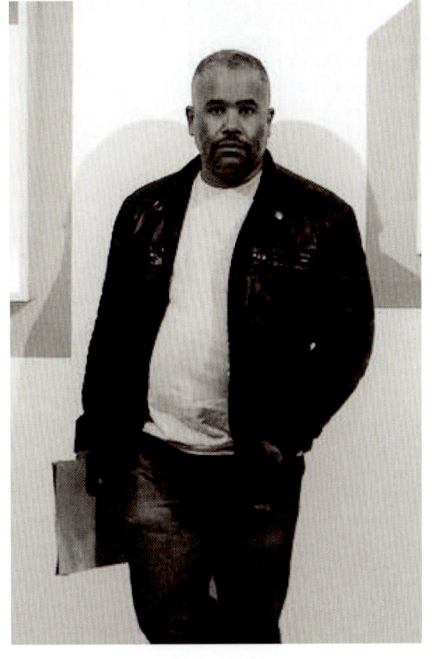

Marcus Jansen, b. 1968, New York, New York is a cartographer of conflict. He has been called a pioneer in redefining urban landscape painting for the last two decades. A former soldier and world traveler since the age of one year old, Jansen is the son of a German businessman and West Indien mother who was first influenced by an emerging and rebellious Graffiti art movement from his home town New York City in 1982. Jansen transforms landscapes into critical social commentary in an era of globalization and a growing new world order while exploring the human condition often working paradoxes and drawing parallels between historic and contemporary events and references.

WWW.MARCUSJANSEN.COM

(facing page) Homeland Security ●
Oil enamels on canvas, 48 x 48 in., 2014

Sugarcoated Revolution ●
Oil enamels on canvas, 48 x 36 in., 2014

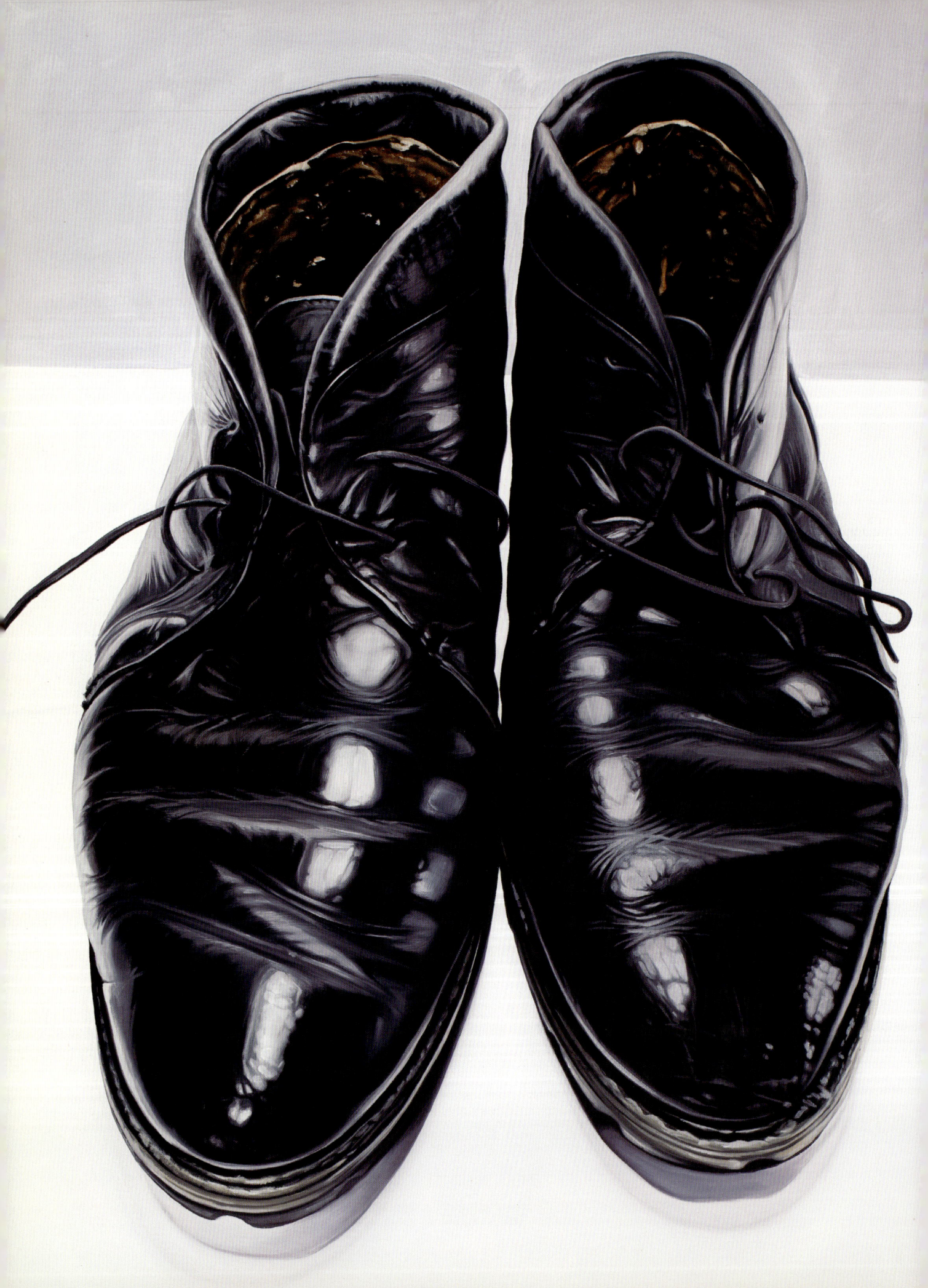

KELLY JO SHOWS

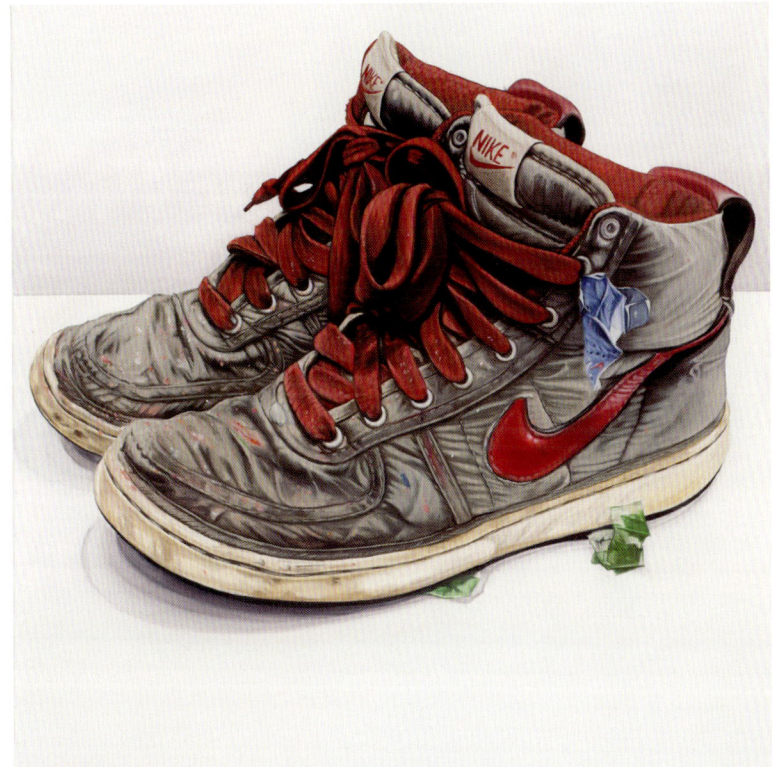

"I have worked on this series for over 6 years. Shoes speak volumes about who we are. After time they develop a character all their own."

This series is about paying homage to a variety of contemporary artists worldwide and being able to connect with them personally. Creating art is my greatest purpose, yet it can become isolating. This series gives me the opportunity to connect with other artists all over the world. To date I have painted over 100 shoe portraits of both world renowned and obscure artists, including: Jamie Wyeth, John Baldessari, Ed Ruscha, Jenny Holzer and the list keeps growing.

I personally contacted artists and asked them to send the pair of shoes that best represents them. The number of positive responses that I've received so far pleasantly surprises me. Most of the shoes

are sent back to the artist but many of them have allowed me to keep them. I now have a wire in my studio with over 50 pairs of shoes strung above my easel. The growing number of correspondence, ephemera and photos that I've collected has become an additional point of interest. Every day I look forward to going to the mailbox to see who has responded. I plan on putting together a book chronicling the portraits, correspondence and contributing artists as a way for people to discover these great artists on their own. I plan on developing this series the rest of my life.

WWW.FEARNOART.NET

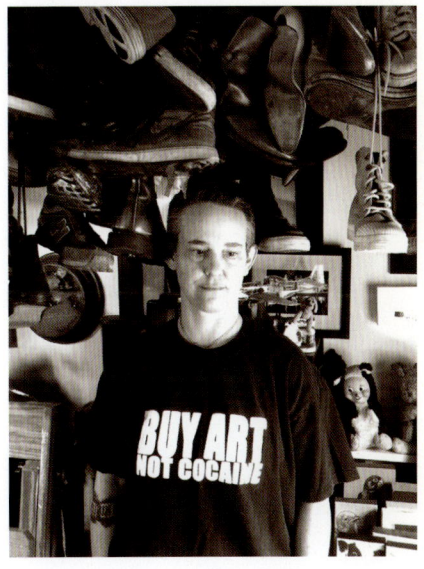

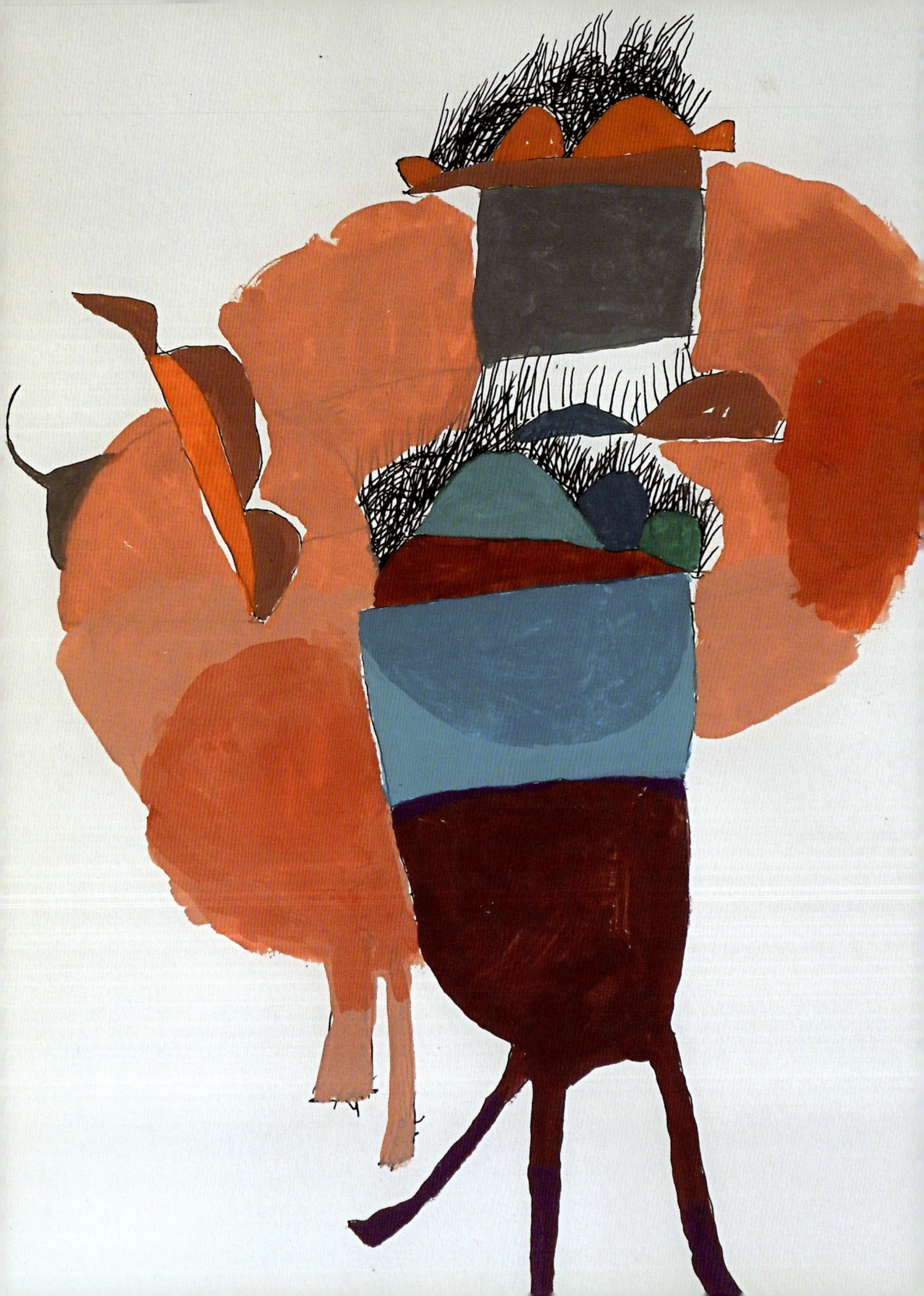

ANNE JOHNSTONE

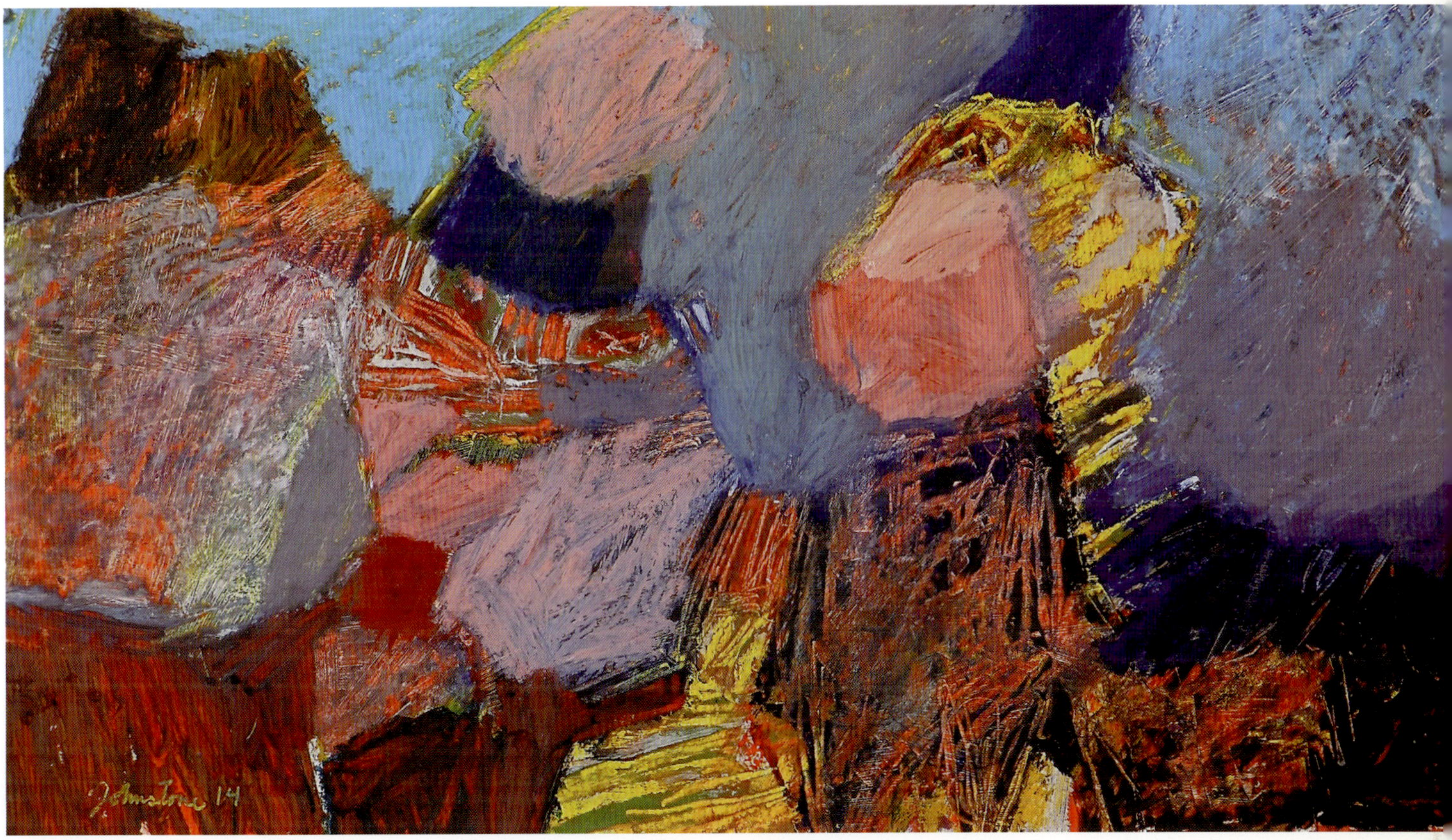

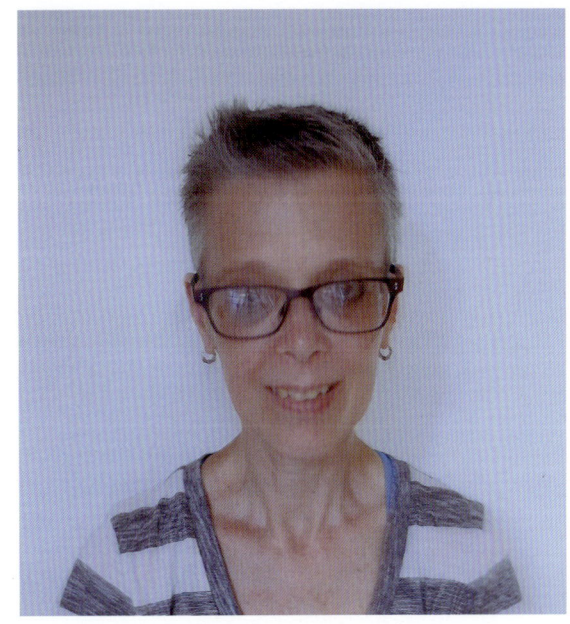

In addition to mixed media painting, I work with oil pastels and in sketchbooks using a variety of media. Layering of images and color are common practices in all of my work. I am fascinated by what's been covered up, scraped away, drawn into, and altered. The finished image has as much to do with what's been covered up or eliminated as it has to do with what's still visible. My processes in creating an image correlate to the way I perceive people: we present to the world selves that are a complex mix of seen and unseen, known and unrecognized forces. The abstract character of my work testifies to the mysteries of what lies underneath the skin.

WWW.ANNEJOHNSTONE.COM

● **(facing page) Counting Sheep**
Mixed media, 9 x 7 in., 2012

● **Queen of Hearts**
Mixed media, 11.5 x 22 in., 2014

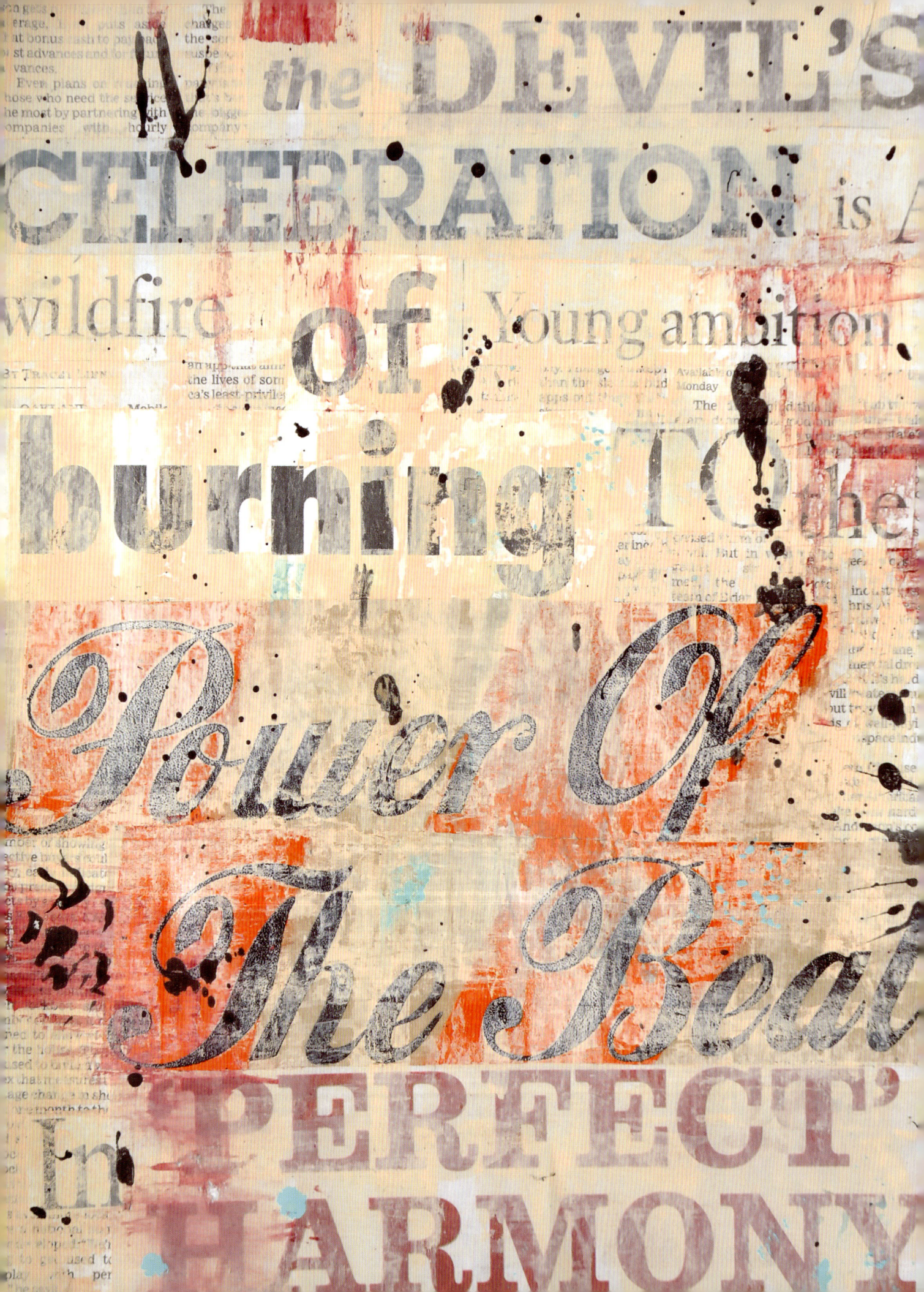

CHRIS JUSTICE

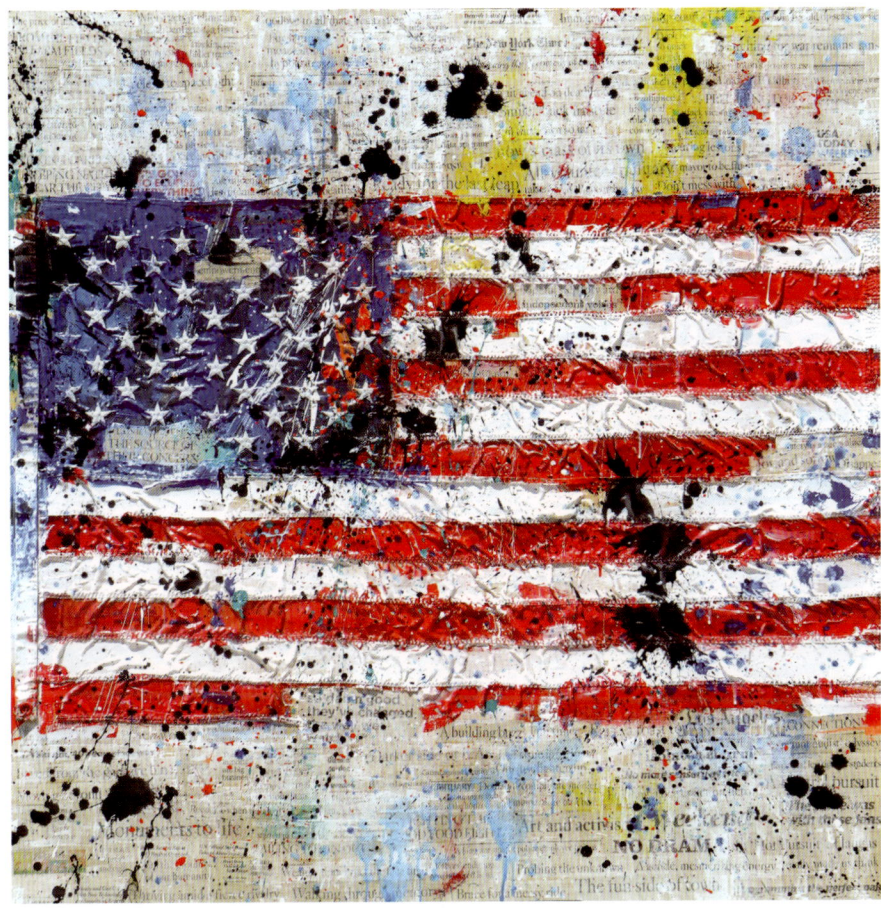

The work is an embracement of my inner madness manifested in reality. It is executed with a strong sense of urgency. I do not create out of choice, I create out of obligation. In simpler terms, the art chose me. I am a strong believer in the notion that art imitates life and vice versa. My work reflects on modern American nostalgia (but not limited to America only) clashing with my functional hoarding of three dimensional materials such as newspapers, magazines, and my beloved collection of tattered American flags compiled from my travels through the southwest. I enhance the work with an array of foreign art materials such as gasoline, beer, fireworks, and flame. Inspiration is a constant trance that surrounds my being. Overwhelming yet liberating, inspiration is something that I live firsthand; therefore, it is what I am. My world is processed by color, which are the most fascinating entities of life, and the paintings exist in a world of their own. What's exciting about the abstract process is that I am creating something that does not previously exist in the world and not only giving it life, but giving it purpose. The purpose of the work is to tell a story. Although I create these works with a story in my heart that represents an experience held significant to my being, it is the viewers job to create a story significant to theirs. It takes immense discipline to allow my paintings to have a mind of their own.

WWW.CHRISTJUSTICEART.COM

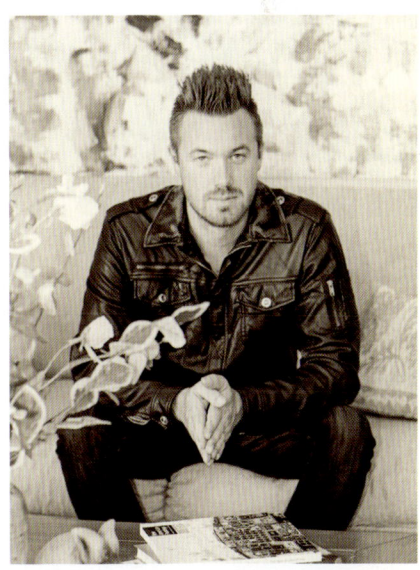

ANGELS in AMERICA

A Gay Fantasia on National Themes

PART ONE:
MILLENNIUM

gels in America

: Just out. Thinking.
per: It's late.
: I had a lot to think about.
per: I burned dinner.
: Sorry
per: Not my dinner. My dinner was fine. Your dinner: I put
it back in the oven and turned everything up as high as it
could go and I watched till it burned black. It's still hot.
Very hot. Want it?
: You didn't have to do that.
per: I know. It just seemed like the kind of thing a
mentally deranged sex-starved pill-popping housewife
would do.
: Uh huh.

Angels in America

joking. . . . I already apologized sixteen times for that,
Mrs. Soffer, you . . . *(While she's fulminating, Roy covers
the mouthpiece with his hand and talks to Joe)* This'll take
a minute, *eat* already, what is this tasty sandwich here
it's— *(He takes a bite of a sandwich)* Mmmmm, liver or
some. . . . Here.

*(He pitches the sandwich to Joe, who catches it and retu
to the platter.)*

(Back to Mrs. Soffer): Uh huh, uh huh. . . .
told you, it wasn't a vacation, it was business
have clients in Haiti, Mrs. Soffer, I . . .
YOU THINK I'M THE ONLY GODDE
IN HISTORY EVER MISSED A C
Don't make such a big fucking. . . .
hold button) You HAG! . . .
If this is a bad time . . .
: Bad time? This is a good time! *(But
me. . . . Oh fuck, wait . . . (Button,
Sorry to keep you holding, Judge Holli
Hollins, sorry dear deep voice you
visit? (Hand over mouthpiece again, to
a truckdriver and he sounds like Kate
ing. Nixon appointed him, all the g
pointees . . . (To Mrs. Hollins) Yeah
how many tickets dear? Seven. For
Street, what? No you wouldn't like L
know. Oh for godsake. . . . Hold. (B
doll, seven for Cats or something, any
don't give a fuck what and neither w
Joe) You see La Cage?*
: No, I . . .

gels in America

: What? *(To Harry)* Hold a minute
Mrs. . . . *(Button)* God-fucking
is . . .
y *(Overlapping):* Roy, I'd really a
Mrs. . . . *(Button)* God-fucking
y *(Overlapping):* Well she was he
af . . .
*(The phone starts making thre
oice.)*
y *(Smashing buttons):* Jesus fuck
(Overlapping): I really wish y
(Overlapping): Baby doll? Ri
*(The phone starts whistling
e: CHRIST!
Ro
y *(Indiscreetly):* Hold. *(Butt*
: Could you please not take
Pause)
I'm sorry. But please. A
(Laughs, then): Right. Sorr
Only in America. *(Pun
's all to fuck off! Tell 'em I
Tell her it's on the way. Tell
I'll call her back. I will ca
borrowed. She's got four hu
. . . Yeah, tell her I said
tent)*
. . . Joe.

Scene 3

*Later th
radio c
audi*

HARPER: Pe
nonsens
dying, ol
When
a spaceship
mering aure
earth. Thirty
atom oxygen mole
explains the fussy veg
rejection of darker ra
without. It's a kind of g
to the creation of the wo
make a spherical net, a

16

ANGELS IN AMERICA

get to me, Joe stays away and
dreams are talking back to me.
MR. LIES: It's the price of rootlessness. M
only cure: to keep moving.
HARPER: I'm undecided. I feel . . . that.

JOE: Oh that's . . . that doesn't make sense. You have all the
time in the world. You could finish it when I'm at work.
HARPER: I'm afraid to go in there alone.
JOE: Afraid of what?
HARPER: I heard someone in there. Metal scraping on the
wall. A man with a knife, maybe.
JOE: There's no one in the bedroom, Harper.
HARPER: Not now.
JOE: Not this morning either.
HARPER: How do you know? You were at work this morning.
There's something creepy about this place. Remember
osemary's Baby?
osemary's Baby?
ER: Our apartment looks like that one isn't that apartment in Brooklyn?
: No, it was
ll, it looked like this. It did.
let's move.
Georgetown's worse. The Exor was in George-
e devil, everywhere you turn, b ddy
Yeah. Everywhere.
many pills today, buddy?
One. Three. Only three.
gent vanishes as Joe enters.)
Pointing at the coffin):* Why are there just two little
ooden pegs holding the lid down?
ISIDOR CHEMELWITZ: So sh out eas
s to.
hope she stays put.
pretended for years that she was already dea
called to say she died it was a surpri
ned her.

I know this is scary for you. But
means to me. Will you try?

me yo hiding B
perso ally wo
the eye and said "h" Forta
Oh and by the way, darling,

ut. For the g ge for the go
covered itself. d position a
ople aren't asha hat like they use
eat thing. The stored w rest
President R one He say "Truth
can be one, country re-
W I need to
be a par up. I
mean, six years ag able,
hopeless, full of uns
fusion and hunger an
HARPER: But it st seems
They say the ozo aye
JOE: Harper . . .
HARPER: And today out th there
was a schizophrenic tr
JOE: Stop it I'm trying to
HARPER: So I.
JOE: You aren't en mak
HARPER: My poi
JOE: It only seems
the smell, J
JOE: You don't Y
JOE: You don't sta

HARPER: Then they went on to a program about
ozone layer. Over Antarctica. Skin burns, b
icebergs melt. The world's coming to an e

Scene 6

*First week of November. In the men's room of th
Brooklyn Federal Court of Appeals; Louis is
sink; Joe enters.*

JOE: Oh, um. . . . Morning.
LOUIS: Good morning, counselor.
JOE *(He watches Louis cry):* Sorry, I . . . I don't know
LOUIS: Don't bother. Word processor. The lowest
JOE *(Holding out hand):* Joe Pitt. I'm with Justice V
LOUIS: Oh, I know that. Counselor Pitt. Chief C
JOE: Were you . . . are you OK?
LOUIS: Oh, yeah. Thanks. What a nice man.
JOE: Not so nice.
LOUIS: What?
JOE: Not so nice. Nothing. You sure you're . . .
LOUIS: Life sucks shit. Life . . . just sucks shit.
JOE: What's wrong?
LOUIS: Run in my nylons.
JOE: Sorry . . . ?
LOUIS: Forget it. Look, thanks for asking.
JOE: Well
LOUIS: I mean it really is nice of you.
(He starts crying again)
Sorry, sorry, sick friend . . .
JOE: Oh, I'm sorry.

28

ANGELS IN AMERICA

JOE *(Making sure no one else is around):* Do I? Sound like
LOUIS: What? Like a . . . ? Republican, or . . . ? De
JOE: Do you mean?
LOUIS: Sound like a . . . ?
JOE: Like a . . . ?
I'm . . . confused.
LOUIS: Yes.
My name is Louis. But all my friends call me
I work in Word Processing. Thanks for the toile

*(Louis offers Joe his hand, Joe reaches, Louis feints a
fo on the cheek, then exits.)*

Scene 7

*A week later. Mutual dream scene. Prior is at a f
makeup table, having a dream, applying the face. H
having a pill-induced hallucination. She ha
time to time. For some reason, Prior has appeared
one. Or Harper has appeared in Prior's dream. It is
ering.*

PRIOR *(Alone, putting on makeup, then examining the re
the mirror; to the audience):* "I'm ready for my close
DeMille."
One wants to move through life with elegan
grace, blossoming infrequently but with exquisite
and perfect timing, like a rare bloom, a zebra orchi
One wants. . . . But one so seldom gets what one
does one? No. One does not. One gets fucked.
One . . . dies at thirty, robbed of . . . decades of m

ANGELS IN AMERICA

HARPER: Valium. I take Valium. Lots of Valium.
PRIOR: And you're dancing as fast as you can.
HARPER: I'm not addicted. I don't believe in addiction
never . . . well, I never drink. And I never take
PRIOR: Well, smell you, Nancy Drew.
HARPER: Except Valium.
PRIOR: Except Valium; in wee fistfuls.
HARPER: It's terrible. Mormons are not supposed to
dicted to anything. I'm a Mormon.
PRIOR: I'm a homosexual.
HARPER: Oh! In my church we don't believe in homos
PRIOR: In my church we don't believe in Mormons.
HARPER: What church do . . . oh! *(She laughs)* I get i
I don't understand this. If I hadn't even see you
and I don't think I did then I think you sho
here, in this hallucination, be se in my experienc
mind, which is where hallucina ns come from, sh
be able to make up anythi that wasn't there to
with, that didn't enter it experience from t
world. Imagination can't e anything new, ca
only recycles bits and p om the world and rea
bles them into vision Am I making sense
now?
PRIOR: Given the circum yes.
HARPER: So when we think we've e the unbe
ordinariness and un truthful ss of our live
ally only the same old ordinar l and falsene
ranged into the appearance of novelty and
thing unknown is knowable. Don't you thin
stressing?
PRIOR: the limitations of the imagination?
HARPER: Yes.

62

ANGELS IN AMERICA

RIOR: Are you one of th
voices?
VOICE: No. I am no nightbird. I am a m
PRIOR: You have a beautiful voice, it sound like
a perfectly tuned, tight string, balar
Stay with me.
VOICE: Not now. Soon I will return, I wi to you;
I am glorious, glorious; my heart, ance and
my message. You must prepare.
PRIOR: For what? I don't want to . . .
VOICE
k and wonde undertake, an
edin mb and straighten, a great Lie
we abol great or correct, with rule sword
and bre of Truth!
PRIOR: What are you talking about, I . . .
VOICE:
I am on my way; when I am manifest our Work
begins:
Prepare for the parting of the air
The breath, the ascent,
Glory to . . .

ANDRZEJ MICHAEL

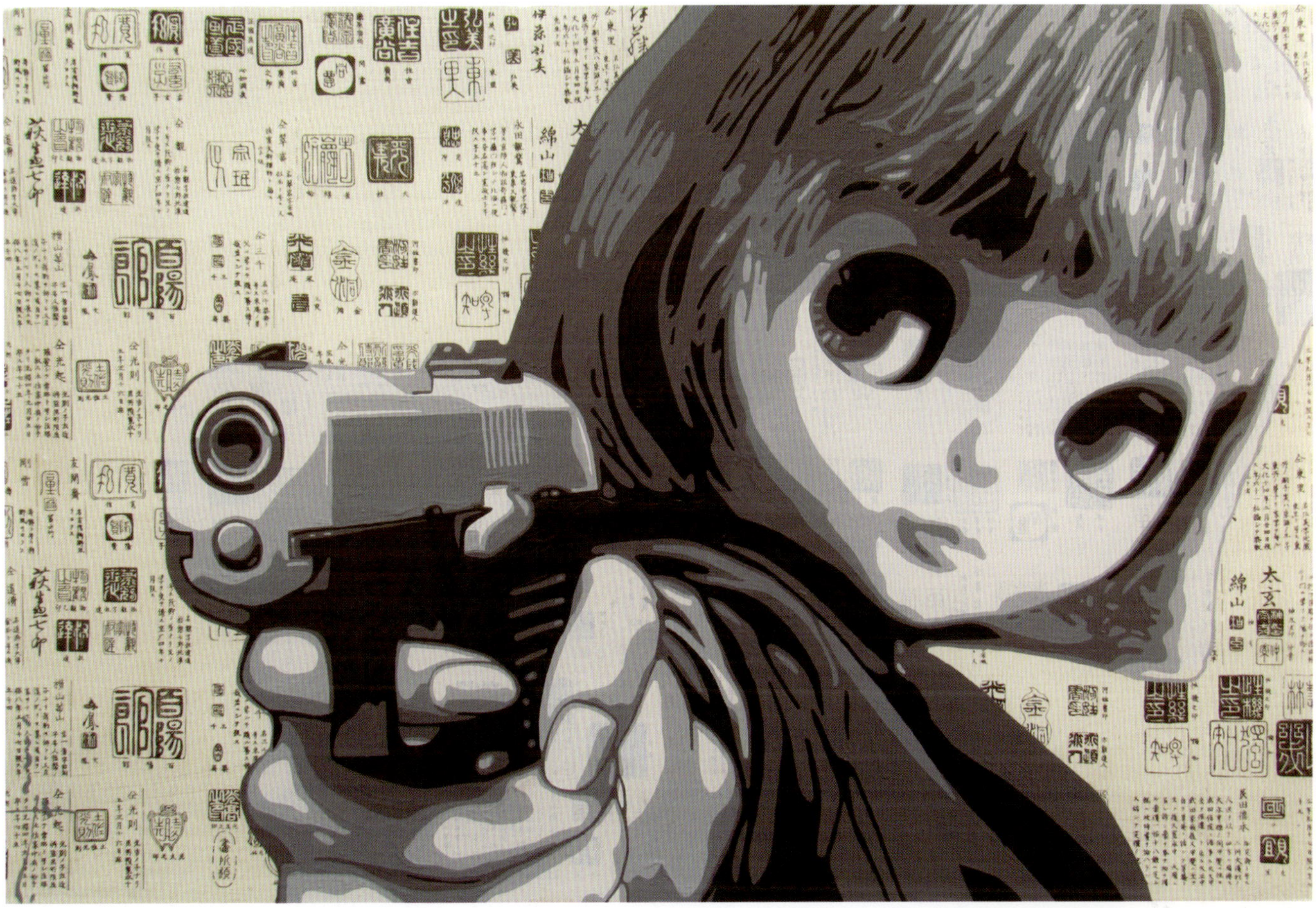

Born in Poland, Andrzej grew up during the years of political oppression and era of communist Poland. There he attended the School for the Arts and Literature. Unconsciously, these primary years were the platform for a deep attraction towards peace, poetry and art as a form of creative preservation. In 1984, Andrzej moved to New York, he consequently received BFA in painting and earned a Master's Degree in Urban Architecture from the University of Pennsylvania. After relocating to the San Francisco Bay Area in 1994, Andrzej's artistic direction began to take shape after integrating Eastern spirituality into his artwork. While Andrzej's current studio is based in Berkeley, his paintings are currently exhibited Los Angeles, the San Francisco Bay Area, Chicago, Dallas, New York,

Boston, Paris, London and Hong Kong. His work is in private collections throughout the United States. Relying on well-known images of man and women in the context of pop art, Andrzej have pulled together elements from mainstream aesthetics, both past and present, to address transpersonal relationships we have to select images. By juxtaposing the sense of identity with text from newspapers and textiles that speak of the social cultural of various decades and cultures, these paintings attempt to make sense of the world encompassing a wider aspect of humankind and the psyche.

WWW.ANDRZEJMICHAEL.COM

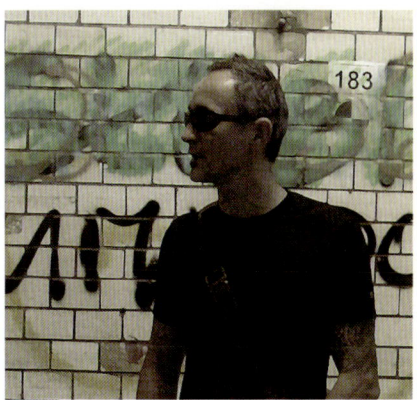

(facing page) Angels in America 01 ●
*Paper, acrylic paint and resin on birch panel,
18 x 24 in., 2013*

My Name is Bond-Lesley Bond ●
*Paper, ink, acrylic paint and resin on birch panel,
24 x 36 in., 2013*

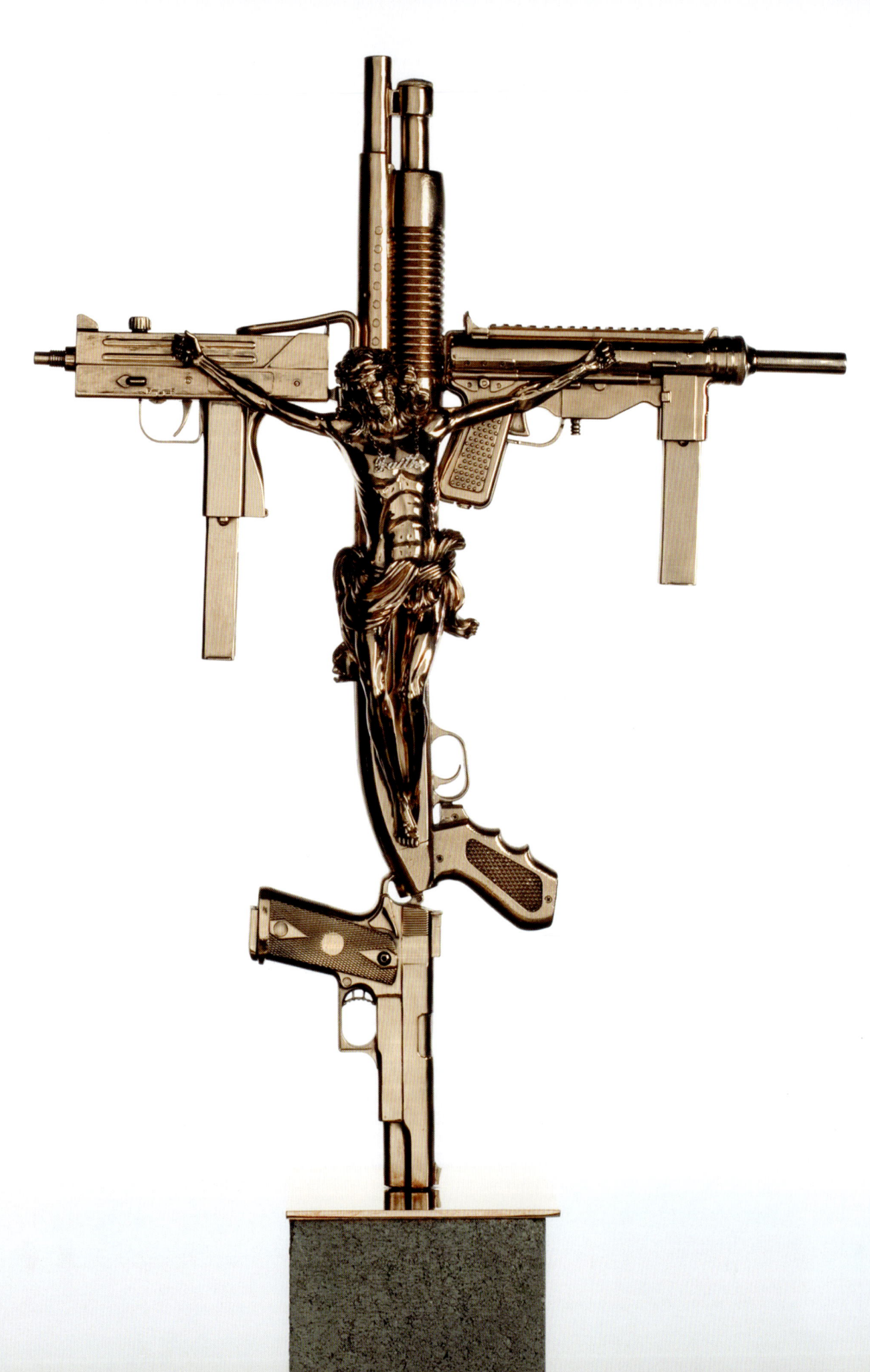

NIMAI KESTEN

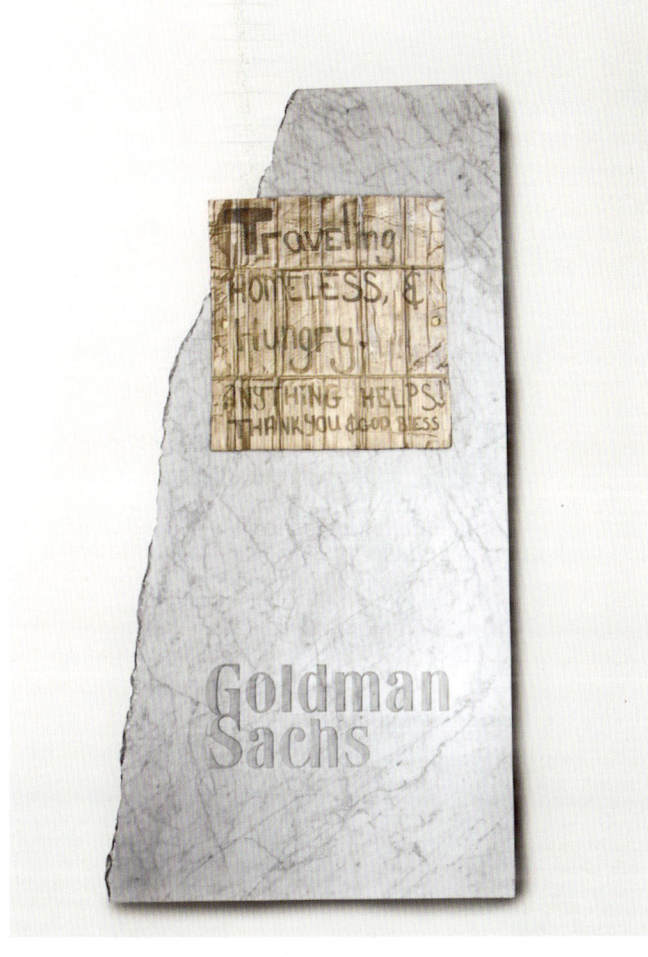

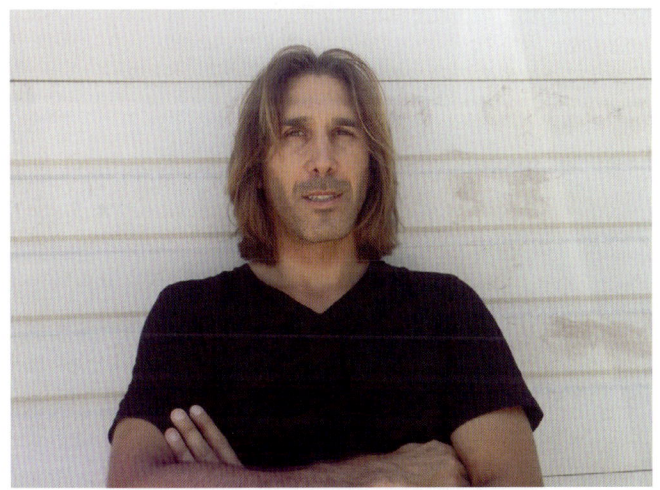

Nimai Kesten is an American contemporary artist articulating his life's journey in a visual dialog that incorporates sculpture, performance and paintings. Nimai Kesten's narrative is unafraid and unwavering and his art is a testament to his courage and vision. Nimai Kesten is a contemporary artist with a practice and focus on socio-political themes. Arguably one of our generation's greatest artists working to challenge a mainstream popular culture consumed with trends and collectable art, Nimai asks the tough questions as he exposes the corruption that resonates in the underbelly of religion, politics and family. The artist's mission is to engage the viewer and question the status quo offering physical evidence through his artistic interpretations of his personal experiences of the crimes committed against him and all of humanity and his sacrifice to hold the oppressor and his cohorts accountable.

● **(facing page) Crucifix**
Cast bronze, polished, set crystal stones, 25 x 34 in.

● **Inaugural Plaque Goldman Sachs**
Carrara marble, polished cast bronze, etched font, 68/33 in., 2013

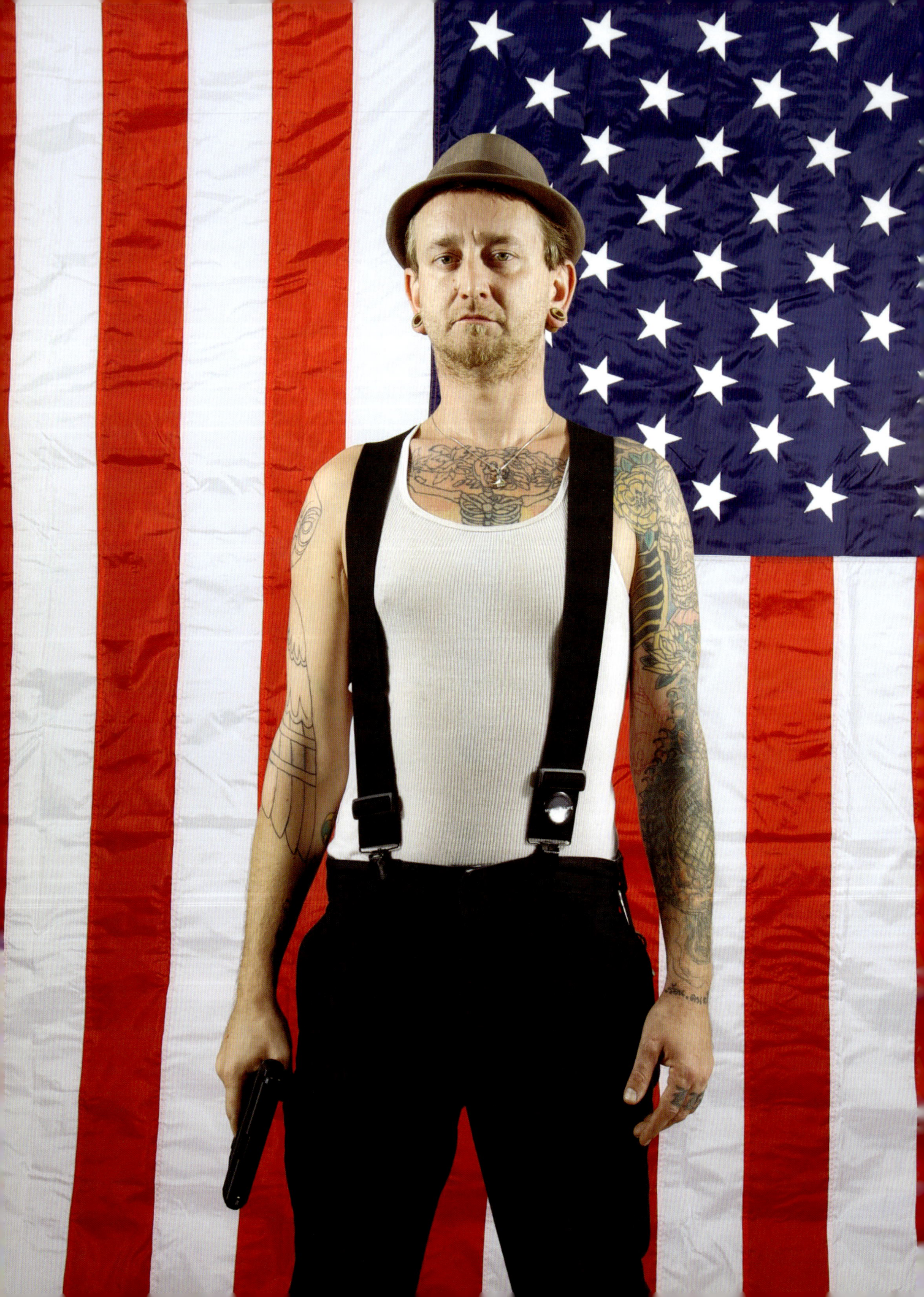

BRUCE KEYES

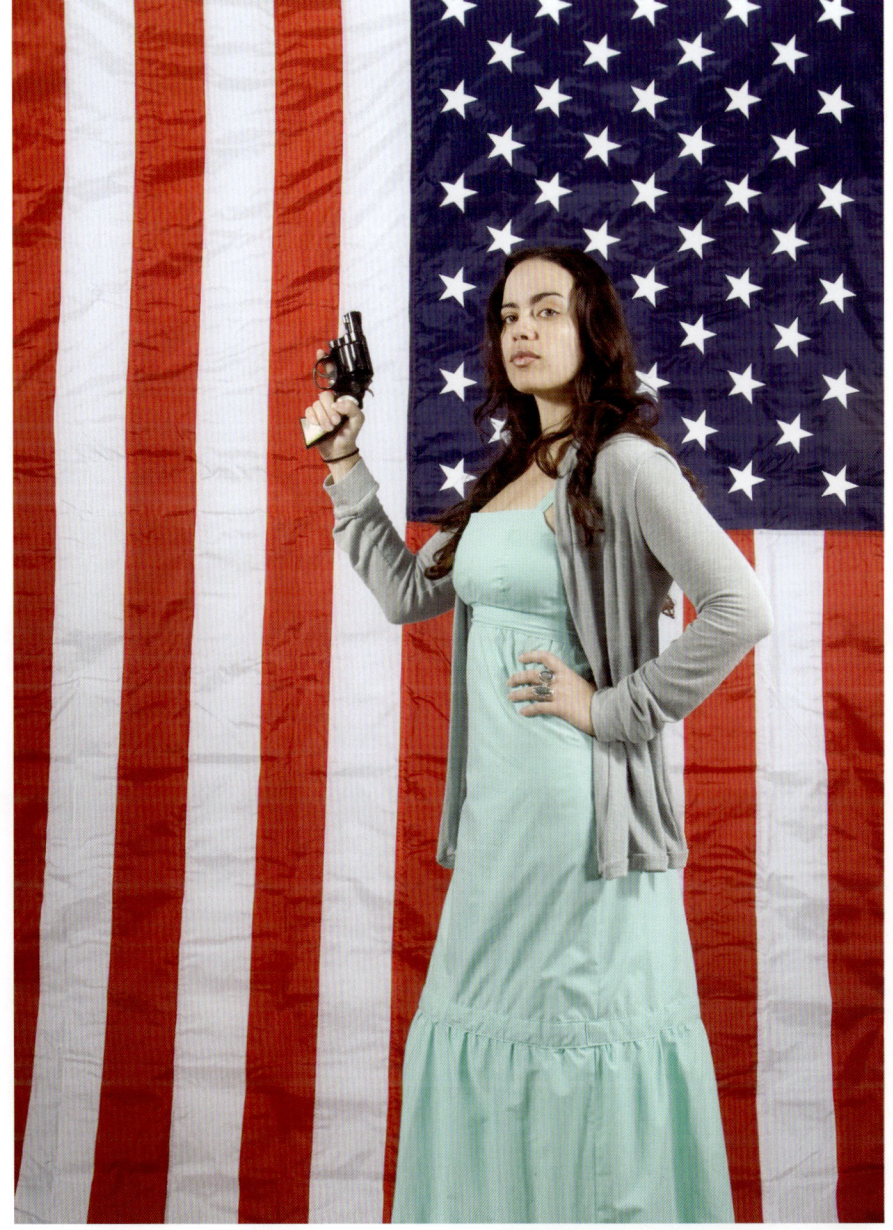

It is this investigation into human nature and the meaning of expression, gesture and timing that Keyes brought to his Weapons of Choice series. Keyes invited an open forum of individuals to be photographed brandishing their favorite weapons. He shot thirty individuals in full figure before an enormous American flag. While the study deals with individual fascination of weaponry in today's society, specifically in America with it's diehard-grip on the 2nd Amendment, there is a duality to the meaning of weaponry in this urban, violent, and yet ethereal image. Keyes provides no definite answer, indicating only that to stand empty-handed before the stars and stripes is not an option.

– ADAM FALIK

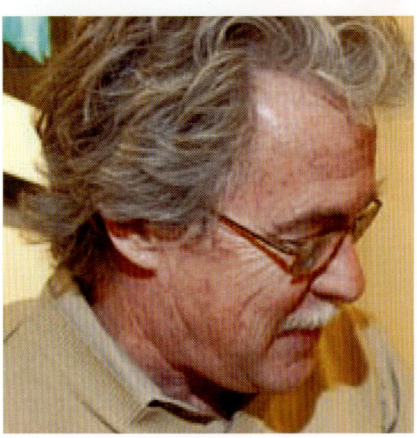

● **(facing page) Chad**
Archival inkjet print, 24 x 36 in., 2012

● **Anya**
Archival inkjet print, 24 x 36 in., 2012

JENNA KNOBLACH

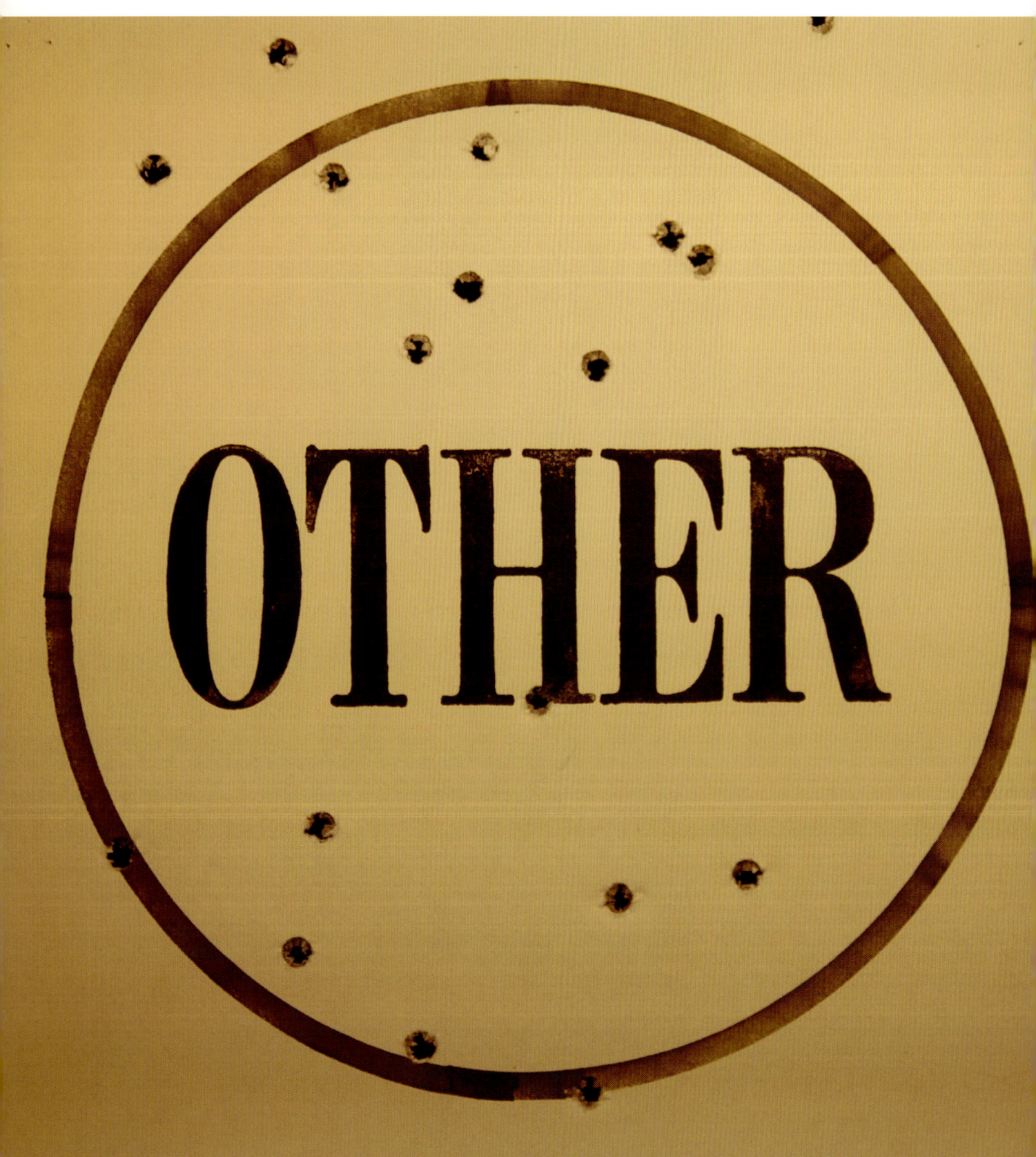

OTHER

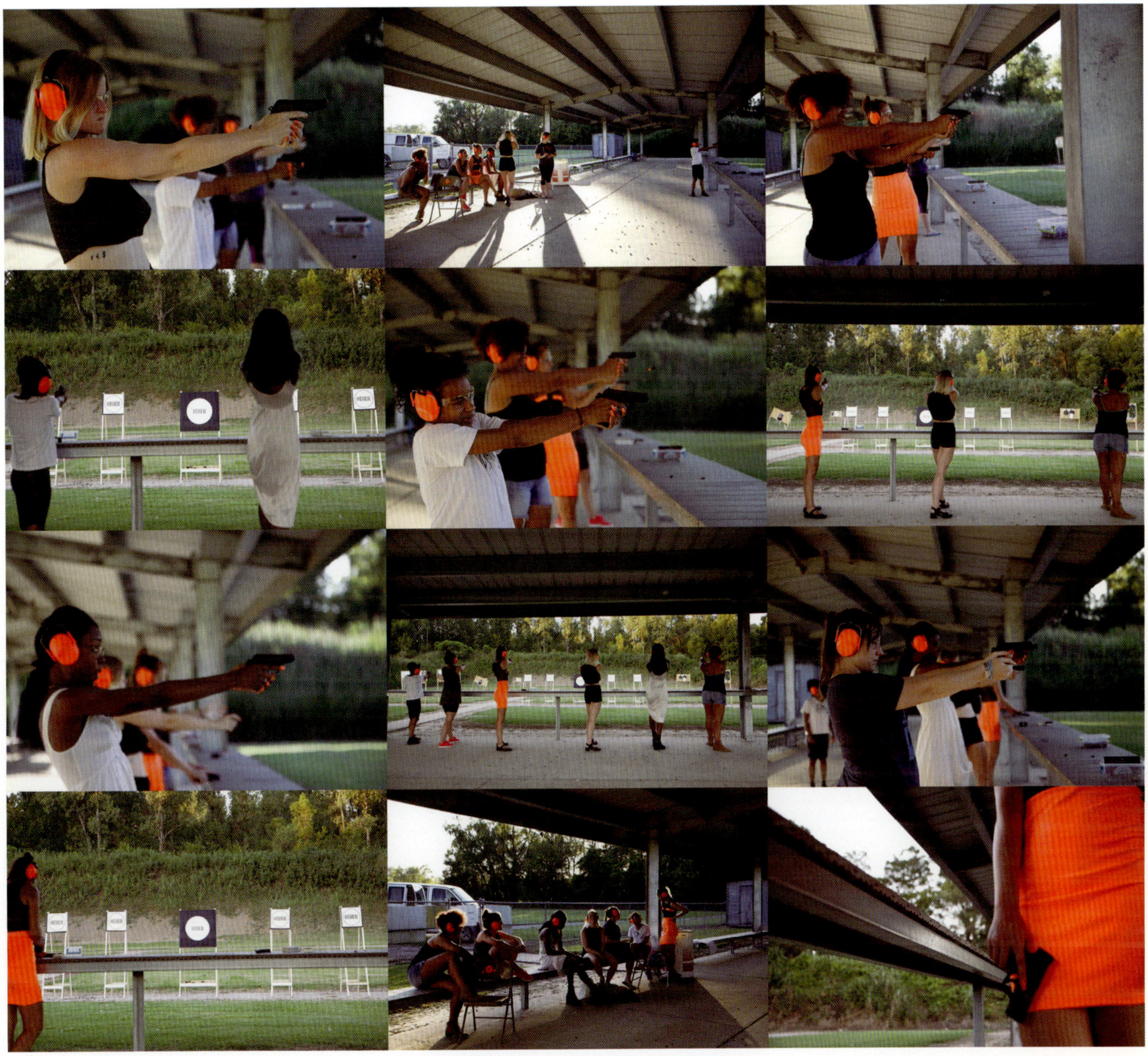

Jenna Knoblach is a visual artist who lives and works in New Orleans. Her most recent solo exhibition was titled Welcome to the #socialartwork and took place at Good Children Gallery. In the past, Knoblach has had work exhibited at the New York Transit Museum, MoMA, LABOR Gallery, UNO St. Claude Gallery, Antenna Gallery, and the Louisiana State Museum.

WWW.JENNAKNOBLACH.COM

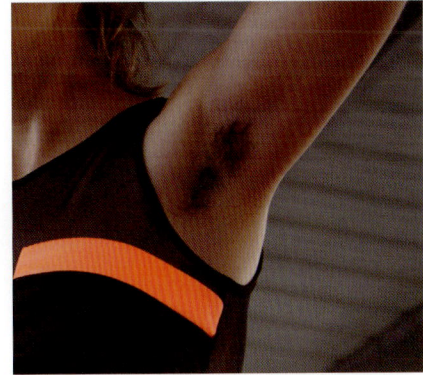

● **(facing page) Title IX**
Letterpress print, marker, bullets, 13 x 13 in., 2015

● **Title IX**
Performance, dimensions vary, 2015

NATALYA KOCHAK

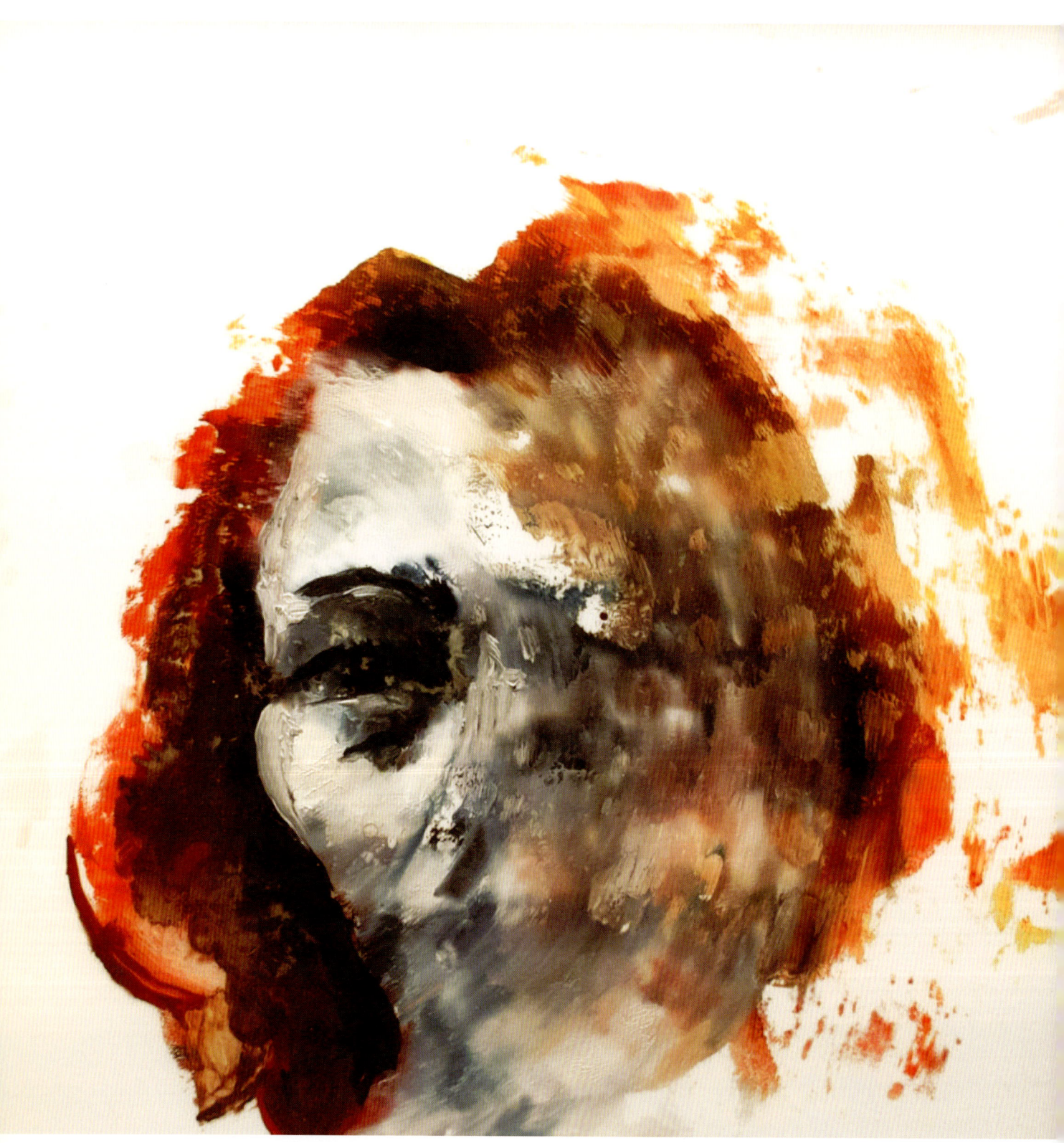

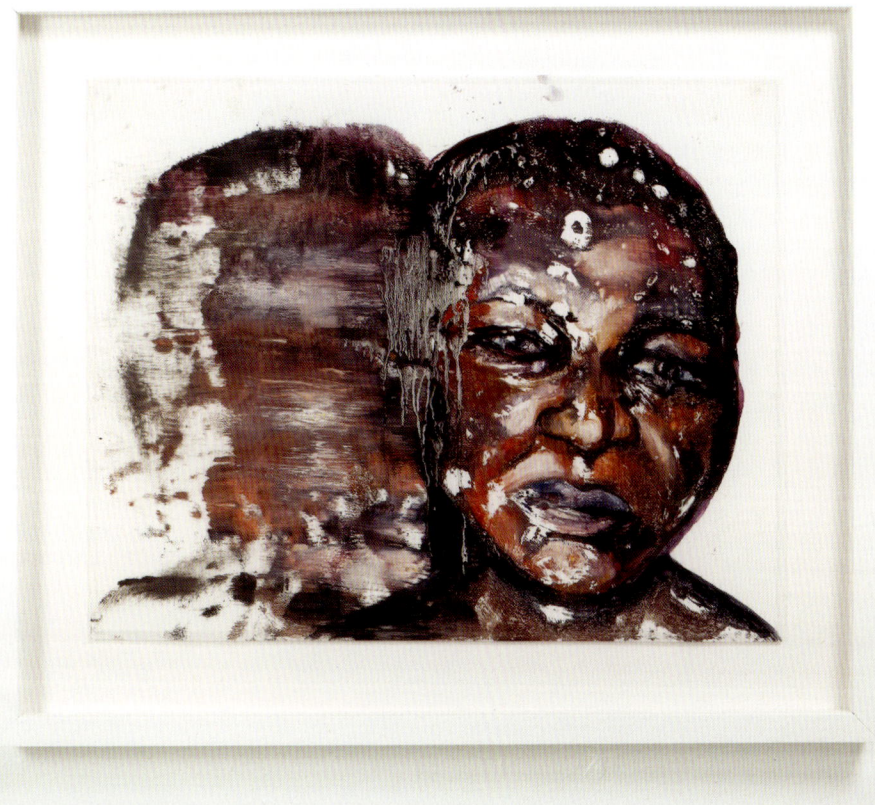

A native New Yorker and graduate of the School of the Art Institute of Chicago, Natalya Kochak delivers in her work a strong yet empathetic approach to humanity in her figurative art. Her childhood was characterized by movement and relocation throughout the United States, and her adult life has seen equal visits abroad. These experiences have trained Natalya's eye and hand to skillfully recognize and capture elements of personal, social, and cultural dramas, from the obtuse to the all but hidden.

Natalya has worked as an Artist in Residence in Berlin and Beijing. Additionally, she received a Kickstarter grant in 2011 for a public works project and the teaching of western artistic methods in Uganda. Now, a resident of Miami, Natalya continues in her practice, a synthesis of painting,

mixed media, and printmaking, to explore the patterns of contemporary culture and the subsequent homogenization and disintegration of the individual.

In the work that Natalya creates she seeks to represent the figure as the malleable reflection of a subject. The figure is set on paper, mylar, or wood panel in much the same way a person is placed into life; with flaws, unpredictable beauties, imprecise edges, and blurred definitions. In her work, however, she uses a mixture of silkscreen, mono print, and collage techniques – usually tools for consistent reproduction – to emphasize the individual imperfections of a single piece, be it an object or a person. While conceptual foundations ground her body of work, the overall emphasis is in the felt experience.

WWW.NATALYAKOCHAK.COM

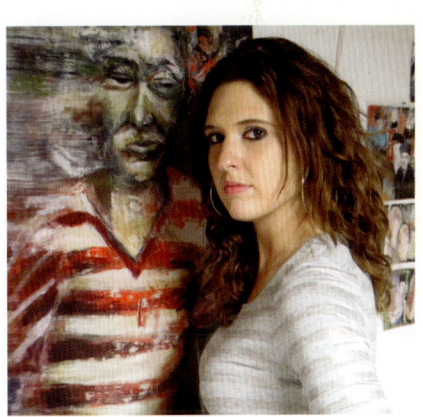

(facing page) Motion Blur #2 ●
Oil on Mylar, 23 x 18 in., 2014

Principal Image #1 ●
Oil on Mylar, 23 x 18 in., 2014

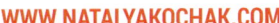

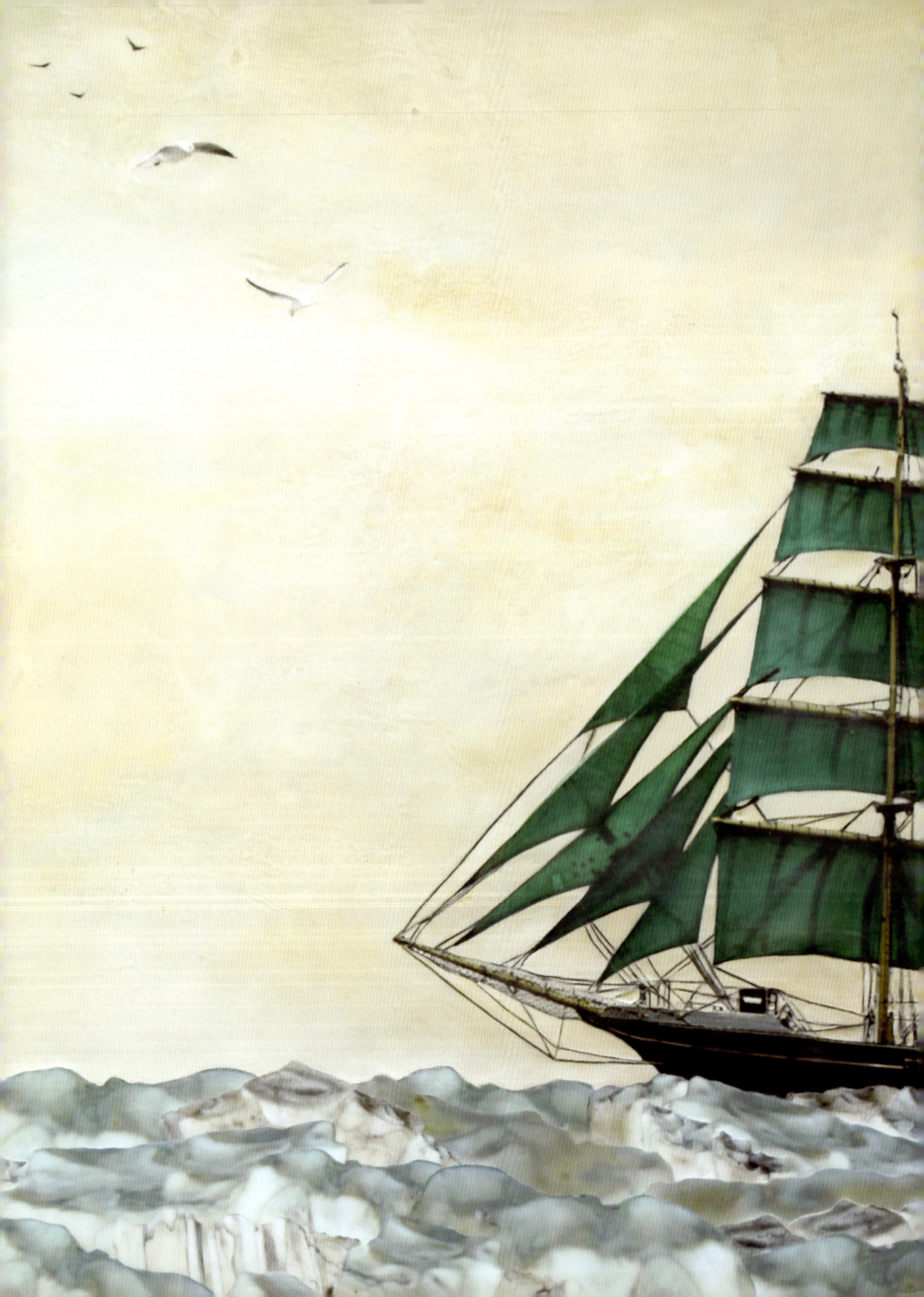

MIRANDA LAKE

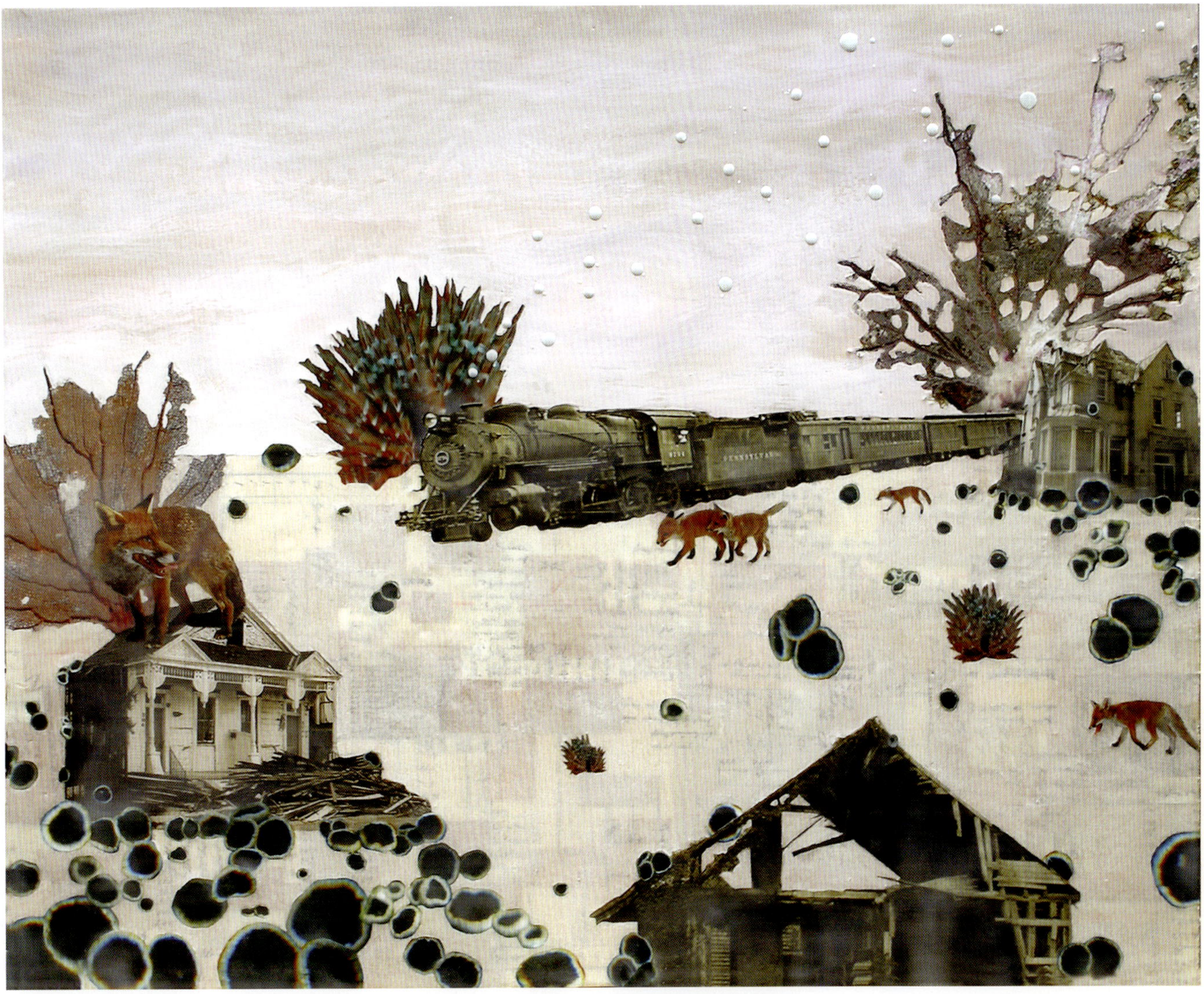

As a self-taught artist and designer based in New Orleans, Louisiana since 1998, my fine art work combines one of the oldest, most archival forms of painting with the digital darkroom creating a bridge between past and present, both personal and collective. I'm inspired not only by the crumbling grandeur of the Crescent City, but also by my love of biology, zoology, travel, sociocultural trending and graphic design.

WWW.MIRANDALAKE.COM

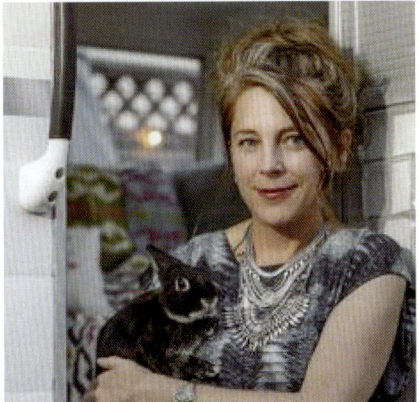

● **(facing page) Halfway Around the World From You**
Encaustic collage, 20 x 15 in., 2013

● **Coaches Long**
Encaustic collage, 24 x 30 in., 2008

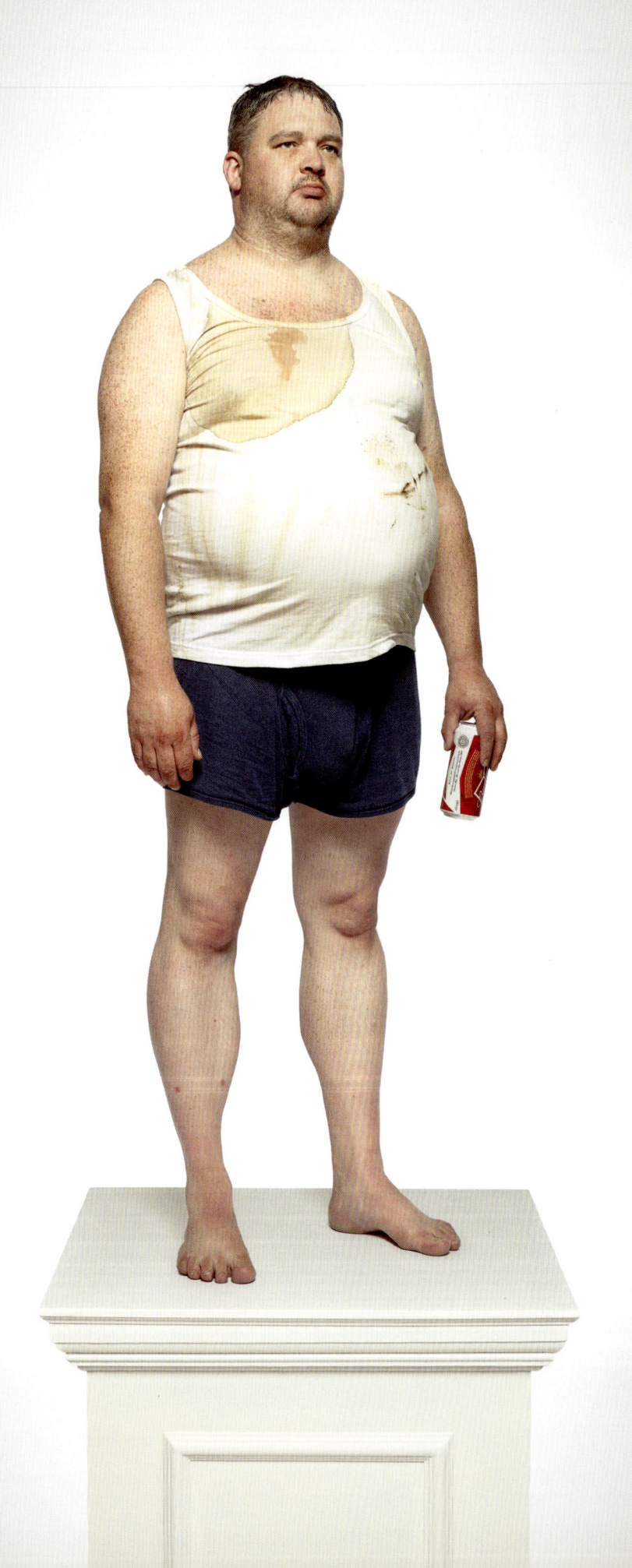

JOHN LAMACCHIA

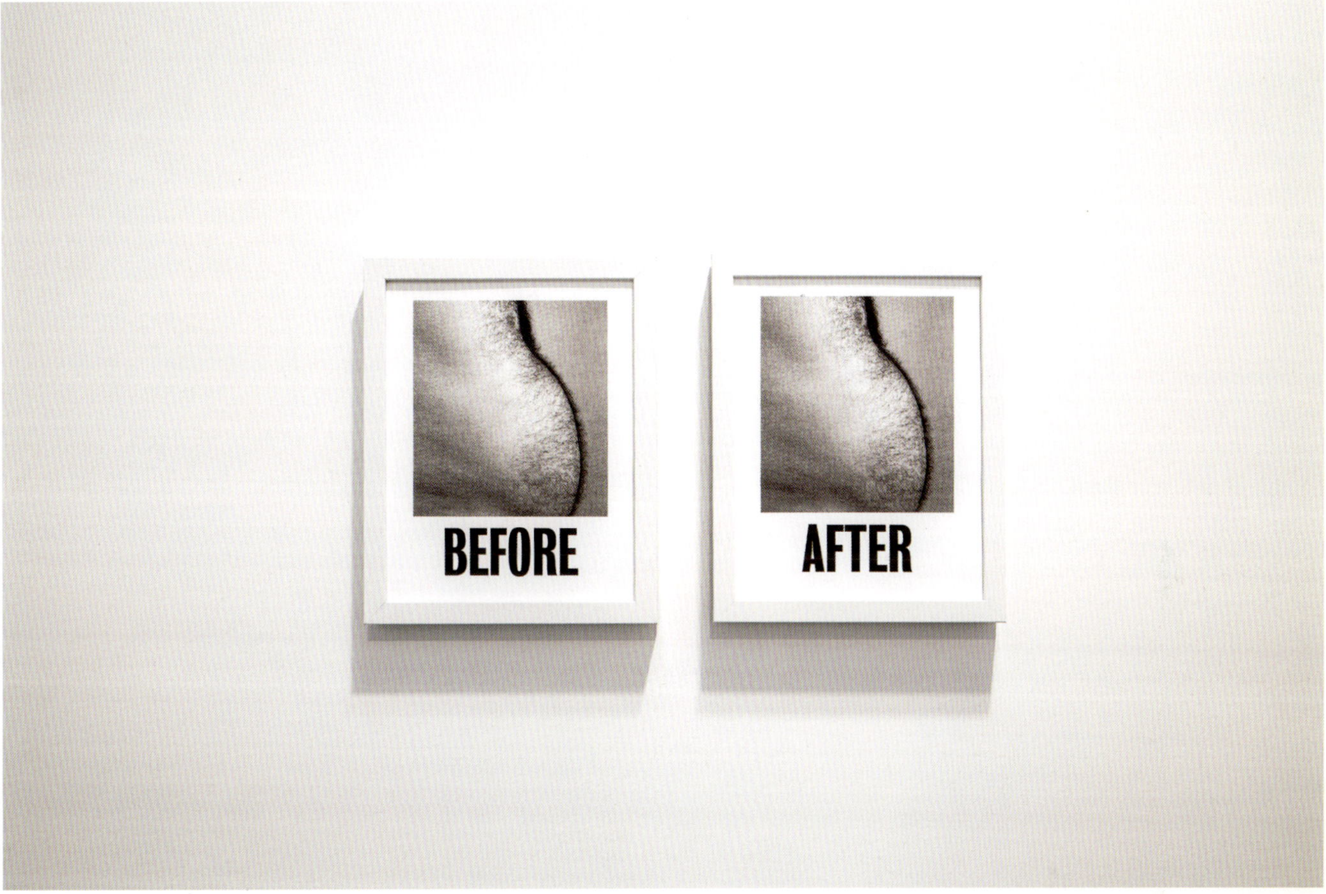

BEFORE AFTER

Akin to Grecian gods and goddesses gloriously posing in their signature demeanors, John LaMacchia's models from everyday life rise on clean cut pedestals, looking into the abyss. In his Statues series, LaMacchia appropriates antiquity's classical notion of aesthetics into a banality of contemporary consumerist culture. Stereotypes of the mundane – from the lady carrying grocery bags to the chunky man devouring his take-out food – gain preeminence and affirmation through the artist's sarcastic deliverance. Known as the perpetuators of victory and status, pedestals in this series elevate 'icons of today' in their trademark postures, not exhausted from wars or drudgery, but from strolling through the aisles or surfing around the channels.

In Before/After, John LaMacchia articulates the notion of purposelessness. Adopting mundane and inherently vapid commercial imagery used mostly in the promotion of dietary or cosmetic products, the artist dismantles what is familiar and convenient into a depiction of the extraneous. Studying the complex desire mechanism of human nature and its reflection on middle-class archetypes, Before/After cuts a slice from the everyday cycle of such figures. Such prosaic imagery coded into the mind of any TV or Internet user is challenged by failure of the end result. The correlation between then and now declines as quixotic anticipations encounter fruitless efforts. Humor, a principal aspect of LaMacchia's oeuvre, indeed claims the final stage, manifesting essential absurdity beneath it all.

WWW.JOHNLAMACCHIA.COM

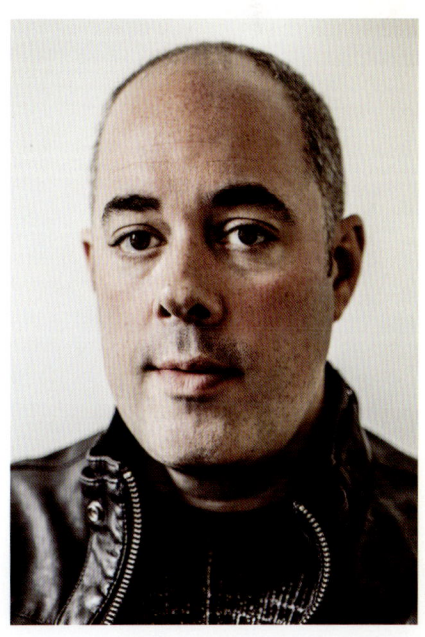

(facing page) Statue, 1 ●
C-print, 30 x 40 in., 2014

Before/After ●
Silkscreen, 8 x 10 in., 2013

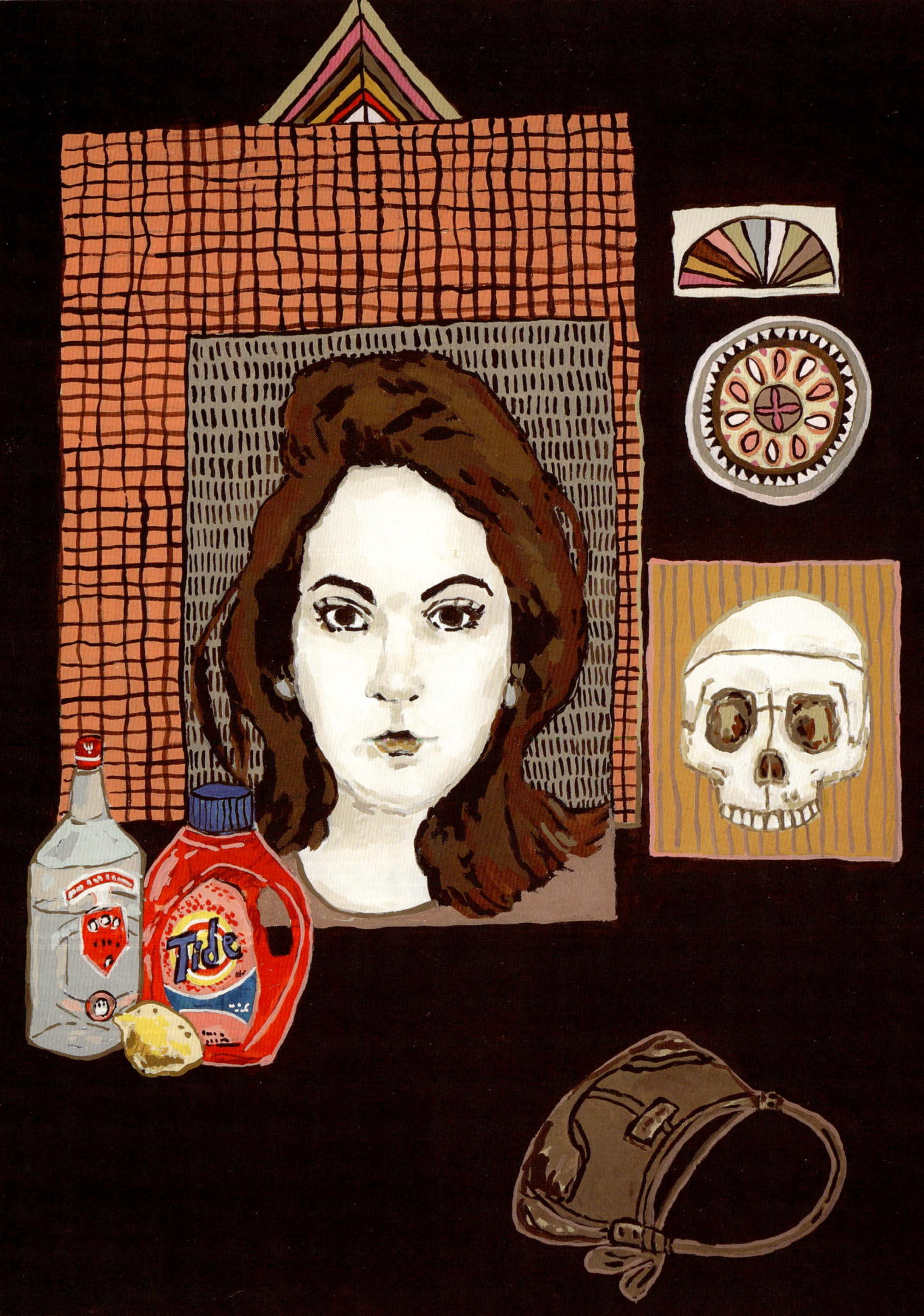

KIRSTIN LAMB

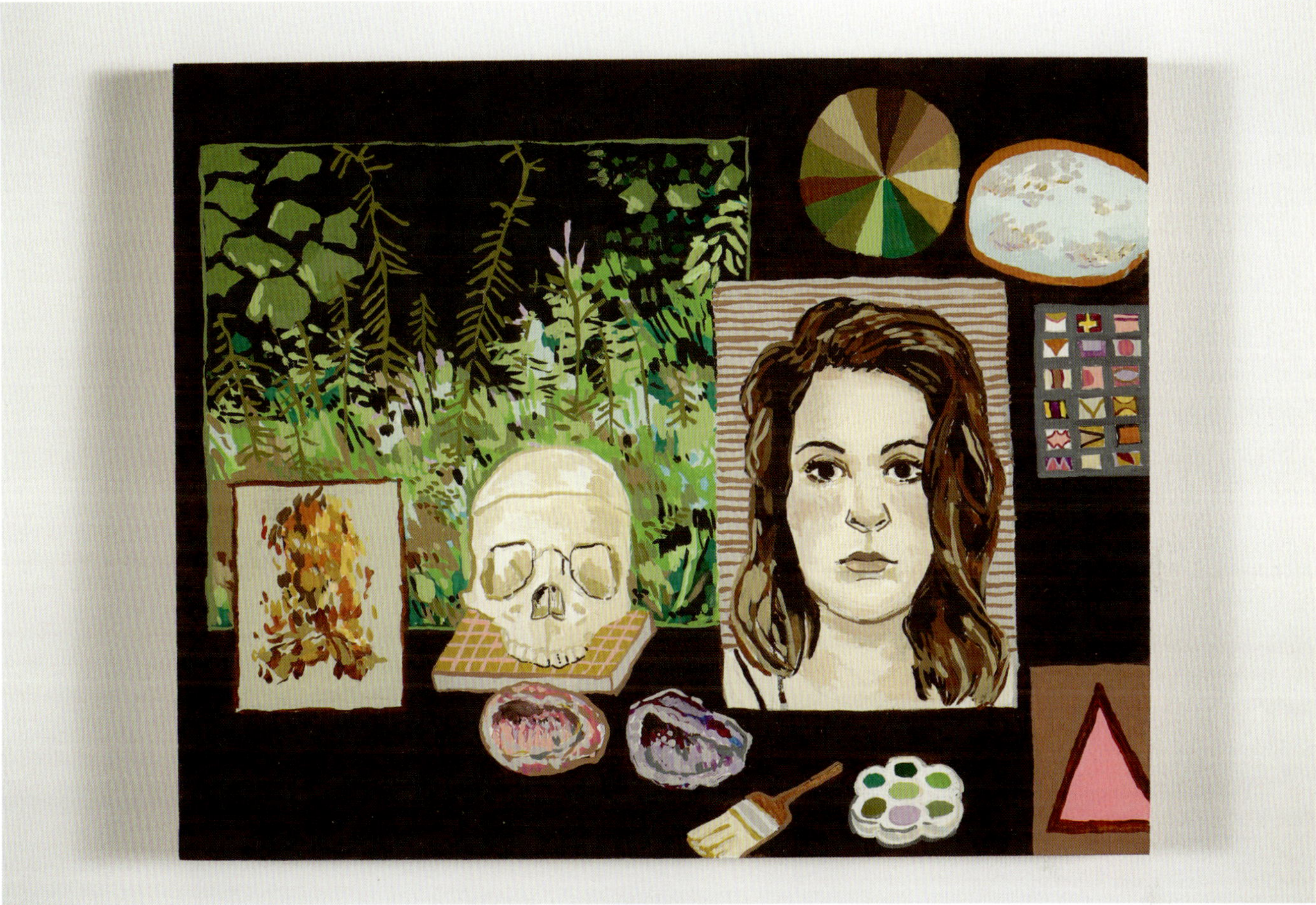

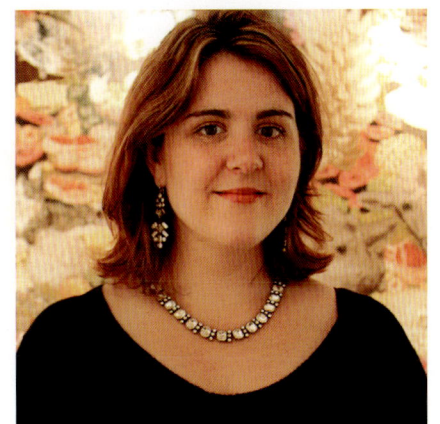

Kirstin is a painter living in Providence, Rhode Island and working in Pawtucket, Rhode Island. Kirstin became obsessed with classical still life and notions of stacking and heaping during her final year of graduate study in Painting at the Rhode Island School of Design in 2005. She began her studies as a literature student at Brown University, graduating in 2001 with Bachelors degrees in both Literatures in English and Visual Art.

WWW.KIRSTINLAMB.SQUARESPACE.COM

● **(facing page) Selfie w/ Tide, Vodka and Skull Painting**
Gouache on paper on panel, 8 x 10 in., 2015

● **Undergrowth**
Gouache on paper on panel, 8 x 10 in., 2014

SANDY LITCHFIELD

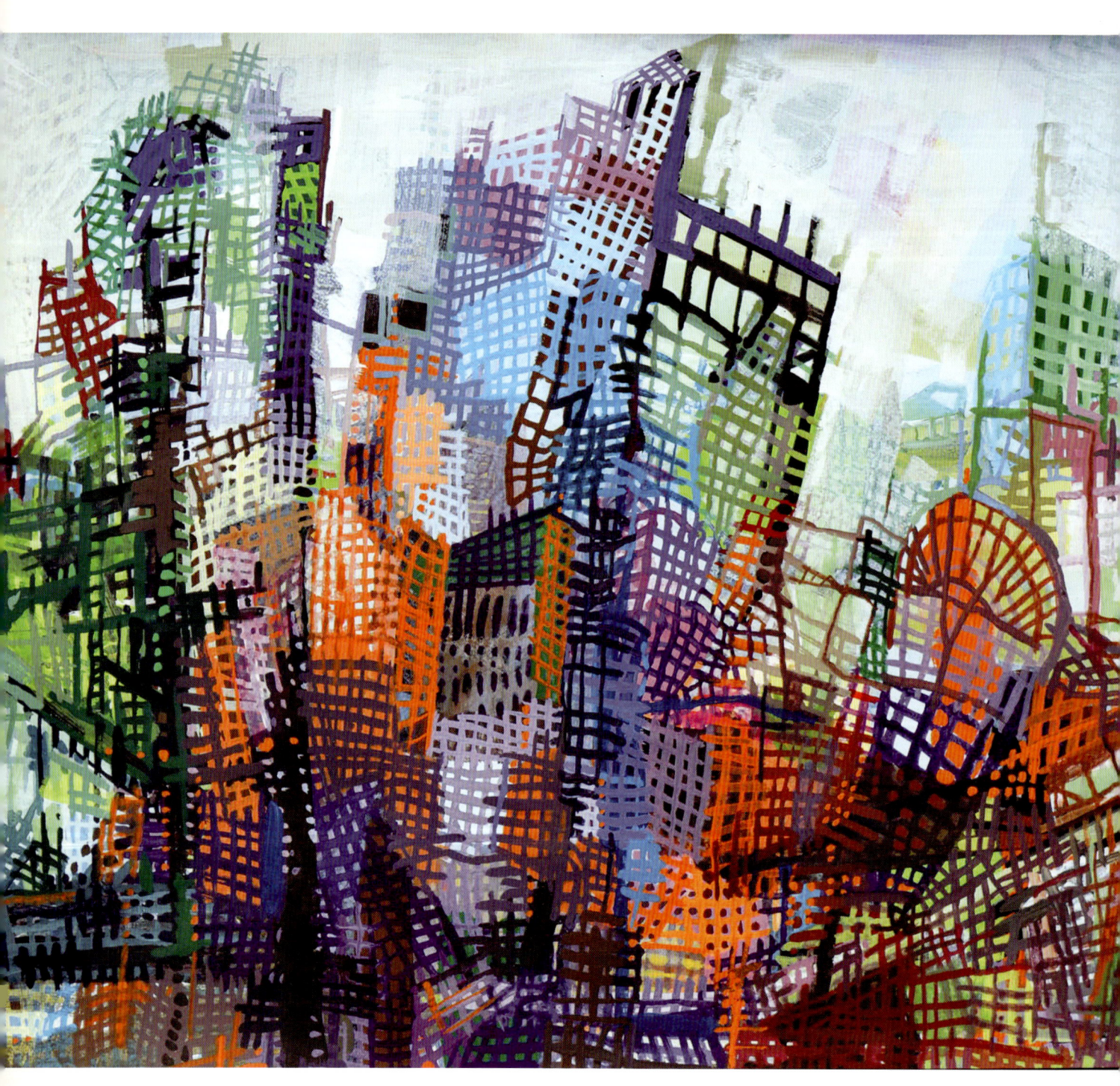

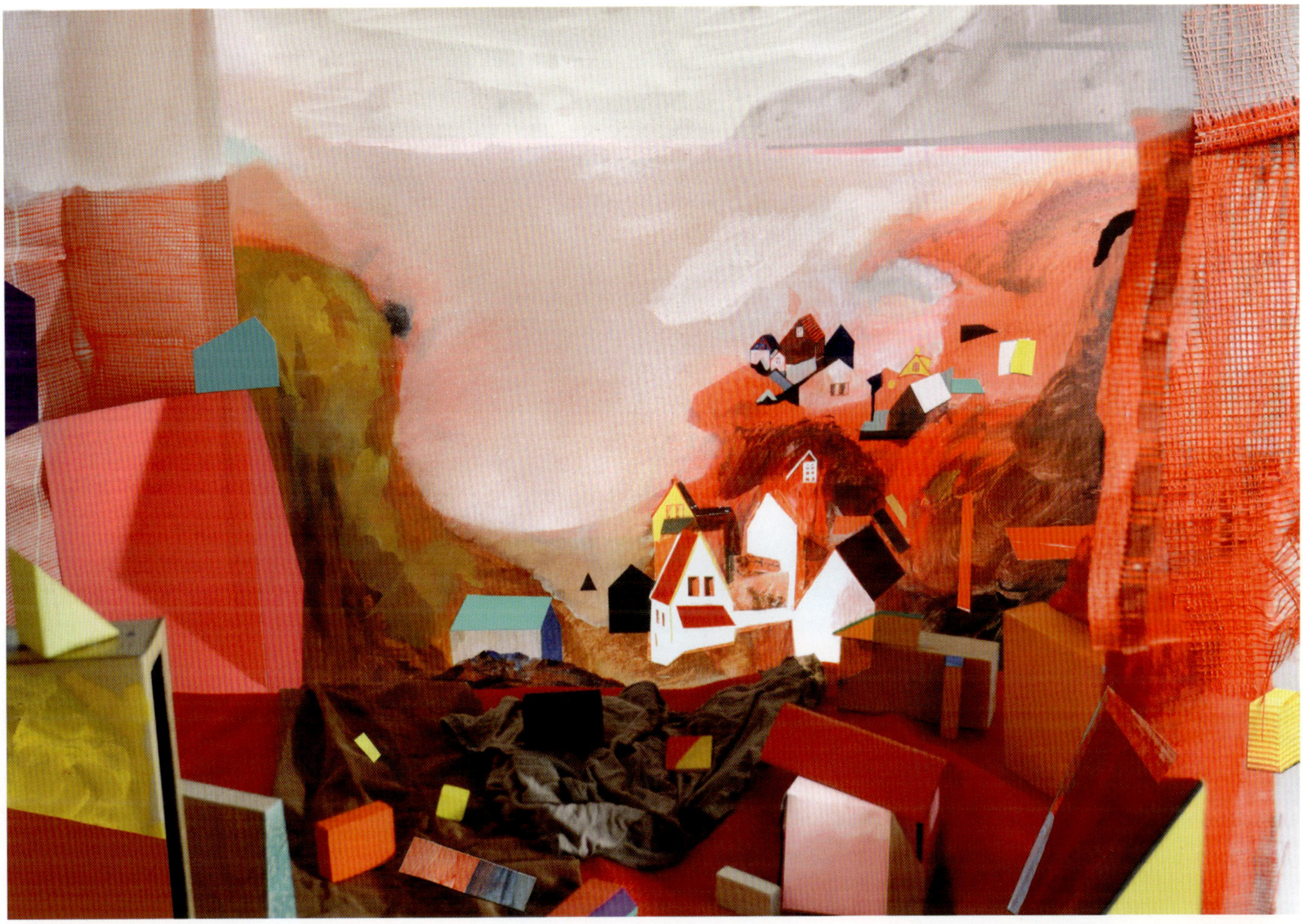

Born in New York, NY, Litchfield currently lives in Amherst, Massachusetts where she is an Assistant Professor in the Department of Architecture at the University of Massachusetts. She teaches art and design at UMass, Amherst College and Mount Holyoke College. Litchfield has exhibited in numerous museums including the DeCordova Museum, The Portland Art Museum and The Hunterdon Museum. Litchfield is a recipient of the Massachusetts Cultural Council Fellowship and the Puffin Foundation Artists Grant Award. In 2007 she attended the Skowhegan School of Painting and Sculpture. She's had solo exhibitions at Carroll and Sons Gallery in Boston, Metaphor Contemporary Art in Brooklyn as well as several New England Colleges. Her work has been selected for review by The Brooklyn Rail, New American Paintings and The Boston Globe.

WWW.SANDYLITCHFIELD.COM

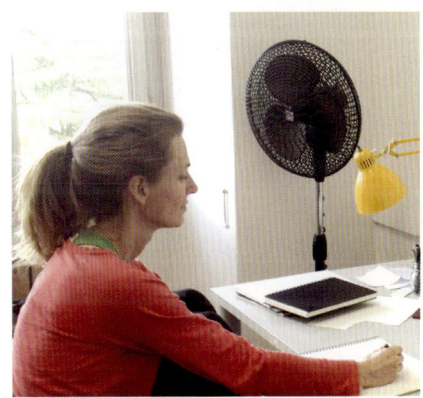

(facing page) Urban Fabric ●
Gouache on paper, 16 x 20 in., 2015

Setting High Hopes ●
Collage, gouache, spray paint, digital print on paper,
22 x 34 in., 2014

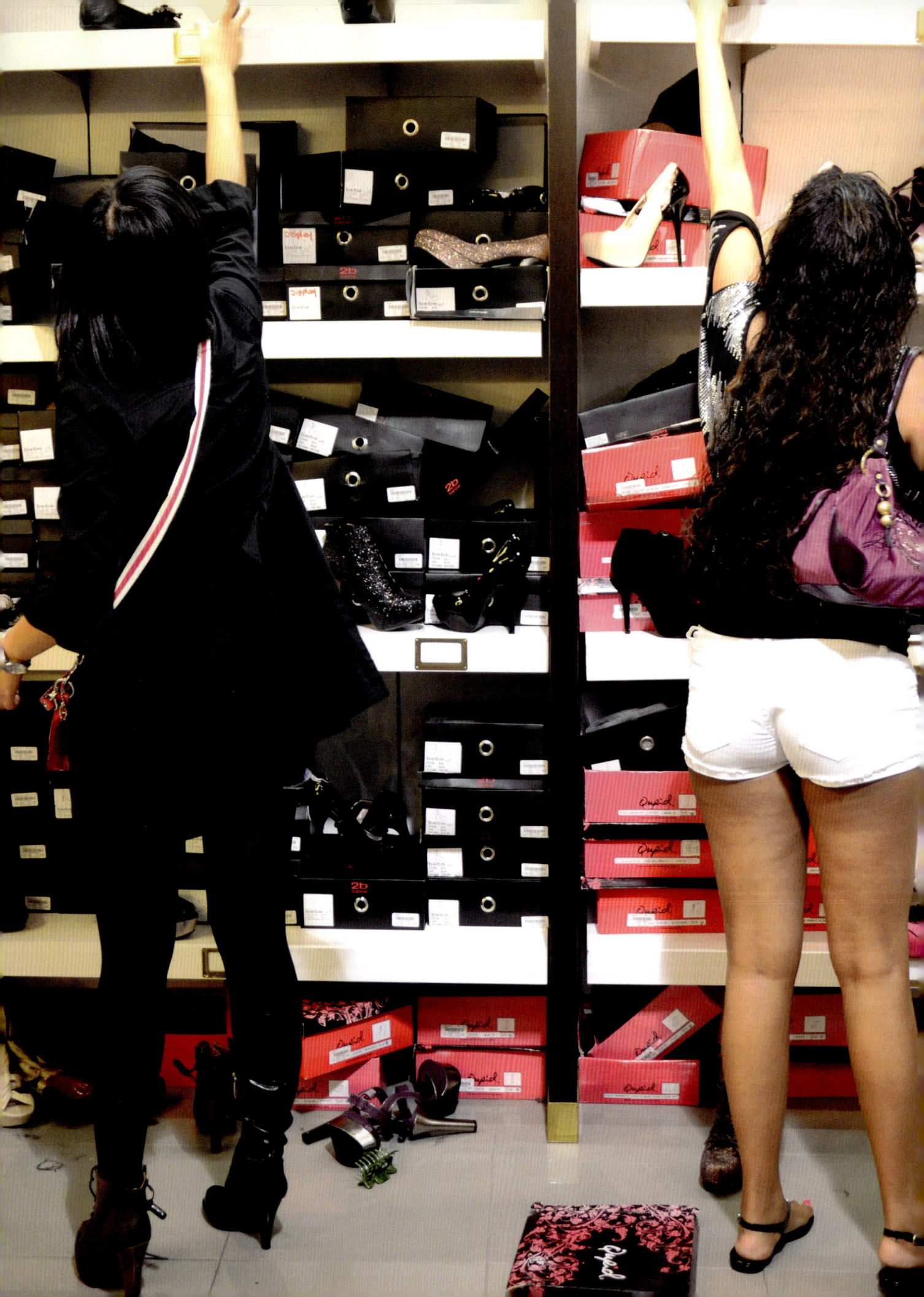

SHERRI LITTLEFIELD

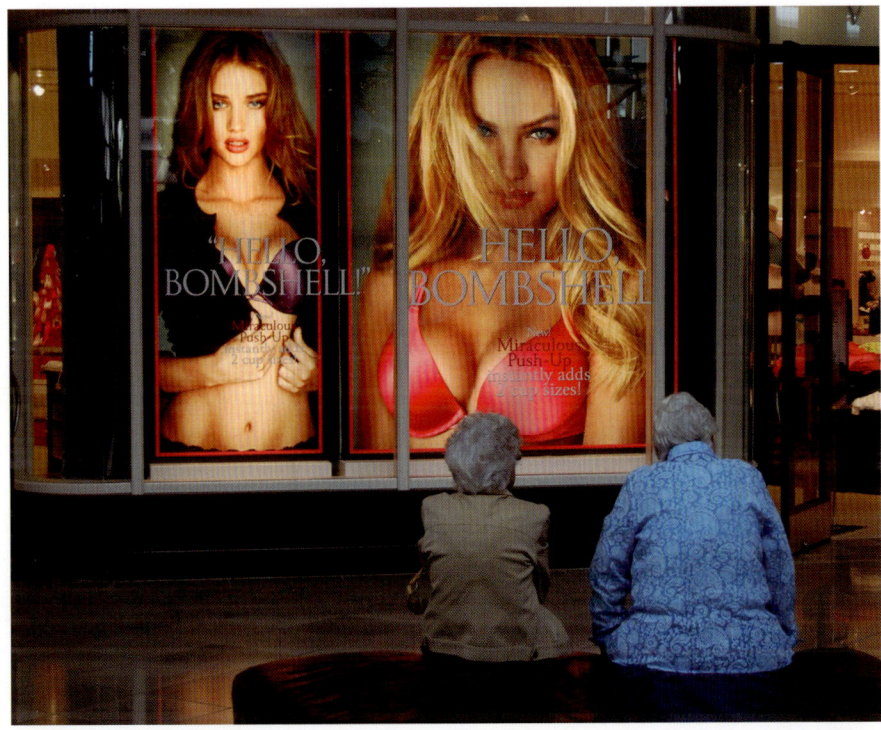

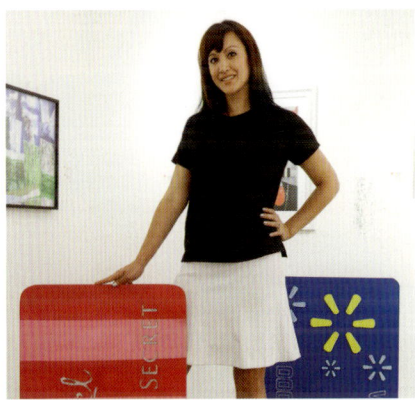

"My art is both a celebration and commentary on the beauty industry and contemporary consumerism. The individuals photographed in the "shopping series" are unaware of their participation in the creation of my work. The large-scale cards in the "swipe" series represent excessive debt Americans face from opening retail credit cards. I do not intend to exploit the subjects or places that I photograph; rather my work comes from a very natural understanding of this environment based on several years of modeling and working in a major department store. I attempt to attach multiple emotions of empathy, humor, and sometimes sympathy – to the moments I capture."

Sherri Littlefield was born in 1987 in Milwaukee, Wisconsin. Photographs from her "Shopping Series" have been awarded and exhibited internationally, including the Brighton Photo Biennial, the Orlando Museum of Art and the Aperture Foundation in New York.

Littlefield earned her MFA in Photography from the University of Central Florida and her BS in Studio Art at Florida State University. An internship at the University of Wisconsin-Madison's Tandem Press, and coordinating events with Snap! Orlando sparked her interest in galleries and art business. After graduate school, Littlefield moved to Atlanta and was soon hired in the sculpture department at SCAD.

Sherri currently lives in Brooklyn with her husband, Andrew. In addition to creating art, Littlefield also manages JanKossen Contemporary Gallery and works at Parsons School of Design.

WWW.SHERRILITTLEFIELD.COM

(facing page) Aldo ●
Digital photograph, 20 x 30 in., 2011

Hello, Bombshell ●
Digital photograph, 16 x 20 in., 2009

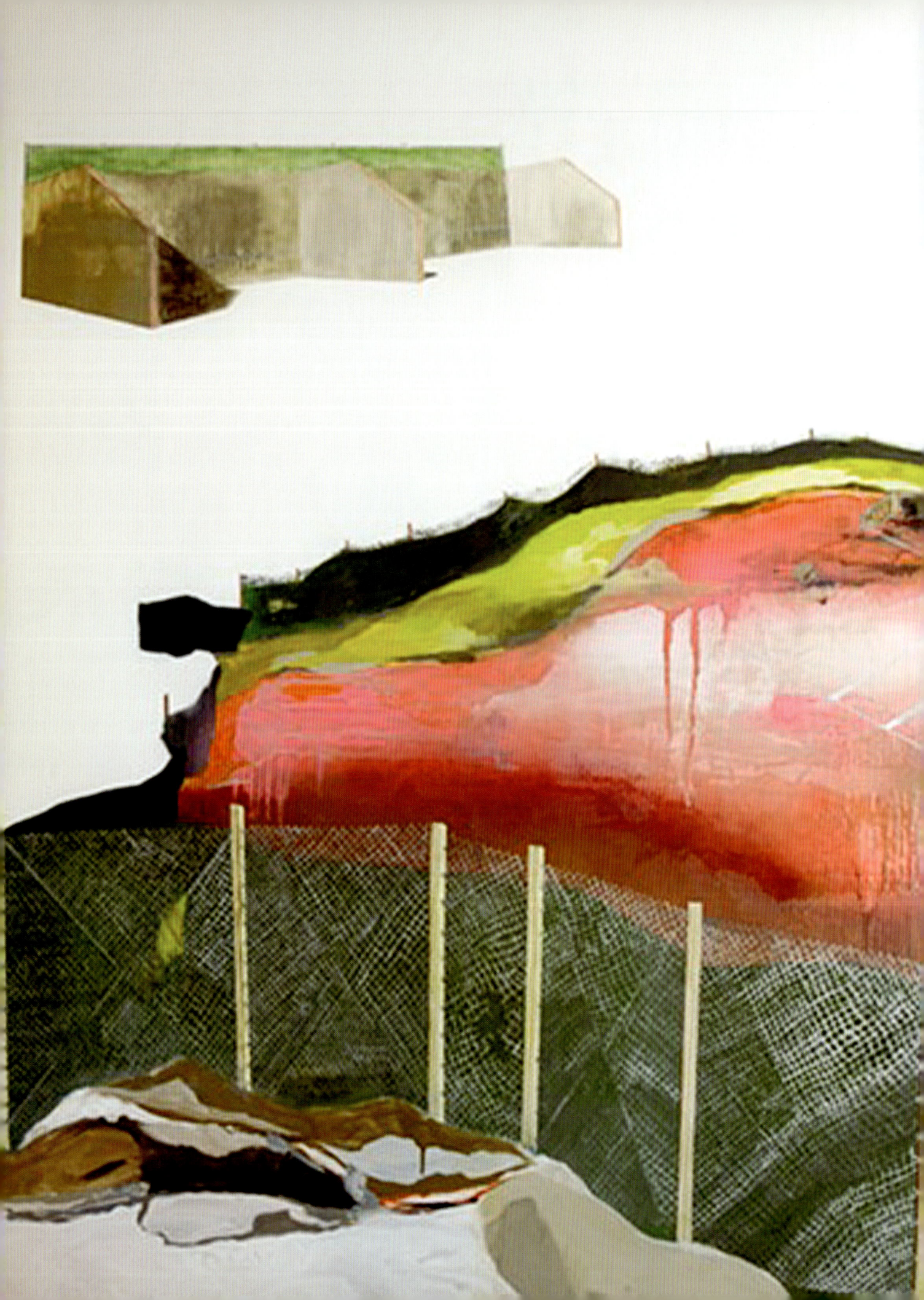

ARIEL LOCKSHAW

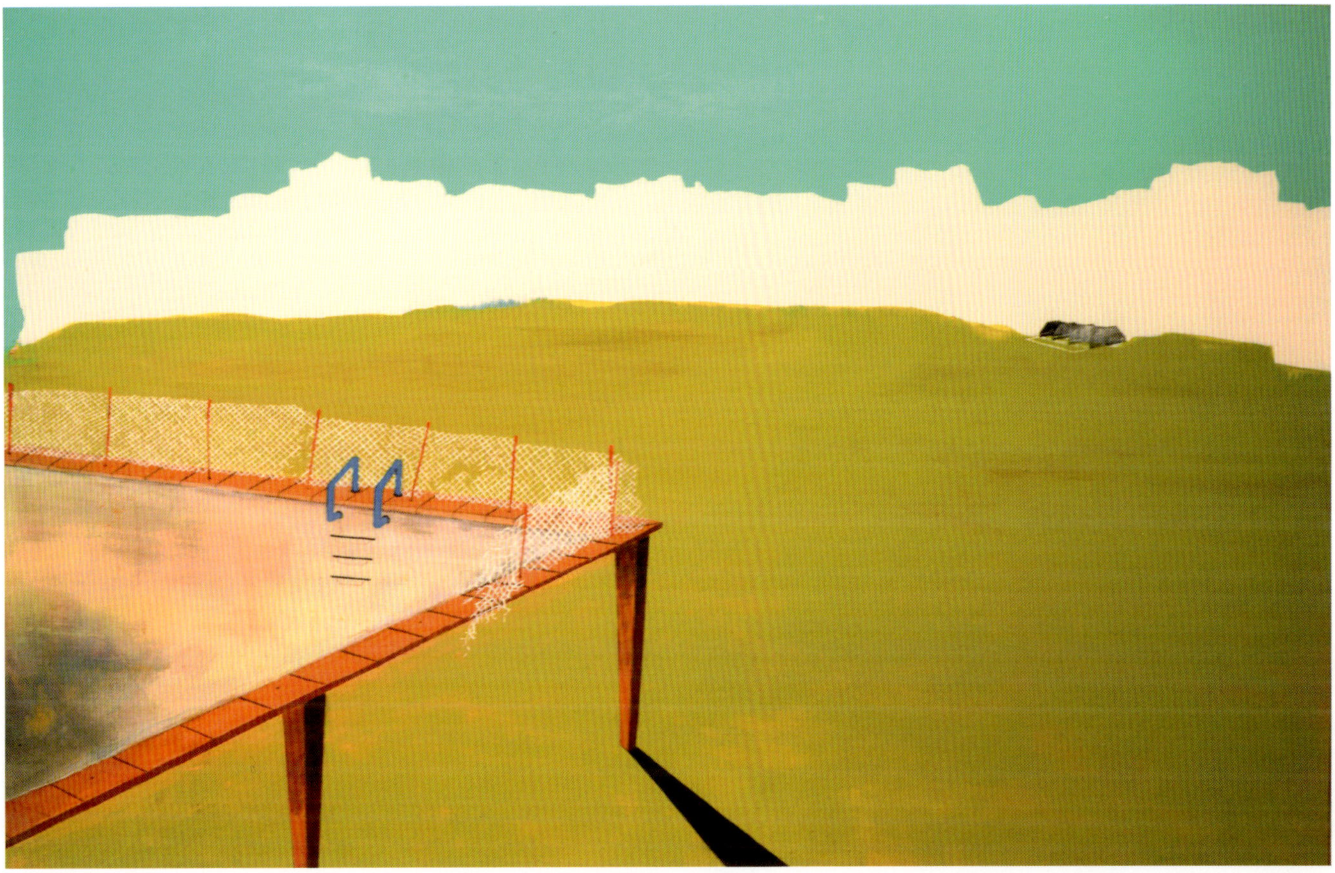

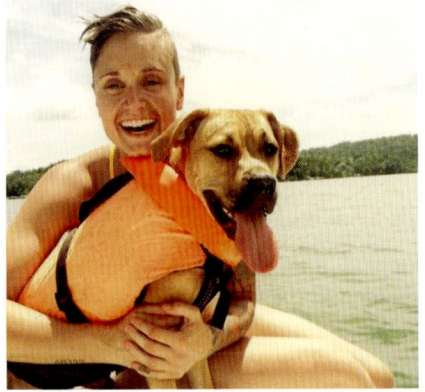

Ariel Lockshaw is a California native and second year graduate student in Painting & Drawing at the University of Georgia's Lamar Dodd School of Art, where she teaches Beginning Painting. True to her West Coast roots, she enjoys surfing, skateboarding, competitive swimming, writing and creating music, and maintains an intimate relationship with the ever evolving local landscape that has birthed so many of her projects and processes. Some of her current conditions/inspirations are that she is teaching a beginning painting class at UGA, training for an open water swimming race in New York, and obsessing over her rescue dog, Scout.

(facing page) Contagious
Oil, Acrylic, Aerosol, Graphite on Panel,
49 x 41 in., 2014

In Your Backyard
Oil, acrylic, enamel on panel, 32 x 48 in., 2014

WWW.ARIELLOCKSHAW.COM

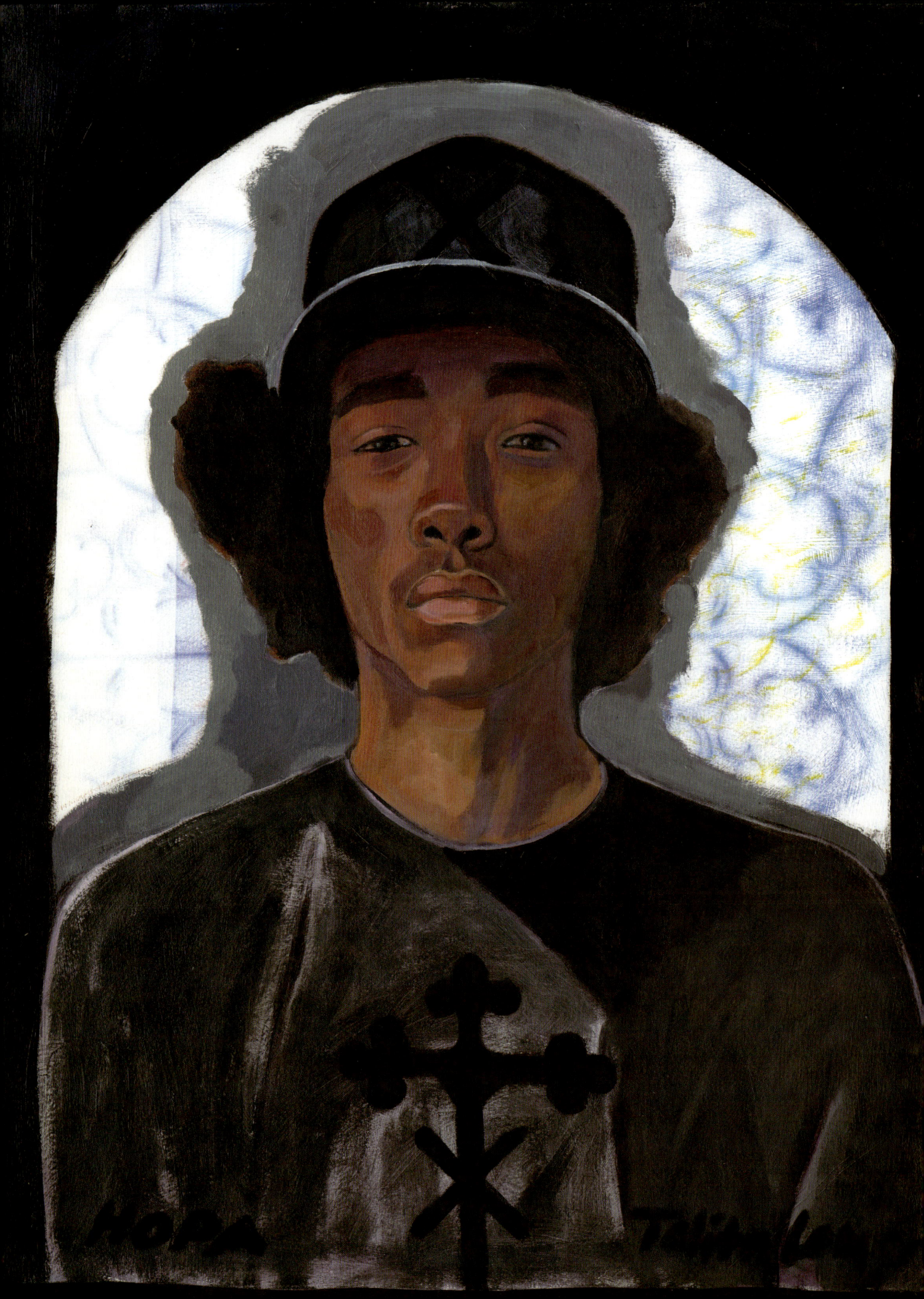

TALITA LONG

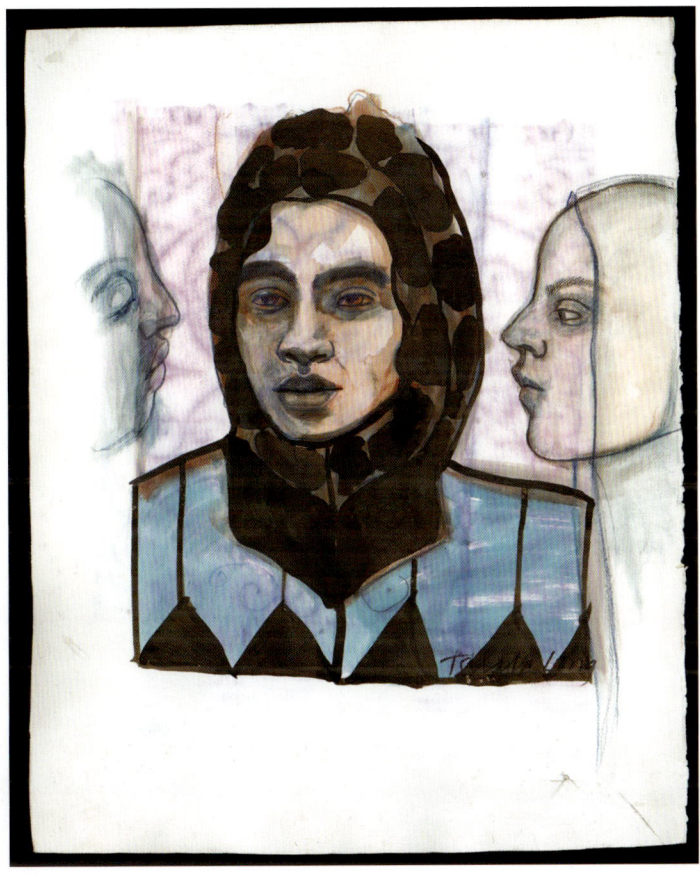

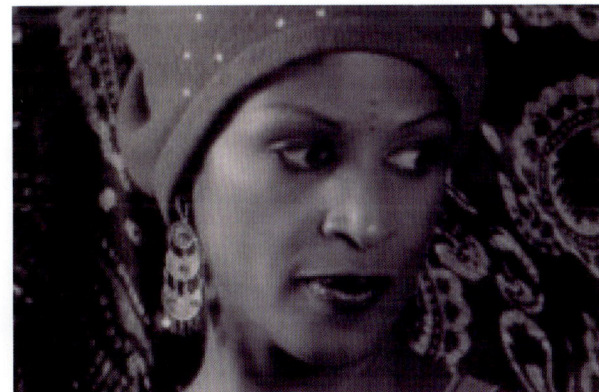

● **(facing page) Hopa**
Oil on paper, 26 x 21 in., 2014

● **Two Angels**
Mixed medium on paper, 18.5 x 20 in., 2014

"My images and my music are the eyes and sounds of where I have traveled and where I hope to venture."

Talita Long has been studying, creating and teaching art for over 40 years. Born in Brooklyn , New York, of Trinidadian parents, Long grew up immersed in the culture of the West Indies... Dance, Calypso Music and the Carnival played an important early influence in her work. Whatever the inspiration, Longs work portrays people and events through a lens of history and fantasy, leaving us not with a clear narrative, but rather a delightful mystery with its meaning open to interpretation.......

Long studied at a number of leading institutions including The Art Students League in Manhattan, Howard University, DC, School of Visual Arts, N.Y., Cooper Union N.Y., where she earned a BFA in Fine Arts.

Through the encouragement from Professor Klabunde at Cooper Union, She relocated to Iowa City and finished a four year study with the Master Printer, Maurice Lasansky and earned an MA and MFA in Printmaking in 1978 at The University of Iowa .Long was the first African American female to earn that degree at the University of Iowa. Long was also mentored by the International artist and Professor, Ben Moss.

After graduation, Long and her eight year daughter Nia relocated to Los Angeles. Long worked for many art organizations. LAUSD's ,Performing Tree, UCLA's Artsreach, Los Angeles County Museum, Afro American Museum. Long was a visiting artist at Dartmouth College and was a professor at Savannah College of Art and Design in the Graduate Painting Department for one year. Through all of her opportunities, Long continued to produce a wide range of work in painting, watercolor, drawing as well as most forms of printmaking. Her work continues to be about the figure, passionately. For a number of years, Long worked with Latin American Artist at the Self Help Graphics Studios in South Central Los Angeles,producing a body of Mono-Prints and Mono Silkscreen prints.

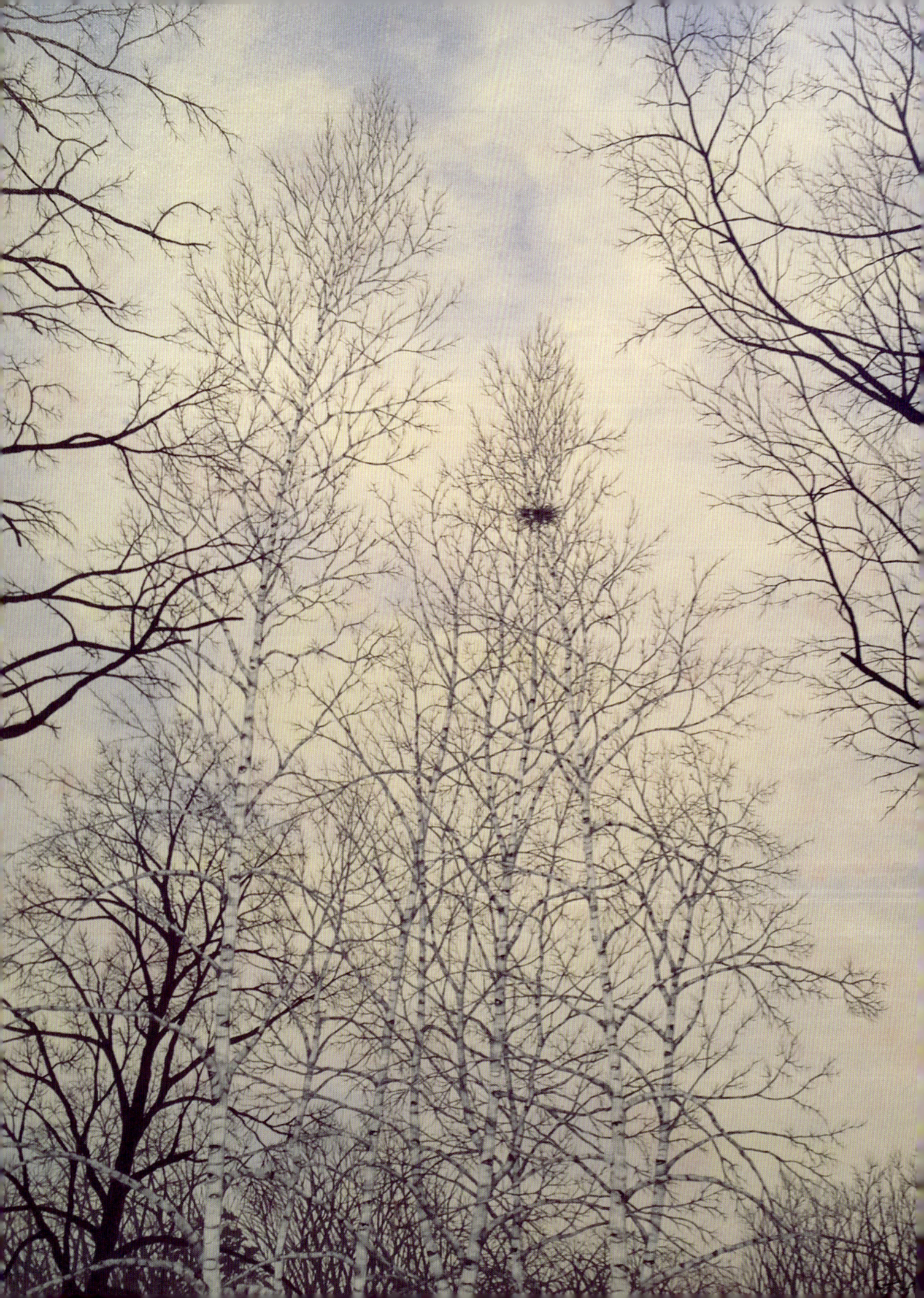

CJ LORI

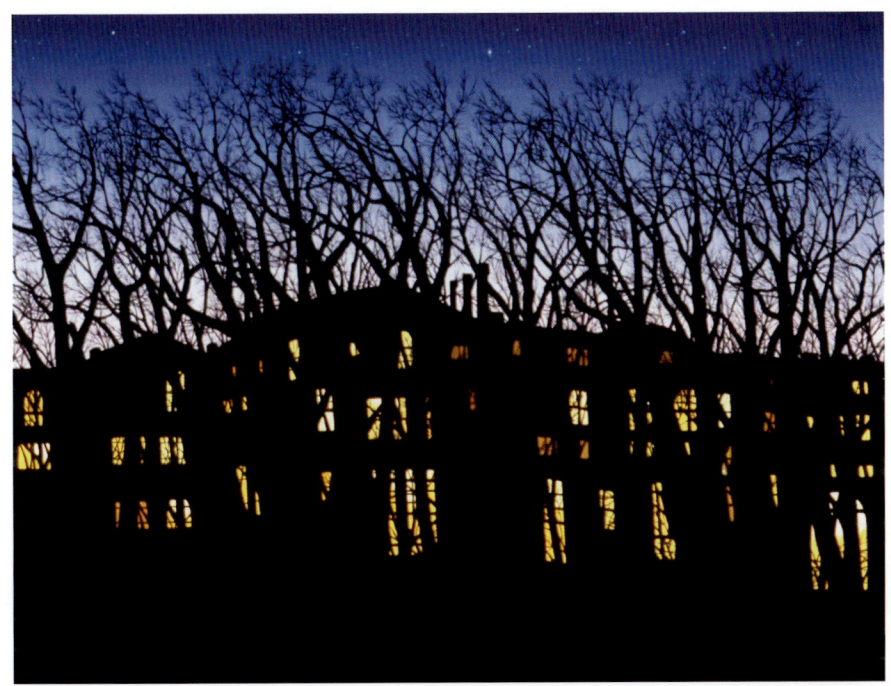

C. J. Lori is an oil painter living in Brookline, Massachusetts. Her work reflects her interest in literature, anthropology and psychology, as well as an abiding fascination with the natural world. Often called "Neo-surrealism" or "magic realism," Ms. Lori's paintings explore the complex relationship between humanity and the environment. She exaggerates or distorts color, form and composition to emphasize sensations that are often contradictory: clarity and mystery, excitement and sorrow, beauty and decay.

Ms. Lori's artwork has been exhibited in solo and group shows throughout New England, and in New York and Chicago. She had a solo exhibition, C. J. Lori: LEAVING, in May, 2015 at Galatea Fine Art in Boston. Her work has been shown at the Danforth Museum in Framingham, MA in OFF THE WALL, Community of Artists, and Figure, Fantasy and Illusion, Selections from the Arthur S. Goldberg Collection. In 2007, she won first prize in Paint!, a national exhibition juried by artist Gerry Bergstein at the South Shore Arts Center.

Ms. Lori is represented by Lyman-Eyer Gallery, Galatea Fine Art in Boston, and 13 Forest Gallery in Arlington, MA. She served in 1997 as First Vice-President of the National Women's Caucus for Art, and for several years as President of the Boston Chapter. Her other interests include reading (especially Henry James), traveling, watching professional football, and walking her dog.

WWW.CJLORI.COM

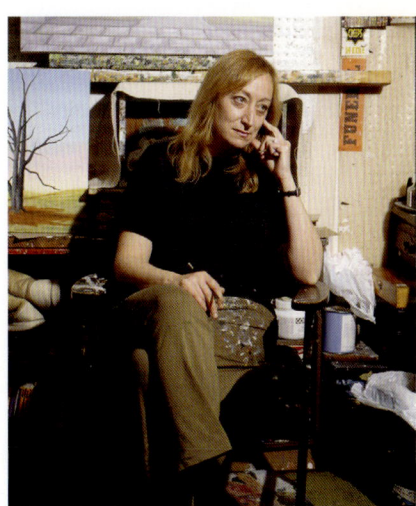

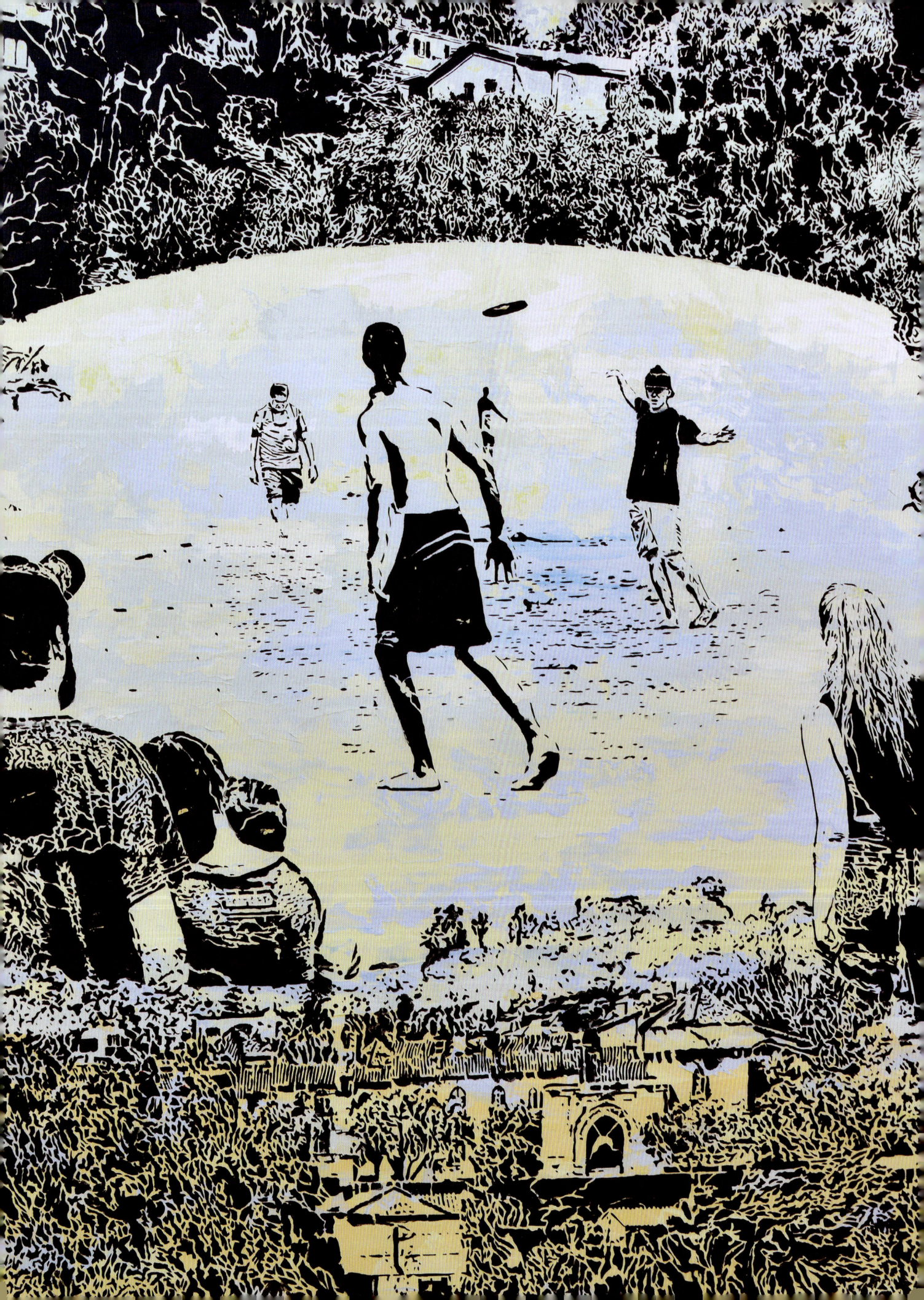

LUCINDA LUVAAS

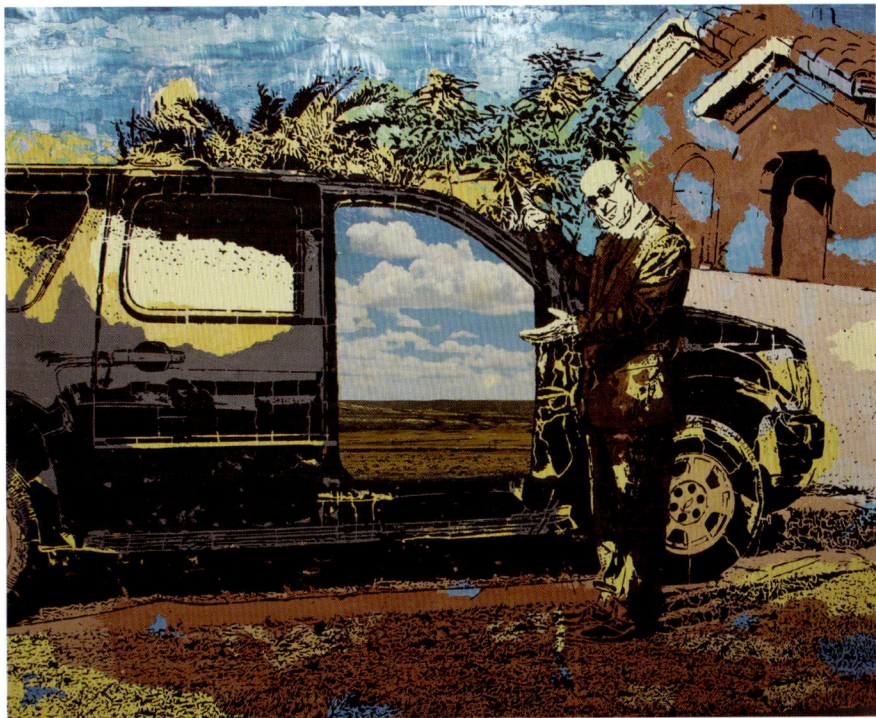

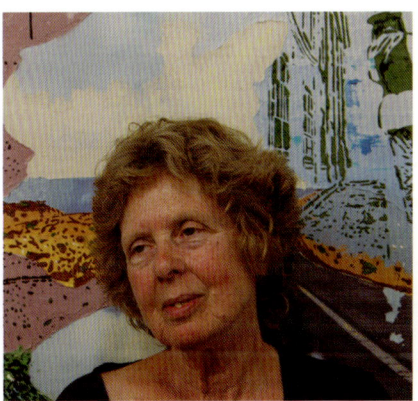

Lucinda Luvaas is a multimedia artist working in fine art and video. Her films and fine art have been screened both nationally and abroad. New York University, The New York Studio School, The Art Student's League, The New School for Social Research. Ms. Luvaas has taught studio painting and mural painting workshops at UCSD, La Jolla, CA, Queens College, the New York City Department of Parks & Recreation, National University, San Diego Campus, CA, John Jay College of Criminal Justice, New York, NY, Teachers & Writers Collaborative, New York, NY, Learning Through An Expanded Arts Program, New York, NY, New York State Community Art Centers and the Southern Vermont Art Center, Manchester, VT. Her multimedia works are part of the Elizabeth A. Sackler Center for Feminist Art at the Brooklyn Museum.

"I've always seen myself as an outsider, an observer, since I was little. I remember being four years old and standing outside my home raking leaves in autumn and whispering, "I will never be like them." I hated the cliques who taunted me in grade school. So, I learned to fend for myself, sharpen my imagination and be alert. I always needed to swim in my own lane, and carve my own story. I very naturally chose art as a way of life because of my need for individual expression."

My first love was drama and film. My visual art reflects my penchant for dramatic scenes and narratives. In addition, I've been musically inclined all my life. I now compose electronic sound not only for my video art pieces, but music written for varied instruments. All my life I've been creatively engaged in making things, and working with others to express their individual hopes and dreams. I truly believe that the imagination and its many forms of expression is mankind's greatest achievement.

WWW.LUCINDALUVAASNEWWORK.COM

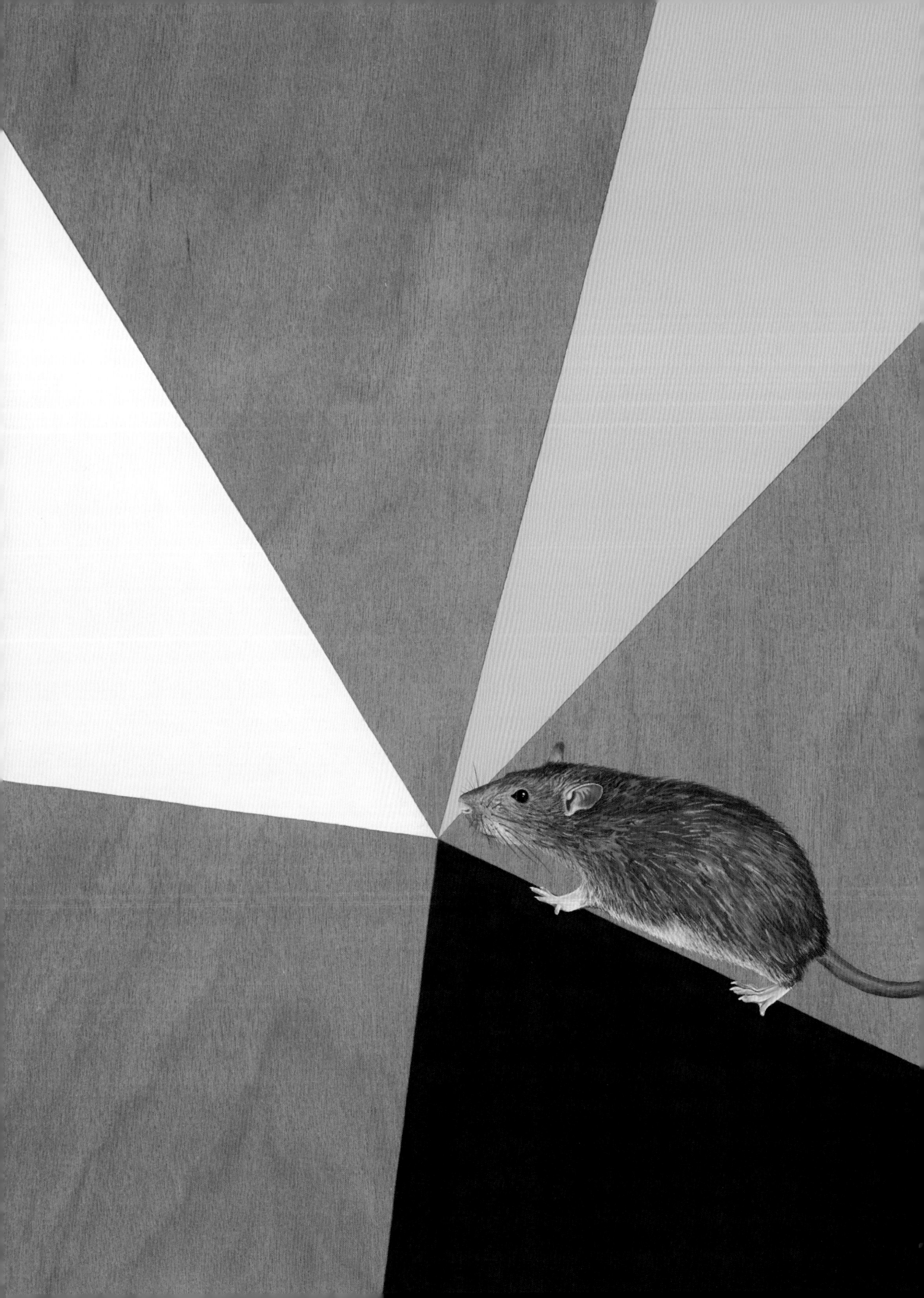

KARA MARIA

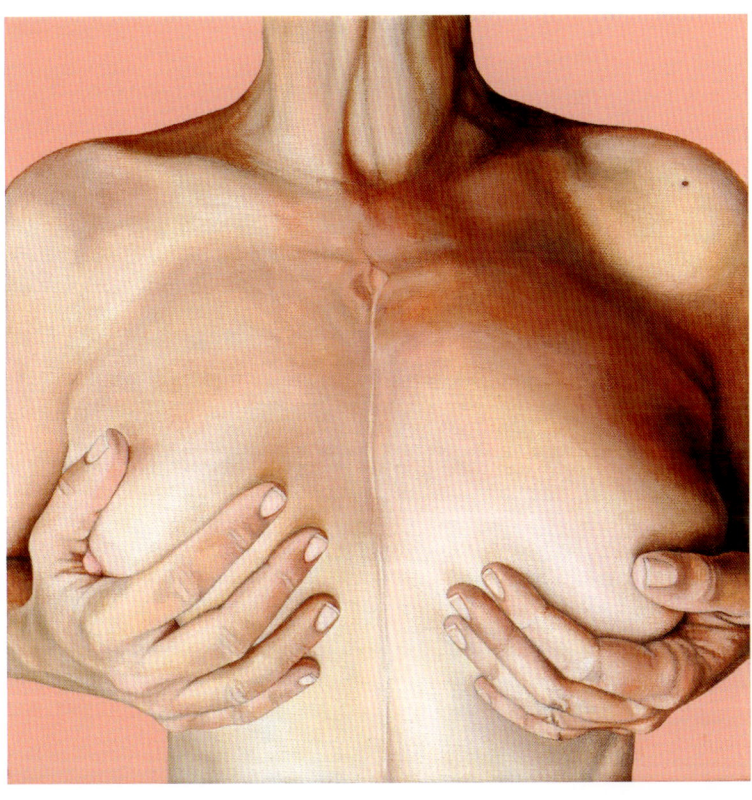

Kara Maria is a visual artist working in painting and mixed media. Her work reflects on political topics—feminism, war, and the environment. She borrows from the broad vocabulary of contemporary painting; blending geometric shapes, vivid hues, and abstract marks, with representational elements.

Maria received her BA and MFA from the University of California, Berkeley. She has exhibited work in solo and group shows throughout the United States at venues including the San Francisco Museum of Modern Art; the Cantor Center at Stanford University; the Contemporary Arts Museum in Houston, Texas; the San Jose Institute of Contemporary Art; and the Katonah Museum of Art in New York; among many others. Her work has garnered critical attention in the Los Angeles Times, the San Francisco Chronicle, and Art in America. Maria has been awarded artist residencies at the Montalvo Arts Center, Recology Artist in Residence Program, Djerassi Resident Artists Program, and at the de Young's Artist Studio. She has been a recipient of many awards and honors, including a grant from Artadia, an Eisner Prize in Art from UC Berkeley, and the Masterminds Grant from SF Weekly. Her work is included in the permanent collections of the Crocker Art Museum in Sacramento, the San Jose Museum of Art, the de Saisset Museum at Santa Clara University, the di Rosa in Napa, Mills College Art Museum in Oakland, and the Nevada Museum of Art in Reno, among others. Maria lives and works in San Francisco; and is represented by Catharine Clark Gallery.

WWW.KARAMARIA.COM

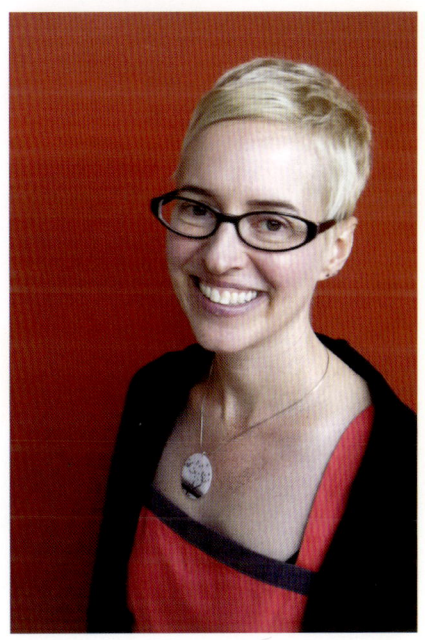

(facing page) Rat ●
Acrylic on wood, 20.75 x 16.5 in., 2014

Breat Portrait #4 ●
Acrylic on canvas, 12 x 12 in., 2012

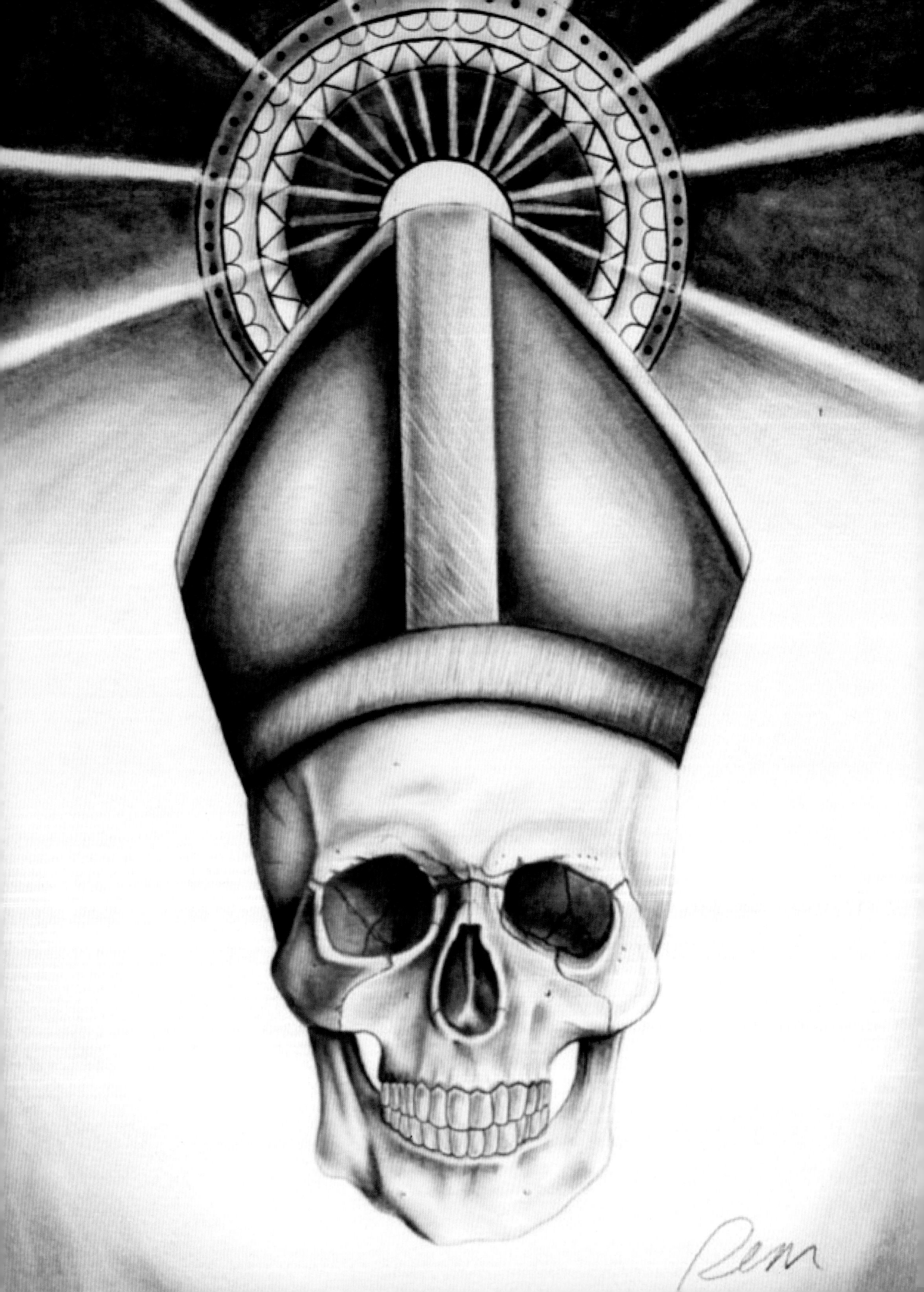

ROBYN MARSHALL

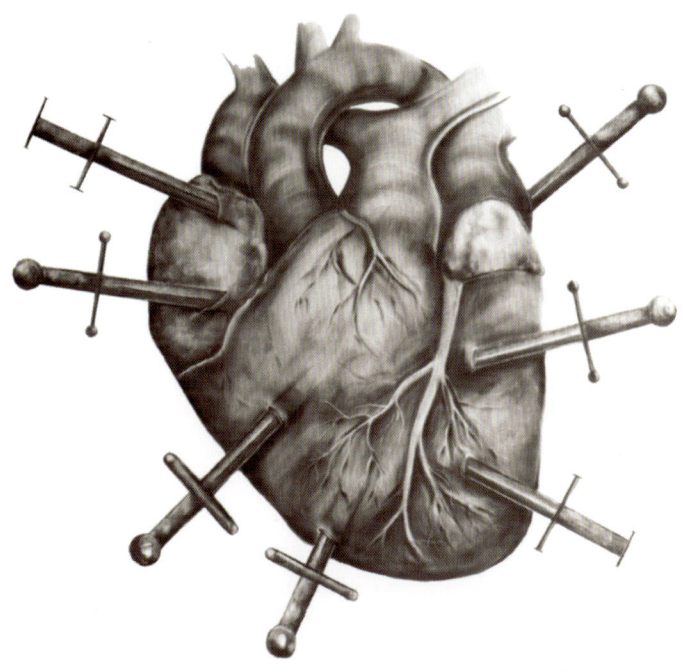

"I have always felt most at home with a pencil in hand, drawing medical illustrations from my father's old biology textbooks. I find the beauty in contrasts with graphite powder and charcoal. I like to show that there can be a soft side to what is usually so hard and strong, like bones. I like to bring what's hiding underneath to the surface and make you face what's hiding. I tone down the graphite to bring emotion to the piece or adjust the scale to increase the dramatic effect. My goal as an artist is to bring beauty to the misunderstood and unseen. I want to make you think in an intriguing new way about the unusual, hidden and forgotten."

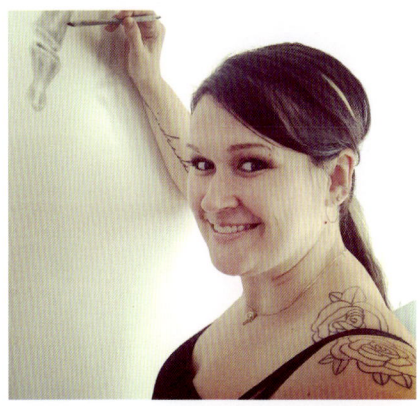

Born in 1983 and raised in Ottawa, Ontario, Robyn had an early love of the arts, despite of never having any formal training or fine art schooling. Her childhood dream was to illustrate medical textbooks and she was always fascinated with skulls and the human body. After settling down in British Columbia and starting a family, Robyn decided to pursue her dream. In July of 2014, on the wall in her kitchen, next to her children eating breakfast at the table, she started her series of large scale medical illustrations and has been going strong ever since. She has been published in over five art reference books and magazines and has been involved in multiple exhibits around Vancouver.

**WWW.ARTISTROBYNMARSHALL.
WORDPRESS.COM**

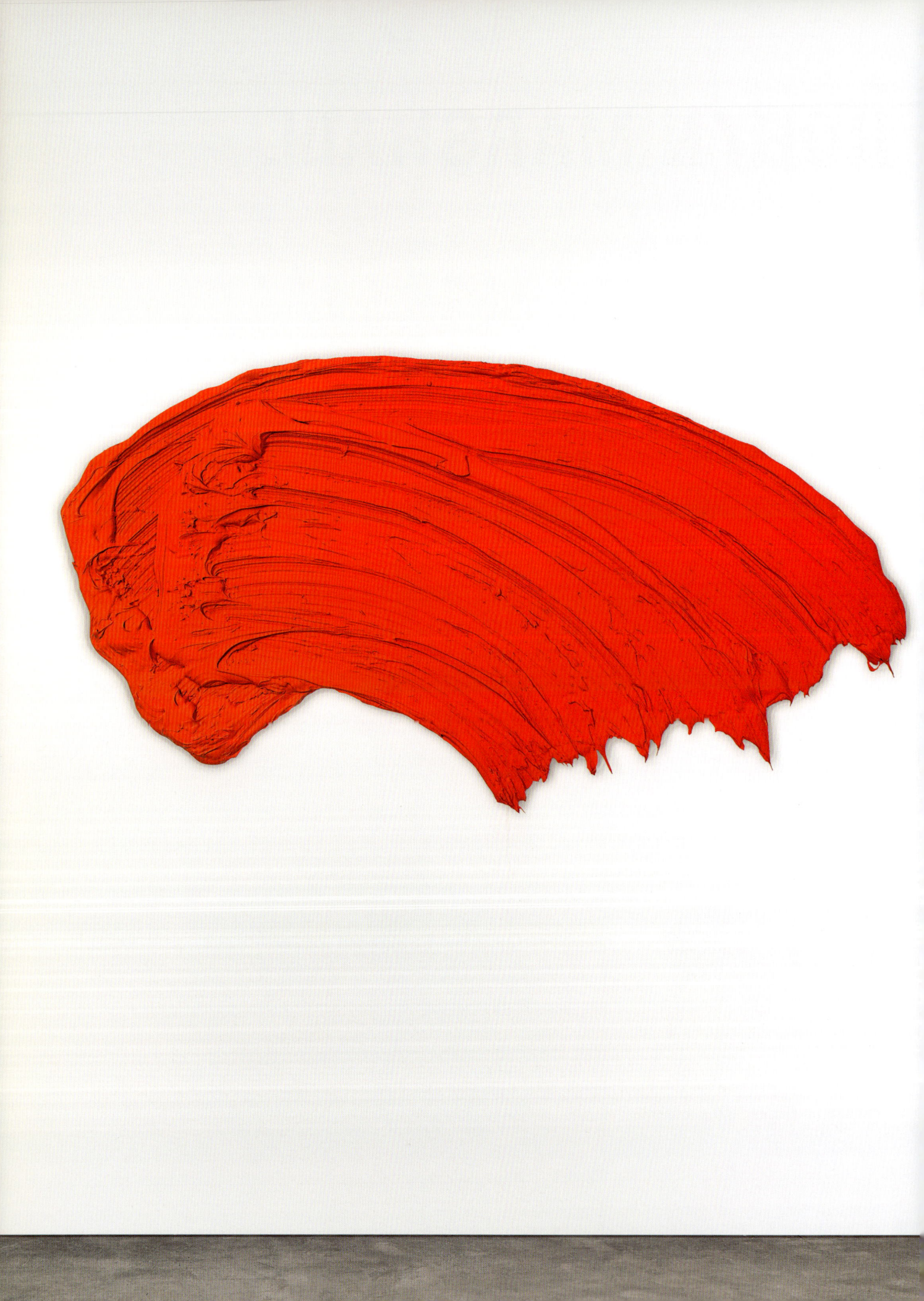

DONALD MARTINY

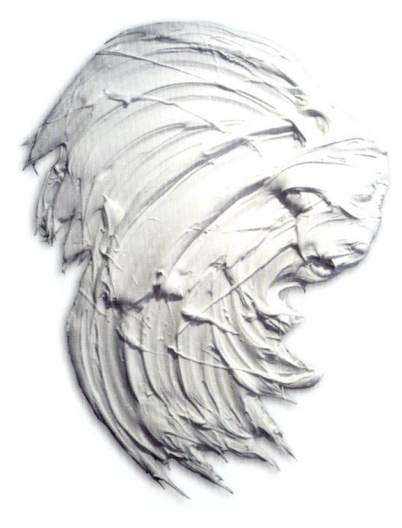

● **(facing page) Opata**
Polymer and dispersed pigment on aluminum, 47 x 92 in., 2014

● **Oscan**
Polymer and dispersed pigment on aluminum, 40 x 31 in., 2014

"Donald Martiny's work forces us to question the established definitions which form the backbone of our understanding of painting as both a pursuit and a product, and of paint as a medium. In challenging the viewer in these ways, it is not only visually exciting but intellectually invigorating."

- PROFESSOR DEBORAH SWALLOW MÄRIT RAUSING DIRECTOR THE COURTAULD INSTITUTE OF ART

Donald Martiny was born in Schenectady, New York in 1953. Martiny, who currently lives and works in Chapel Hill, North Carolina, studied at the School of the Visual Arts, The Art Students League in New York, New York University and the Pennsylvania Academy of Fine Arts. His work is in private collections in Amsterdam, London, Paris, Philadelphia, Washington DC, San Francisco and Los Angeles.

WWW.DONALDMARTINY.COM

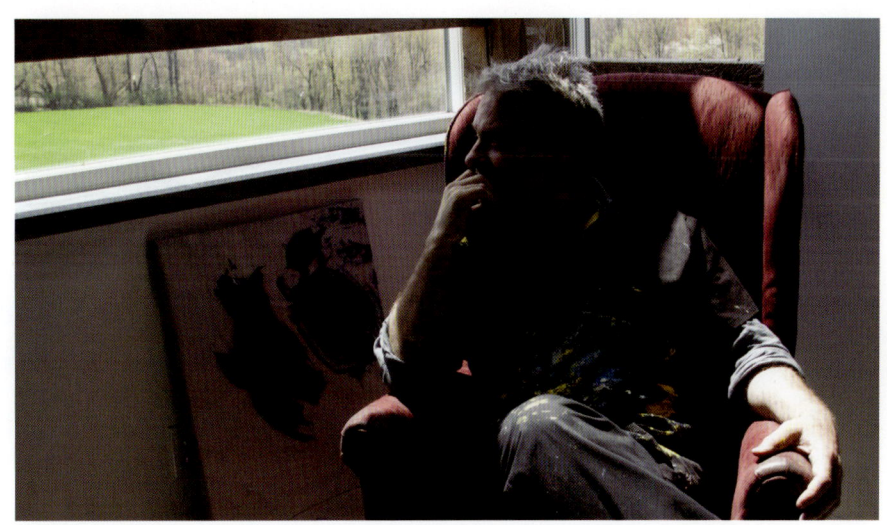

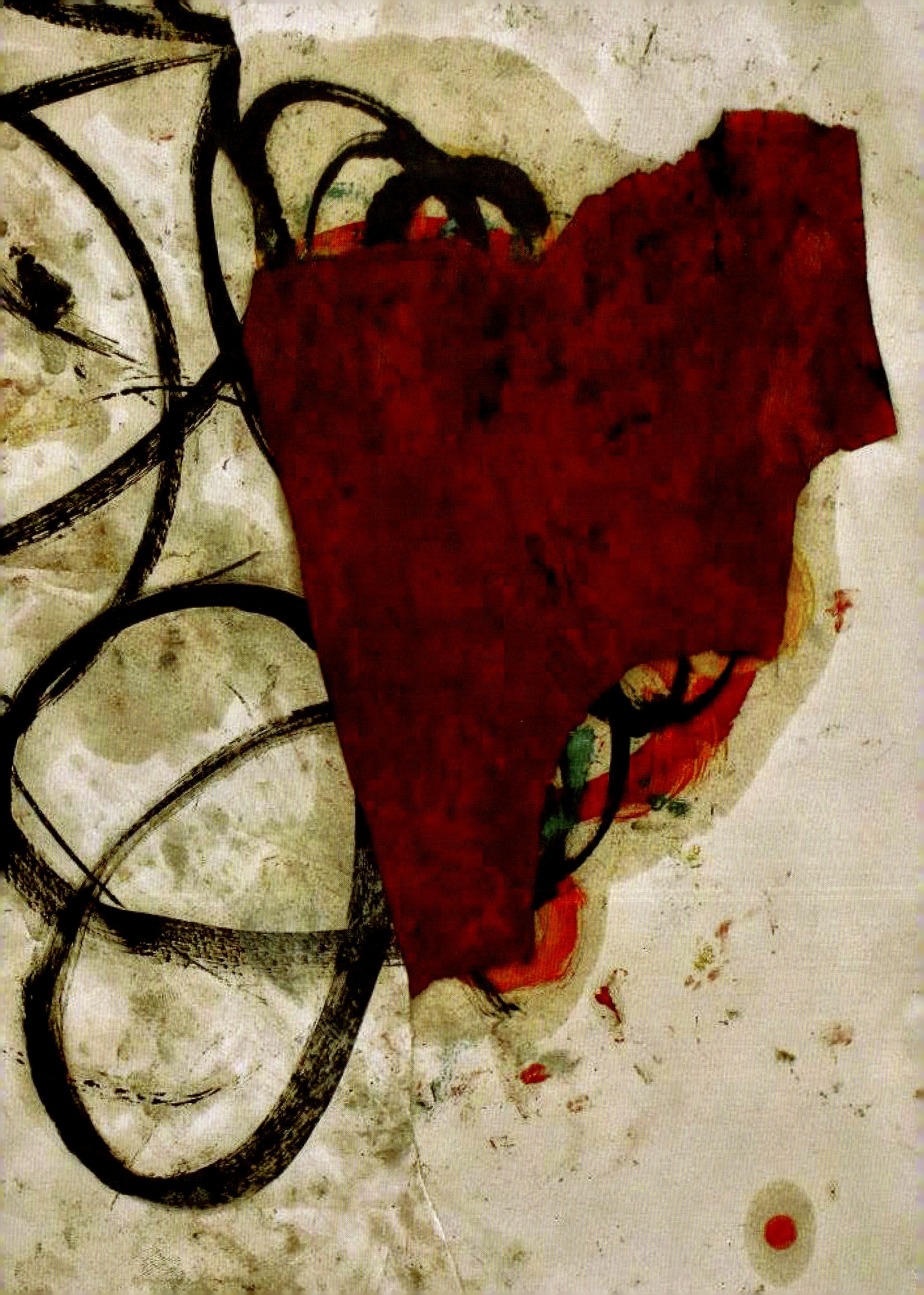

HILDY MAZE

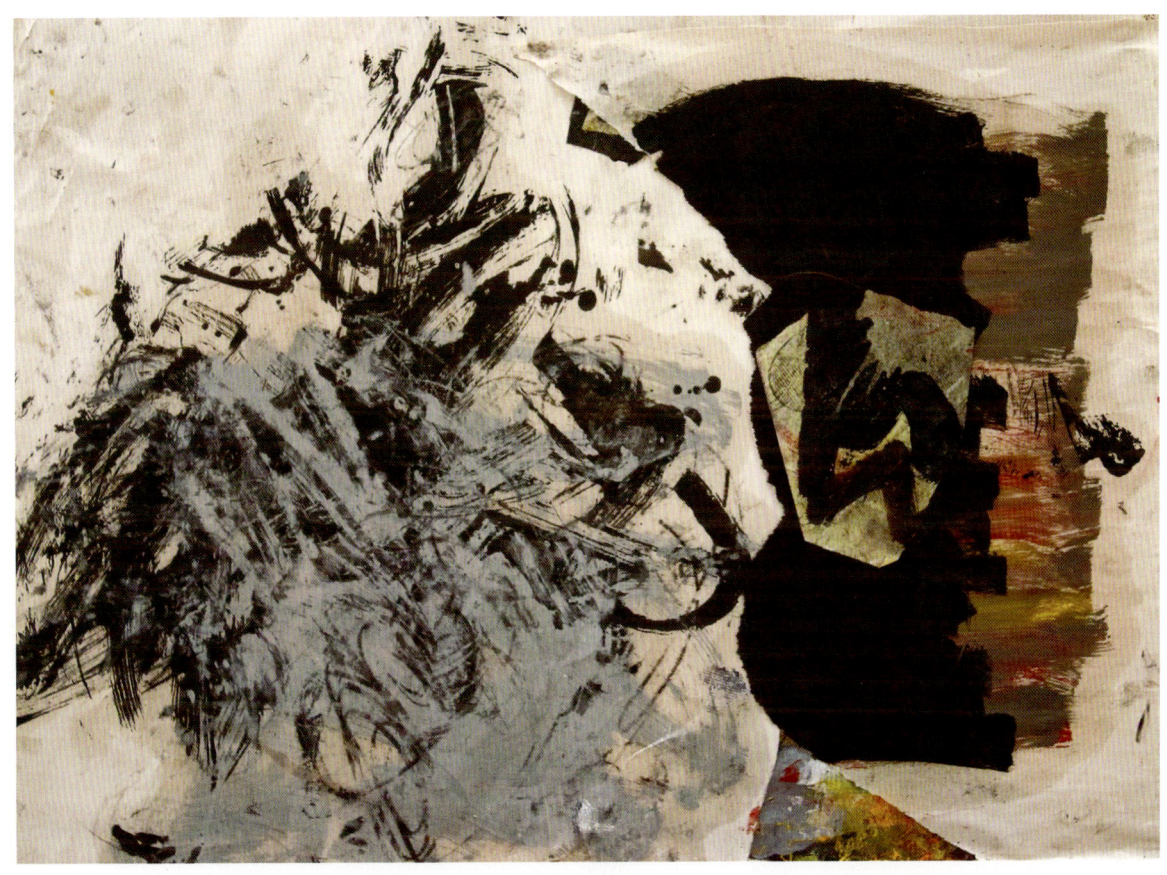

"I consider my work abstract contemplative. A way of looking at the image of ourselves, a self that keeps changing trying to keep alive the fiction of its existence."

Using various techniques I look at how we manifest our world and our grasping at a self through thoughts, emotions and the delusory notion of "I" and "mine," self and other, and all the concepts, ideas, desires and activities that sustain that false construction. I invite you to move into a space of speculation beyond the boundaries of the image into your own mind. Paper is used as the ground which most imitates life. Touched in any way there's a response; a finger print, wrinkle, rip,drip or tear which becomes texture and language. My creative practice is to cut thru to how this illusory discursiveness obscures the basic nature of mind. I examine how and why we create

various discontents as distractions from the truth of impermanence and non-existence of 'I am' putting endless effort into trying to solidify our lives, grasping at the ungraspable. I try to counter-act this culture of speed and information overload with each image and title as a flirtation with the possibility to recognize the basic pristine nature of mind's emptiness, clarity and equality continually awake and aware. The fact that we need to grasp at all and continue grasping shows that in the depths of our being we know that the self doesn't inherently exist.

WWW.HILDYMAZE.COM

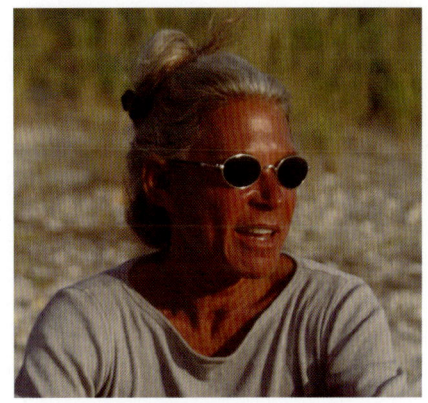

(facing page) From the immediate previous moment no clue what happens next... ●
Oil on paper collage, 23 x 29 in., 2015

Beneath the Turbulence ●
Oil on paper collage, 30 x 36 in., 2015

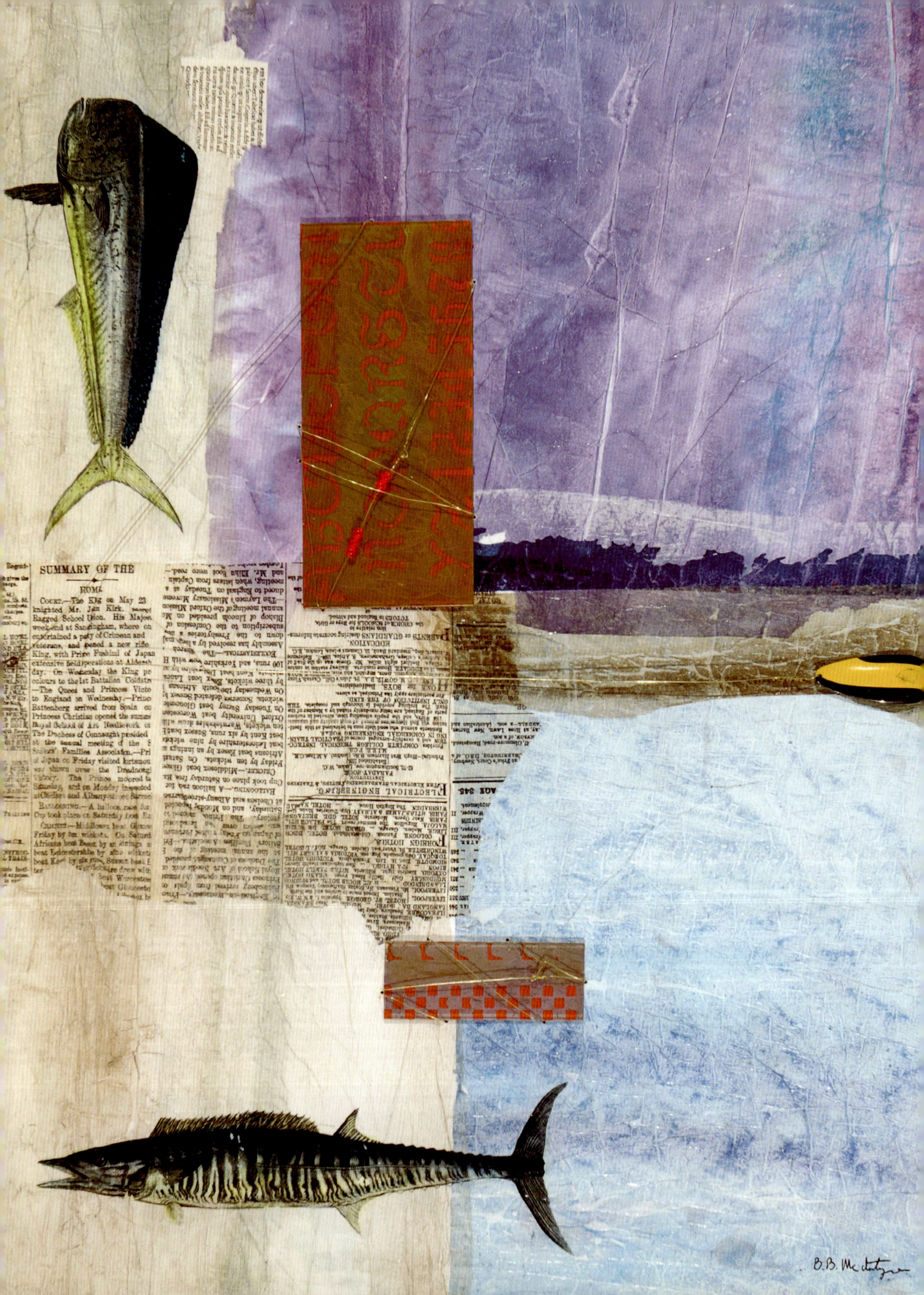

BB MCINTYRE

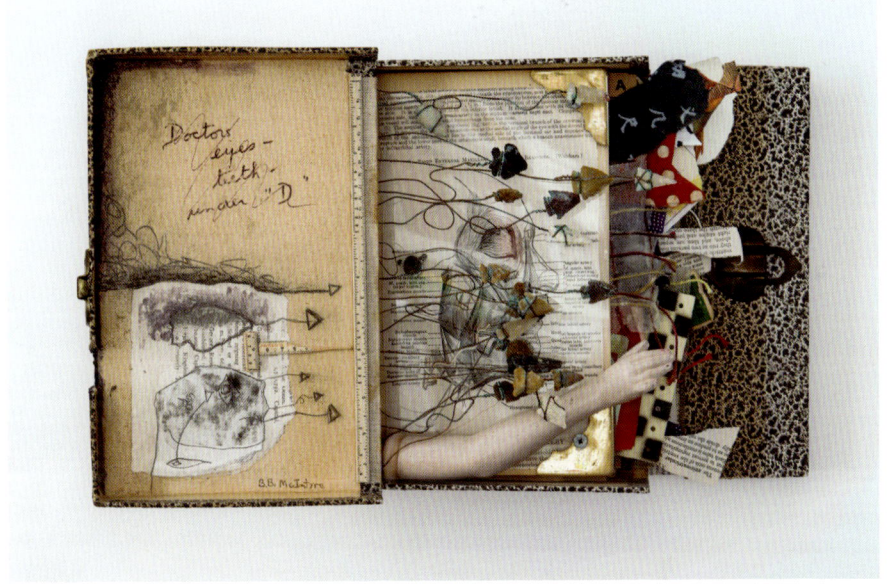

"Assemblage for me is about discovery......of connections to the feelings of attachment we have to these items. Assemblage is a challenging art form, in that, it is thought provoking, makes one wonder, this is part of the mystique. My work tends to be about searching for what is inside, for what strengths and values we already possess, but may have lost sight of. Utilizing vintage and used items is a theme in my work and brings for me a sense of finding worth (a rediscovery) in things that may have been discarded."

Irreverence, imagination and whimsy are immediately evident in McIntyre's found object art. B.B. (Barbara Baker) McIntyre is a classically trained artist and earned a BA-(Fine Arts Major) from UCSB. She worked almost exclusively in paper collage for many years and then gradually her pieces seemed to grow off the paper and become 3 dimensional with the use of Found Objects.

For over 15 years, her assemblage art work has been shown in Juried and invitational Shows across the USA, Tokyo, Japan and Berlin, Germany. She has won many awards and has pieces in both private and public collections. Her work has an eye for composition and a compulsion for texture in the form of massed objects- like a group of bottles in place of a torso of a woman, porcelain feet for hair or a group of vintage keys set into an old croquet ball.

WWW.BBMCINTYRE.COM

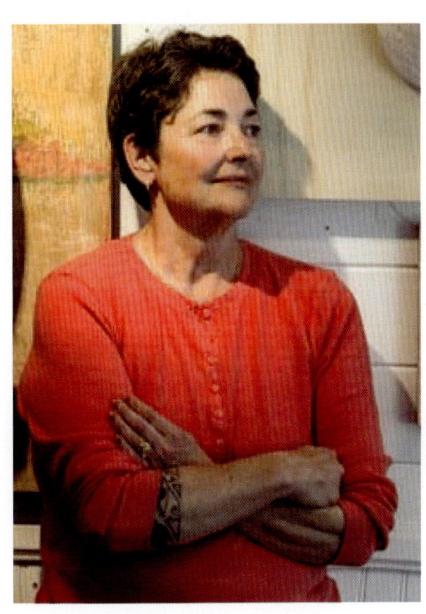

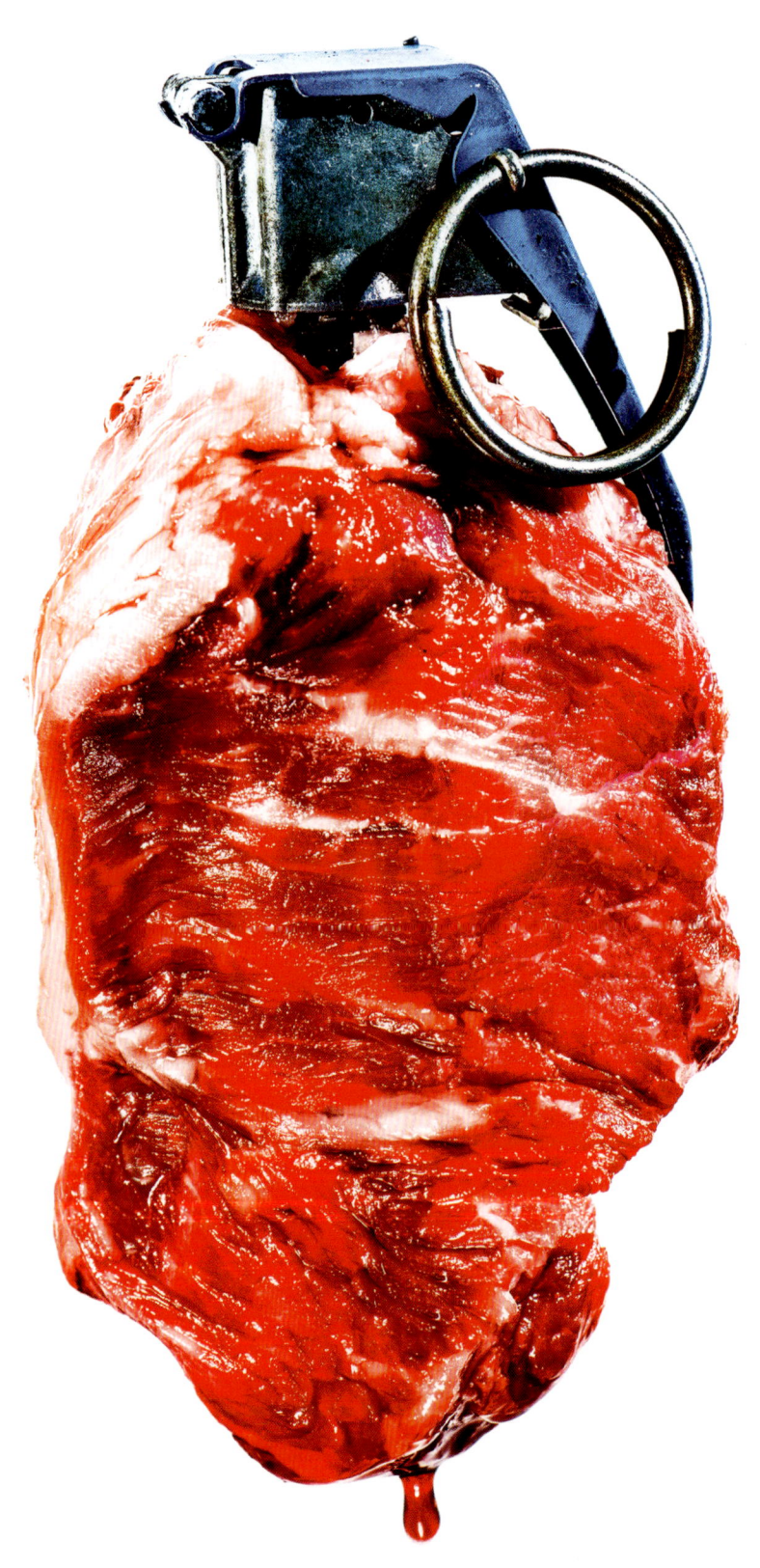

MATTHEW MCKEE

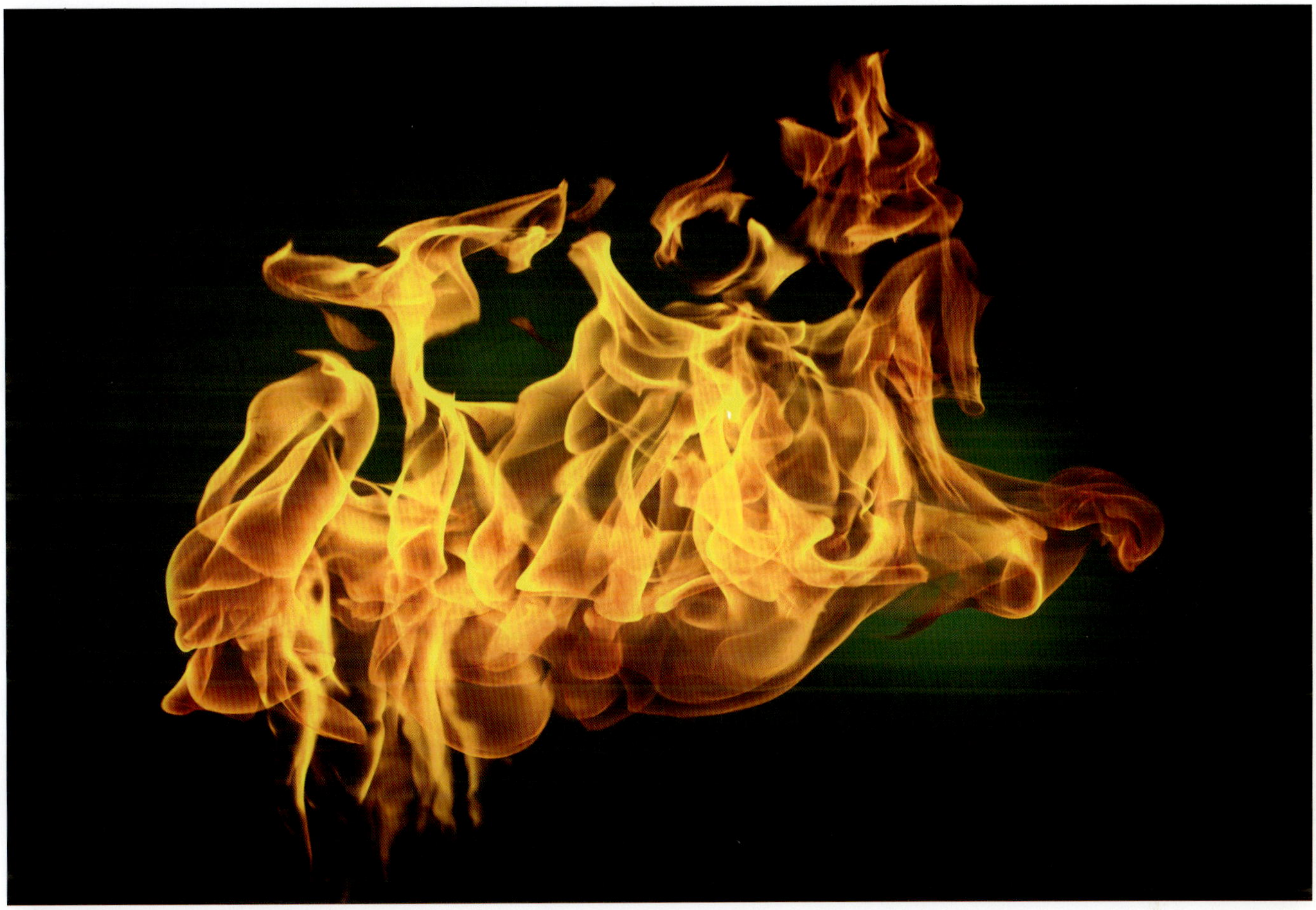

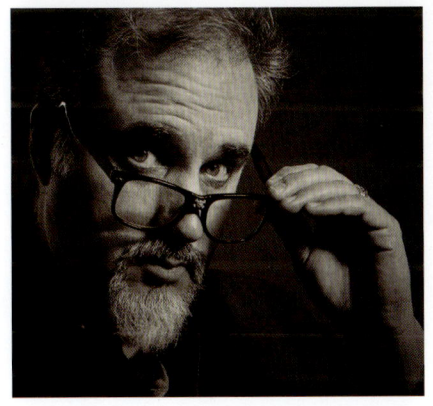

Matt McKee creates concept-driven, painterly photographs that reference human psychology and modern culture. His moments are not captured but are carefully crafted slices of time, designed to puncture the ever increasing surface tension of our day-to-day visual static and make the viewer pause.

His drive to create survived 10 years of higher education at 5 different institutions, before graduating from the Rochester Institute of Technology and settling into the Boston area in the 90's. He shows regularly in the New England region and his work is shown in public and private collections internationally.

WWW.MCKEEPHOTOGRAPHY.COM

● **(facing page) Hi Steaks!**
Dye sub on aluminum, 40 x 50 in.

● **Lig na Baste, aka Paiste.**
Dye sub on aluminum, 24 x 36 in.

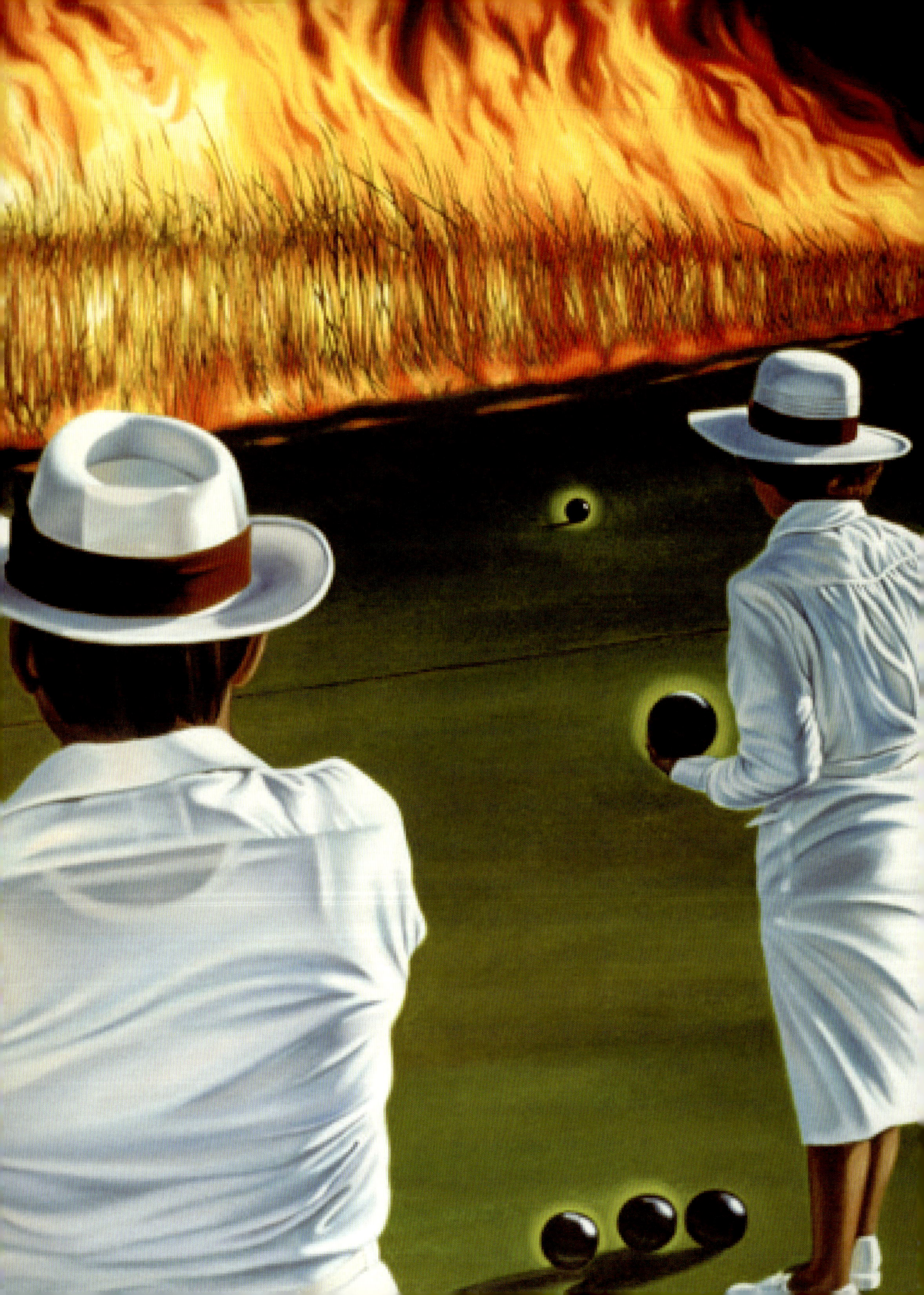

MARILYN MURPHY

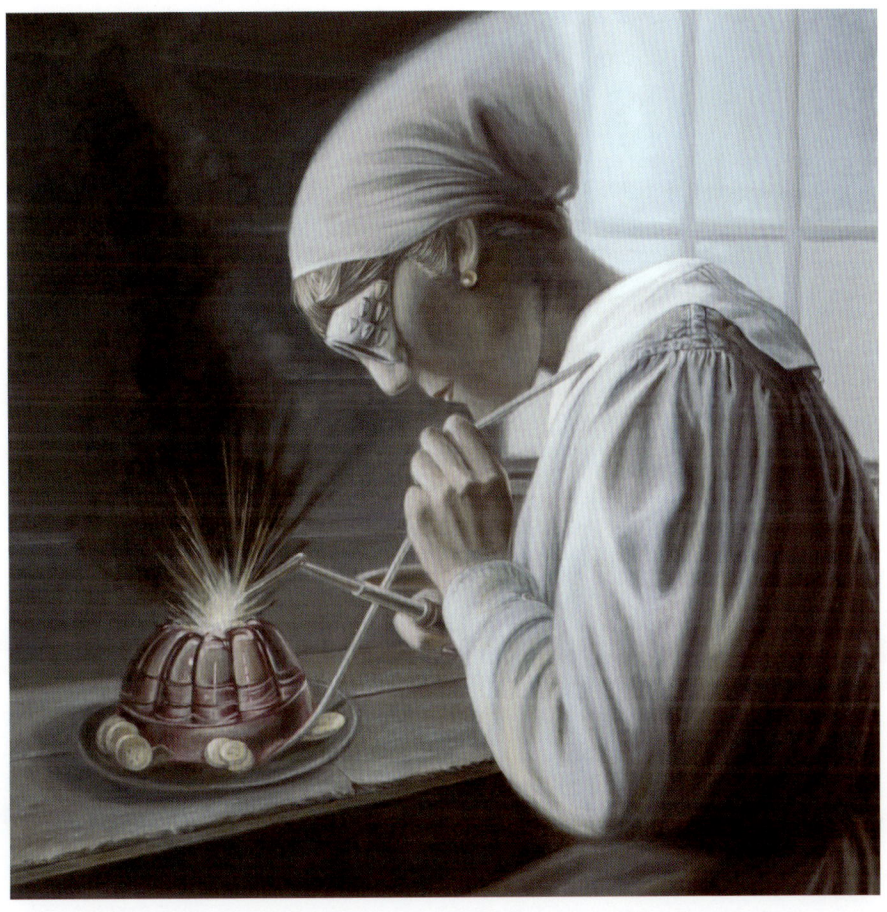

A Professor of Art at Vanderbilt University (BFA Oklahoma State University, MFA University of Oklahoma), my artwork has been shown in more than 390 exhibitions nationally and abroad. In 2012, I was part of a two-person exhibition at the Huntsville Museum of Art and in 2008 had a mid-career survey at the Frist Center for Art in Nashville. My work is represented by Adler & Co in San Francisco, Carl Hammer in Chicago and Cumberland Gallery in Nashville.

My paintings and drawings create curious situations that often explore the themes of people working, the act of seeing or the elements. Having long had a fascination with the magazines and ephemera of the 1940's and early 1950's including the instructional photographs in Popular Science and Film Noir, people or objects in my work are taken out of context or scale to create an implied narrative. While occasionally my art has a political element, many of my pieces comment upon the act of seeing, the creative process or some aspect of human experience.

WWW.MARILYNMURPHY.COM

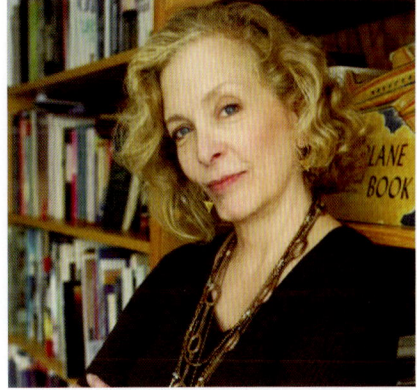

SHEILA NEUFELD

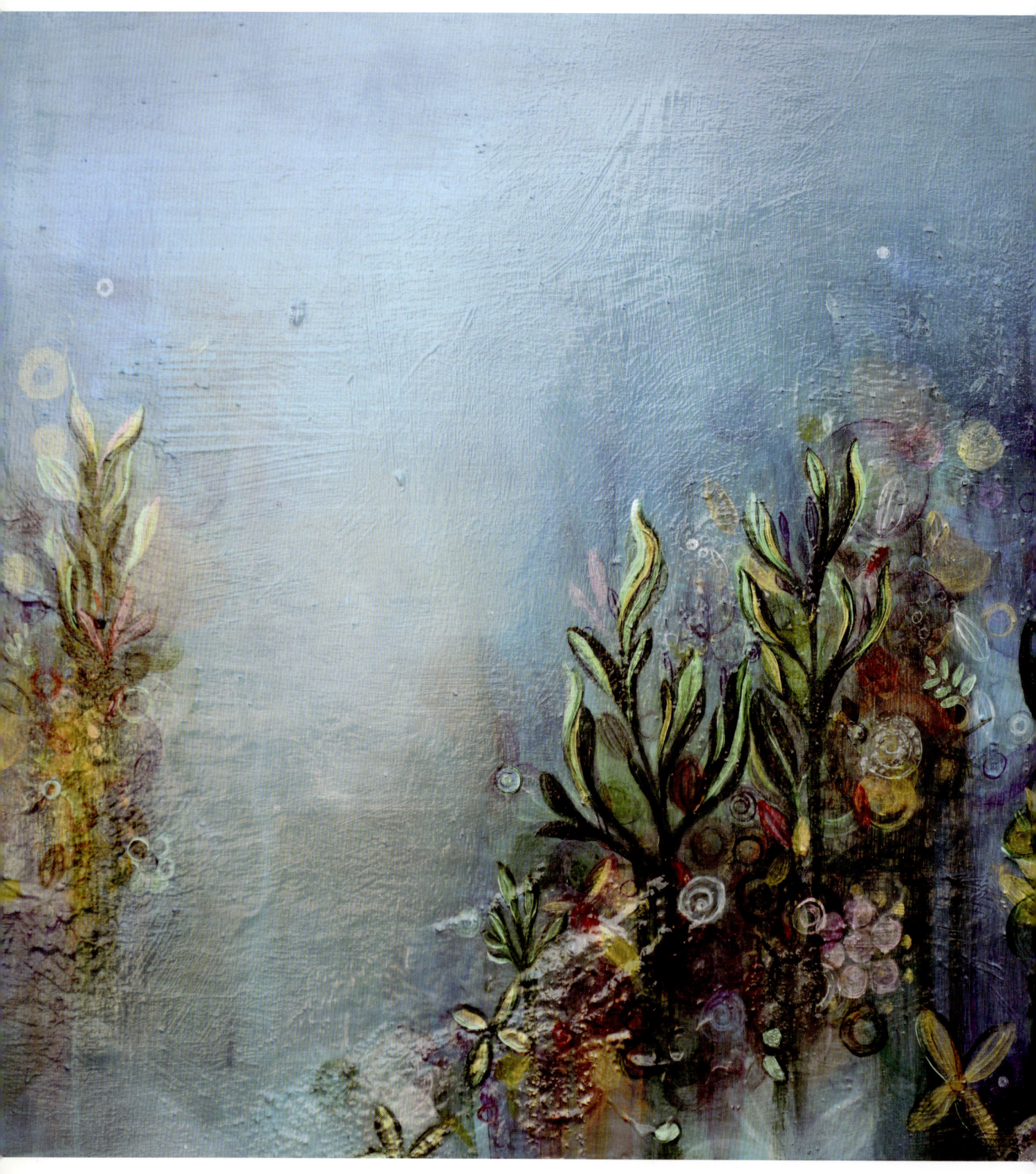

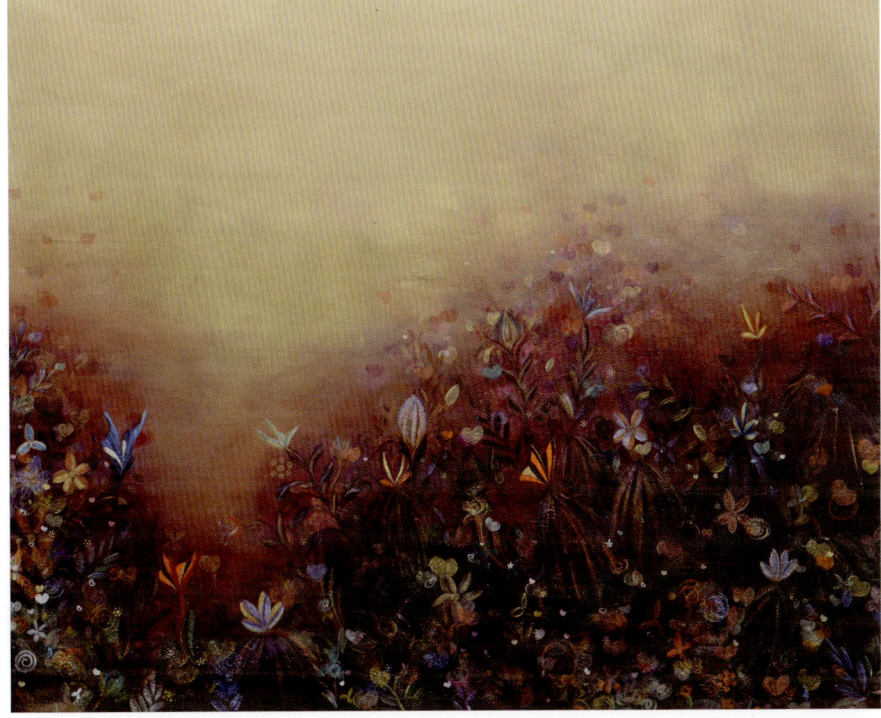

"Through the creation of art I become like a child full of wonder to the doorway of life's mysteries and to the essence of love that is a part of us. As I create layer by layer deepening into my artistic experience I become aware of life; its complexities and infinite possibilities."

Sheila Neufeld is a Canadian artist living in Vancouver, British Columbia. She completed her art studies at Langara College in 2004 and made a pivotal decision one year later to invest her savings into her first major show. Its success made her decide to commit to her art full time. Since then her art has been commissioned and collected across North America and she has exhibited at a number of art galleries and trade shows with her most recent major exhibition at Artexpo in New York City.

Sheila's paintings are dramatic yet delicate; powerful yet peaceful. These opposites are carefully achieved through an intricate process of building up thin layers of color and texture resulting in radiant, shimmering compositions full of depth and emotion. Her paintings are often described as expressive bursts of beauty, joy and love. While capturing the imagination of our expanding consciousness, Sheila's paintings reflect her passion for spirituality and mysticism surrounding the unity of all life.

WWW.SHEILANEUFELD.COM

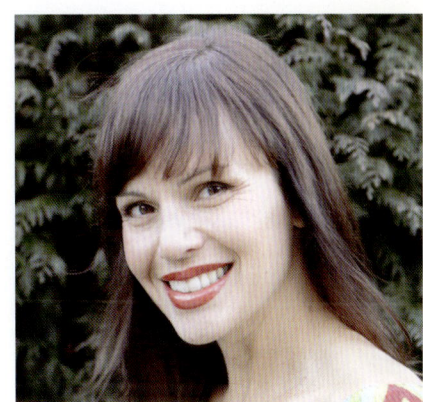

TOSHIKO NISHIKAWA

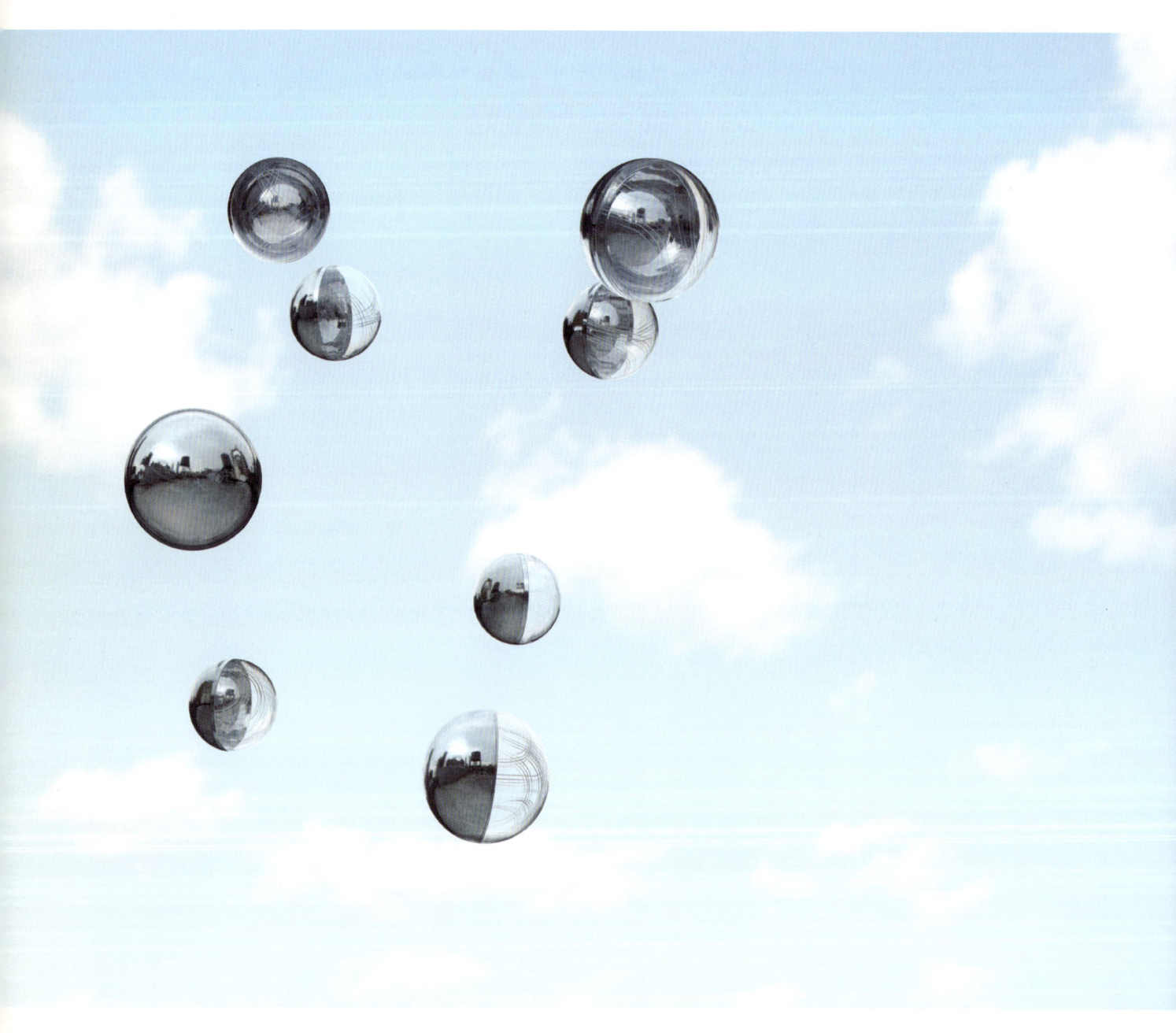

"Living as a woman is so wonderful, living as an artist is so interesting. Living as a human being is just an amazing experience to me."

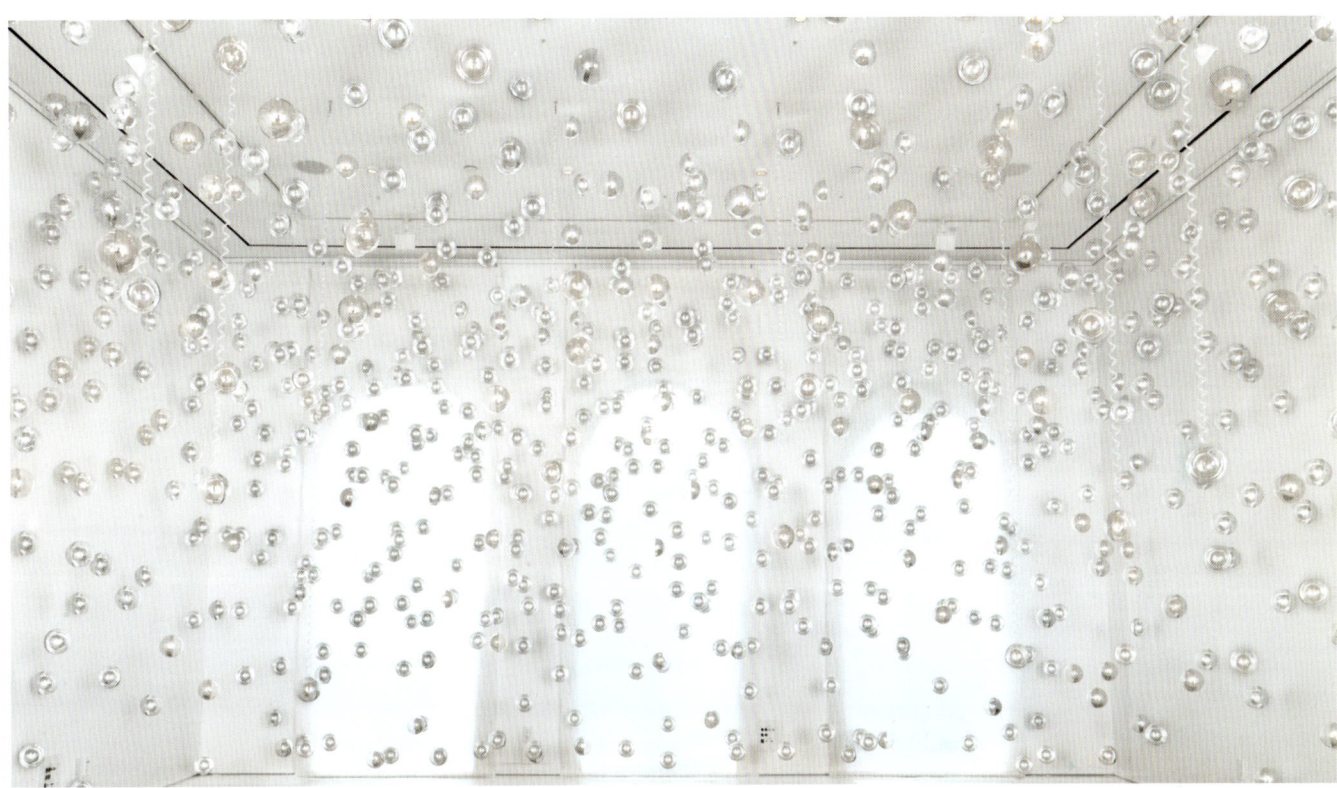

"The time is passing through my existence
There is my existence in one passing point
of evolution of mankind."

I was born to be a medium that gives birth to art works. It is the unification of the feeling of incredible waves of emotion and birth of unknown dimension that humans can never see through their eyes as actual shapes or words, but can see and feel in their imagination. The position of light or where people stand will change the vision of my art works dramatically, so the work can not be completed without human imagination. I would like my art to reach and influence all people around the world and be appreciated by those who previously had no interest in art. By looking at my artwork, I wish for all of them to have an opportunity to be free from the object world. I want to give them the opportunity to use their imagination to grow out of their bodies and experience the richness of our souls. I am just a medium, not a scientist nor a philosopher, so I just wait for that moment in time that energy comes and bears the things that should be born.

Agony and unimaginable pain let me know how heavy my role is.

WWW.TOSHIKON.COM

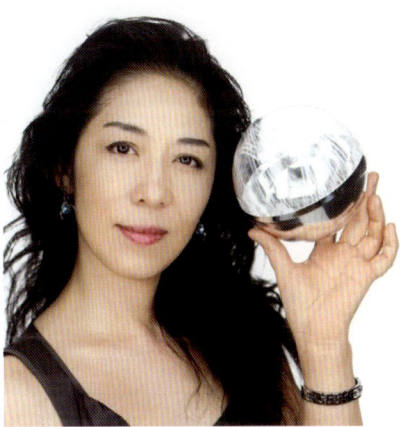

Senbazuru room installations ●
Images courtesy of the Vilcek Foundation (orbs)

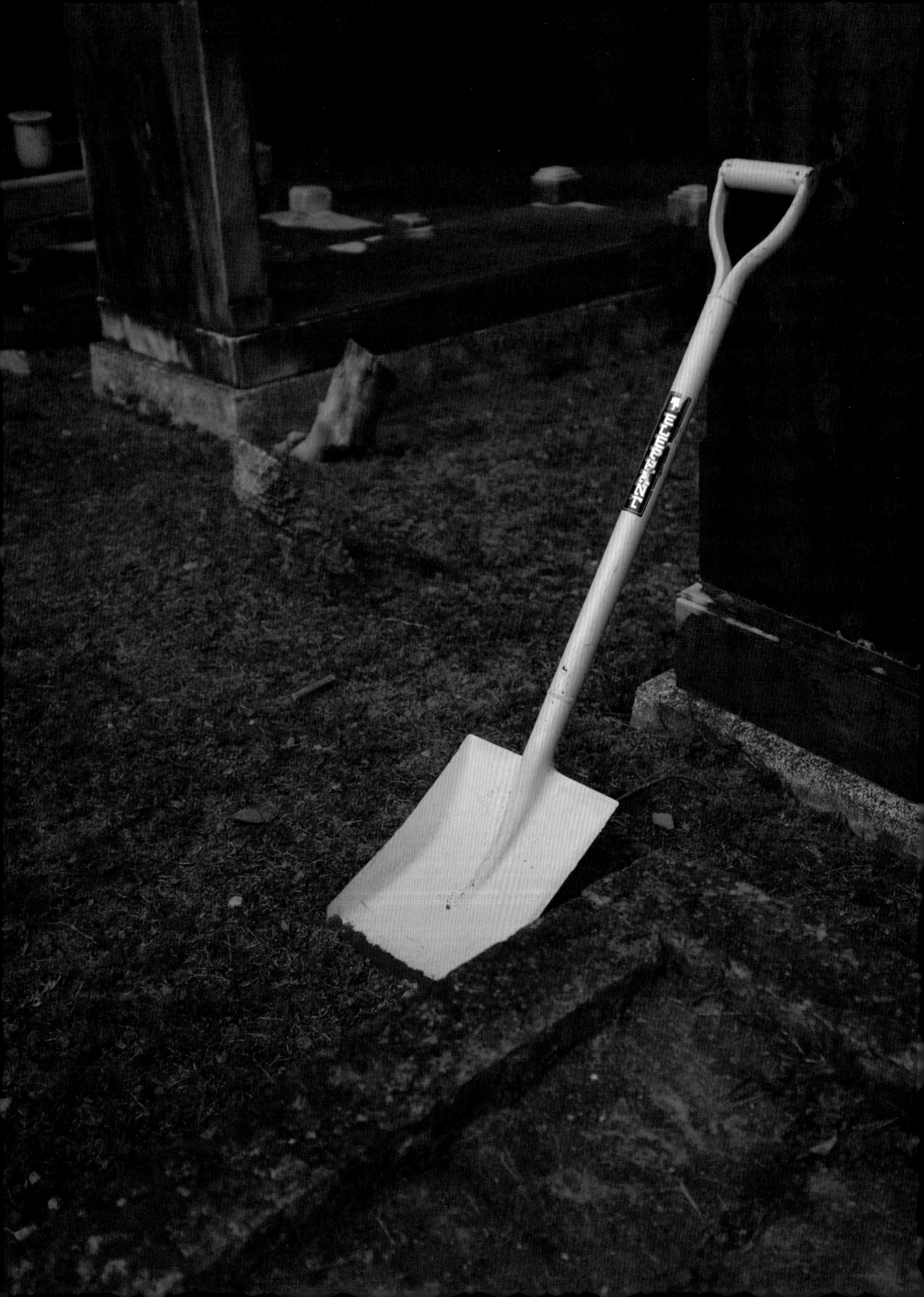

KINGA OWCZENNIKOW

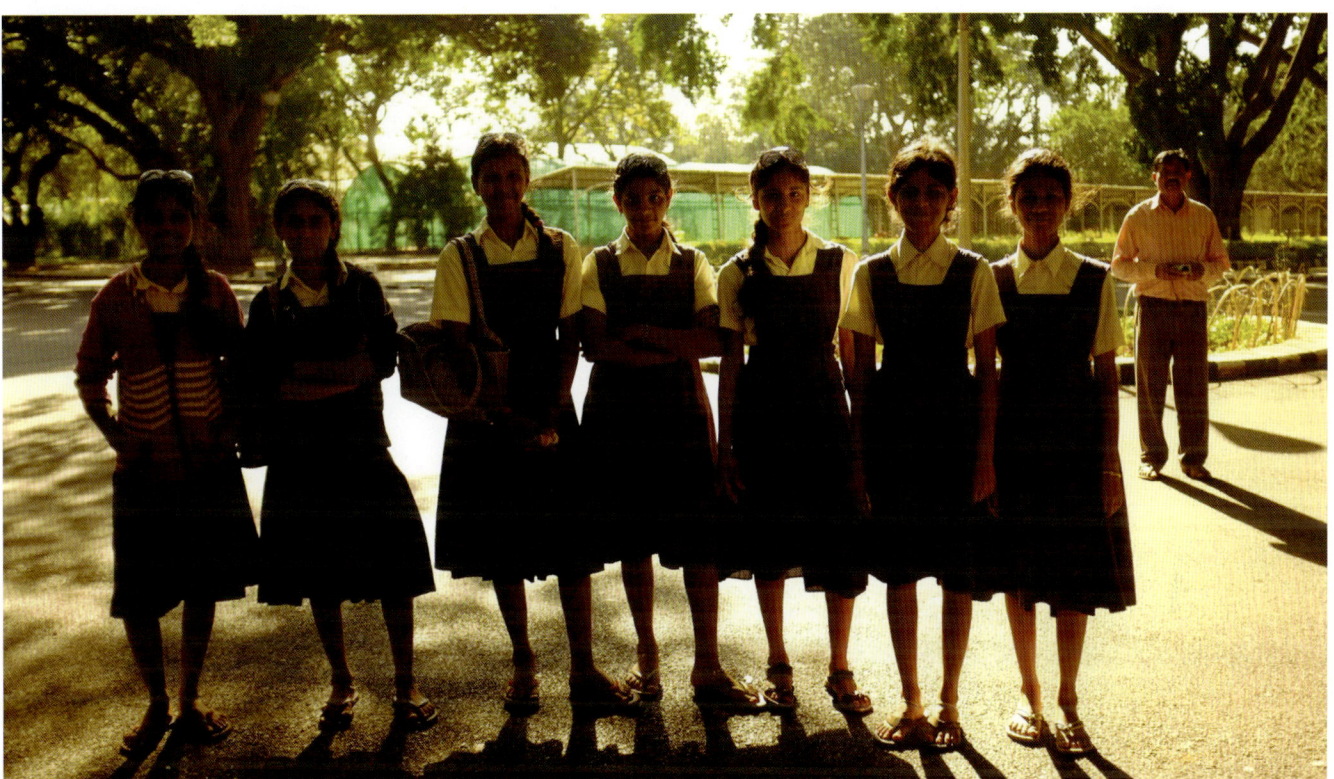

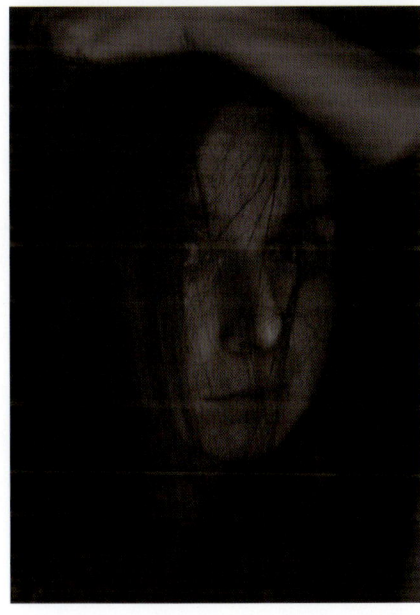

Kinga Owczennikow was born in Poland's south-western province of Lower Silesia but chose to live abroad for most of her adult life. Ever since being a little girl, she had a strong longing to get to know different cultures, and always felt a citizen of the world. Photography seemed like a natural step following her passion for traveling. After completing an intense term at Warsaw School of Photography & Graphic Design in 2012, she became seriously interested in the medium. It allows her to discover the world again and again by offering a very unique kind of focus. This way it has slowly made her believe in its exceptional voice. She is currently based in Hong Kong and continues studying the art of photography at own pace, with accreditation of the University for the Creative Arts in the UK. Her work is strongly influenced by leading nomadic lifestyle and naturally accepting the constant change within it.

HTTP://CARGOCOLLECTIVE.COM/
KINGAOWCZENNIKOW

● **(facing page) Happy Valley Hong Kong**
Color photograph, 2012

● **Untitled: Bangalore India**
Color photograph, 2012

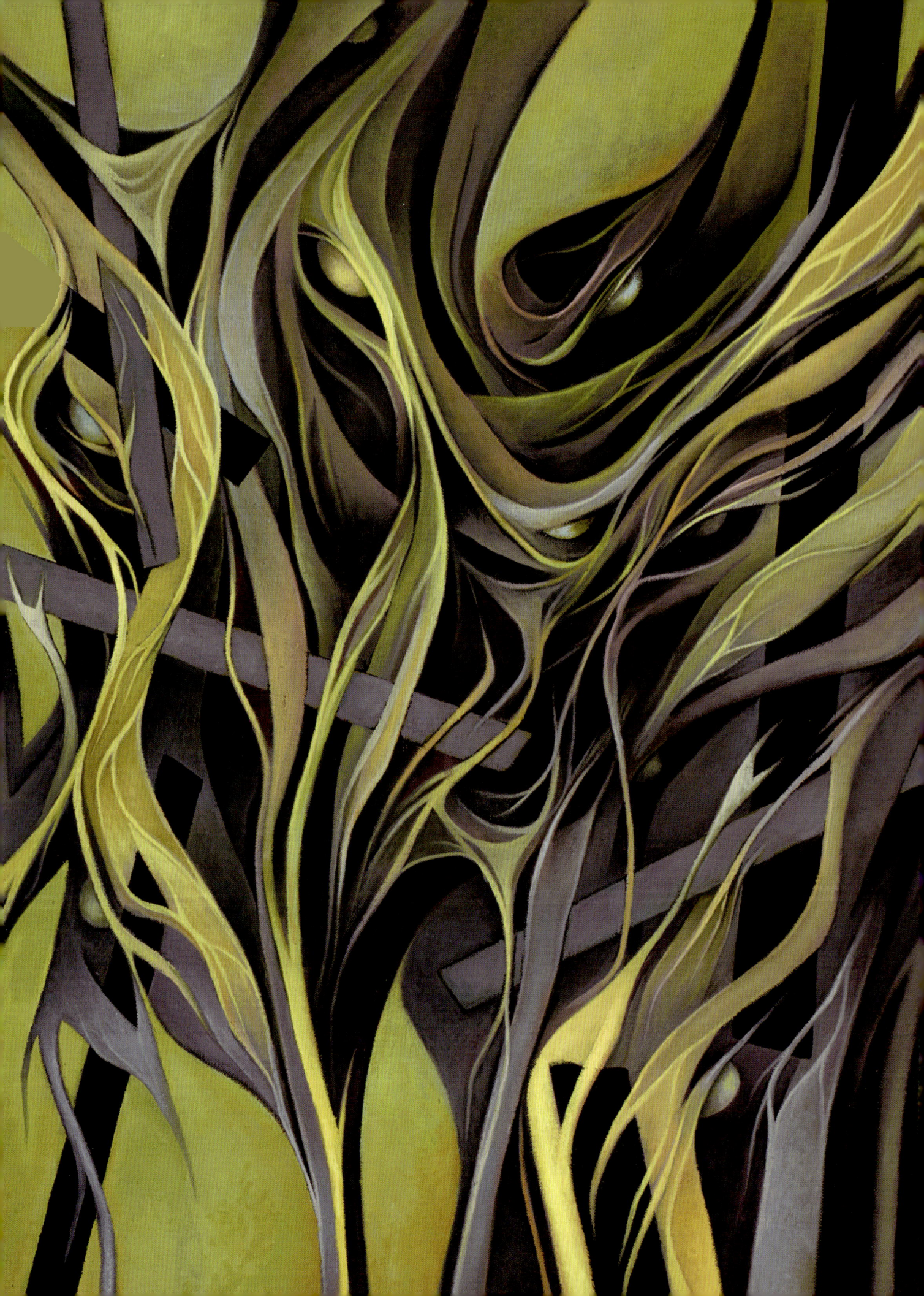

RONALD OWNBEY

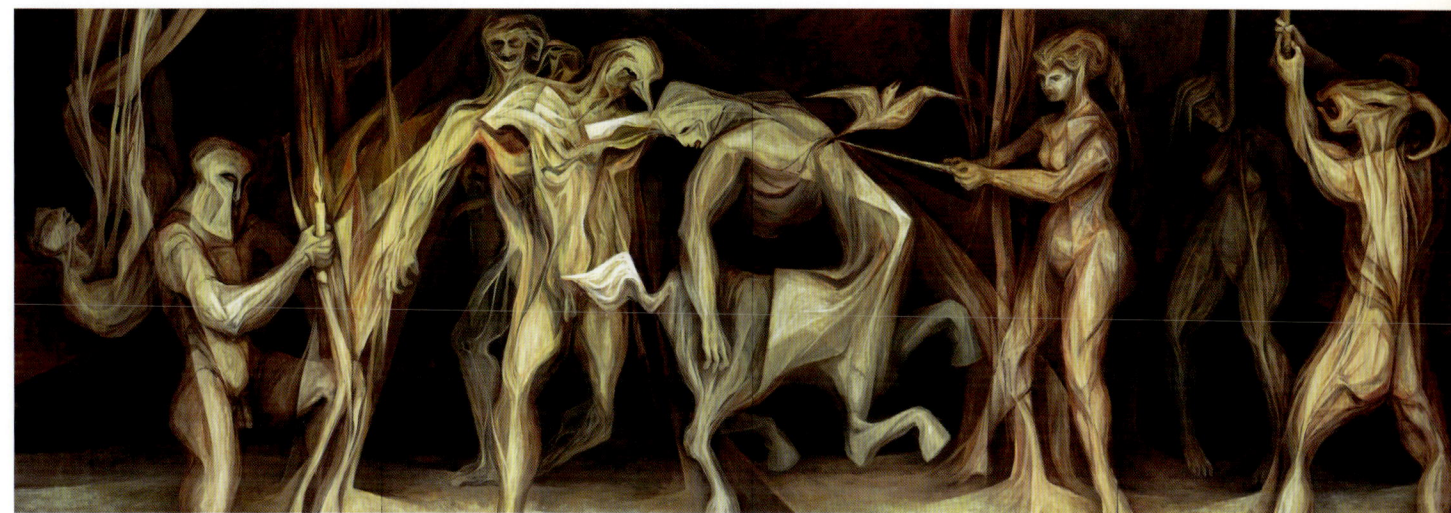

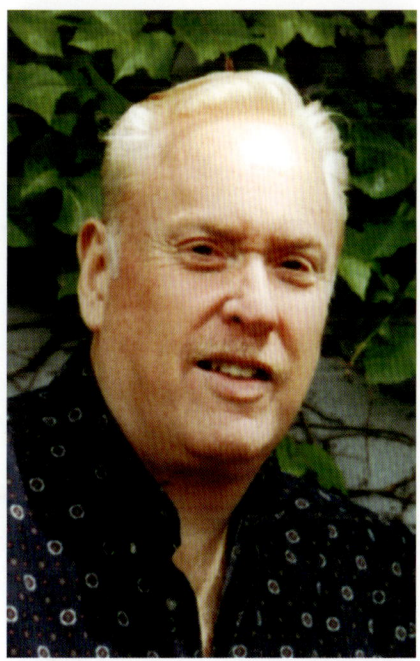

The ideas for my work are very personal reflections and interpretations of my fantasies, emotions and reactions in response to my relationships, my family, and the history and state of the world and the moment in time in which I exist. The chaos, complexity, serenity and vastness of the universe and our world and the great variety of all living things at all visual levels that nature and God have created energize my creative spirit. The tearing apart, discovery and reinterpretation of systems, colors, shapes, space and lines mirror the constant changing thoughts and formations found in my inner soul and the universe.

My work is very biomorphic, plant like, of faces and the inner and outer appearance of the human body and animals, and the microscopic close-up of other living organisms. My work has a strong symbolic and surrealistic tone, monochromatic at times but usually with strong shapes, color and value contrasts. The ideas formulated in my mind are filtered through my heart after much contemplation and travel through my hand onto the paper or canvas. The process is mysterious, frightening, exciting and introspective all at the same time during the struggle and the moment of creation. The final birth of the work is but a small morsel of the inner spirit and the process that allows that to happen is the most important part of the experience.

WWW.RONOWNBEYARTIST.COM

● **(facing page) Conflict**
Oil on canvas, 22 x 24 in., 2015

● **Not Less Through the Loneliest Air I Descended**
Oil on canvas (in four sections), 144 x 48 in., 1964

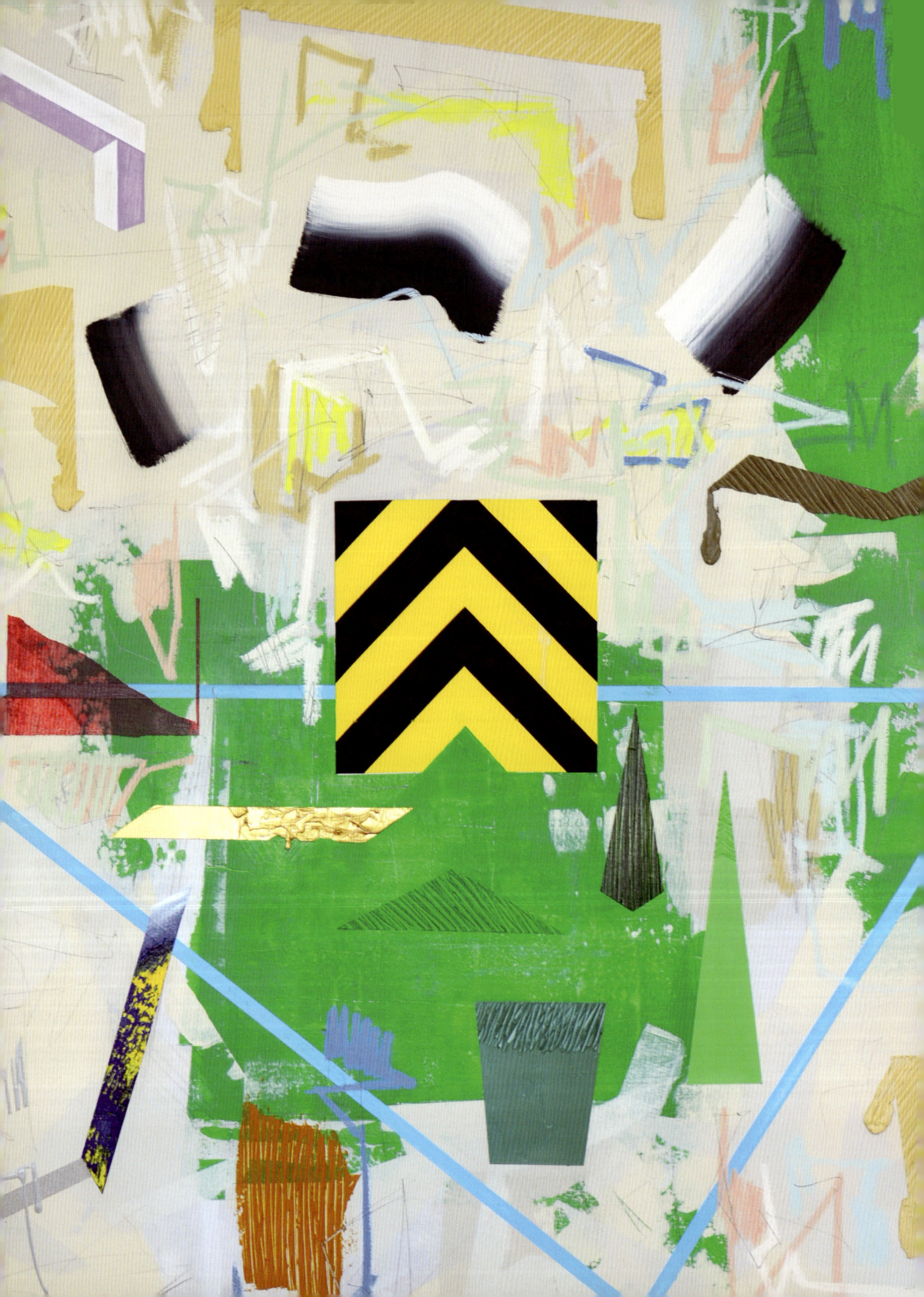

HEEBEOM PARK

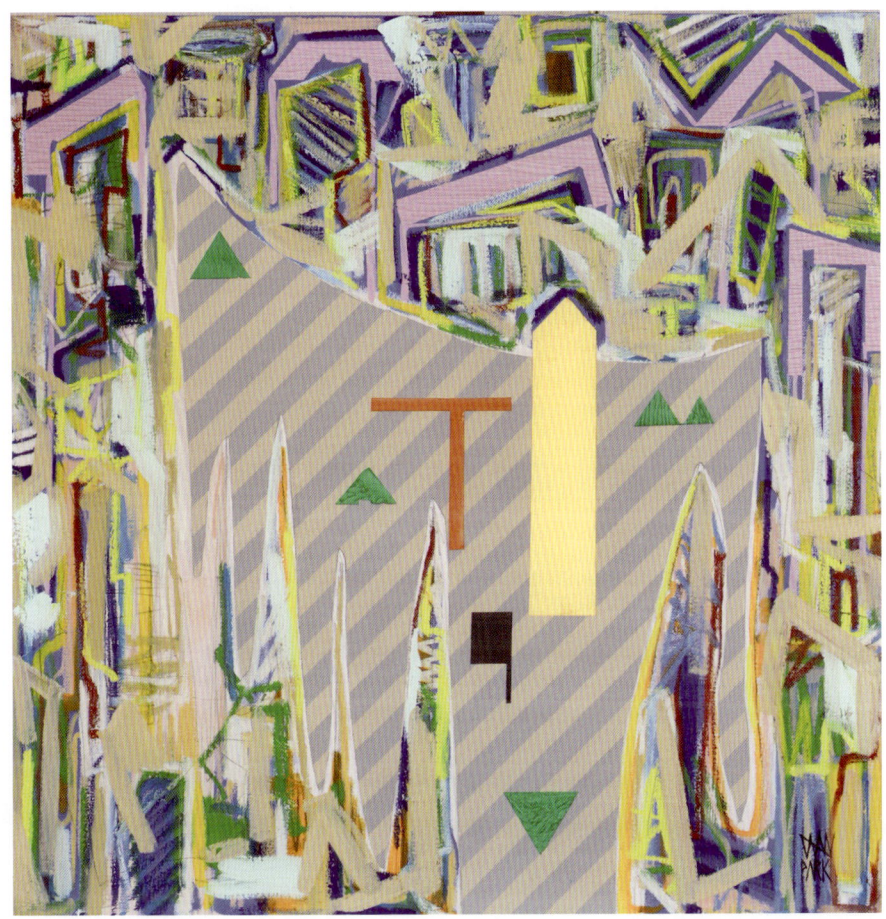

"Everyone dreams of freedom and although it is impossible to reach a true level of freedom in a life which is so bounded by rules and limitations."

Born on November 17, 1978 in Busan, South Korea and grown up in Seoul and Busan both cities. I studied at School of Art & Design High School and Art school of Daegu University in South Korea. Currently, I live and work in New Jersey and New York.

I seek to find the world in dichotomy and harmony in difference, contrasting and juxtaposing contrasting elements, directly transport this idea onto the canvas. For instance, if there is a stop then there is a movement, if there is a creation then there is extinction and if there is law then there is lawlessness. Through this observation of object by lines, shapes,

colors and compelling forms that is my tools of expression. In my paintings you will find a lot of straight lines and irregular lines, bright colors but dark colorless, shapes and repetitious forms of different sides of shapes which tell a story of how complex our daily lives can be yet at the same time it can be simple. What results is a reconfiguration of space and time that infuses new meaning into the ordinary symbolism of our modern world.

WWW.HEEBEOMPARK.COM

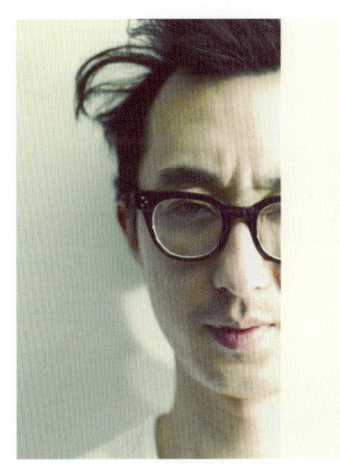

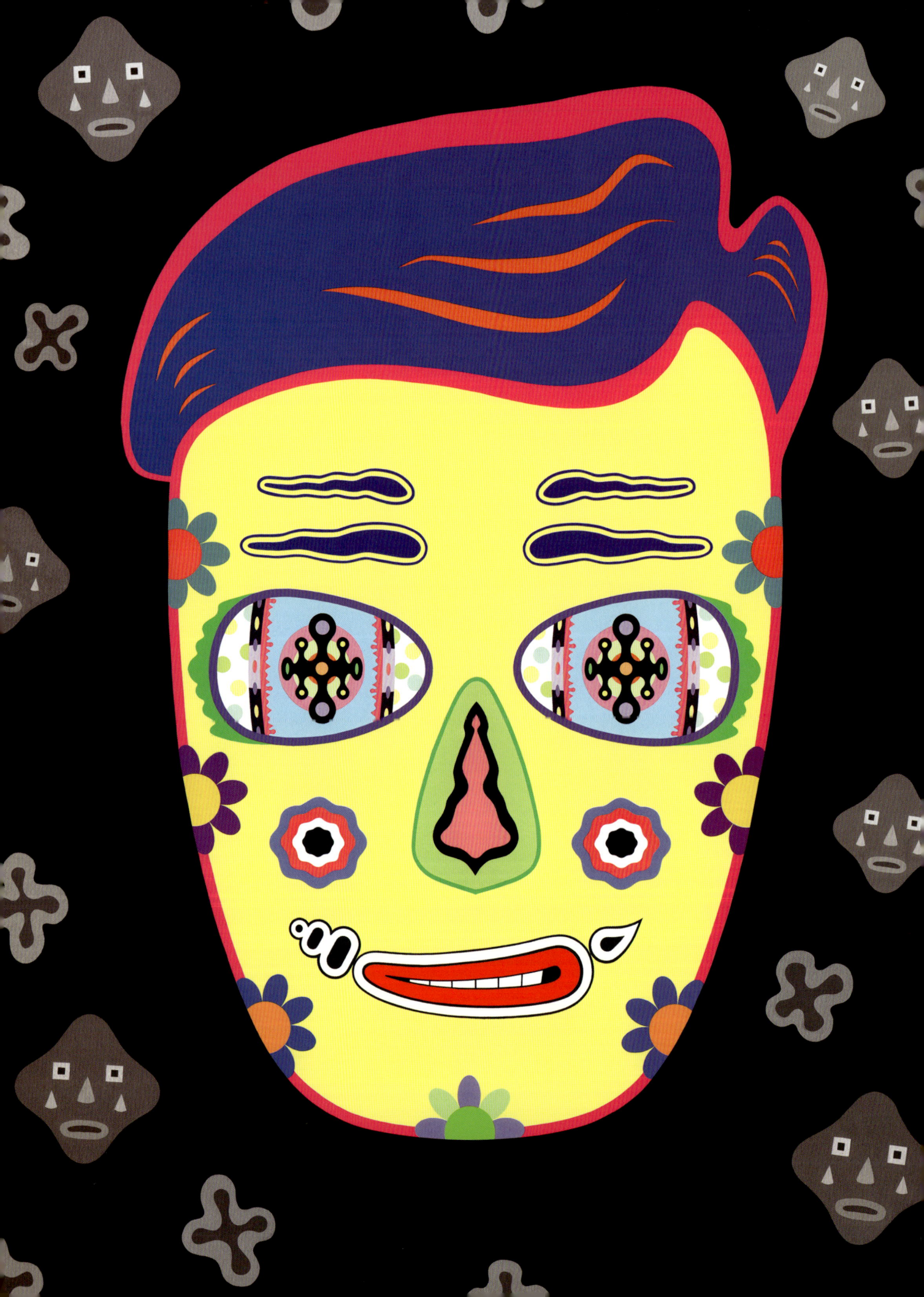

LOU PATROU

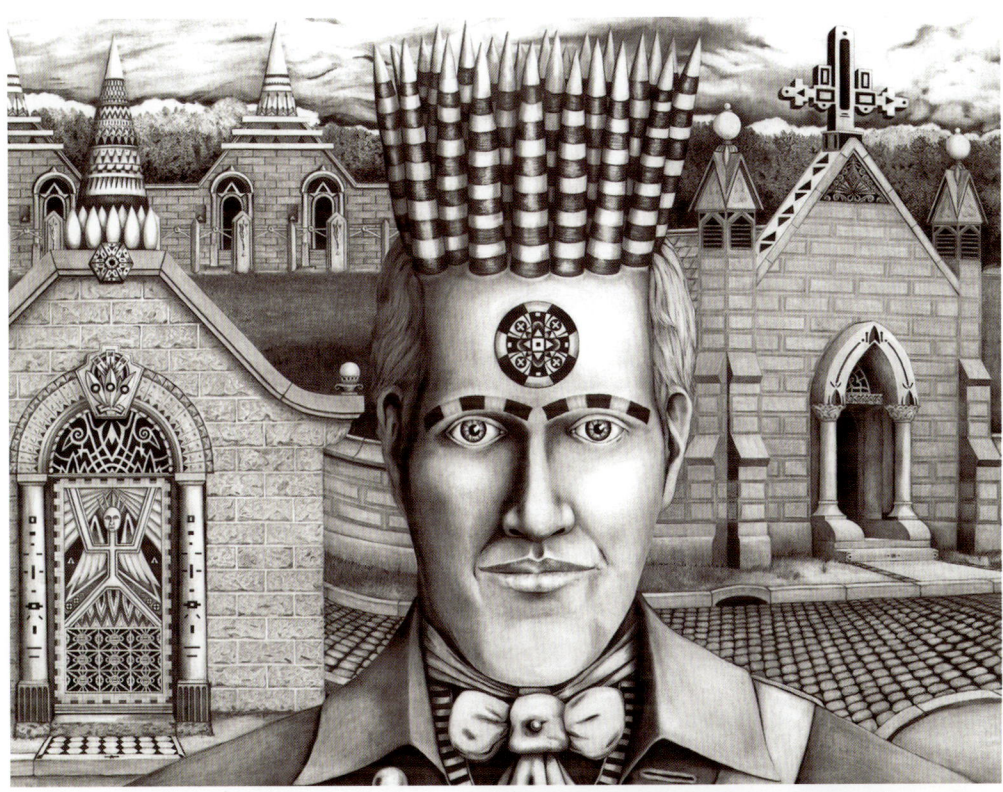

Lou Patrou has been drawing and painting faces since the 1960's and has been steadily creating a body of work with a portfolio that spans over four decades. Patrou's work is difficult to categorize because he doesn't always use the same artistic language, repeat the same disciplines or follow a straight direction with his work. One thing you could say is that he is obsessed with making faces and finding new ways to create designs and forms out of them. Lou is able to successfully jump between several styles and techniques. His work can go from tight graphic pop art, rendered whimsical and kitschy pieces suggesting patterns to visceral narratives in pencil or pastels.

While working in a large fine art graphics house in Los Angeles in the mid 80's Lou started experimenting with reproducing his images as fine art photographic reproductions and various substrates as installation pieces.

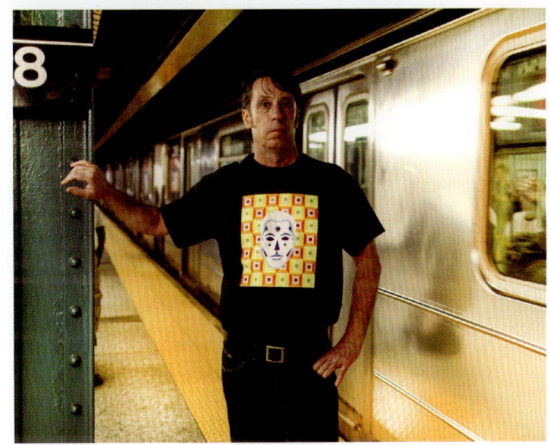

● **(facing page) Ricky**
*Acrylic on watercolor paper,
40 x 60 in., 2014*

● **Cemetery**
*Graphite drawing on paper,
18 x 24 in., 2004*

WWW.PATROU.COM

ANITA PELTONEN

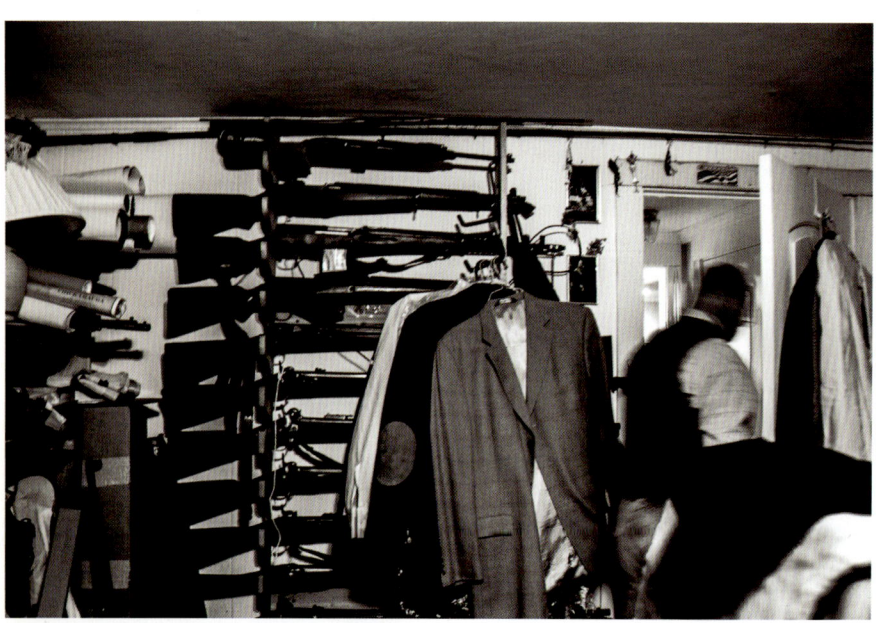

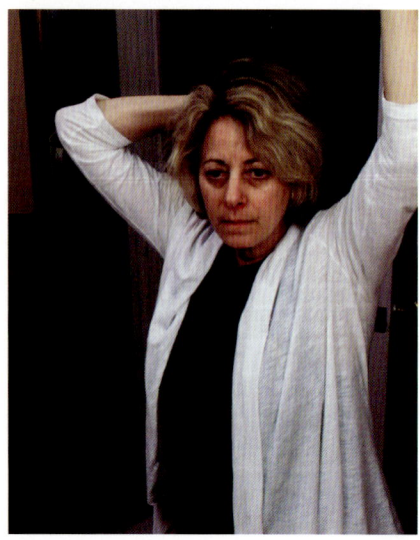

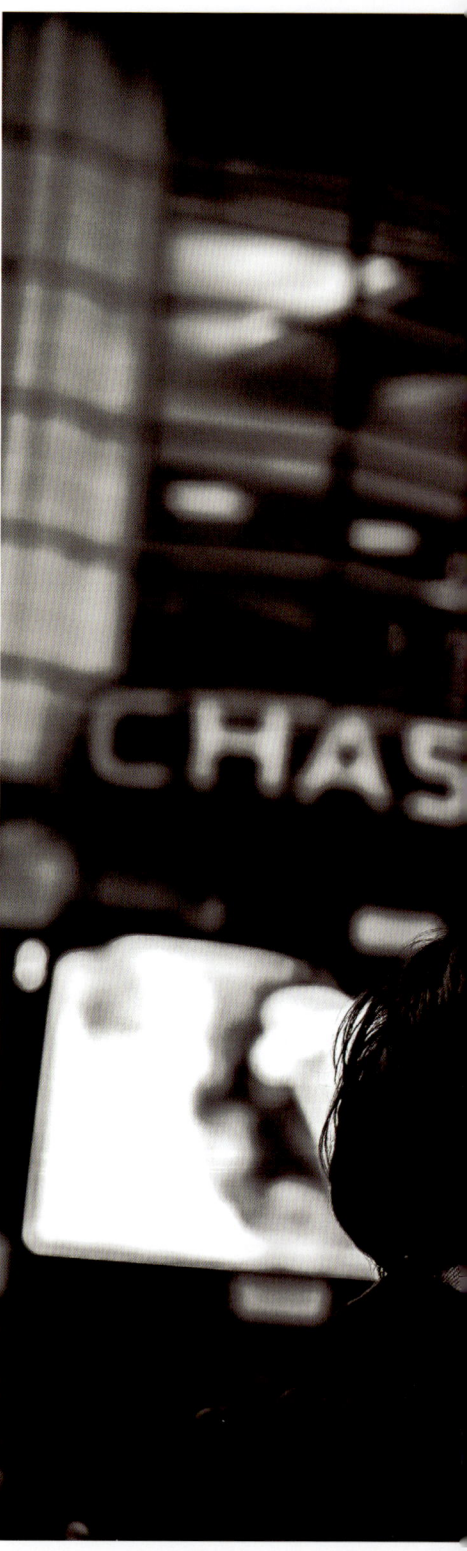

A native of New York City, Anita Peltonen has lived in Montreal, Helsinki, and London. She now lives in upstate New York, with fly-bys through Washington, D.C. For decades a reporter, editor, and foreign correspondent, Peltonen is moving into photojournalism and library science.

Anita Peltonen's photos have appeared in The New York Times, F-STOP Magazine, the Duncan Miller Gallery, Humble Arts Foundation NY, and the International Center of Photography publications.

WWW.13MOONFACE.WIX.COM/
ANITAPELTONENPHOTOG

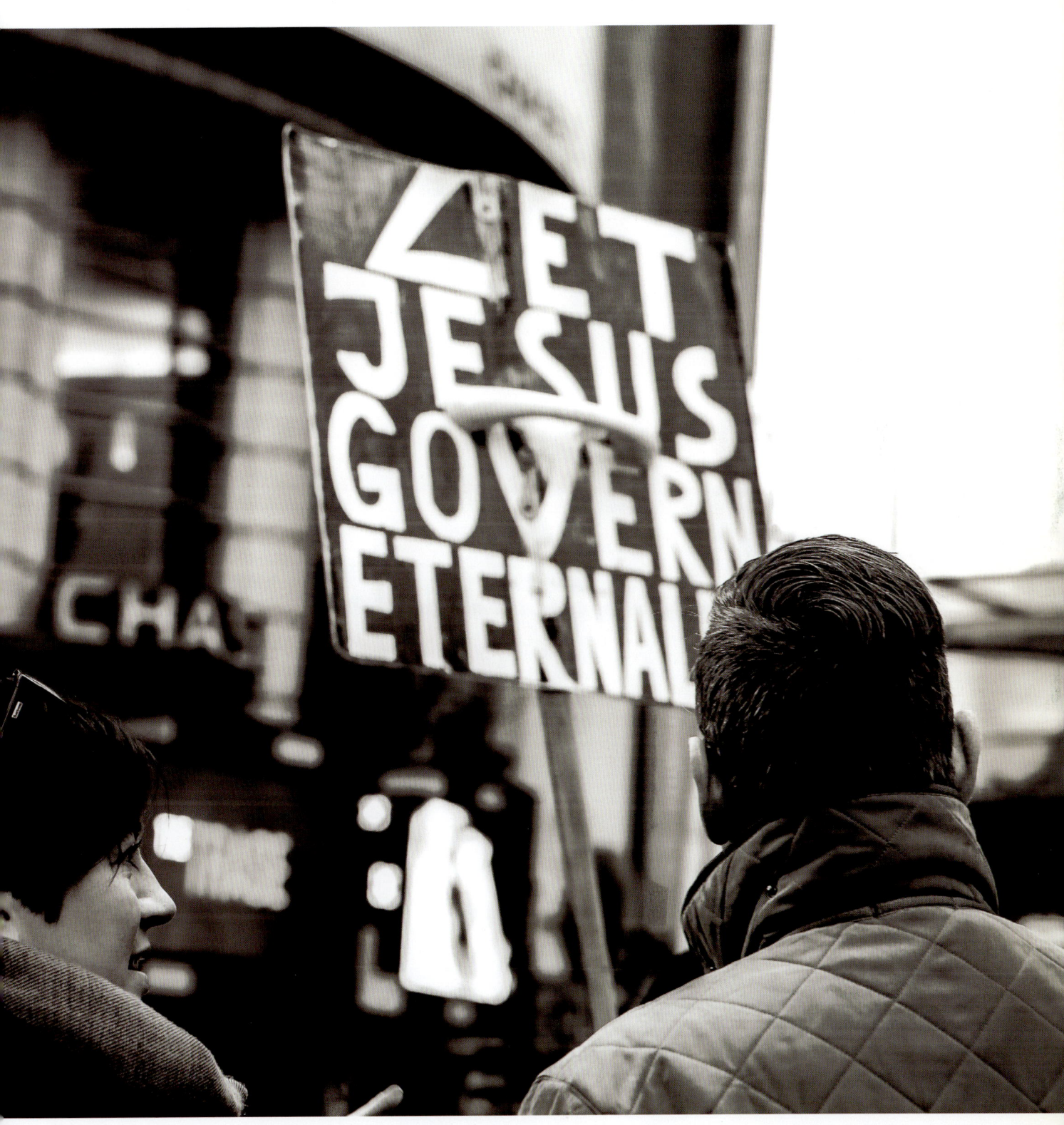

(facing page) **His Collections** ●
Digital, 51 x 34 in., 2015

Christ Still Lives in Times Square ●
Digital, 57 x 38 in., 2015

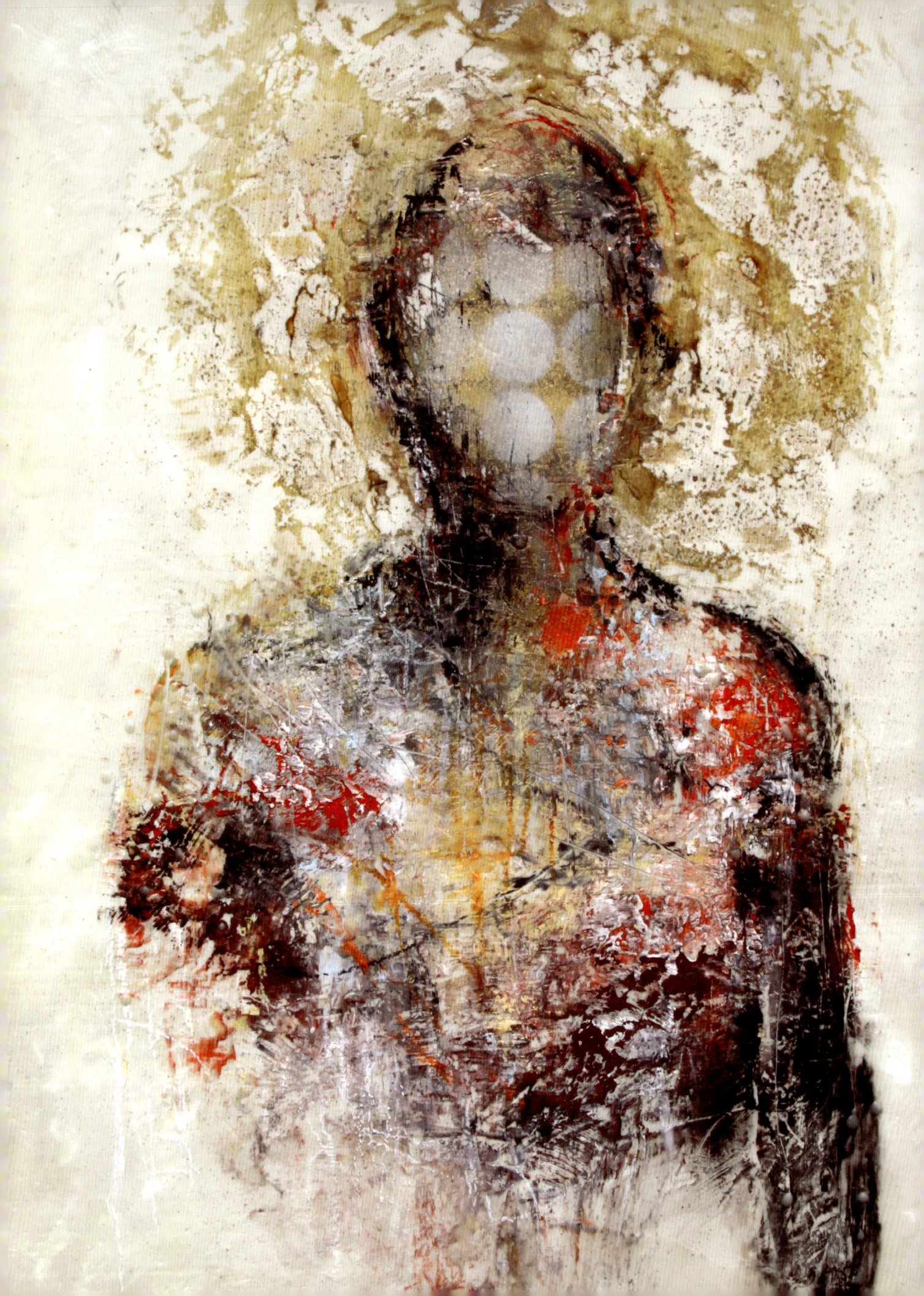

JAMES PETRUCCI

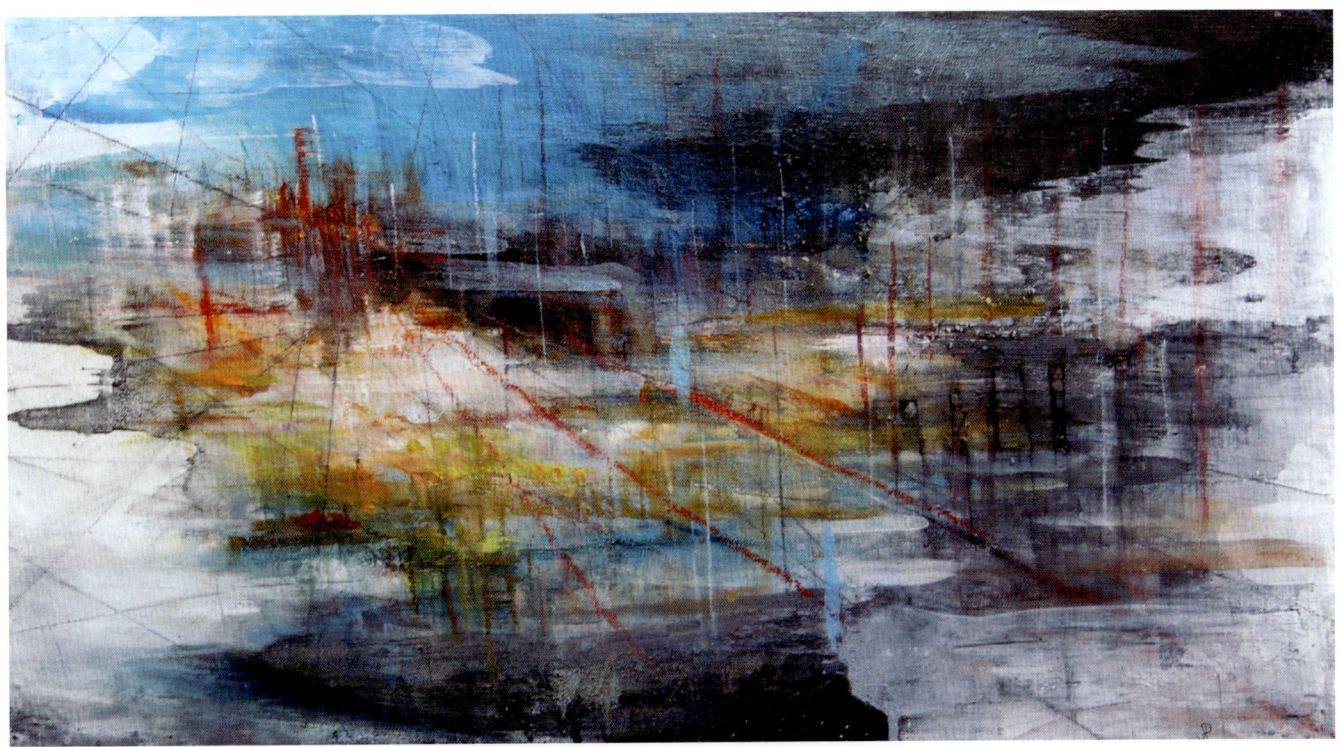

"In my work I tend to oscillate between landscapes and the figure. The main theme present through out all my work is that of passing of time and how it affects this temporary space we all occupy. Everything that makes up our world is in a constant state of flux- everything moving towards it's own end. This finite amount of time defines and gives meaning to true beauty."

My landscapes are layered memories eroded by time. Sun bleached nostalgia of a moment that cannot be repeated. My figurative work embraces the construction/ deconstruction process. While I set out to break down the figure it is important to retain the human spirit. The figures in my work are intended to be anyone and everyone yet I hope balance that ambiguity with human emotion. I want to explore the concept that we are more than just the physical and to express that spark that makes us each unique. I work with a variety of media including oil, acrylic, ink, oil sticks, beeswax, and spray paint. Using mostly palate knives and untraditional mark making tools I hope to tell a story in the fragmented layers.

WWW.JAMESPETRUCCI.COM

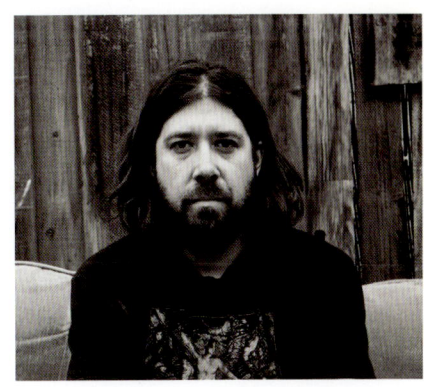

(facing page) Vessel #1 ●
Mixed Media (oil, Beeswax, spray paint, and Shellac) on Paper Mounted on Panel, 22 x 34 in., 2015

Velocity #12 ●
Mixed Media (acrylic, gesso, pastel, charcoal, and graphite) on Panel, 12 x 24 in., 2014

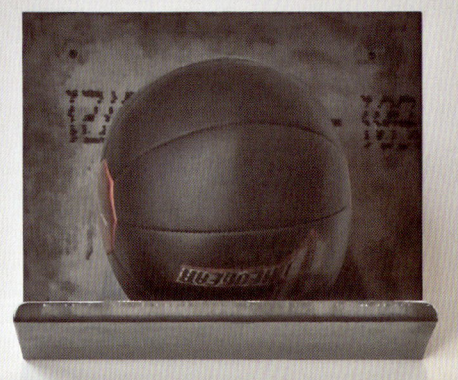

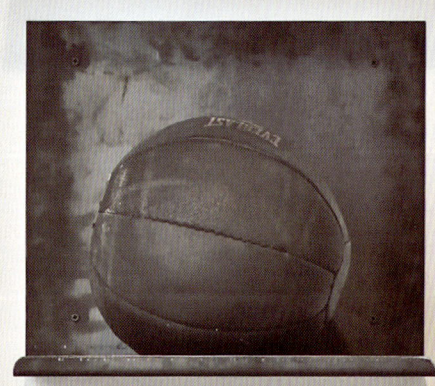

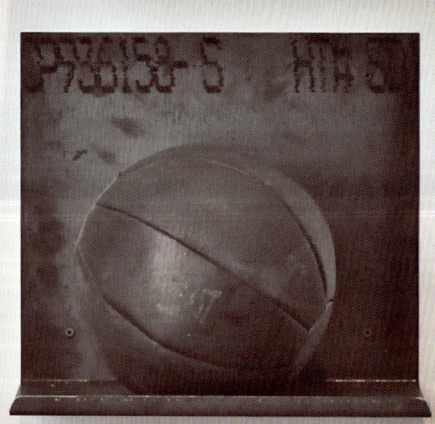

MICHAEL PRIBICH

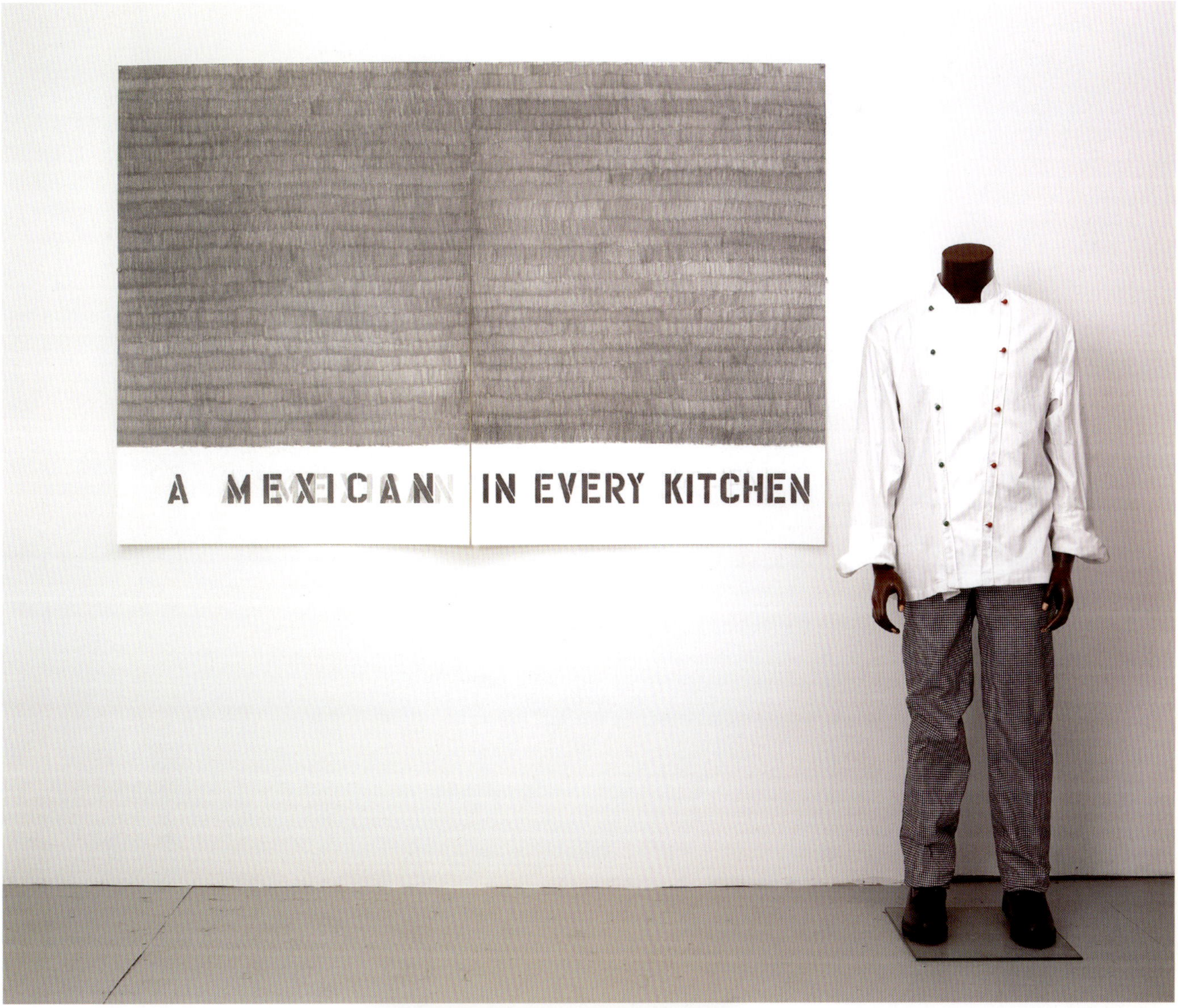

A MEXICAN IN EVERY KITCHEN

● **(facing page) Medicine Ladder**
Bent steel, medicine balls.
55 x 16 x 12 in., 2015

● **Mexican in Every Kitchen**
Graphite on paper, diptych
Standing figure with cotton garments
66"h, 50 x 76 in., 2007

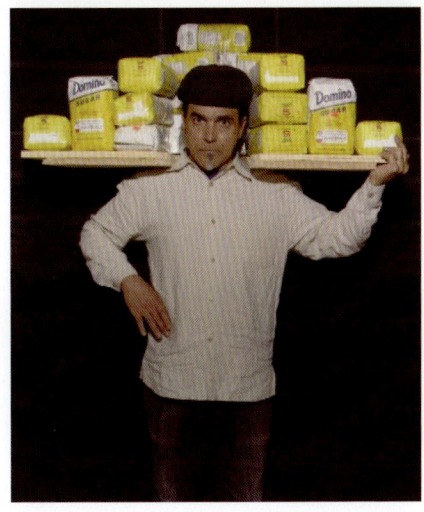

Michael Pribich grew up in Northern California and currently lives in New York City. He received an MFA degree from Hunter College, NY. He is interested in the artist role in advancing ideas and conversations that lead to continual growth and change. He has completed projects with the Public Works departments in Sacramento and Woodland California. His observations form a critique of the working and living conditions of those on the periphery. The disparity between classes inform his use of materials with a coded language of irony, and wit.

WWW.MICHAELPRIBICH.COM

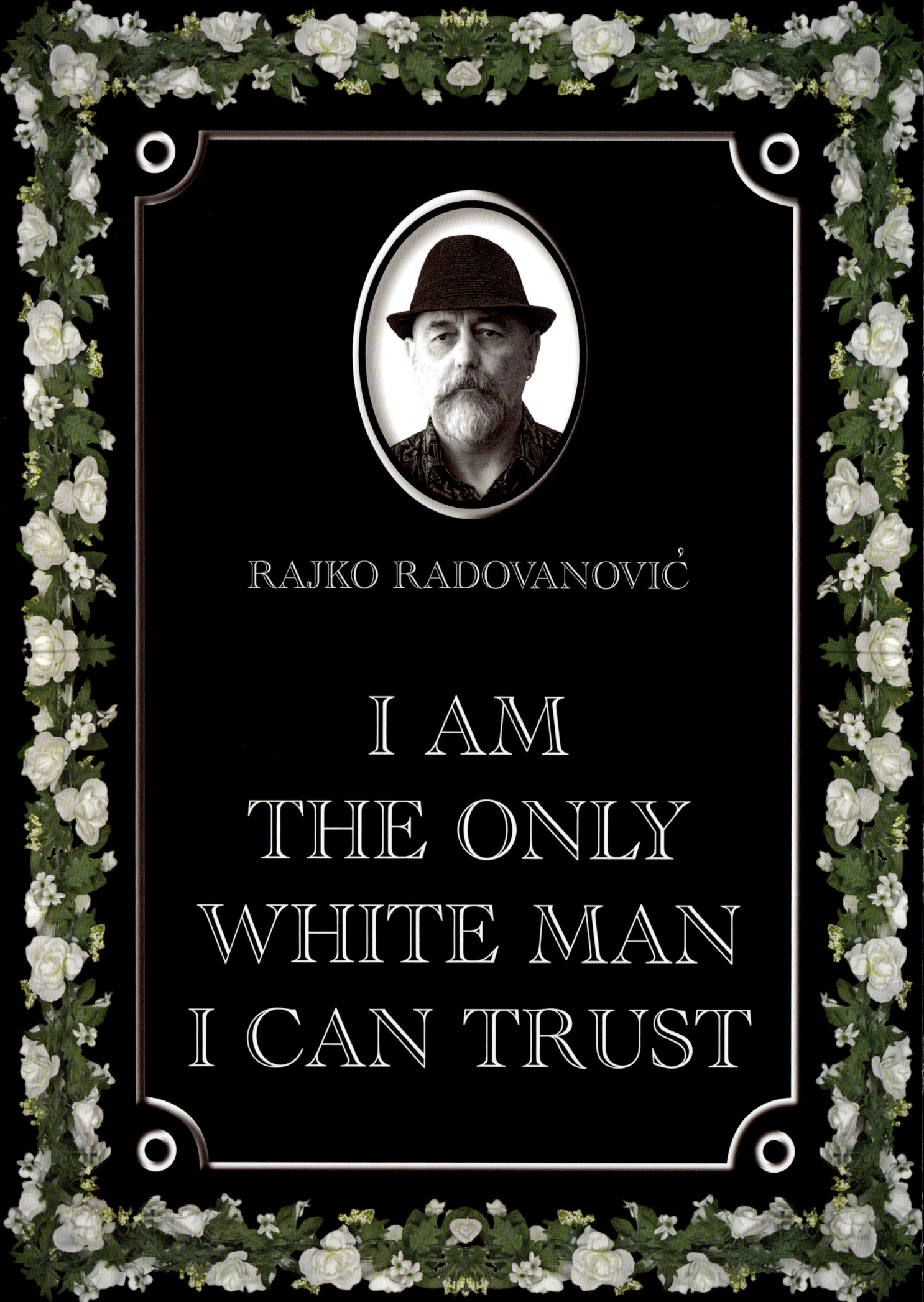

RAJKO RADOVANOVIĆ

A PRECONDITION OF DOING VIOLENCE TO ANY GROUP OF PEOPLE OR NATION IS TO MAKE THEM LESS THAN HUMAN

● **(facing page) Futility of Identity**
Digital print, acrylic paint on archival paper, 35 x 28 in., 2012

● **A Precondition**
Digital print on archival paper, 31 x 25 in., 2008

"To this day, art seems to me the only attempt to deconstruct the daily consent of bearable normalcy. Once one realizes the meaninglessness of one's own environment the only remaining choice is to start to learn how to live with that fact. For [me] art has been and still is a clear modus of existence for an individuated human being."

Rajko Radovanovic was born in a country that no longer exists. It is good to know one's own roots and where we all came from but he no longer believes that the concept of 'home' or that of 'belonging' can be dictated solely by the physical place of birth or by contemporary concepts of 'nationality'. The notion of self-identity is a spiritual choice rather than a political 'given'. Living and working as an artist in a range of different countries Radovanovic has witnessd how modern political establishments, through their use of the media, have promoted the notion of 'other' as a modern definition of 'enemy'. It is through this manufactured concept of

'difference' that moral justification is sought for inflicting violence towards fellow human beings.

Until recently Radovanovic was used to being defined by geographical displacement-my 'foreign' surname. In his new environment of New Orleans, that profiling has now become 'visual' in character. By widening my frame of reference and working directly with people with differing experiences and backgrounds to my own I am continuing to explore current concepts of 'identity', 'home' and 'belonging'.

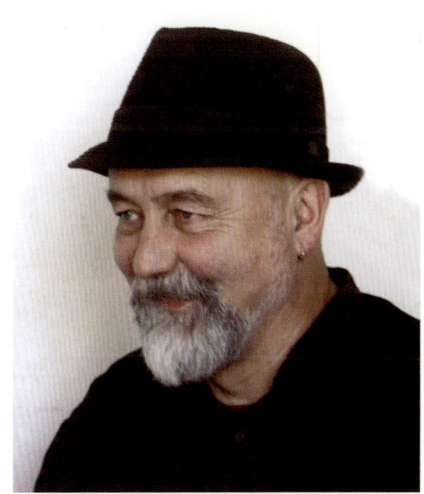

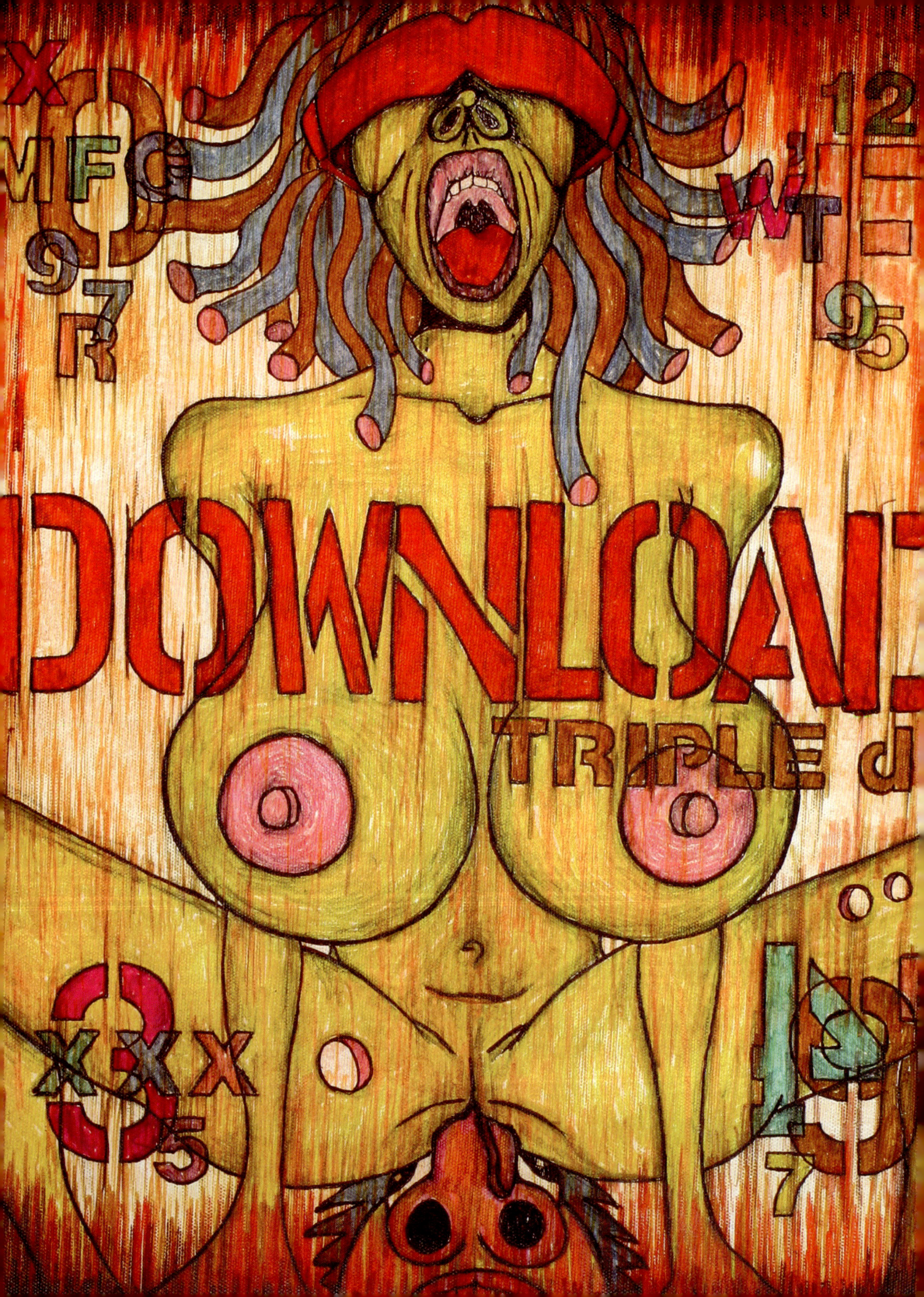

RALPH ROETHER

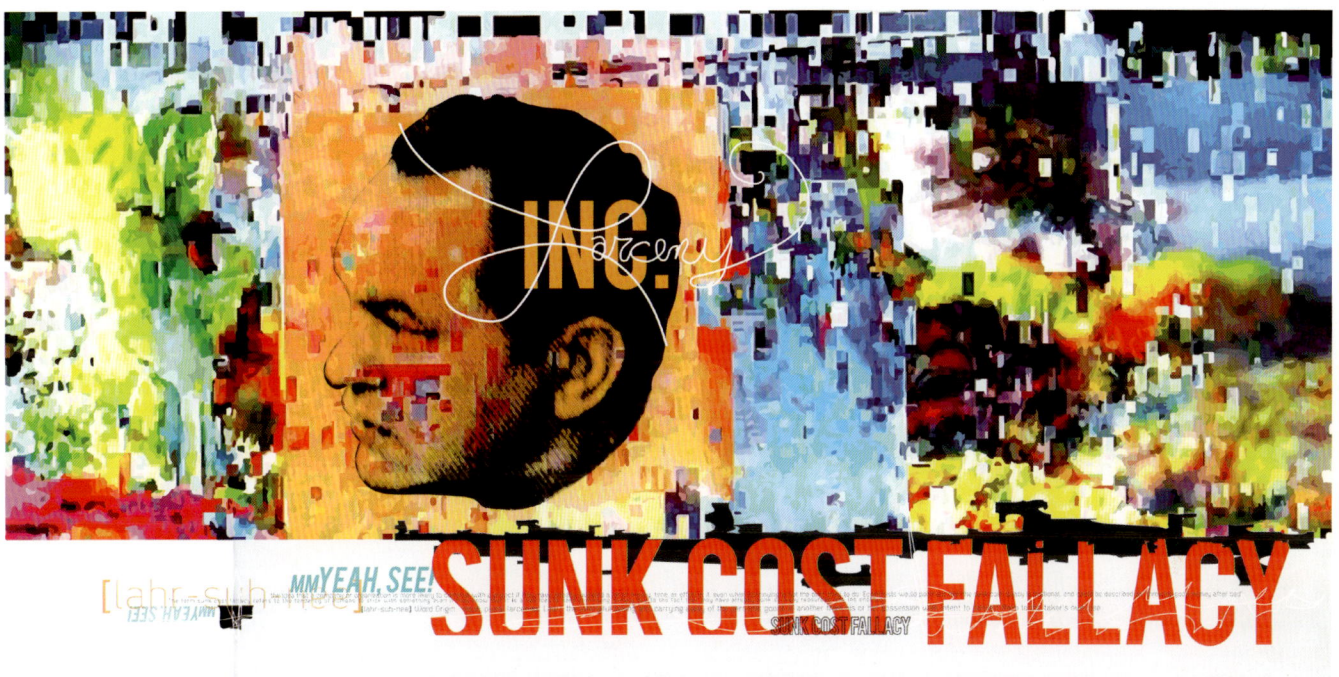

Ralph Roether is an award winning, professional graphic designer, illustrator and artist based in central Illinois. He was born in the city of Chicago, grew up in southern Illinois and settled in the center, where he earned his degree in Graphic Design at the University of Illinois at Urbana-Champaign. His talents were first recognized in the fourth grade where he was then partnered up with the high school art teacher to further develop his artistic skills. He is currently very active in the local art scene doing volunteer and graphic design work for 40 North, the Champaign County Arts Council. He is also a member of the Vault artist collective in Tuscola, IL.

His mediums of choice include markers, ink and pencil work on paper. He frequently works with acrylics and mixed media on wood panels or doors. He also creates digital illustrations from his original artwork and photography. His subject matter ranges from playful imaginative cartoon type doodles, and ones with sexual fantasy themes. He is also a portrait artist that often combines his love of typography. Ralph's work has been featured in many local art festivals and one man shows, as well as Dirty Detroit/Dirty Show and in Studio Visit Magazine Volume 29.

WWW.RALPHROETHER.COM

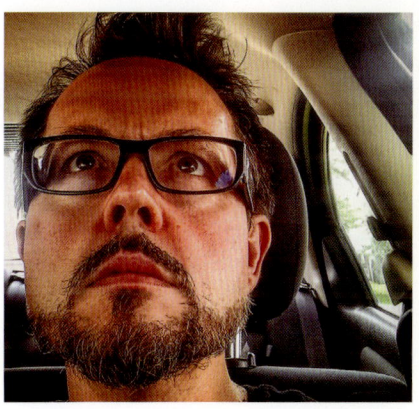

(facing page) Download ●
Mixed media on canvas, 18 x 20 in. 2009

Sunk Cost Fallacy ●
Digital print, 16 x 8 in., 2015

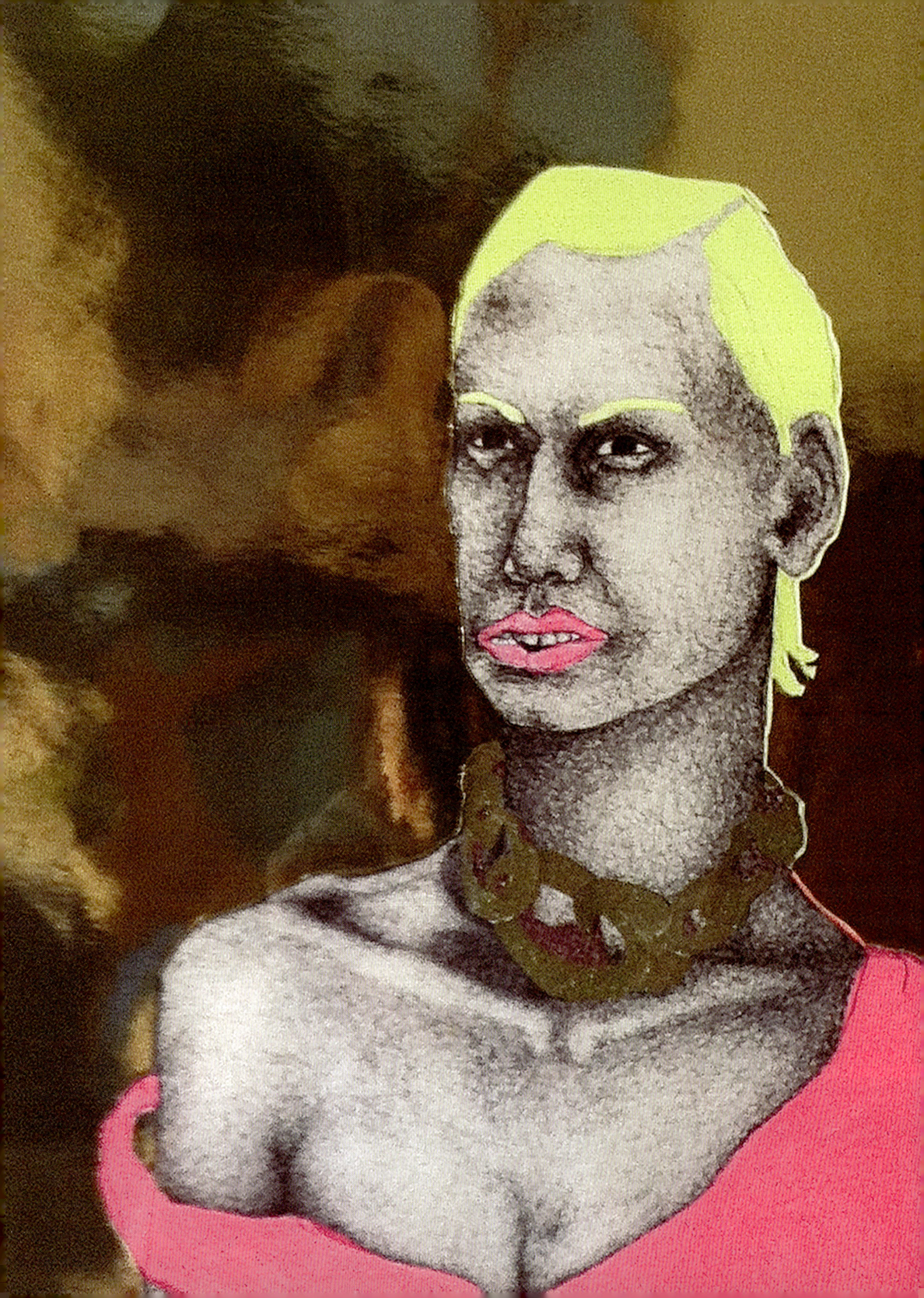

LINDA SERRONE ROLON

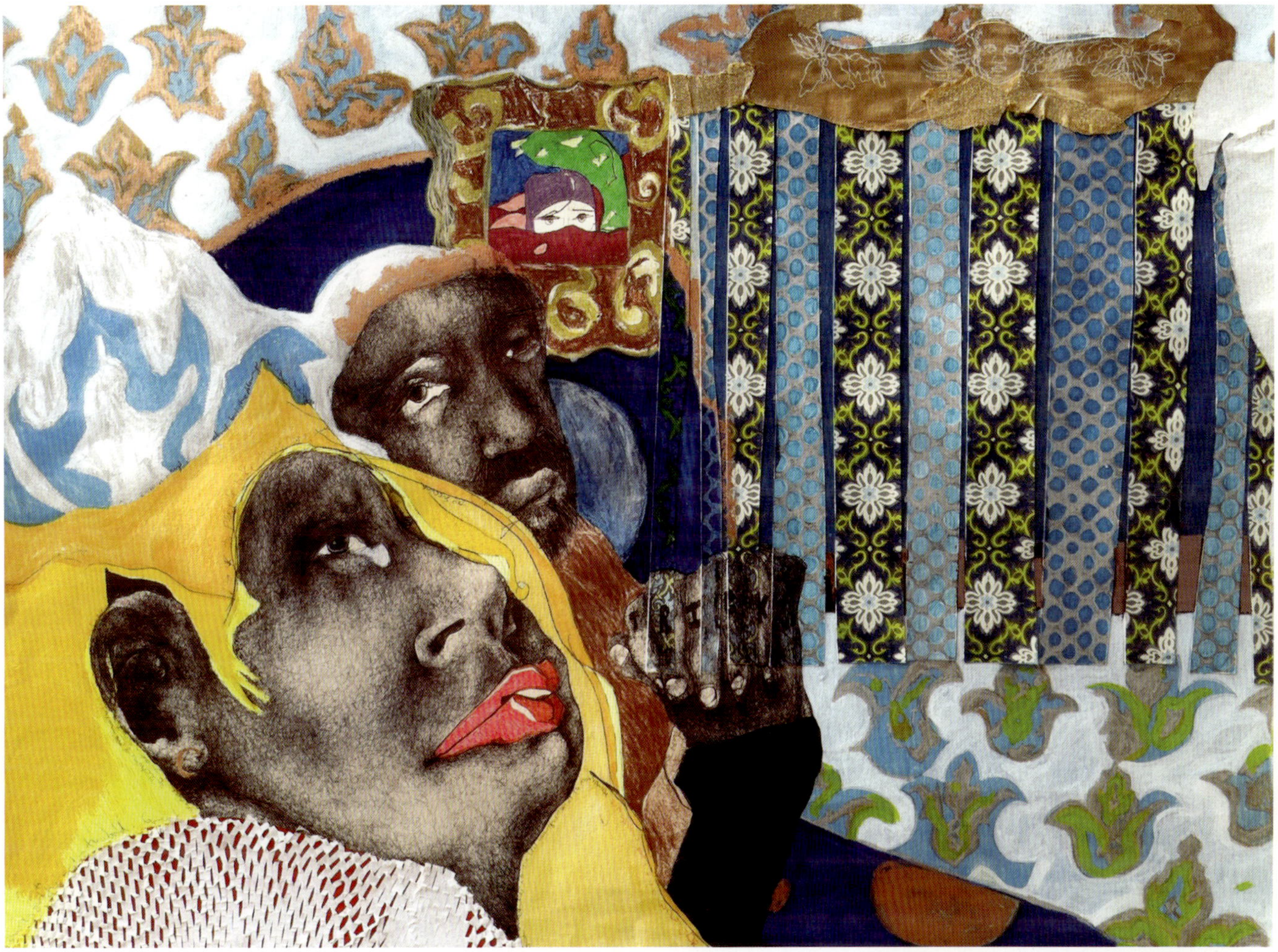

Linda Serrone Rolon was born in 1974 and raised in the boroughs of NYC. Serrone Rolon was raised in an untraditional fashion that forced her to be the observer she is today. At a very young age she traced everything in sight. This created a strong muscle memory of the human face and a trust in herself and how a drawing unfolds. She holds a BFA in painting (2001) and also has taught studio art classes, on and off in Manhattan, Maryland and Brooklyn, for the past 17 years. Her studio remains in Brooklyn, NY.

Linda Serrone Rolon's primary medium is oil paint but she often works out her ideas with a Ballpoint pen on paper. Serrone Rolon always filled sketchbooks but since the birth of her child (2008), working on paper became a more convenient spring board.

In her most recent work, Serrone Rolon distorts situations using color and patterns that are pleasing at first glance. But as you get closer and look a bit longer the intensity of a glance or a positioning of a hand starts to speak volumes. The layers and layers of material(s) in her paintings are created until she can feel the temperature of a character's skin. And with the works on paper, the layers of ink and glitter and more ink makes the paper seem wet or heavy with content that keeps getting covered up. During her process there is a subconscious reality that occurs. And for her, the process is magic.

WWW.LINDASERRONEROLON.COM

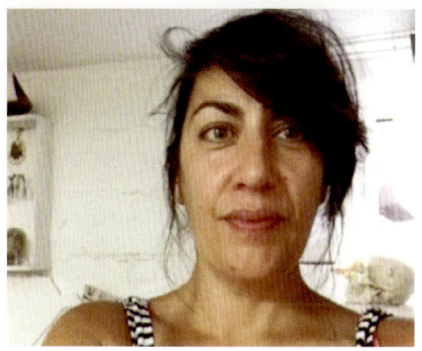

(facing page) Destination of What is III ●
Ballpoint, gold mylar & mixed media on paper
18 x 14 in.

Trick, 365 Days of Rehabiliation... ●
6 years later
Ballpoint & mixed media on paper, 23 x 30 in.

RAINBOW HUSTLER

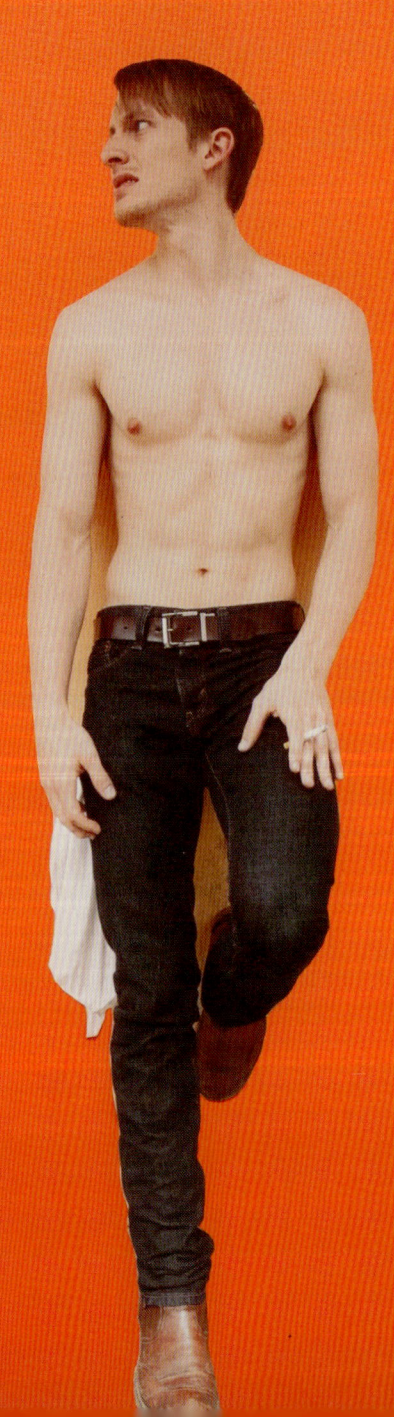

TERRENCE SANDERS

A MAN CALLED ME A NIGGER PERHAPS HE COULDNT PRONOUNCE MY AFRICAN NAME MAYBE IT WAS MY UNFLINCHING GAZE ENVISIONING MY ANCESTORS IN CHAINS CONJURING MASTER RACES CRIMES ANGAINST HUMANITY THE RAPE OF AFRICAN PUBESCENT GIRLS IS DOMINANT IN MY HUE ENGULFED BY CONDESCENDING IRREVERENCE SOLIDIFIED BY GREED AND CONTEMPT STOLEN AND SOLD INTO SLAVERY BY AFRICAN EUROPEAN AND AMERICAN STRIPPED NAKED OF NATIVE TONGUE CULTURE FAMILY AND HOMELAND WHEN I A M OF NO FURTHER USE AS A MUL E OF CAPITALISM THEY DENY ME AN EDUCATION AND CALL ME IGNORANT THEY DENY ME WORK THEY INFLICT FOR FEAR OF A BLACK PLANET IMPRISON BLAC K YOUTHS FOR FEAR OF A REVOLU TION RAPIST MURDERERS LI ARS THIEVES YOUR SERVANTS CONTINUE TO WORK WITHOUT COMPLAINTS THEY SIP CHAMP AGNE AND EAT HOR D OEUVRES

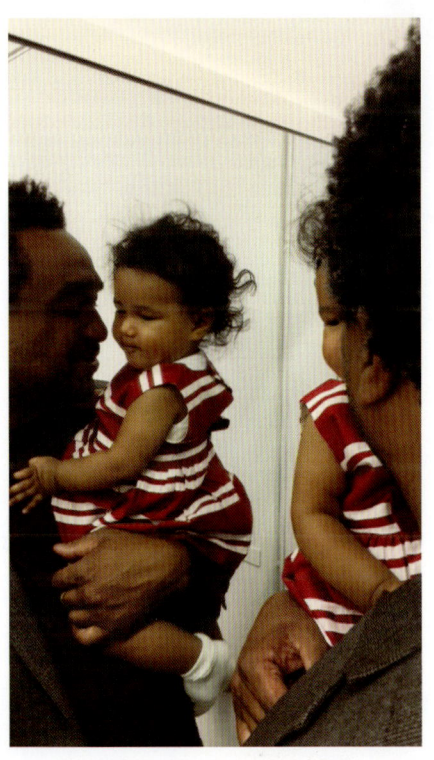

I feel a strong responsibility to provide the viewer with stimulating visuals that speak in an equally distinct language. These tableaux initiate a vibrant dialogue between subject and viewer. Collecting reference and materials from photo archives, the internet, academic papers and mass culture periodicals, I transform the data collected to create works that reflect the world's turbulent, terrible and beautiful past. Examining the human condition, the exploration breaks social and cultural barriers. The resulting pieces ask the viewer to synthesize many threads of thought and provoke critical thinking. The viewer draws new conclusions atop already layered narratives. I will continue to expose systemic corruption and abuses inherent in contemporary structures.

WWW.TERRENCESANDERS.COM

● **(facing page) Rainbow Hustler**
Mixed media on canvas, 35 7/8 x 60 in., 2011

● **Nigger**
Mixed media, 124 x 60 in. 2011

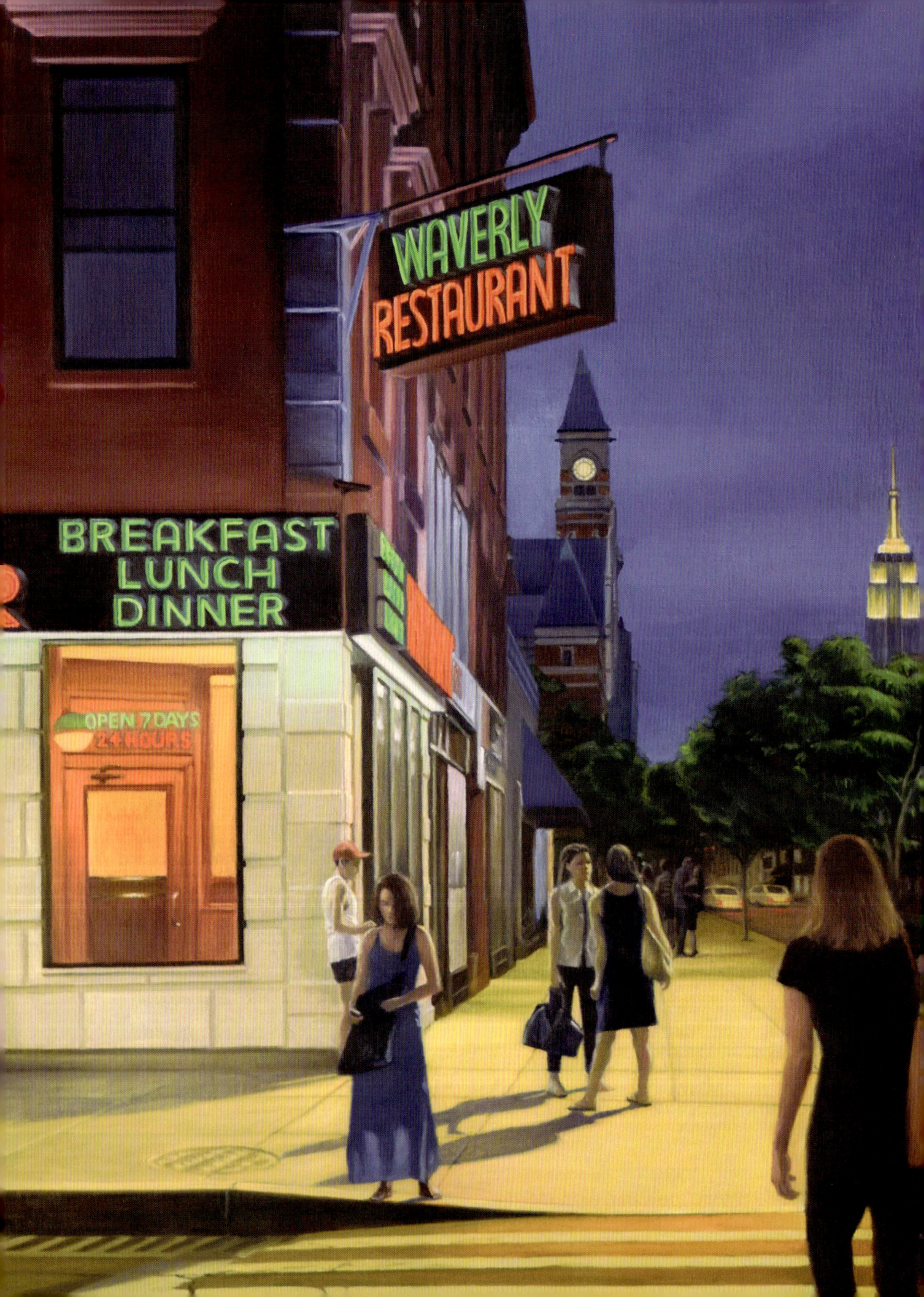

NICK SAVIDES

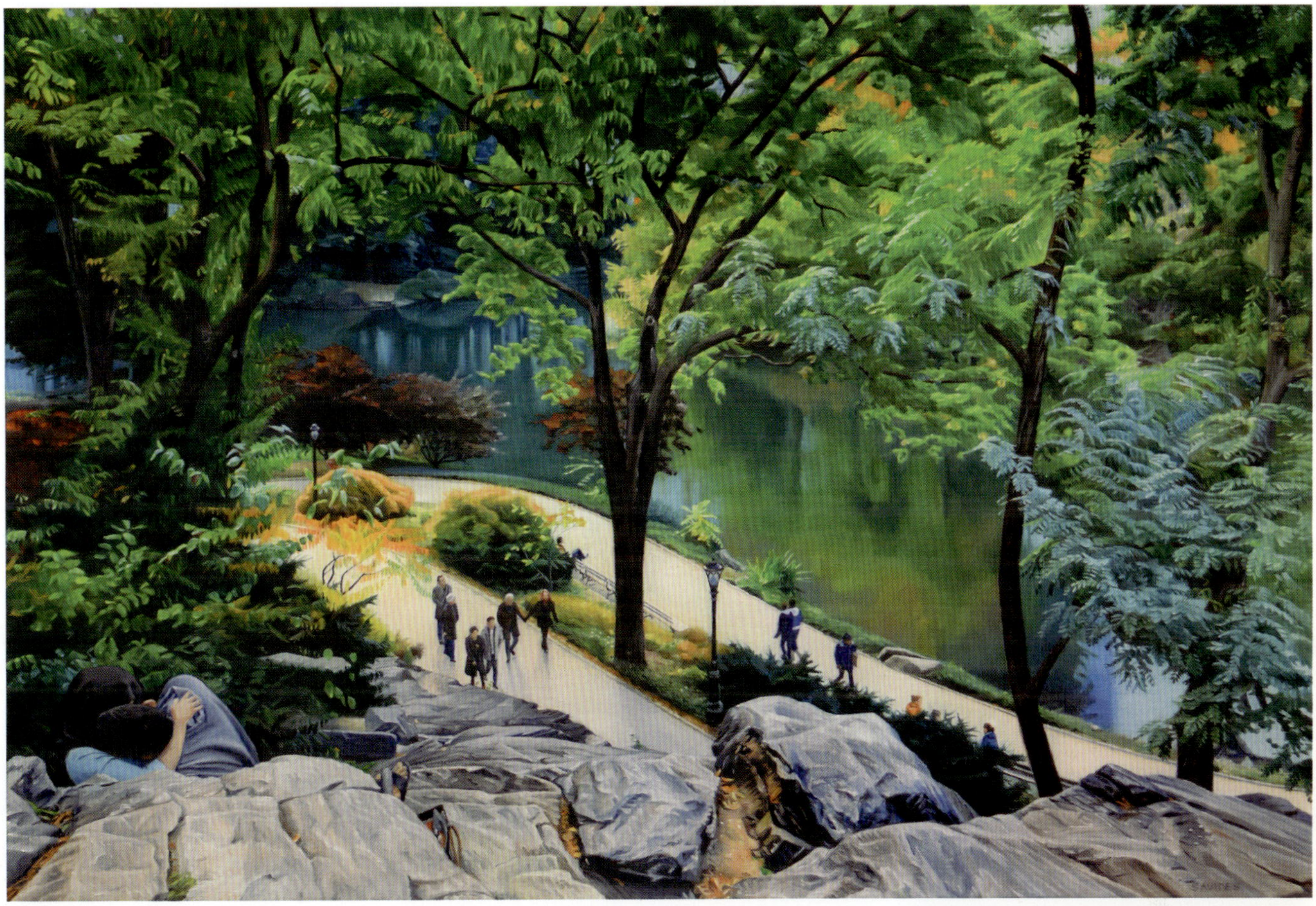

Nick Savides learned to paint from his mother at three years old and hasn't stopped since. Inspired by the works of Edward Hopper, the quiet energy within his art captures a palpable sensation of both light and place. The paintings' range encompasses urban scenes and architecture, landscapes, the figure and portraiture.

After studying under Paul Georges at Brandeis University, Nick began a career as a Realist painter. It was then that the effects of light became and stayed a key ingredient in his paintings. The paintings capture a sense of time and place with a certain understatement, as many of the titles would suggest, such as "Wall Street – Early Morning". They grip you by inviting you in with the familiar and showing you more than you expected. As Val Schaffner writes, "Beyond the carefully rendered beauty, complexity, and calm of his art, there is mystery: a sense of something about to be discovered."

Since his first solo show in 1980, he has exhibited in many group and solo shows in New York City, as well as Massachusetts, Long Island, Upstate New York, Connecticut, and New Jersey. His work is included in numerous private and public collections, and was featured on June Middleton's "Minding Your Business," which aired in 2010. Twice published by Nabi Press, he had a retrospective of his work at the Berkeley College Gallery in 2012, and his work is on the cover of the 2015 William & Mary Review.

Nick lives and paints in Brooklyn.

WWW.NICKSAVIDES.COM

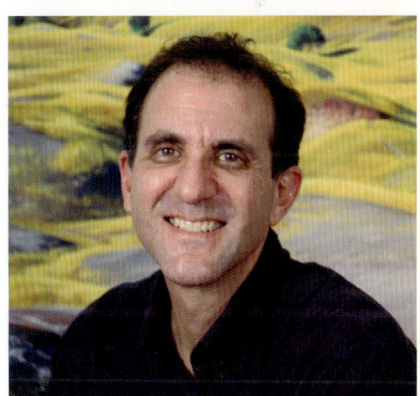

(facing page) Waverly Diner ●
Oil on linen, 42 x 36 in., 2014

Lovers in Central Park ●
Oil on linen, 36 x 54 in., 2015

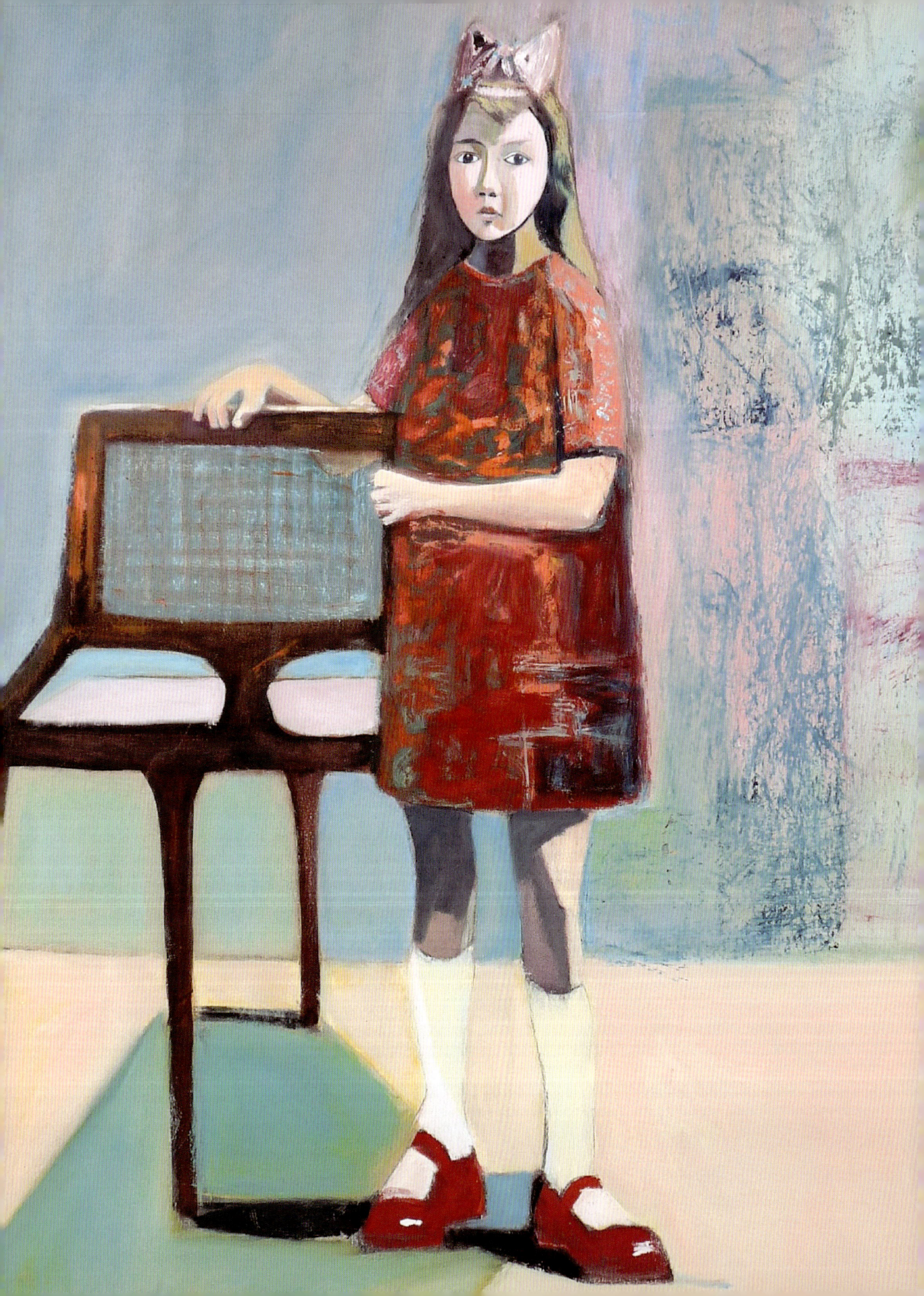

CAROLYN SCHLAM

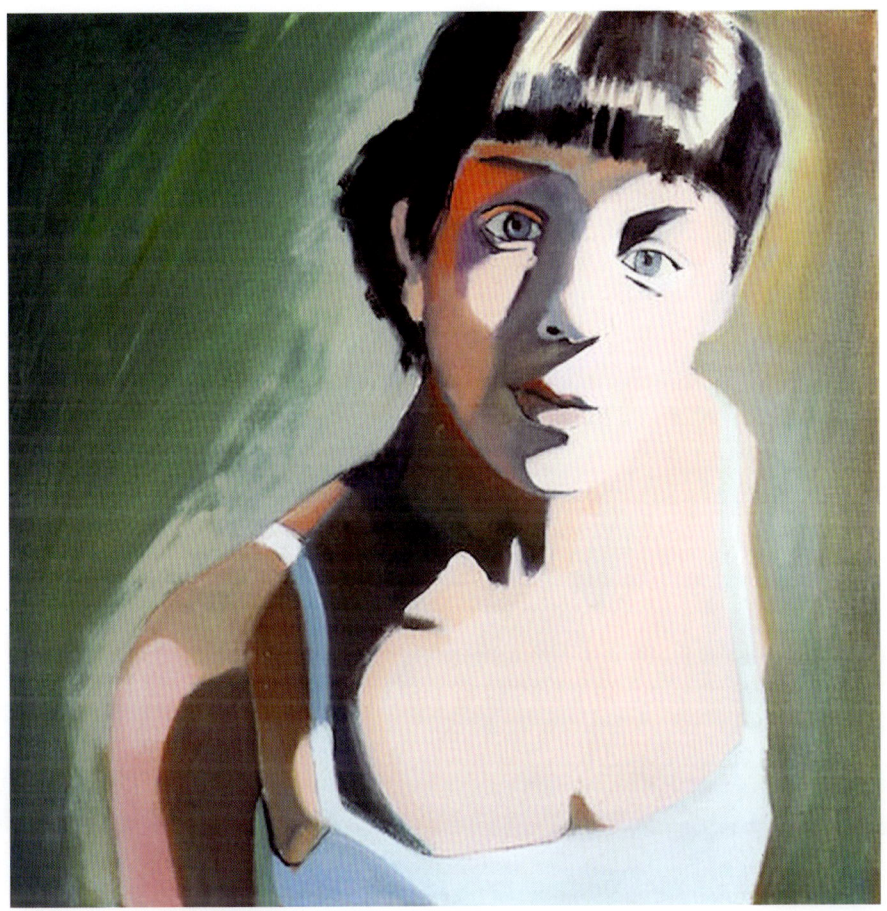

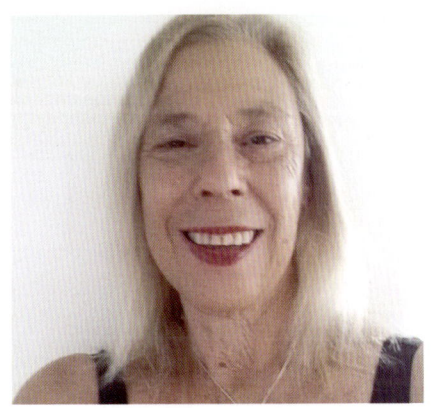

I am a figurative painter, sculptor and glass artist. My portraiture is modern and narrative; to peer below the surface and express the ineffable peculiarity of human emotion is always my intent. A kind of longing to be witnessed is at the heart of my imagery. I am currently working in oil, ink, mixed media, glass and wood.

In 2013, I was named one of the finalists in the Smithsonian Museum Portrait Competition and my work, "Frances at 103" was exhibited at the Museum, and was subsequently acquired by the Smithsonian. I am now at work on "In Bloom", a proposed exhibition of 100 works of feminine portraits and floral motifs.

I am the author of a treatise on art called "The Creative Path: Process and Practice" which is represented by Schulman Literary Agency in New York. I have also written a sequel for children called "Art Smarts" and have contributed samples of my work and illustrations to many other books.

I maintain a wonderful studio in Taos, NM where I live in a cohousing community. The studio is a veritable playroom with areas for my serious work in oil and glass, as well as a workshop for the folk arts I practice for soul repair: my soft dolls for children and glass dolls for adults have cheered many. I believe that all of our being, even our frivolous side, can be gloriously represented in art.

To do so is the purpose and the joy of my life.

WWW.CAROLYNSCHLAM.COM

● **(facing page) Little French Girl**
Oil on canvas, 50 x 36 in., 2014

● **I Wonder**
Oil on canvas, 24 x 24 in., 2014

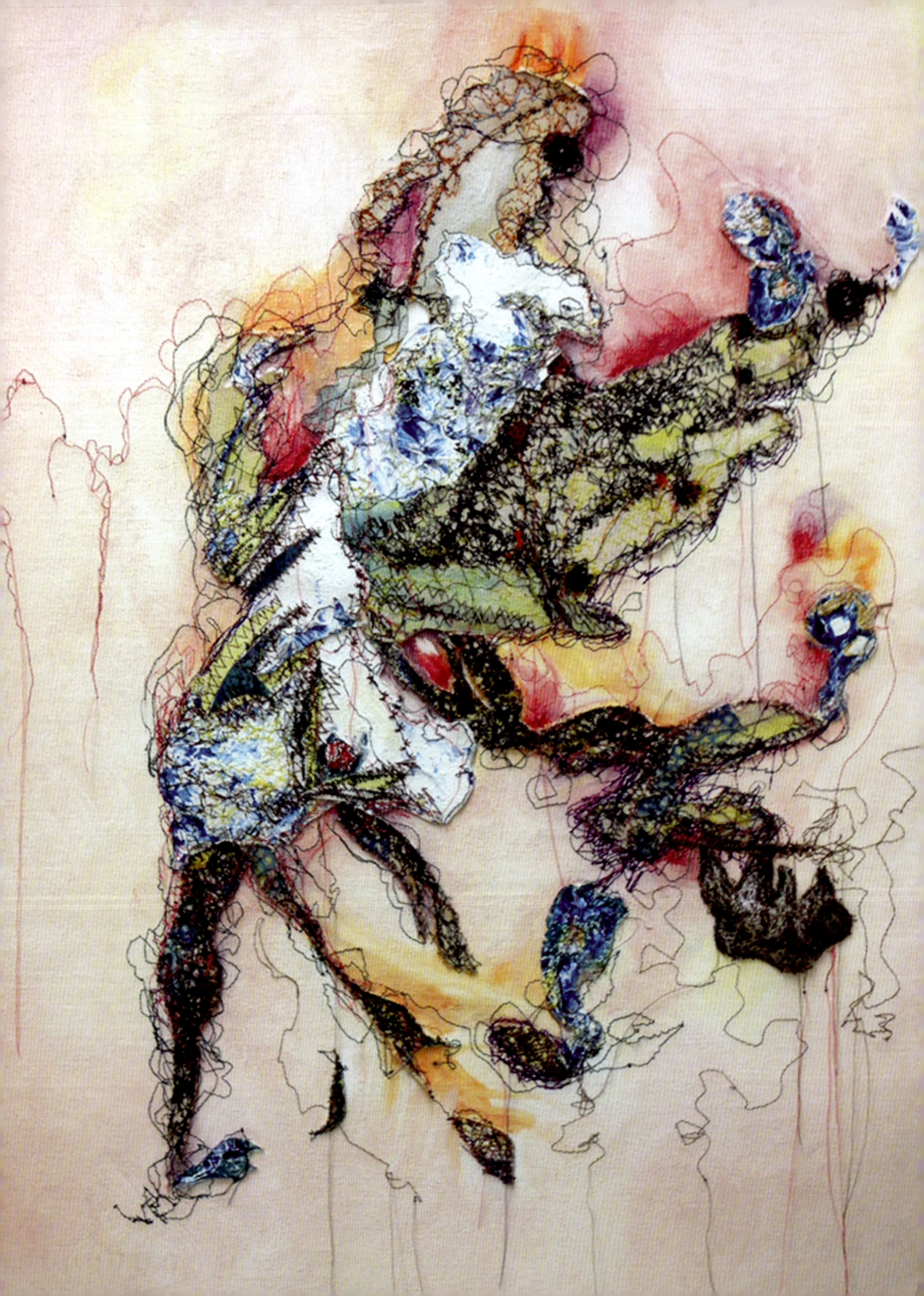

ON KYEONG SEONG

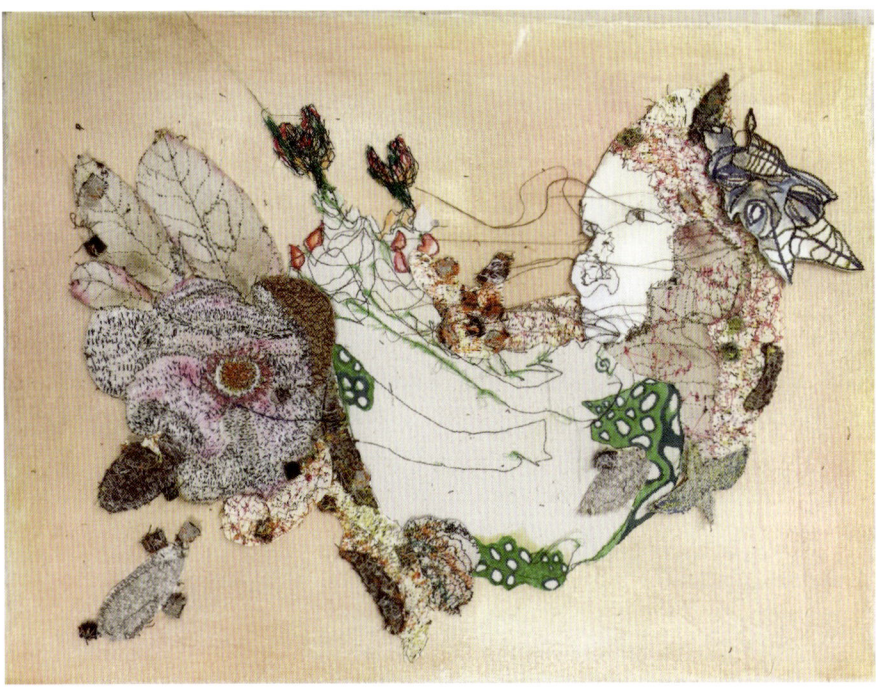

● **(facing page) The very place where I was made**
Stitchery and oil, 18 x 24 in., 2015

● **Imagine the shimmer of high noon**
Painted and sewn collage, oil, and needlework, 22 x 28 in., 2014

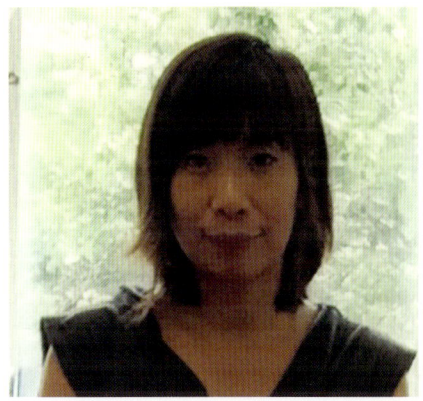

"My inspiration for those work comes from multiple sources; my interest in cell biology, particularly in relationship to pathology and human mortality, a love of nature, concern for the environment, and feminist ideas around women's labor, as well as a latent interest in a general form of feminist idea."

On Kyeong Seong presents a body of work consisting of displaying biomorphic abstraction developed through unconventional means such as sewing machine as well as painted and sewn collage used to build up a relief surface on the canvas. The abstractions generally take the form of an isolated figure surrounded by the canvas, but also sometimes represent an environment of interrelated forms. The forms evoke association with cell biology, natural microscopic forms, bodily organs, flowers, and carnivorous plants and other combinations of flora and fauna. Adding to the sense of strangeness and grotesqueness is the use of dangling threads that sometimes look like manmade screens, plant filaments, or human hair.

By observing nature under magnification for a discovery of its mystic and magical sense,

Seong often find that shapes and forms have distinctive features as the disparate, the unusual, and the monstrous objects through which perfection and imperfection versus beauty and ugliness exist side by side; by revealing these contrasting ideas, my works of art portray them in both. Hence, her works of art, in providing distorted realities of nature through my abstract ideas, describe that all beings can exist alongside and appreciate both beauty and ugliness. Seong begins her work by using the sewing machine as a tool to create automatic drawing gestures and to get away from overly determined painting marks.

She completed her MFA in 2014 while working as the director of children education in Korea. On-Kyeong continues her own studio practice and resides in Greater Boston Area, MA. Her organic-ornamental

compositions combine the sense of mysticism of the Mother Nature and the expressive and autonomous world of my own, translated to the visual language of abstract painting. Her works traverse the fragile line between collage making, painting, and embroidery. The paintings of abstraction serve as the base of her artworks, the collage strengthens the imagery by combining her previous ideas with new ones, and the embroidery offers a unique texture that is actually designed to be pleasing to the touch and made possible the expression of automatism and gestural movements in magnificent nature world.

WWW.ONKYEONG.COM

JAMEL SHABAZZ

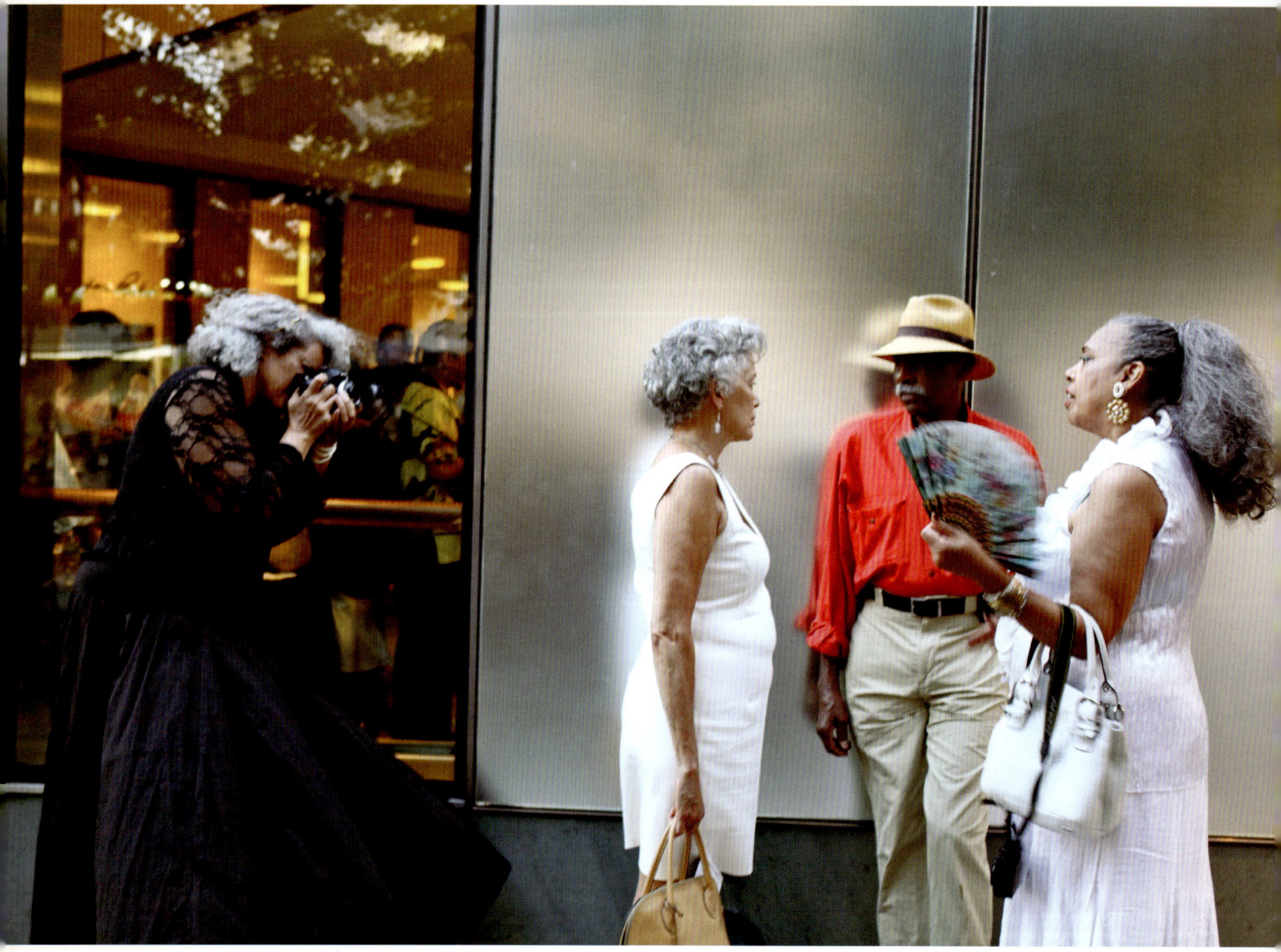

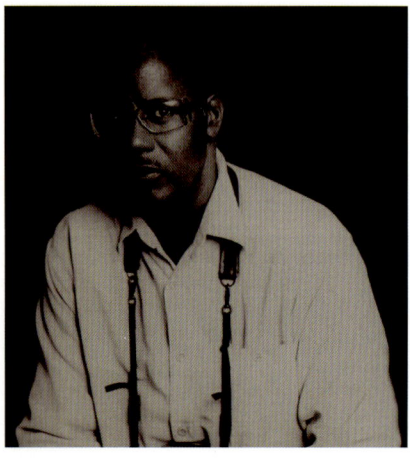

JAMEL SHABAZZ was born and raised in Brooklyn, New York. At the age of fifteen, he picked up his first camera and started to document his peers.   Inspired by photographers Leonard Freed, James Van Der Zee, and Gordon Parks, he was marveled with their documentation of the African American community. In 1980 as a concerned photographer with a clear vision he embarked on a mission to extensively document various aspects of life in New York City, from youth culture to a wide range of social conditions. Due to its spontaneity and uniqueness, the streets and subway system became backdrops for many of his photographs.

Shabazz says his goal is to contribute to the preservation of world history and culture. In the past 10 years he has had over two dozen solo exhibitions; "Men of Honor", "A Time Before Crack", "Pieces of a Man", "Represent", When Two Worlds Meet", "Back in the Days," and "Seconds of my Life," which have been shown from Argentina to

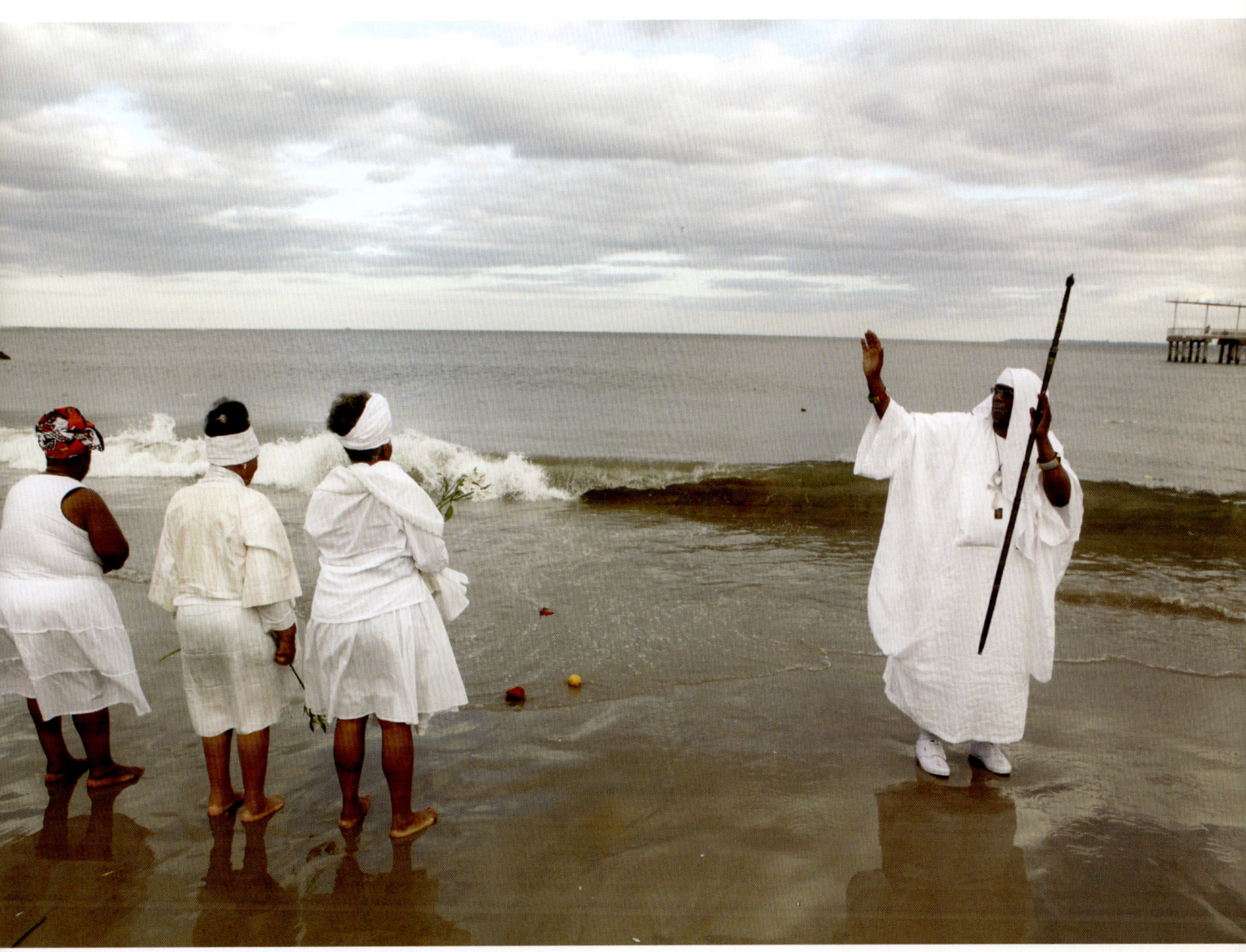

The Netherlands, England, Italy, Germany, France, Japan and throughout the United States.

An even longer list of group showings include Art Basel; Miami, the Brooklyn Museum, the Newark Museum, the Contact Photo Festival, the Victoria and Albert Museum, The Studio Museum in Harlem, Duke University, and the Adidas Photo Festival in Ethiopia.

Over the years Jamel has volunteered, working with a wide range organizations centered on inspiring young people in the field of photography and social responsibility.

Shabazz is the author of 6 monographs.

WWW.JAMELSHABAZZ.COM

(facing page) Four Shades of Gray ●
Digital C print, 11 x 14 in., 2012

Tribute to the Ancestors ●
Digital C print, 11 x 14 in., 2014

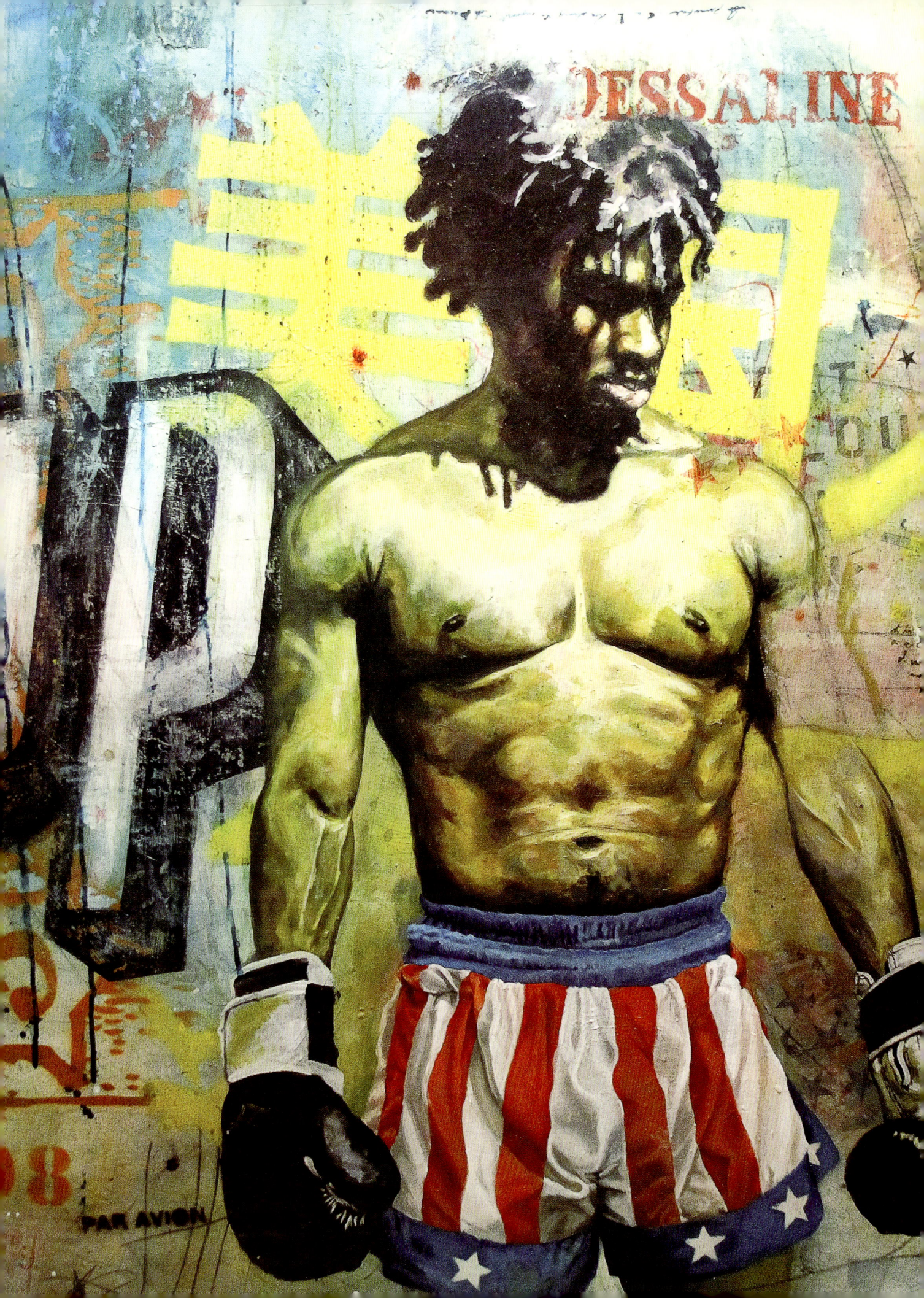

GREGORY ST. AMAND

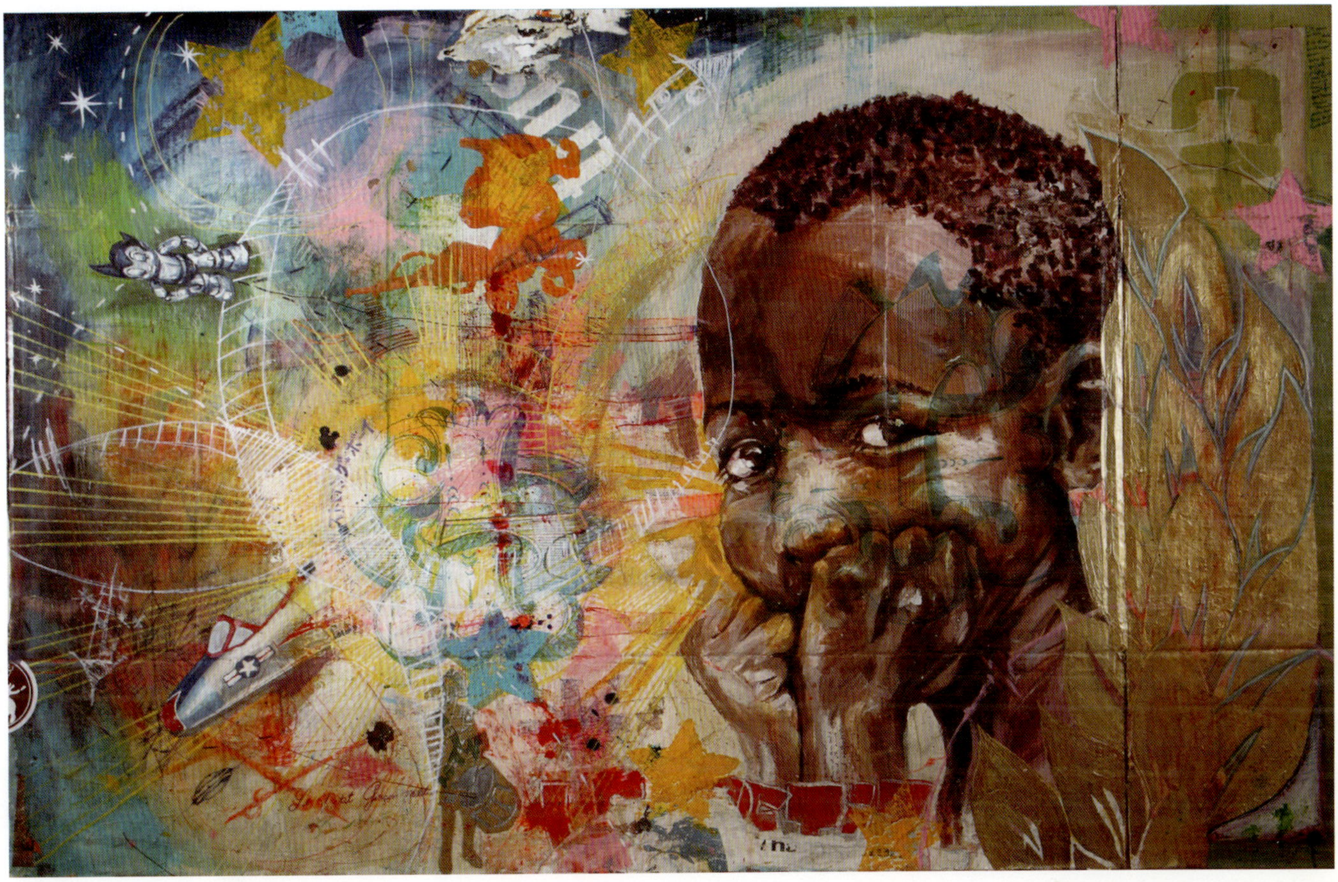

Gregory Saint Amand's art is both playful and sharp with astonishing depth, expressed through layers of symbols and contemporary esthetics of lines and iconography while creating an interesting balance with figurative subjects. It pushes visions of the west and the east through the eyes of boy who grew up in a Haitian family. His extraordinary colors offer a new language of depth and boldness and gives a sense of freedom, to a romantic nostalgia. It creates an anticipation of great joy that is heart warming, and pleasing to the eyes. The rudeness of the brushstrokes make the work inviting and hypnotizing and masterful. Every time you look at it you discover something new hidden in the layers, increasing the charm of the work.

Gregory employs a wide range of art medium techniques such as inks, acrylics, pen, markers and various others he paints on canvas wood and even cardboard. St Amand paints humanity and its varied cultural languages that clearly and surprisingly peek through his art leaving the feeling that it only could have been expressed in such a way. His art communicates visual language that seduces one another into dialogue.

Gregory was born in New York, but raised in Haiti from age 1 with his grandparents who called him GOGO, before returning to the US in his later teens. Gregory St.Amand attended college at THE COOPER UNION for the Advancement of Science and Art. Winning a full 4-year scholarship earning his BA Degree.

WWW.IKNOWGOGO.COM/

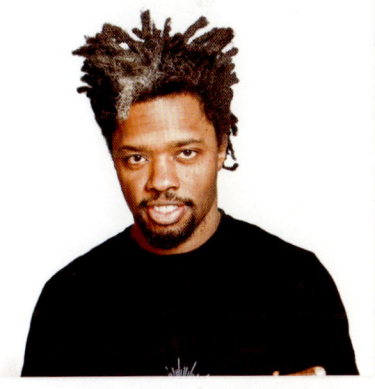

(facing page) The American Fighter ●
Mised media, 65 x 64 in., 2015

Frere de Astro ●
*Mixed media, acrylic, links & alkyd,
48 x 73 in., 2010*

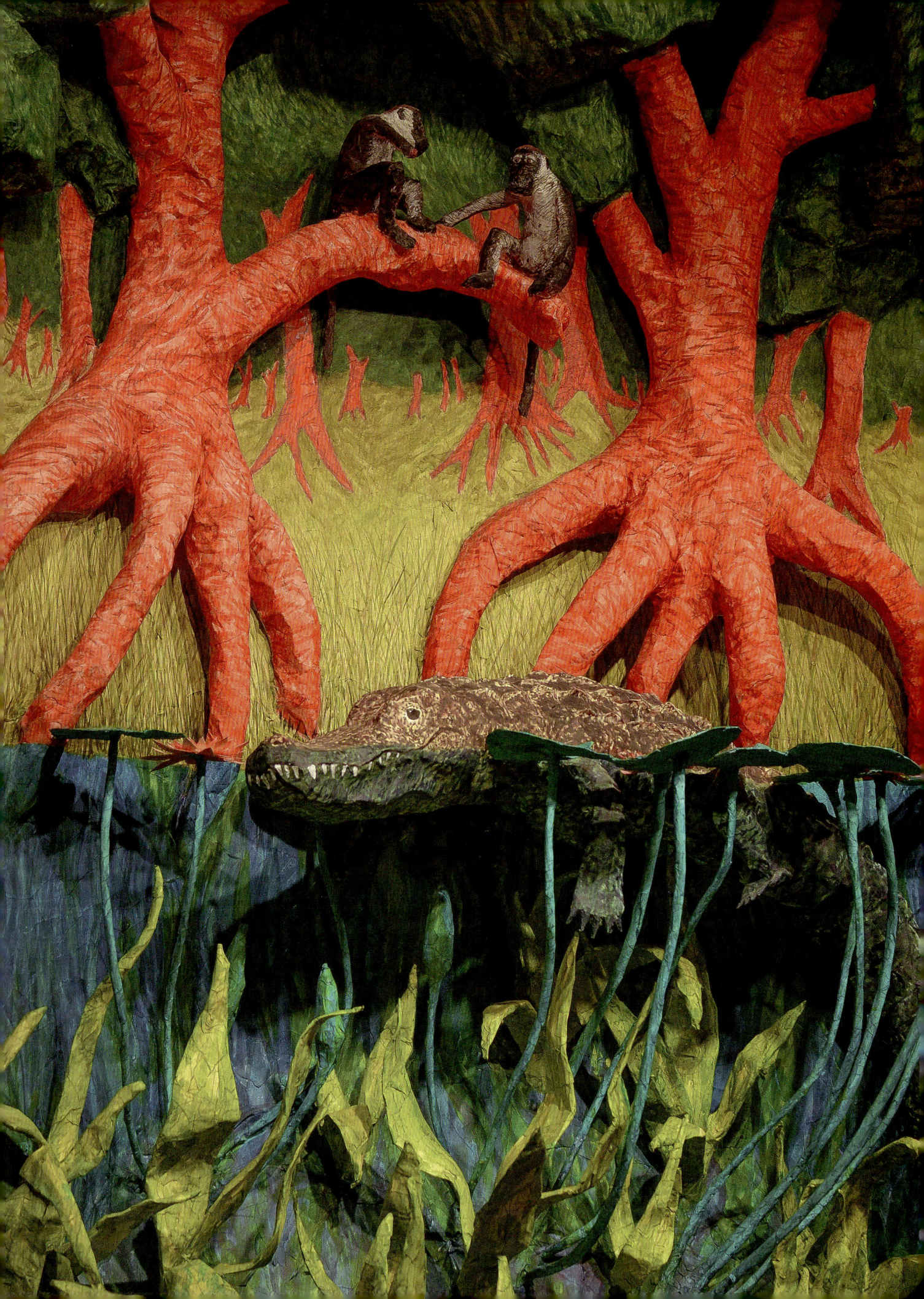

ALFRED STONE

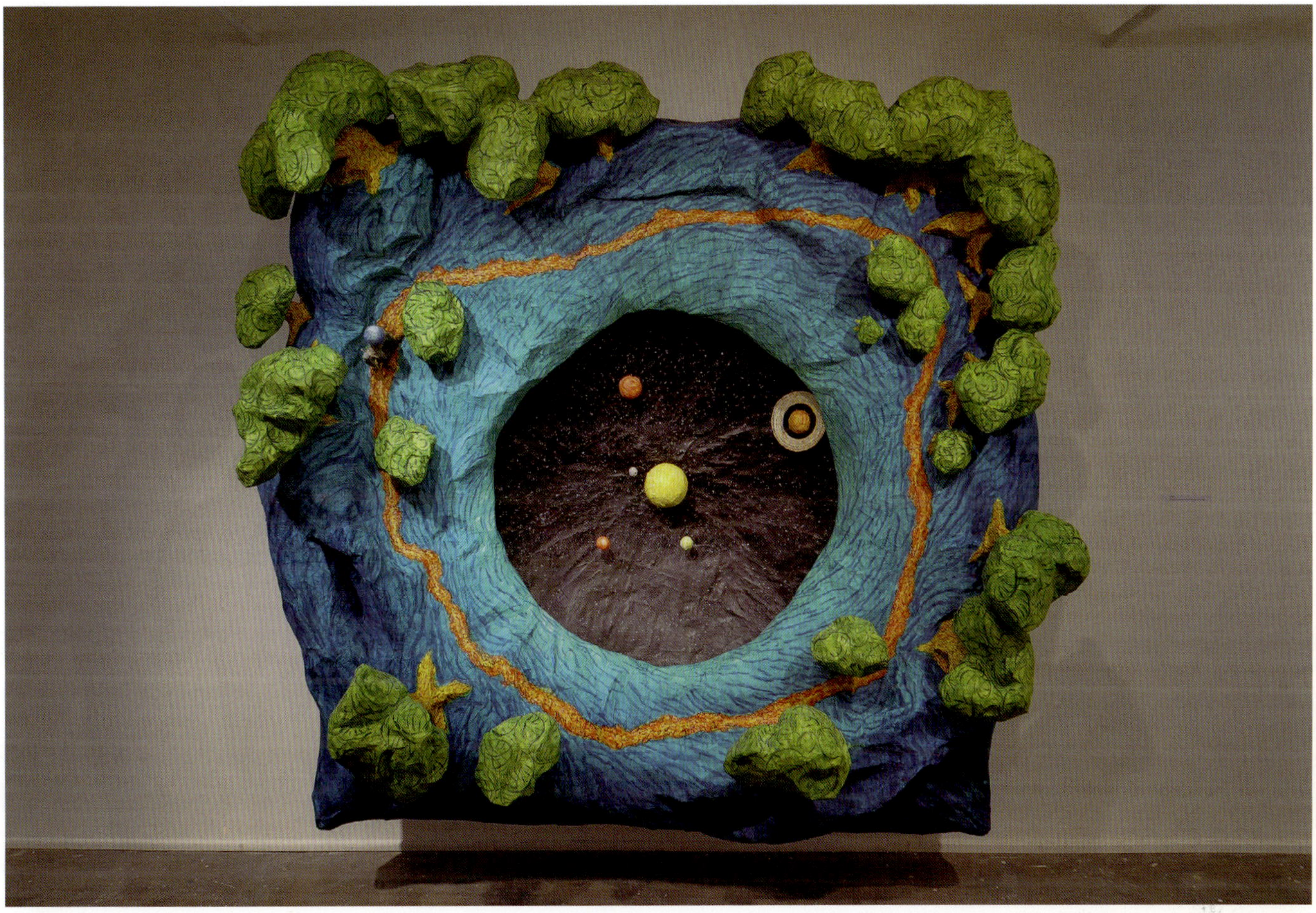

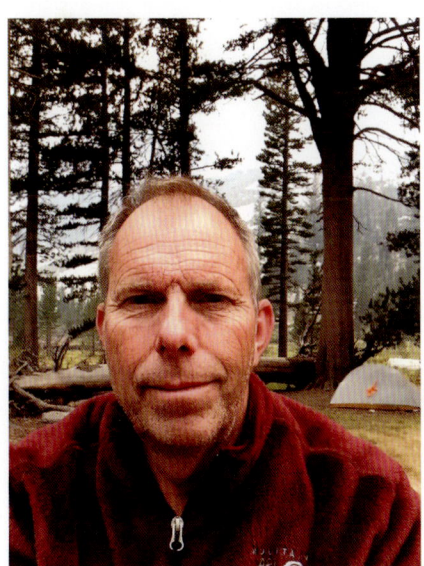

"So what do we see and why? We all approach the art work independently within a shared environment, looking, imagining, creating."

The Imagery, themes and concepts which Stone"s work is rooted in, arrive from his interest in cultural anthropology and our cultural environment. He's questioning perception; the act of looking and its mediation and effect. With the understanding that our culture is a mode of measurement of comparison and context, and in such there are no "absolutes". What Alfred is exploring is how we exist in participatory universe, our awareness of physical phenomenon and how they are defined by the questions we ask of them and the limits of expression.

WWW.ALFREDSTONE.COM

(facing page) See No ●
Ink on paper over wire and wood,
88 x 62 x 28 in., 2011

Center ●
Ink on paper over wire and wood,
80 x 82 x 27 in., 2008

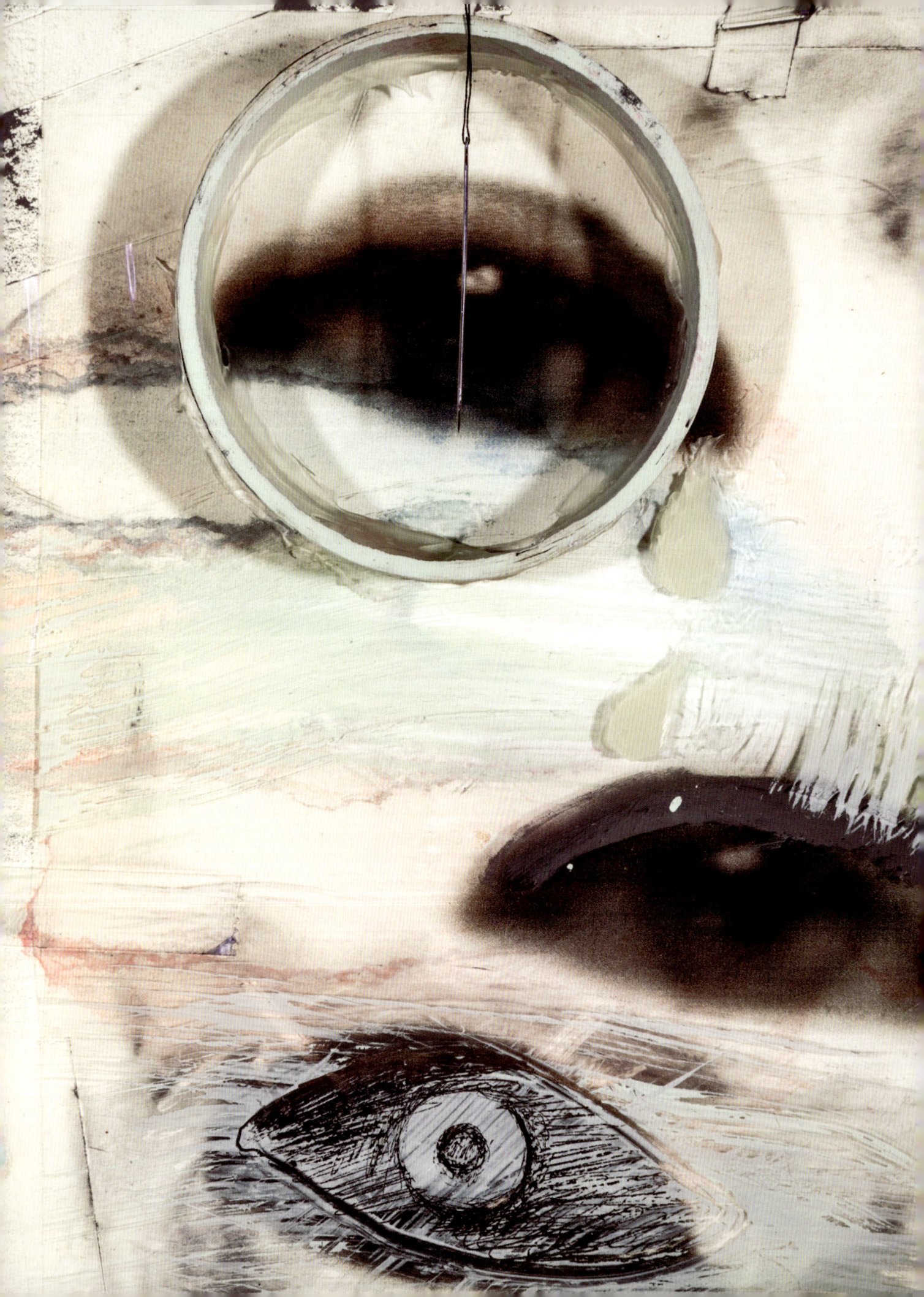

PAM SUTHERLAND

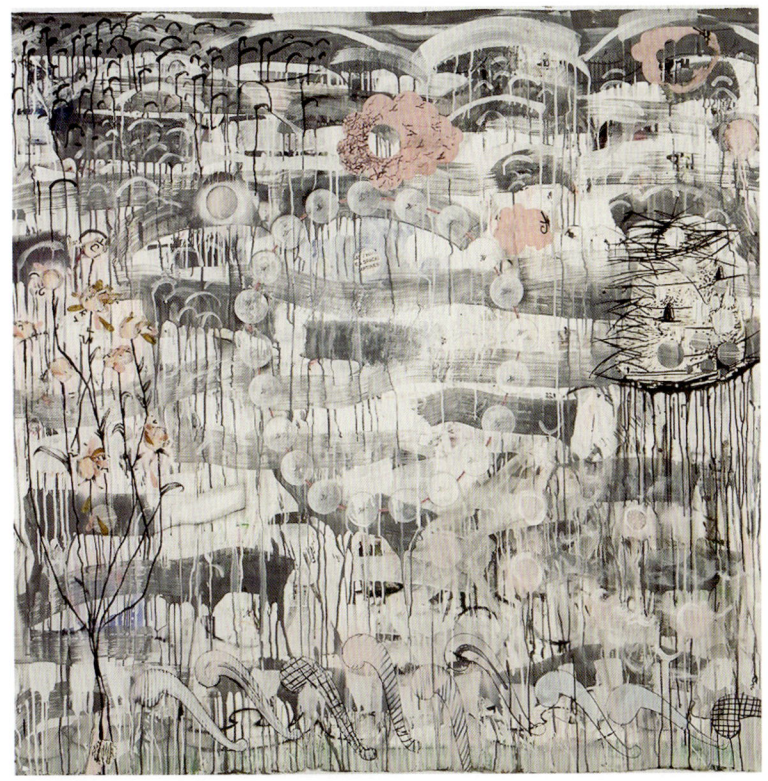

"I am interested in the space between sentiment and formalism. My work, by appropriating and adding to the collected evidence of my life, pays homage to art's unique ability to give permanence to the fleeting."

Pam Sutherland is an artist residing in Richmond, VA who works in drawing, collage and installation.

Pam received the Virginia Museum of Fine Arts Fellowship in 2004 for Drawing. Solo shows include Souvenirs of Daily Life at Second Street Gallery in Charlottesville in 2001; one heArt, an installation at the Orange Door Gallery in Richmond in 2003; New Drawings at ADA Gallery in 2004; Too Much Sugar at Main Art Gallery in September 2006; and both Esoteric Blanket in January 2007 and Ghosts from a Middle Place in February 2010 at Kathryn Markel Gallery in NYC. She exhibited her sculptural paintings in Acts of Arrangement at the Page Bond Gallery in Richmond in September 2103 and most recently revealed her series Gray Matters at the Workhouse Art Center in Lorton, VA as part of the VMFA's Professional Fellowship 75th Anniversary exhibition.

Pam's work was published in the Open Studio Press' Studio Visit in 2008. Finally, she is the 2009 recipient of the Theresa Pollack Prize for Excellence in Fine Art given by Richmond Magazine. Her work is in several public collections including the University of Virginia, the Federal Reserve Bank, the Try Me Collection and Wachovia Securities.

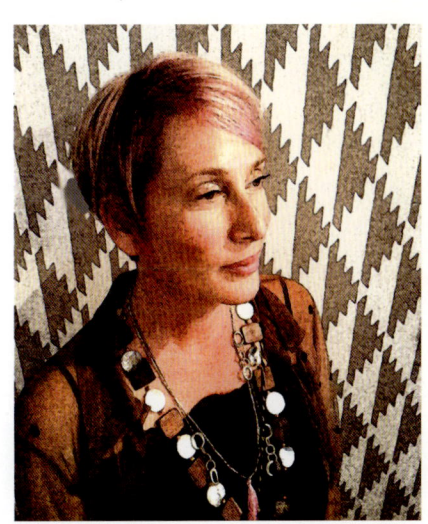

WWW.MAPANDERSON.COM

DAN TAGUE

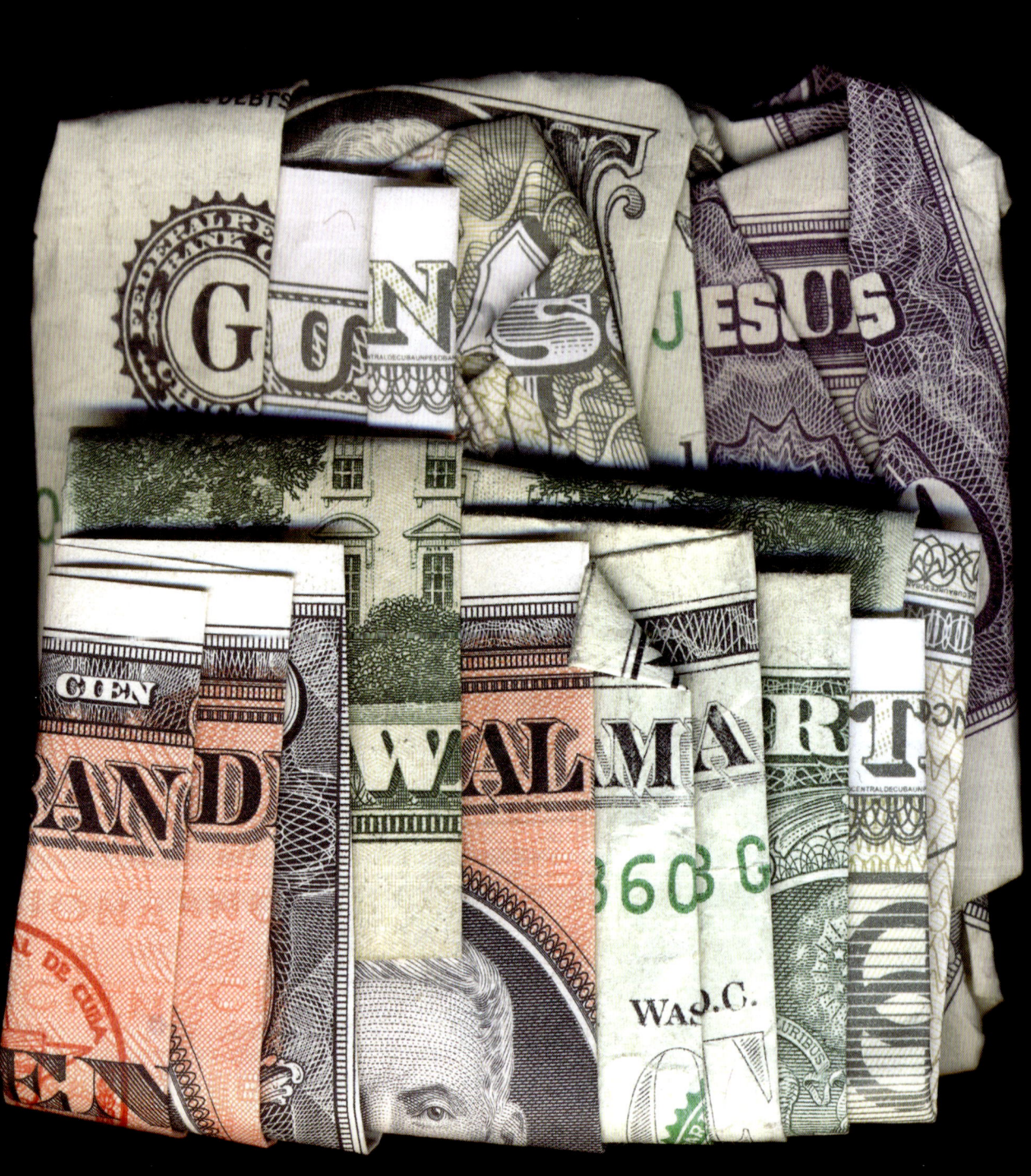

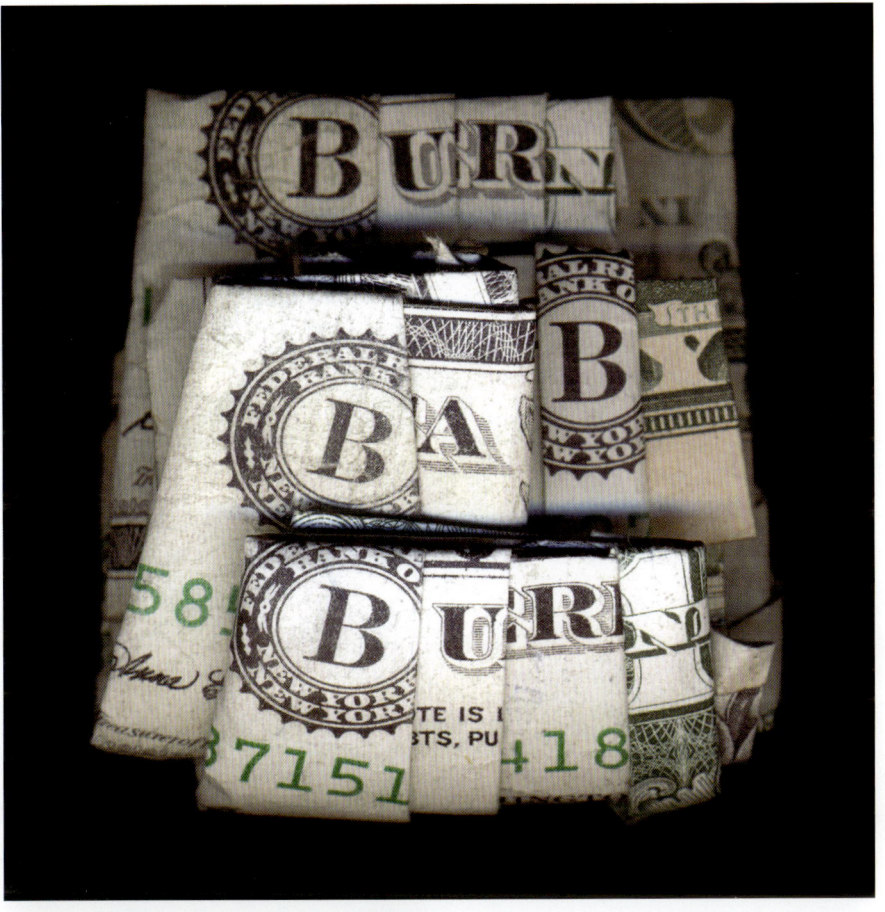

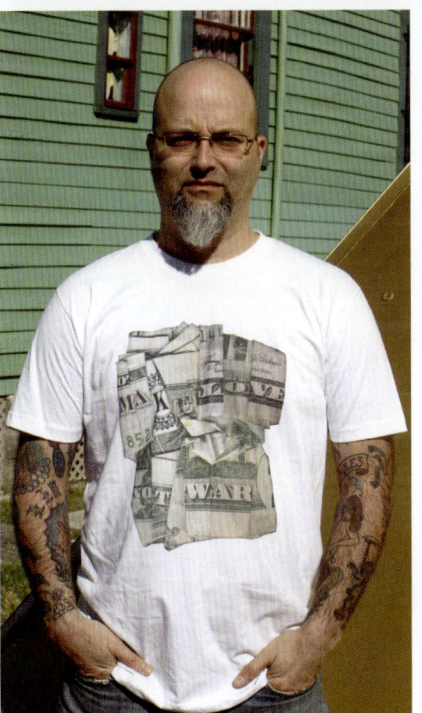

The many nuances associated with the dollar bill serve as an unrelenting source of inspiration for me as I fold the monetary engravings obsessively to reveal messages. These manipulated promissory notes take on new meanings as the messages are realized in the ready-made light of the U.S. currency. At the very core of this fiscal narrative is the tug-of-war between politics and the pursuit of happiness. This photo series offers a moment of reflection to further consider the good, bad, and the ugly in these portraits of a monetary centric world.

WWW.DANTAGUESTUDIO.COM

ADRIAN TONE

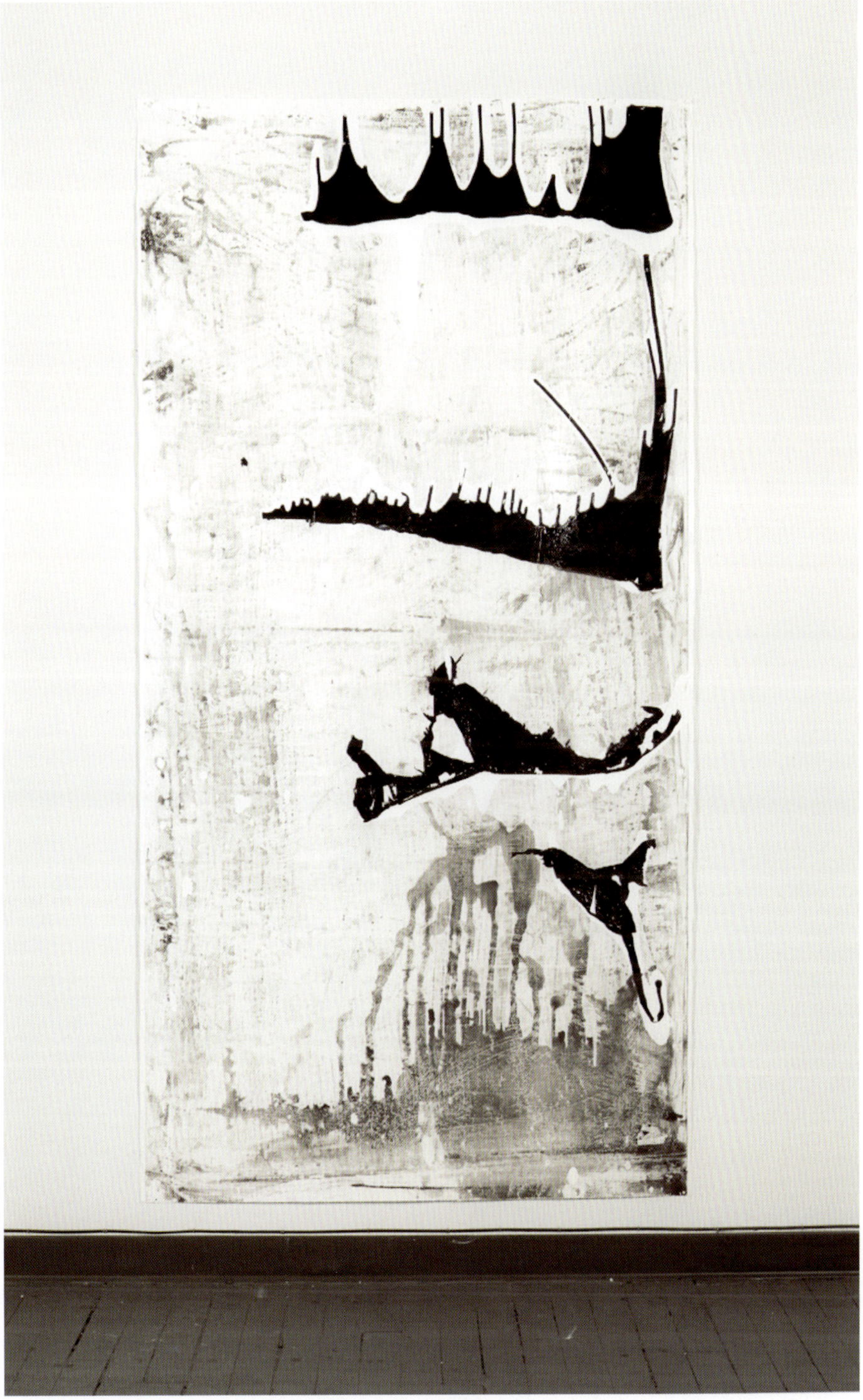

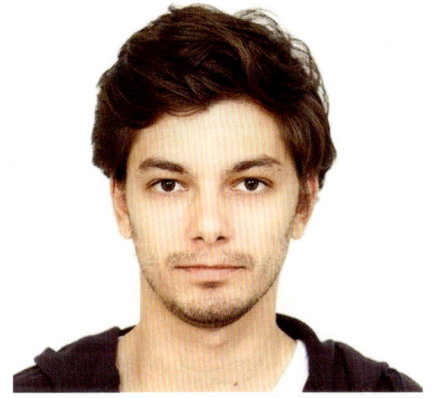

I make big pictures that are meant to seem quick and intuitive, like sketchbook drawings. I am attracted to the freedom to experiment that comes so naturally when working small and want to bring that same sense of immediacy into the large works. It is important they don't look contrived. They are a flash snapshot.

The pictures are either 4x8 or 8x8 feet, made on standard sized sheet material. I paint on sheets of Polyethylene, a plastic used in commercial packaging. Once finished I transfer the resulting marks onto their final support, watercolor paper. The finished work is both a print, a transfer, and an original at the same time.

In these works I primarily use 2 types of marks: a washing and a scraping. The paint material is first applied with a roller (not a brush). I then proceed to wash it down with a washcloth and scrape it away with a scraper until I am left with something that resembles a bi-product, a remnant of a painting, the discarded side of a decalcomania experiment.

WWW.ADRIANTONE.COM

● **(facing page) Untitled**
Acrylic on watercolor paper, 48 x 96 in., 2014

● **Untitled**
Acrylic on watercolor paper, 96 x 48 in., 2015

AMY KANKA VALADARSKY

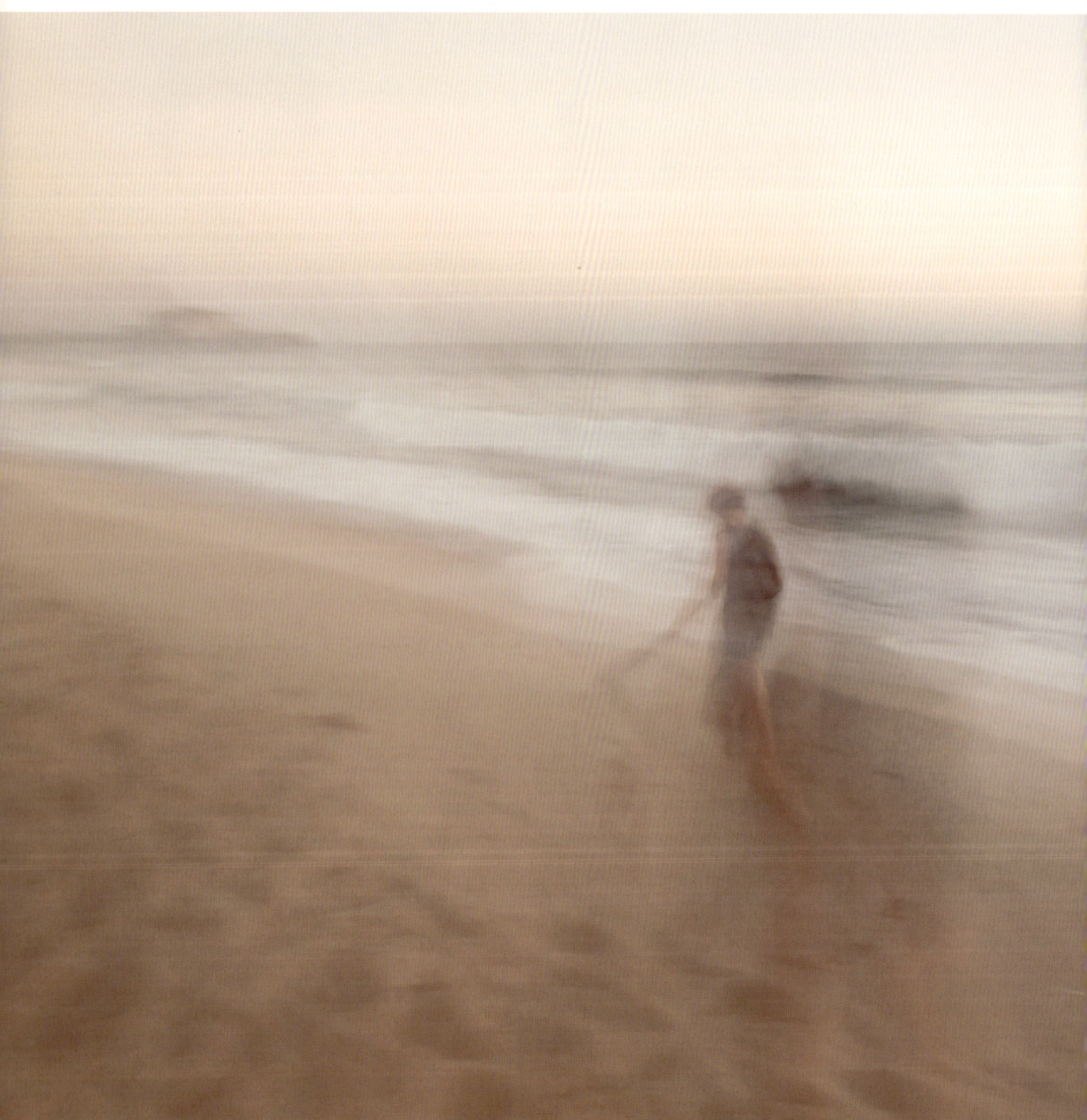

"We see what we know until we know who we are, then we see what we feel." — Ernst Haas

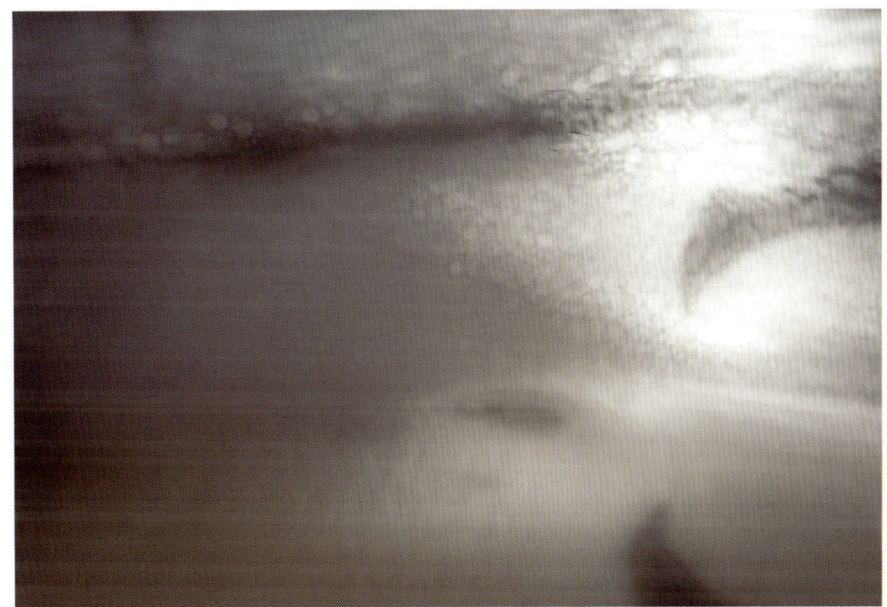

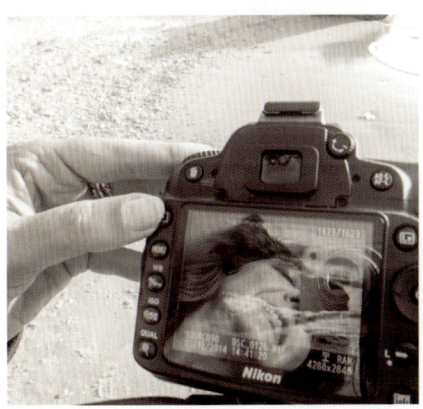

For most of my life, almost until the age of 50, I 'saw what I knew'. Born in Romania in 1964, my family moved to Israel when I was 8 years old. Following the family tradition, I studied computer science and moved straight into a hi-tech career. For 25 years, I used creativity to solve software problems (and raise children) with brief escapades into drawing lessons and weekend gardening. A crossroad in my professional life triggered the question I never asked before: 'What do I really want to do?' Easier asked than answered. I knew I want to let the 'Creative Me' take front stage, but it took almost three years during which I became a certified goldsmith before I fell in love with photography. For me, photography is an internal journey. Like dreams, photography has a way of making thoughts and feelings surface, giving them visual shape. I am still amazed how the eye understands before the mind does. Still surprised to see new facets of me in the images I create.

WWW.AMYKANKAPHOTOGRAPHY.COM

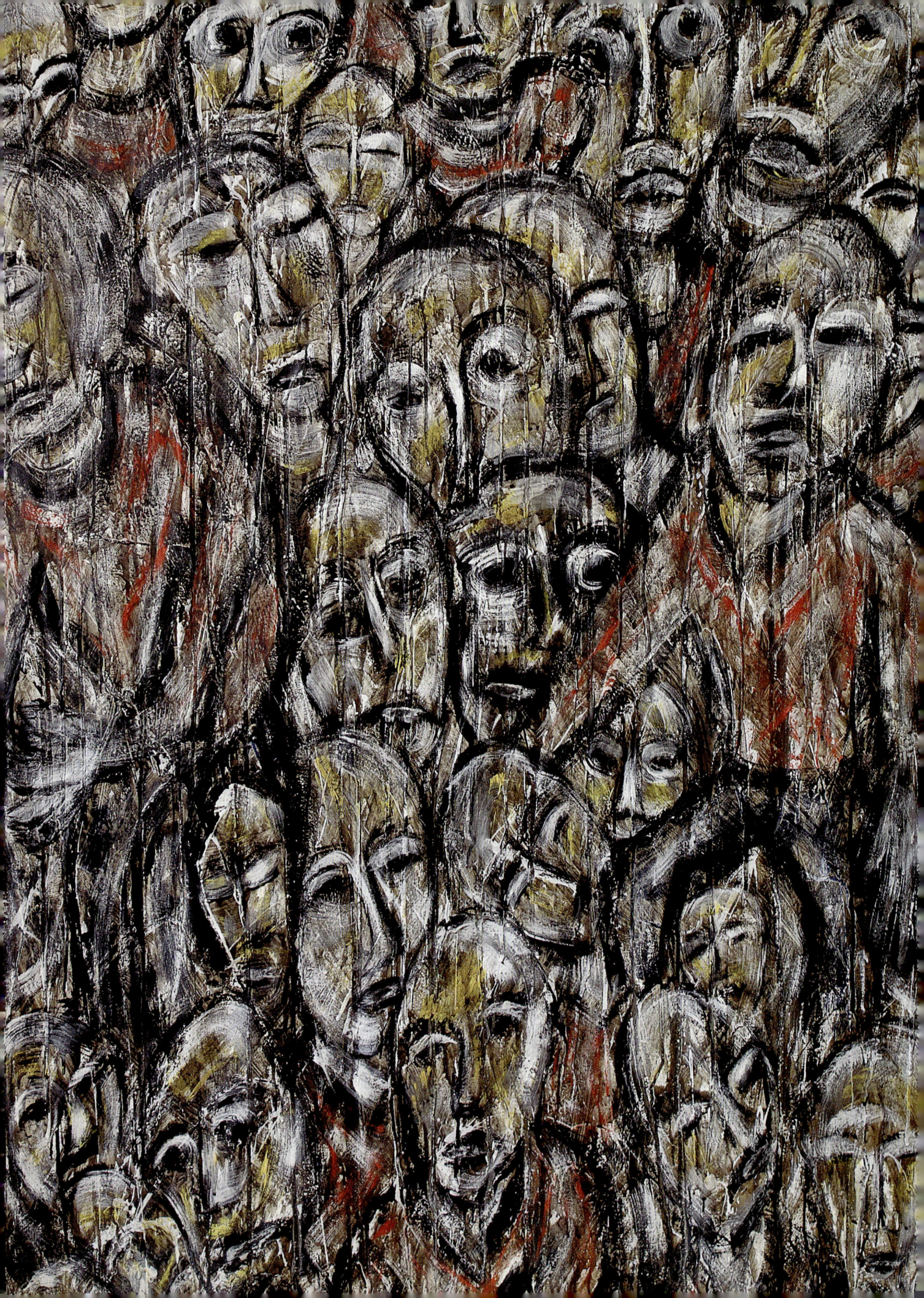

JOHAN WAHLSTROM

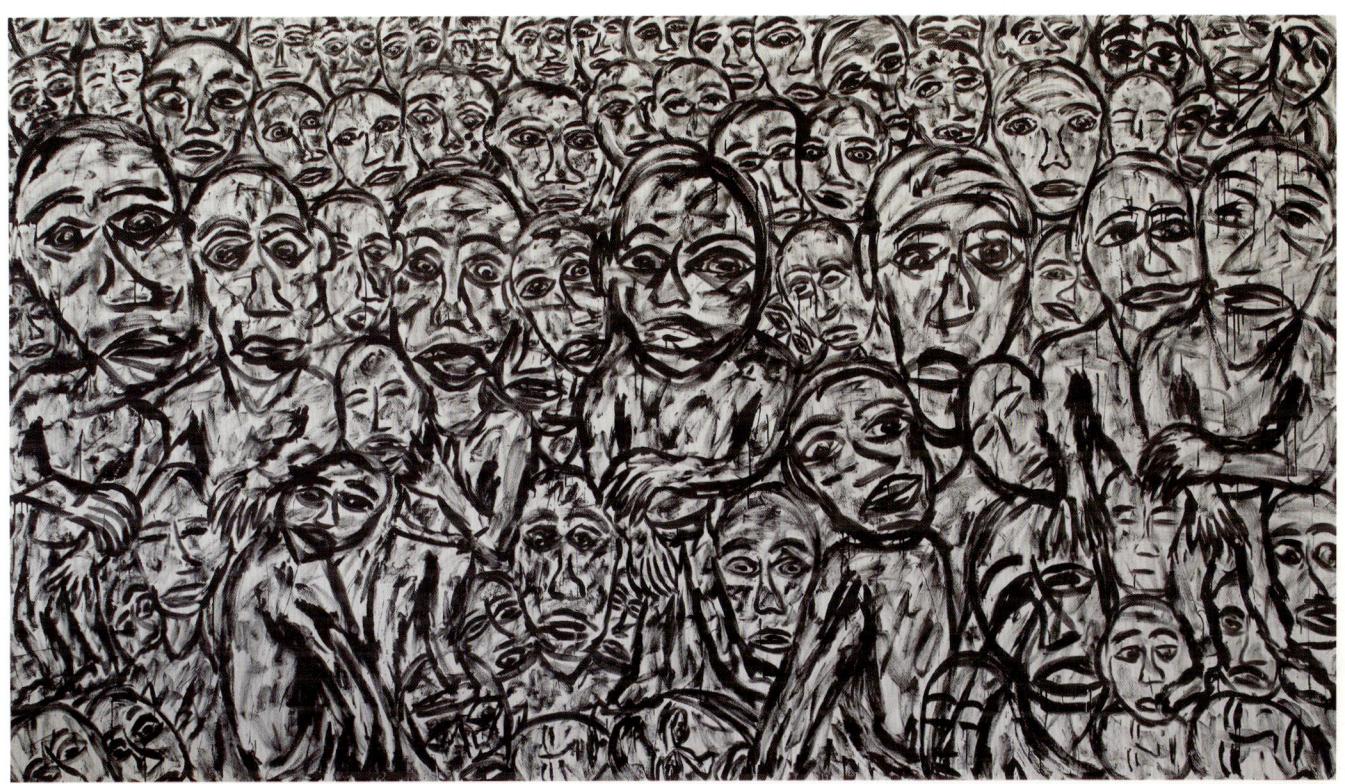

"I paint to keep myself insane. I paint anxiety to be calm. I paint war to have peace. I paint sadness to be happy. I paint the dark to be in the light. I paint death to be alive. I paint a story so that I don't have to tell a story."

Born 1959, Stockholm, Sweden. Lives and works in New York City & Malaga, Spain. He is a fifth-generation and internationally recognized artist, exhibited in New York, Boston, Los Angeles, Elmhurst/Chicago, Miami, London, Berlin, Milan, Amsterdam, Madrid, Barcelona, Zurich, Amsterdam and Stockholm to name a few.

"Evocative artist Johan Wahlstrom aims to encourage the celebration of daily life and incite happiness through the acceptance of reality. His emotionally charged neoexpressionist paintings are a contemporary hybrid of Jean DuBuffet's chaotic geometric canvases and Jean-Michel Basquiat's subversively scrawled social critiques. Wahlstrom works in series

that function as pointed signifiers to his artistic intention. His work aims to elucidate the uncontrollable nature of reality in an effort to embrace the small sufferings that signify life. Wahlstrom's work continues to gain attention fuelled by his overwhelming desire to connect with humanity in the hopes of provoking conversation. Pushing his abilities to the limit, Wahlstrom transcribes visual stories to enact societal change by illustrating the erratic and confusing nature of human existence."
-Kirsten Nicholas.

WWW.JOHANWAHLSTROM.COM

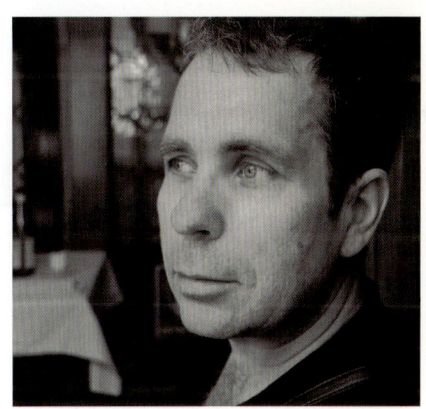

(facing page) Private Prison ●
Acrylic, Color Pigments, Silver and Pear Metal, Varnish on Canvas, 79 x 47 in., 2014

Waiting for Godot ●
Acrylic on Canvas, 11.5ft x 6.6ft, 2013

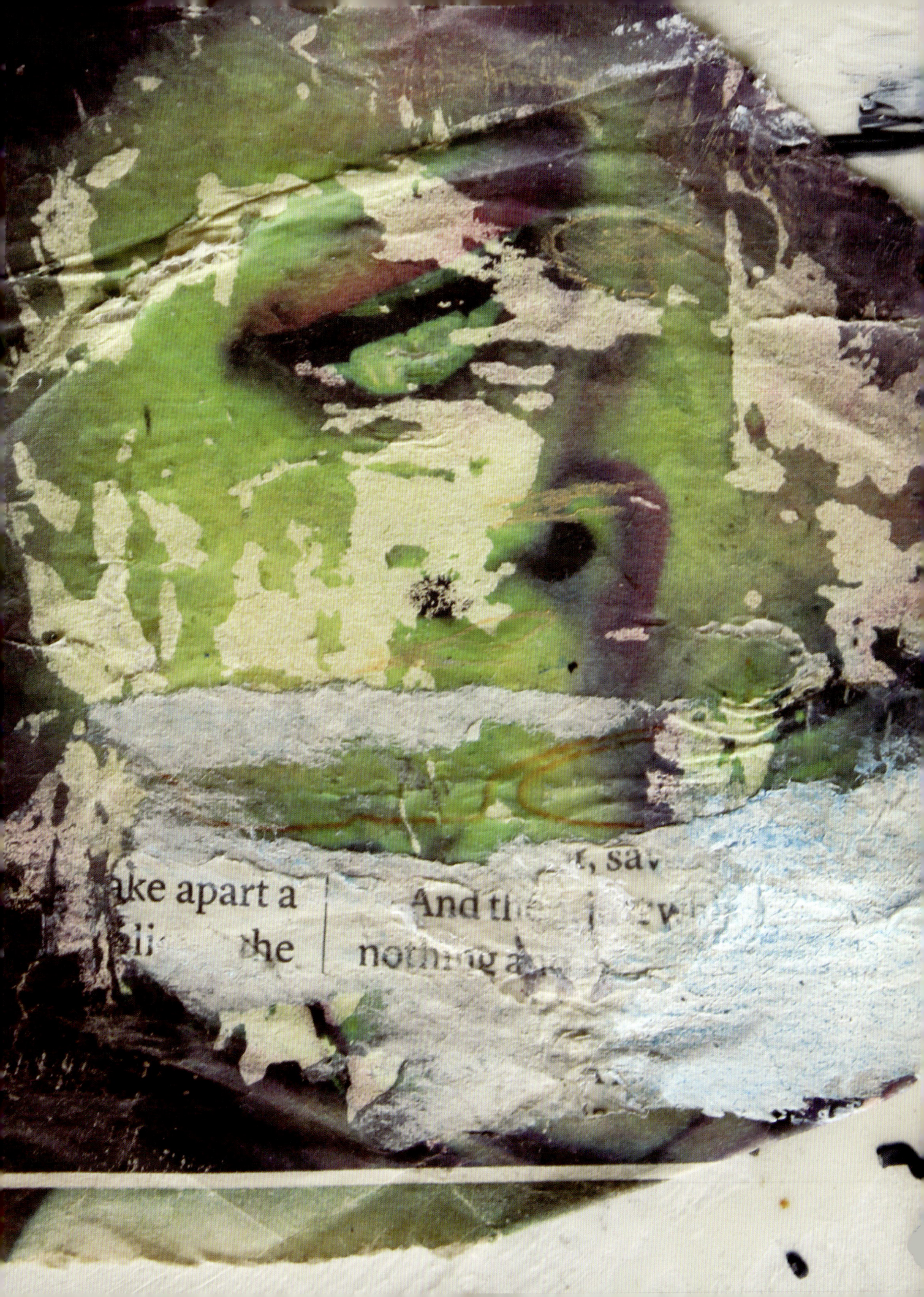

MARILYN WALTER

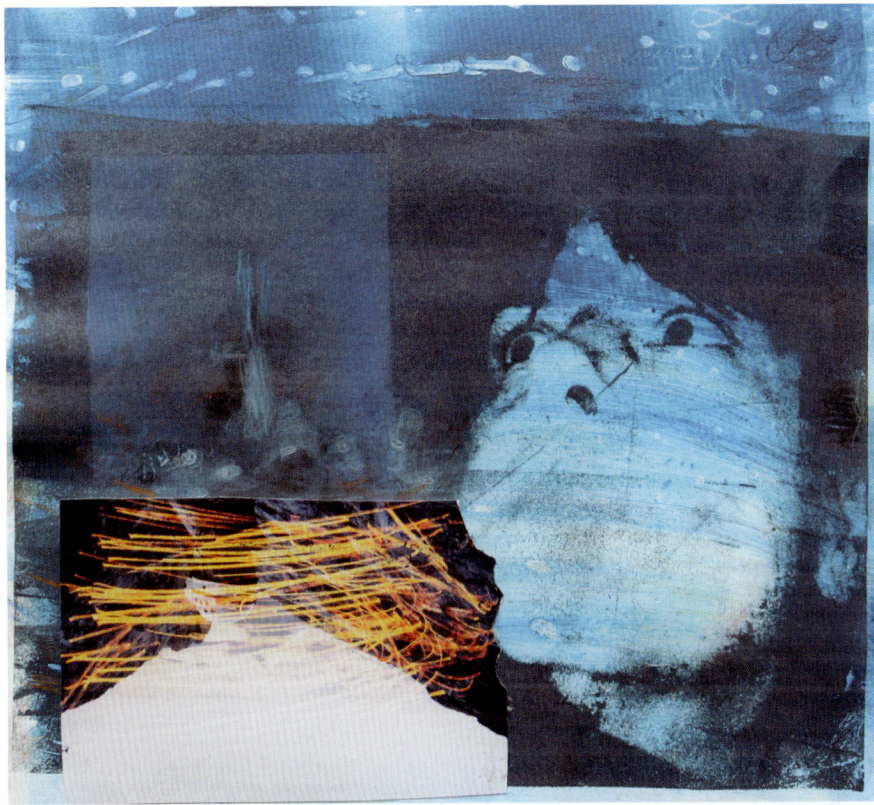

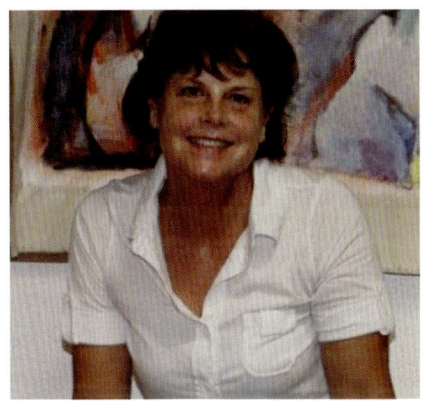

● **(facing page) Feeling Drawn to Words**
Acrylic paints, inks, marker, pencil, on plastic, transfers, on board, 4 x 4 in., 2012

● **Real Values Comes with Madness**
Monoprint, paper litho, pencil, collaged photo piece 8.5 x 11 in.

"The swirling, poetic moments, when I close my eyes and allow real and invented experiences to intersect, inspire my current mixed media paintings on paper, canvas and panel. People, places, thoughts, shapes and colors from everyday life move like quick films or snapshots; mysterious picture dramas shift between the seen and unseen, moving from the transparent to the obscure; and patterns, events or phrases become volatile and unsettling in my art. I document and observe these unfolding events, which engage the imagination and create a sense of place."

Marilyn Walter currently lives in West Palm Beach, Florida and works at her studio at The STUDIO 1016, 1016 Clare Avenue, Building 5. Walter is an avid educator who taught visual art classes for the Council Lifetime Learning Program at the National Council of Jewish Women New York Section. She also worked with the Intergenerational and Art & Memory workshop series. Walter attended Fairleigh Dickinson for her BA and continued her education at Parsons for teaching. In 2011 and 2012, she participated in the School of Visual Arts Summer Residencies in Painting & Mixed Media and Printmaking & Book Arts. Since participating with NYC HomeBase IV, a Social Engagement Project, Walter is currently experimenting with the incorporation of social interactions into her art.

Her process in creating art is to erase, inscribe, trace, incise, collage and transfer the resultant marks and images onto paper, canvas, wood, plastic or Plexiglas. Colors, shapes, movements, textures are repeated on multi-layered mixed media surfaces, becoming collages of traces. She reaches the desired result when the patchwork of translucent plastic, paper or blackboard paint seamlessly incorporates the surrounding elements. Growing up in Kuwait and Iran has allowed Walter to combine my passion and knowledge of both Eastern and Western cultures in my art. The influence of pattern, multiples and use of space viewed in her childhood are visible in the digital technology and printmaking processes that I use in creating my current work—a confluence of the timeless and the present.

WWW.MARILYNWALTER.COM

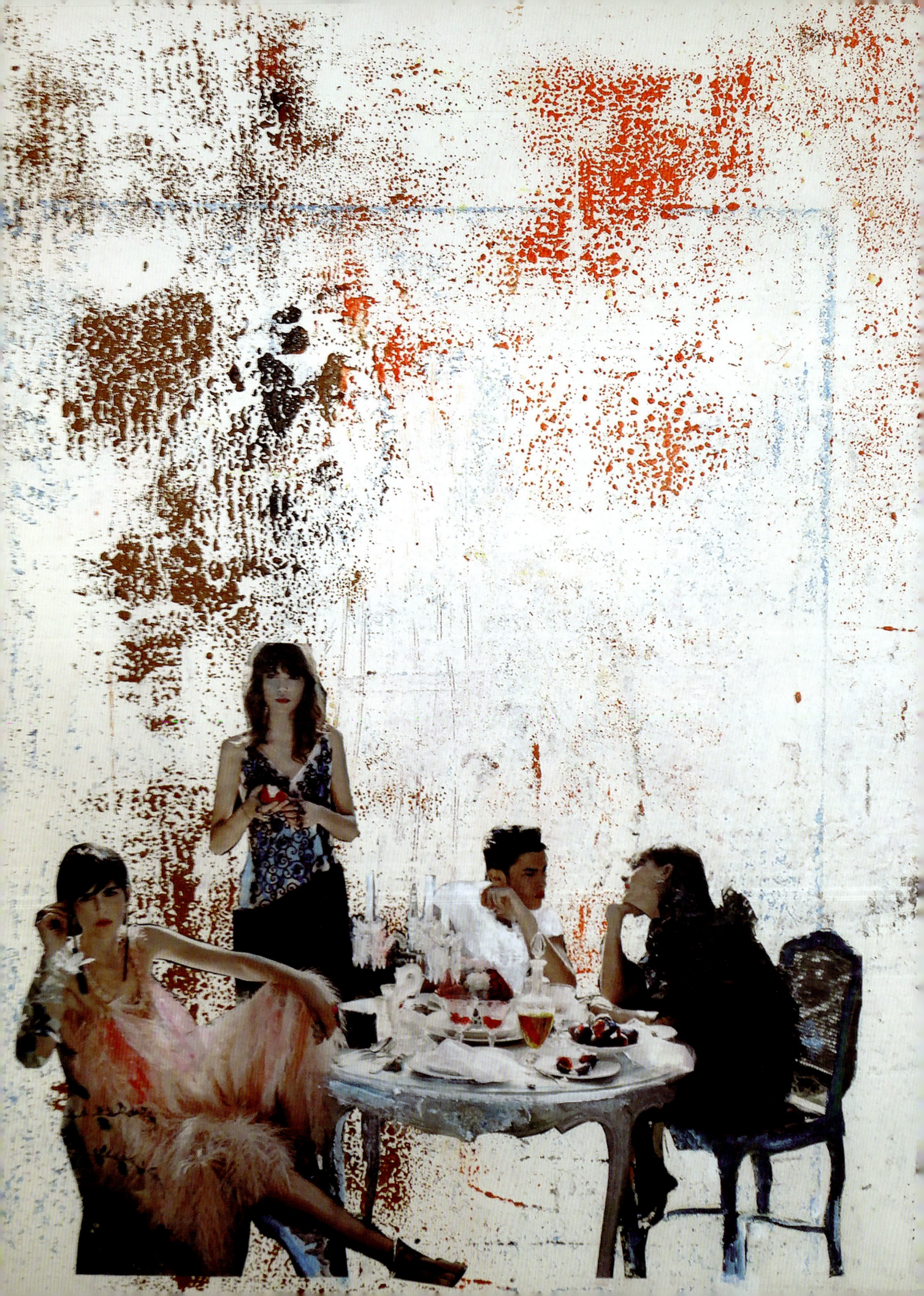

SIRARPI HEGHINIAN WALZER

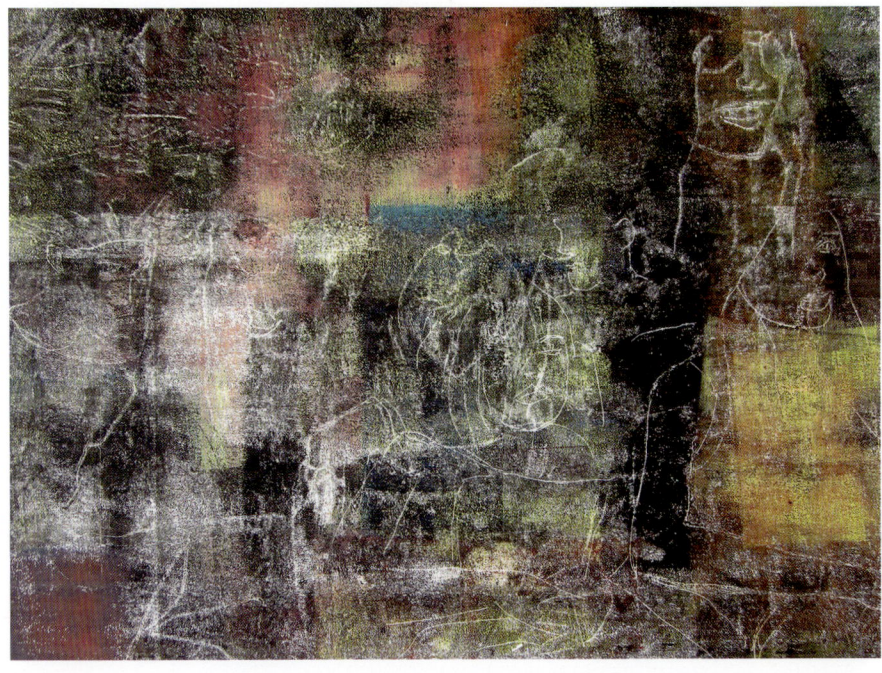

"My mixed media abstractions echo the ideas and values that take center stage in my thoughts -- an ongoing tension between freedom and containment, edging both the artist and the viewer closer to that place where chaos can erupt into clarity, and memories are distilled into single dramatic moments. I use the color white to suggest purity and simplicity, and to act as a unifying field for deliberately juxtaposed disparate images. The forms and exaggerations of color choices are metaphors for a search, with clues to content and interpretation, representing different layers of life, alluding both to what is present and what is missing."

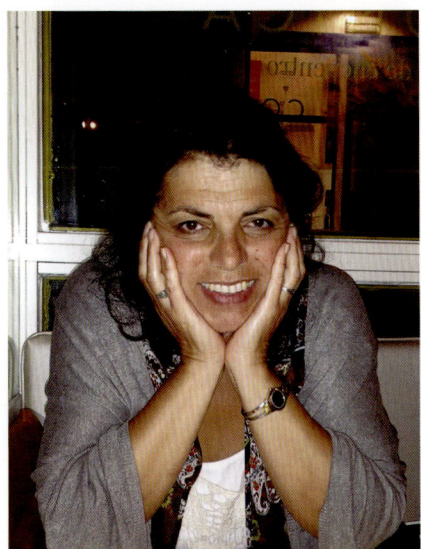

Sirarpi's artwork is in many collections nationally and internationally. She has received awards and exhibited her work, including installations, in galleries throughout Europe and the United States. She lives and works in Lexington, Massachusetts.

Sirarpi is an artist member of Gallery263 in Cambridge, MA and Gallery Z in Providence, she serves on the boards of Cambridge Art Association and Non-Profit Net in Massachusetts. She is the principal of Consult and Design, a small-business IT consulting firm. She is the co-founder and director of Art Without Borders, an online community that champions the rights of artists.

In Europe, Sirarpi worked with artists Andrej Woron, Milan Knížák, and Peter Erskine, and in the USA, with Timothy Harney, Jon Imber and Ati Gropius. As an engineer at Biotroniks in Berlin, Germany, her team designed pacemakers. At Honeywell in Lexington, MA, she worked on infrared imaging systems. Sirarpi studied biomedical systems engineering at Boston University and painting and stage design at the Academy for Fine Arts "Die Etage" and Hochschule der Kunste in Berlin, Germany.

WWW.SWALZER.COM

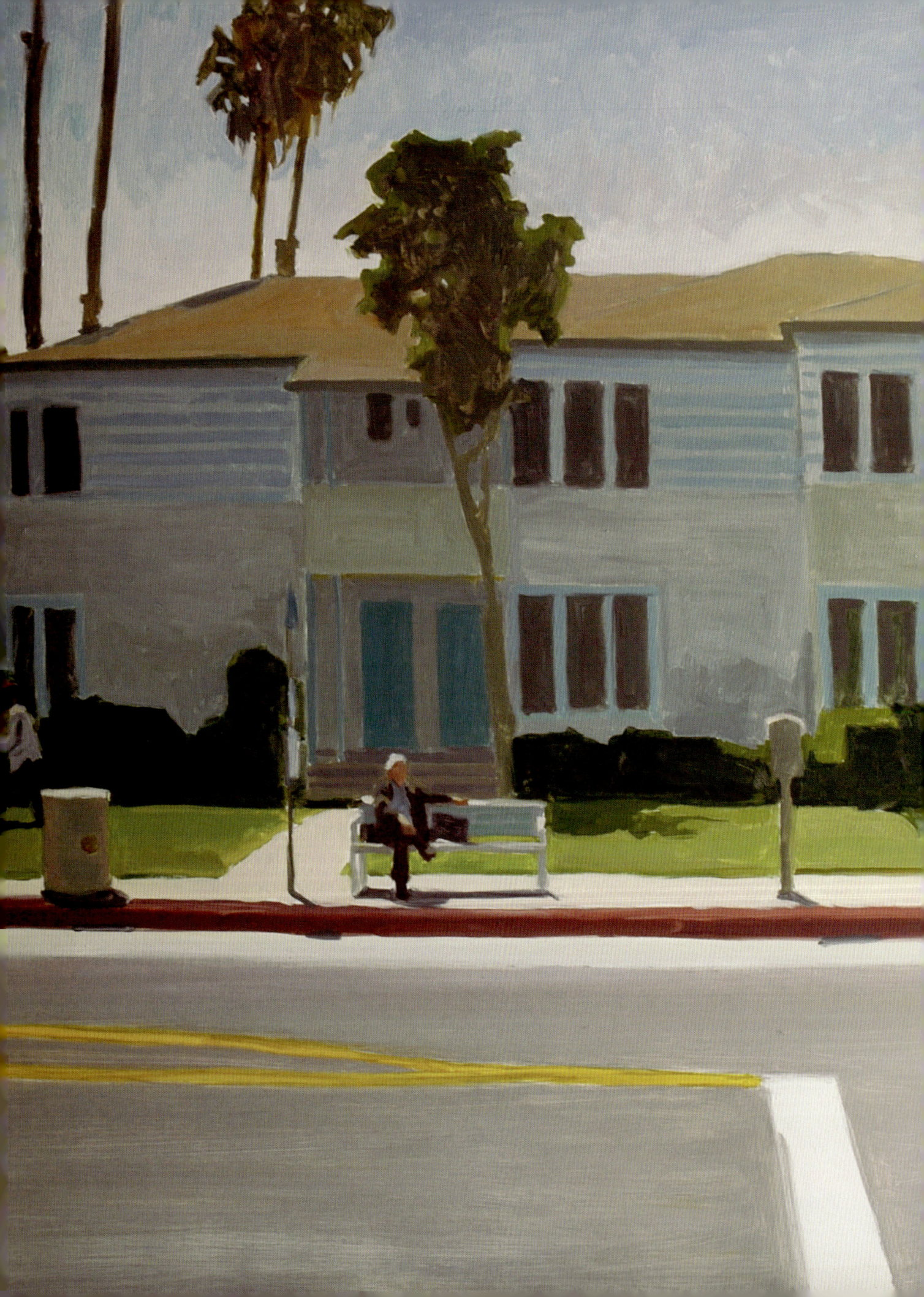

ANNE WARD

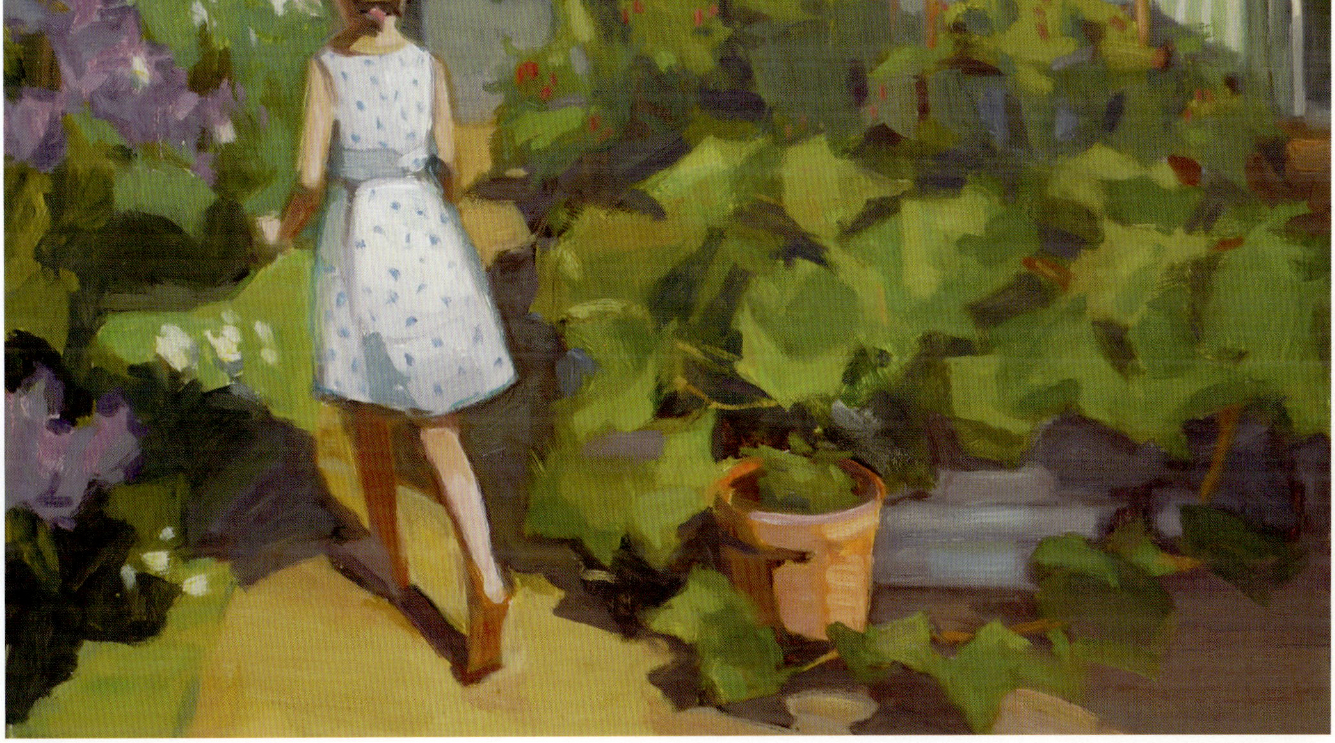

"I am inspired by the transitional and transformative nature of light. I'm endlessly curious about the combination of light, pattern and color. Light is my greatest teacher and I will be its humbled student for all of my days."

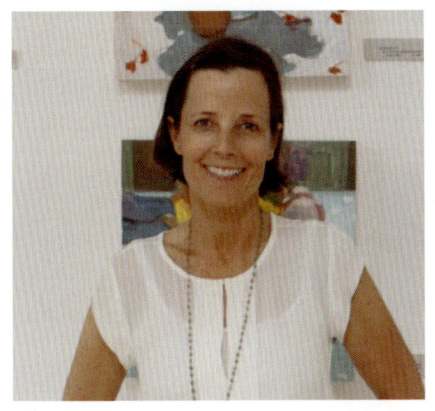

Anne Ward is dedicated to painting with the intention of capturing quiet spaces and the light that envelopes them. She decided to pursue painting after working for writer/director Lawrence Kasdan on several films. It was while living in France that Anne discovered the thrill of painting outdoors with an easel and returned home fully devoted to the pursuit of painting. Though primarily self-taught, she has also studied with painter Joseph Mendez. Anne is an Artist Member of the California Art Club and the Oil Painters of America. Her paintings reside in many private collections. She lives and paints in Los Angeles with her husband author/painter Ian Roberts.

WWW.ANNEWARD.COM

● **(facing page) Waiting**
Oil on panel, 23 x 25 in., 2009

● **Free**
Oil on panel, 12 x 16 in., 2014

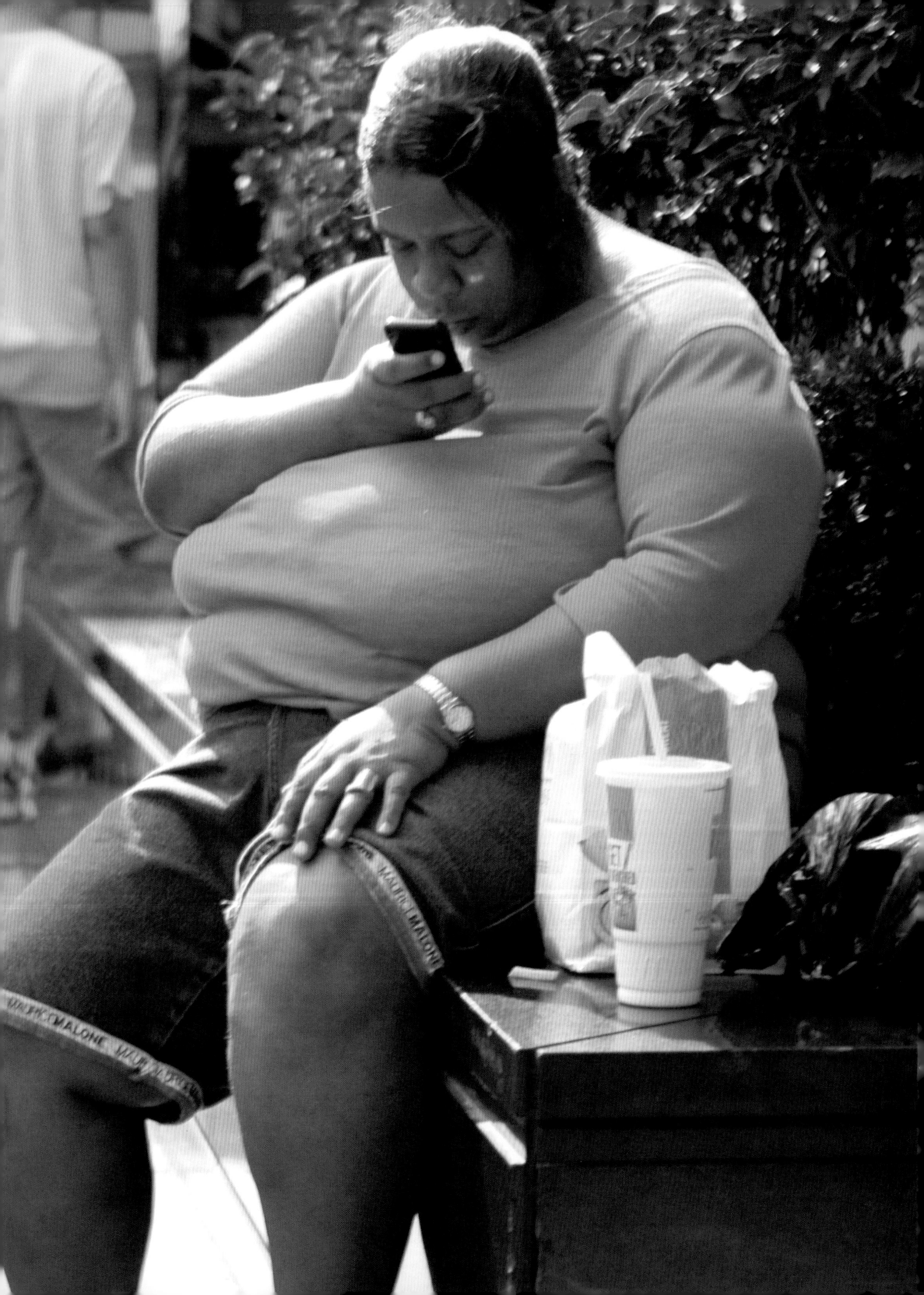

DANA WEST

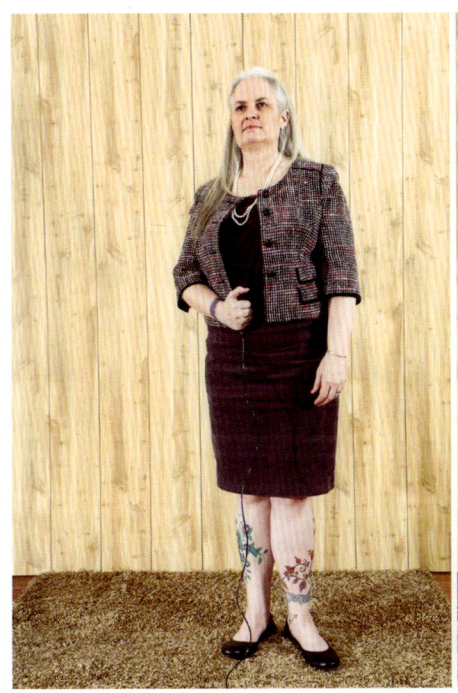 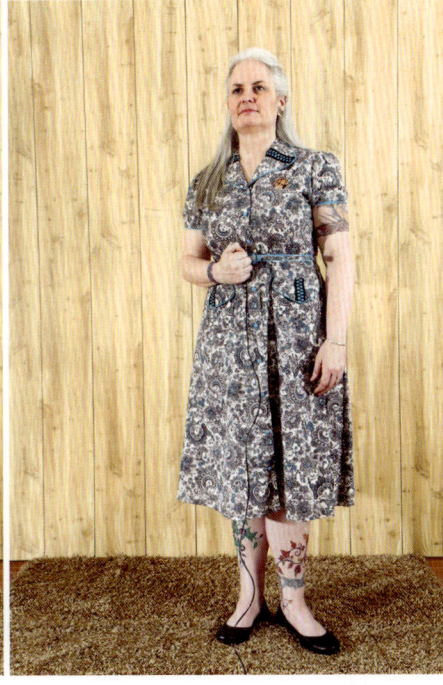 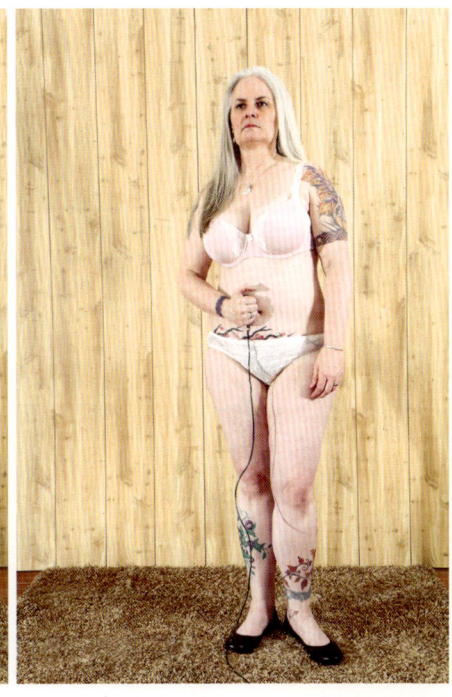

"Who are we, as individuals and as a collective? How do we take what family, religion, and society thrusts upon us and overcome to become the person we choose? "Like their personal lives, women's history is fragmented [...]" – Elizabeth Janeway.

Dana West was born in California, spending most of her life living in the deserts of the Southwest and Southern California. She received her BFA from The School of the Art Institute of Chicago (SAIC) in 2013. Now a Chicago based artist, Dana is also a staff member of the SAIC Photography Department. Dana has exhibited from San Francisco to London and has work in the permanent collection of the Joan Flasch Artists' Books Collection. Dana's work is an exploration into the contemporary fabric of women stained by living. Whether it's the self-portraits of "Stand Up Straight" or the photographs and transcribed text of "i love you too.", Dana draws on personal life experience as both the artist and the subject in much of her work. Her personal history mirrors that of other women faced daily with identity, religion, and cultural norms and expectations.

Photographs tell lies through slivers of reality. How much do we rely on images to provide memories of personal experience, how is collective memory of past events shaped and preserved, and how do they overlap, coexist, and inform each other? The process of making art is a way for me to deconstruct, abstract, and build connections from personal narratives, including image and text through photography and artist books."

WWW.DANAWESTPHOTO.COM

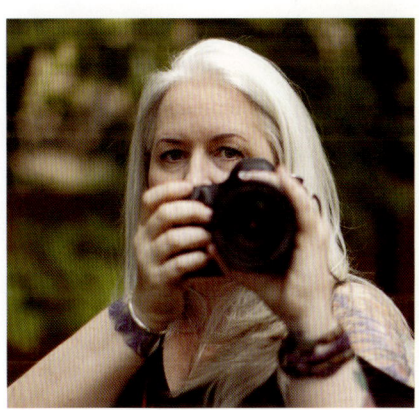

(facing page) #38 from the Street Series ●
Archival inkjet print, 2012

Stand Up Straight triptych ●
(from the Stand Up Straight series)
Archival inkjet print, 2013

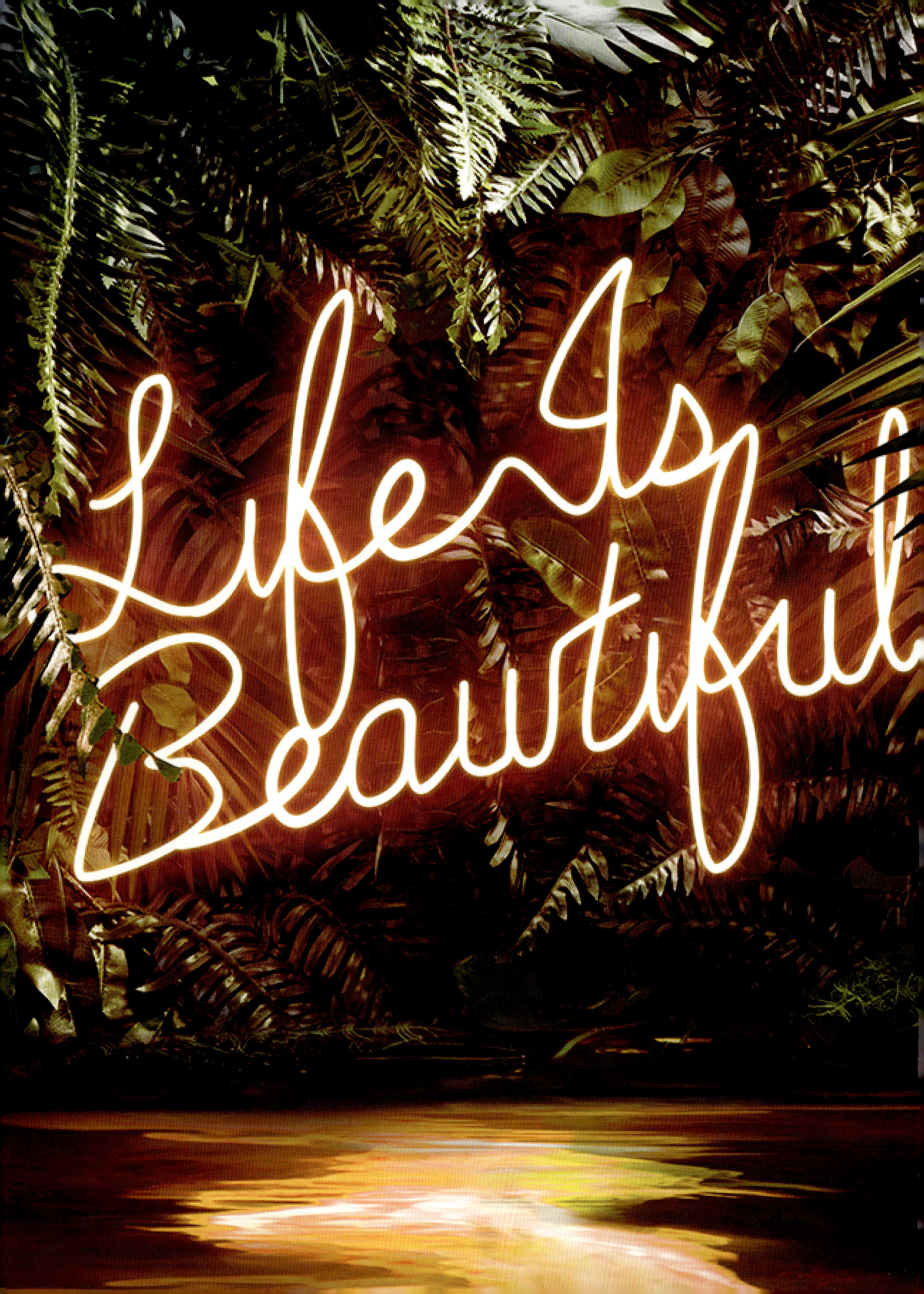

YEE WONG

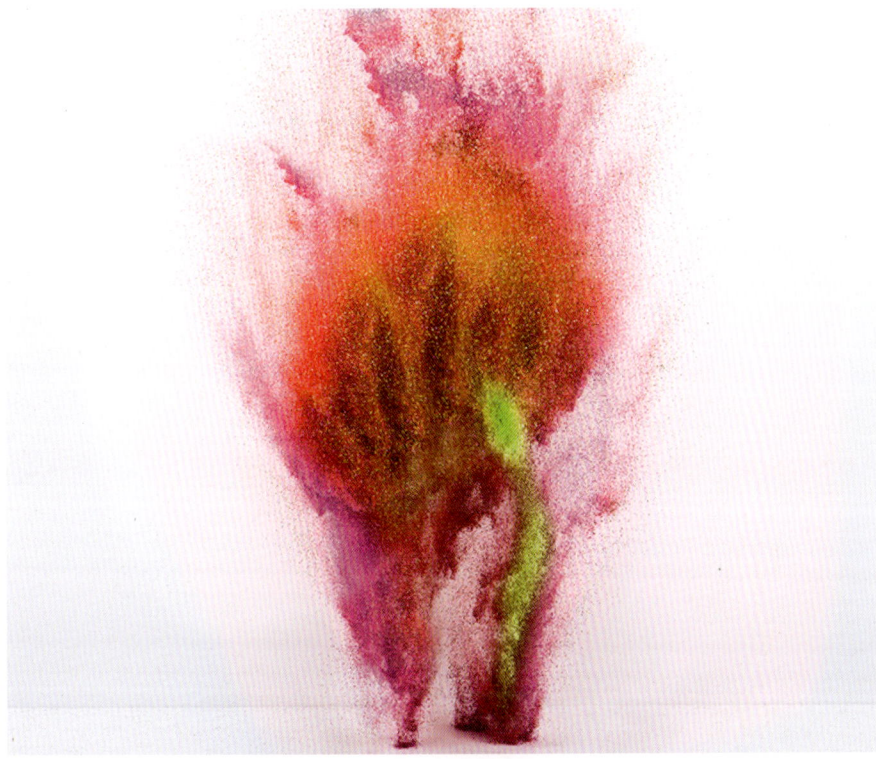

● **(facing page) Disco in the Jungle:
Life is Beautiful**
Photographic paper, 50 x 60 in., 2012

● **Powder Movement: Flaming Red**
Photographic paper, 50 x 60 in., 2009

Yee Wong is a well-known contemporary Asian-American artist. She specializes in digital arts, graphic design, and 2-D and 3-D art. Her works often capture the unusual nature of objects used in daily life, which she uses to express her emotions to give life to her art. Yee also believes that an artist's heart is shown through his works. While some artists want to show a more negative side of life, Yee's works expresses the nice quality of everyday objects, revealing their beautiful side. And she does it in a hyper-realistic way that most people might not even notice in their daily lives. According to Yee, "While in this world already filled with lies and corruption, I think there is a need to create art that gives a space for my viewers to breathe and see the beautiful side and hope of this world.

Yee has worked and lived in New York for decades. She moved to America at a young age and started to explore the flourishing art and pop culture scene. Yee said in a recent interview with Cult Collective, "I have lived in the US for most of my life. I am used to the western culture and at the same time I also have Asian values because of my roots. It may sound a little schizophrenic . . . but it is actually a blessingbecause it has made me a well-rounded, worldly person with a broader view" (http://goo.gl/XxG3TA). Yee's Asian roots and western experience make her work appealing to a global audience, thereby expanding the exposure of her art. Her career now takes her between New York and Hong Kong.

HTTP://YEEWONG.TUMBLR.COM

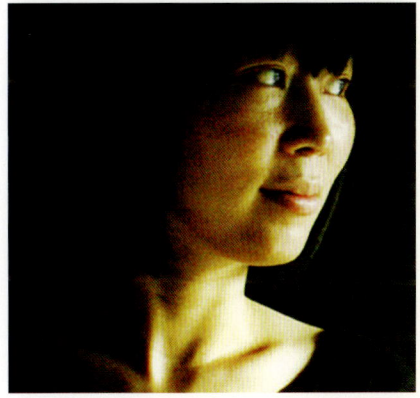

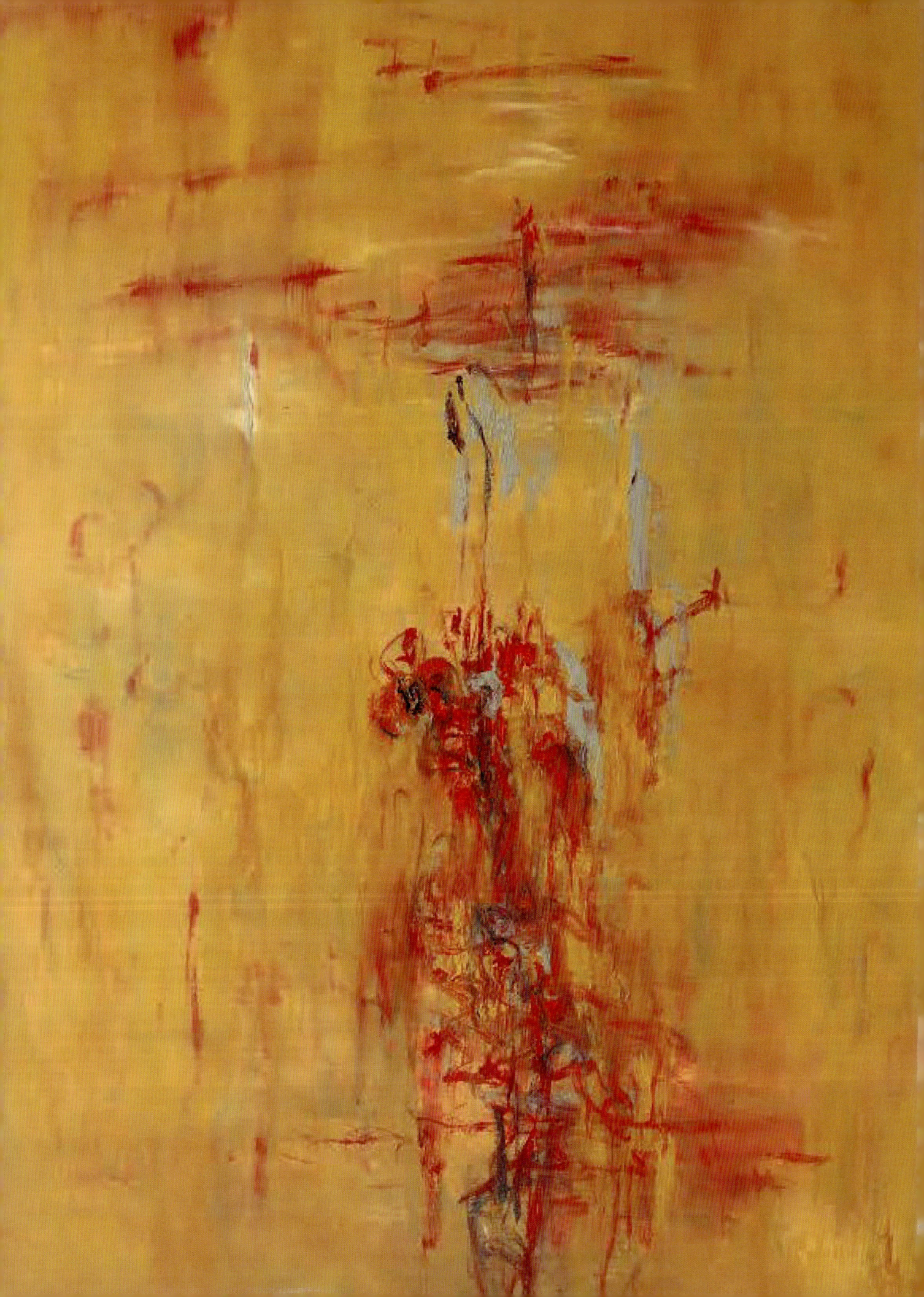

WEI XIONG

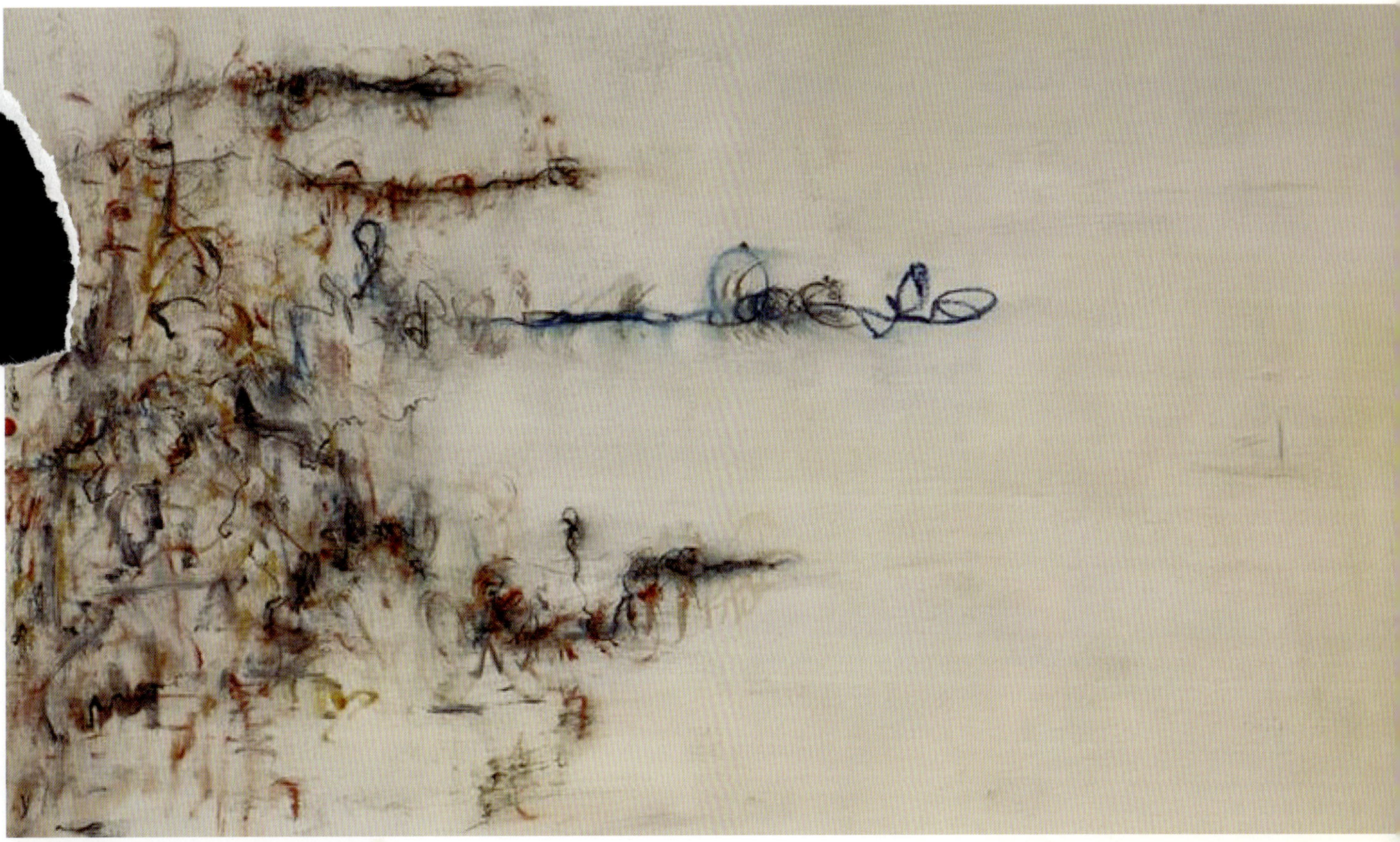

Xiong, Wei was Born 1965 in Chengdu, China and educated in USA. Inspired by Zen study and Minimalism I started to practice art since early 90's. Exhibited both in USA, Europe, Taiwan and China during these twenty years and collected by a few of museum. Now live and work in Los Angeles and China.

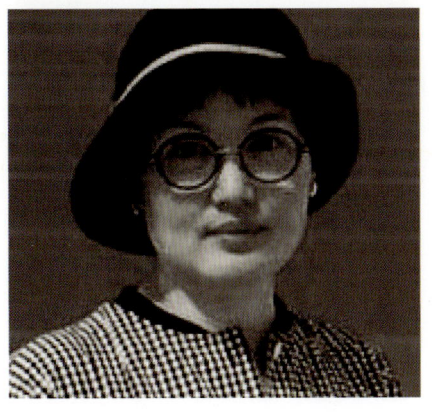

● **(facing page) Untitled**
Oil on board, 20 x 29 in., 2011

● **Untitled**
Oil on linen, 29.2 x 33.4 in., 2011

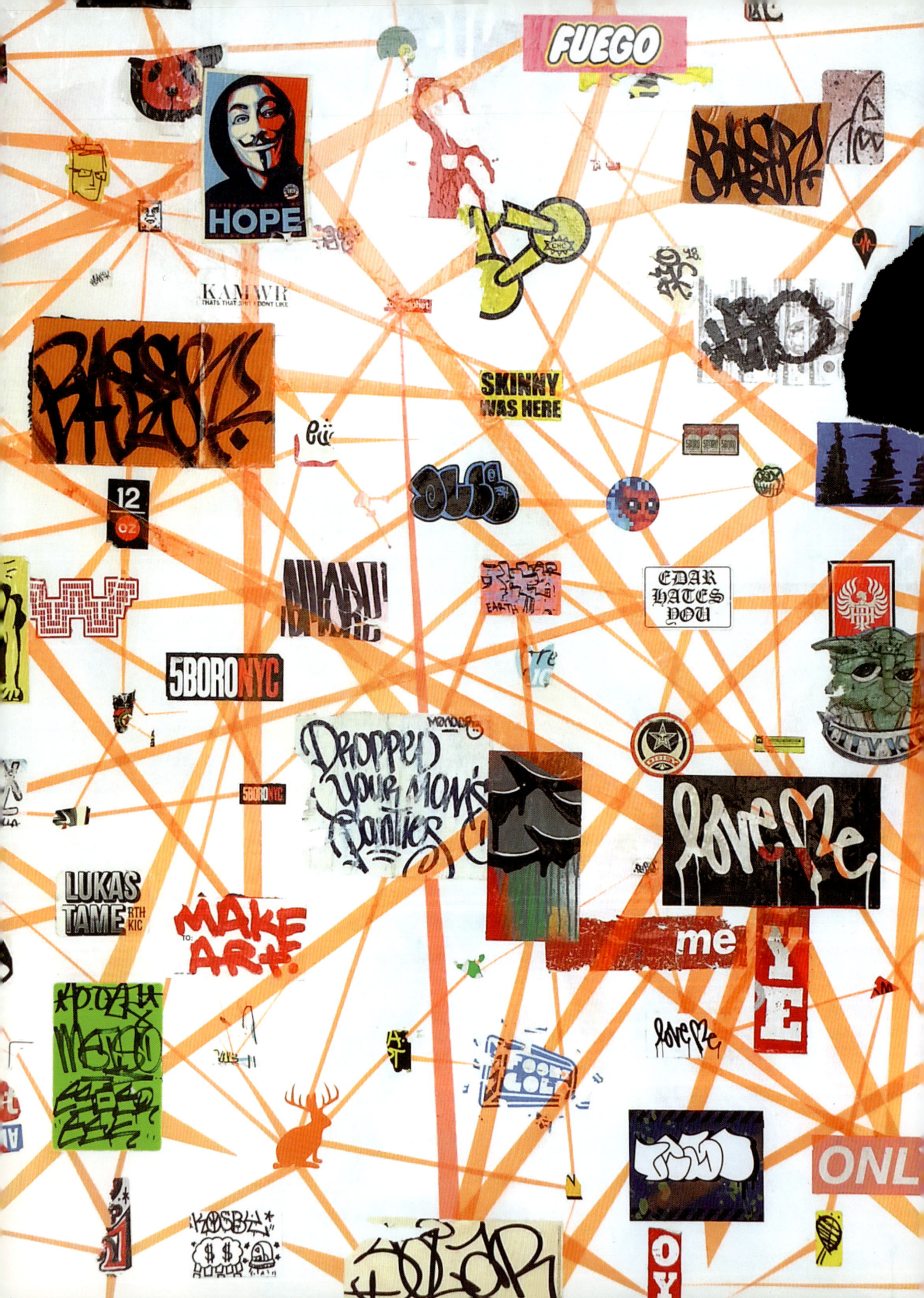

EGON ZIPPEL

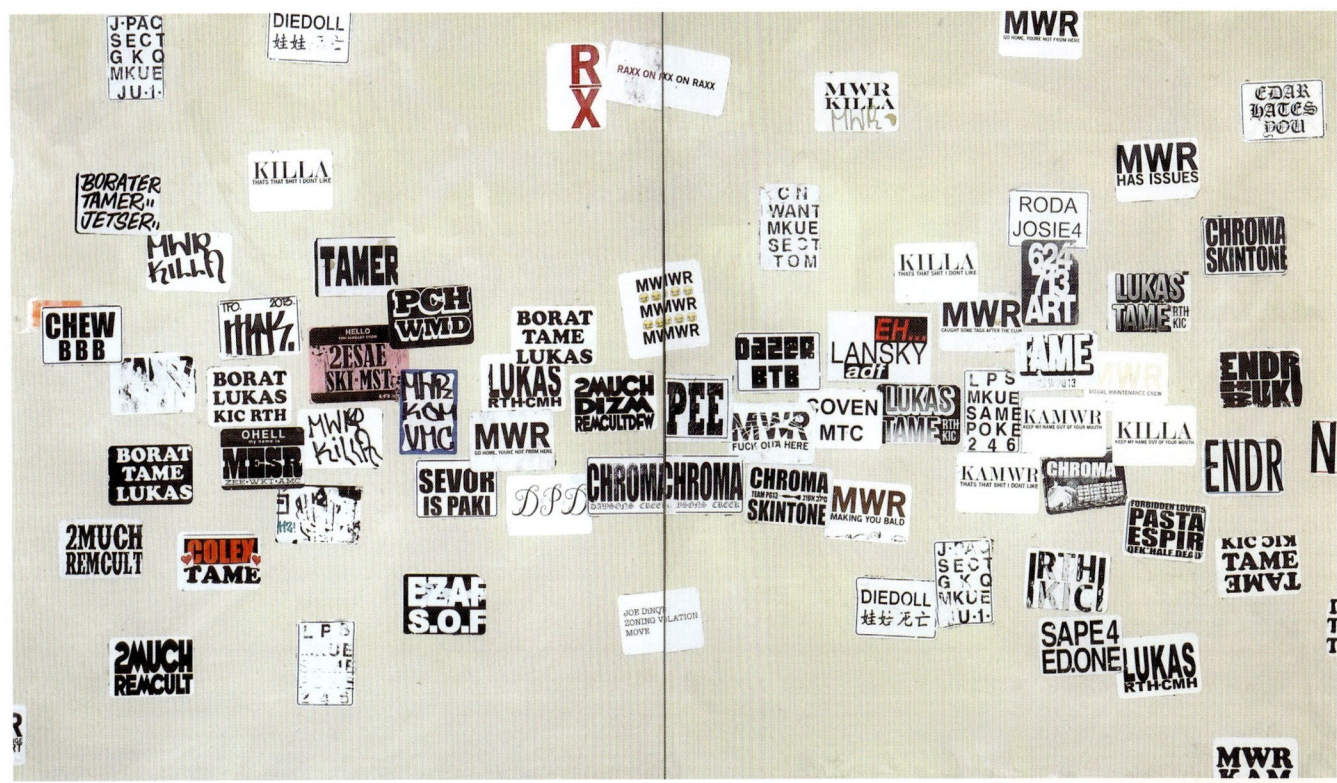

Egon Zippel was born in Timisoara, Rumania in 1960 to German parents. When Nicolae Ceaușescu rose to power in 1964, the Zippels presciently fled to Heidelberg, Germany, to begin life anew. Egon studied graphic design at the University of Mannheim whence he received a Fulbright Scholarship comprising an introductory month at Georgetown University in Washington D.C. and the academic year of 1984-85 at the University of Texas in Austin. Over the next few years Egon studied computer graphics at the New York Institute of Technology and finished his postgraduate studies at the Institute for New Media at the Staedel Art Academy in Frankfurt from 1993-94.

During the early '90s he lived primarily in Italy until eventually settling again in NYC in 1996. Currently he maintains studios in both New York and Berlin. Egon believes in both predetermination and free will. Wrestling with this contradiction makes daily life rather complex. The "Devandalizing" series involves recycling "communication" from appropriated stickers, graffiti "tags" on visitor ID labels and similar items, and other fragments of urban signatures found on the streets of various cities around the world. He regroups these artifacts of urban life onto canvases in defined, yet chaotically linear, circular, or random compositions, which emanate contemporary culture.

The work straddles numerous fences and encompasses sevxeral categories: Painting, conceptual art, and collage all come into play as he vandalizes the vandals. Yet, Zippel has "immortalized" the stickers by scraping them from their ephemeral placements on city streets and re-affixing them to canvas. Weathered and tattered, fragmented and battered, he feels that their war-torn condition confirms their authenticity. With a multi-edged blade Egon Zippel has developed a new twist on urban archeology.

WWW.EGONZIPPEL.COM

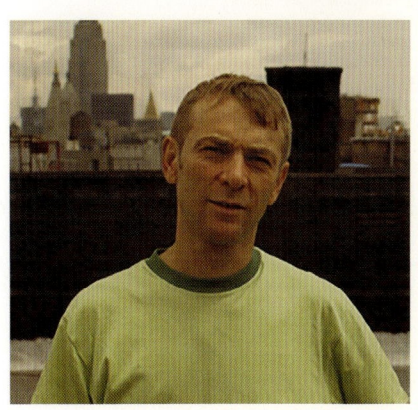

(facing page) HOPE, ENTANGLED ●
Graffiti tags and stickers harvested from the streets of New York City and applied to canvas. 48" x 48", 2014

2MUCH ●
Graffiti tags and stickers harvested from the streets of New York City and applied to canvas. Diptych, each panel 30" x 30", 2014